W9-ABB-912

Islam Assembled

DAYAN CENTER FOR
MIDDLE EASTERN AND AFRICAN STUDIES

ISLAM ASSEMBLED

The Advent of the Muslim Congresses

Martin Kramer

New York **Columbia University Press** *1986*

DS
35.7
.K7
1986

Library of Congress Cataloging in Publication Data
Kramer, Martin S.
Islam assembled.
At head of title: Dayan Center for Middle Eastern
and African Studies.
Bibliography: p.
Includes index.
1. Islamic countries—Politics and government.
2. Islam—20th century. 3. Near East—History—
1517-   . I. Merkaz Dayan le-limude ha-Mizrah
ha-tikhon ve-Afrikah. II. Title.
DS35.7.K7 1985   909'.097671   84-21407
ISBN 0-231-05994-9

Columbia University Press
New York   Guildford, Surrey
COPYRIGHT © 1986 COLUMBIA UNIVERSITY PRESS
ALL RIGHTS RESERVED
PRINTED IN THE UNITED STATES OF AMERICA

The Dayan Center for Middle Eastern and
African Studies
The Shiloah Institute
Tel Aviv University

THE DAYAN CENTER, through the Shiloah Research Institute and its other constituent units, seeks to contribute by research, documentation and publication to the study and understanding of the modern history and current affairs of the Middle East and Africa. The Center, with the Department of Middle Eastern and African History, is part of the School of History at Tel Aviv University. This study appears in the Center's Monograph Series.

To my parents, Anita and Alvin

CONTENTS

PREFACE

"If a scheme on these principles could be carried into effect, it would be the greatest event ever known in the annals of Mohammedan history."

—Shaykh Mustafa al-Maraghi,
on his congress proposal of 1915.

LATE IN THE last century, Muslims, separated by distance, language, and history, first thought to make their world whole by assembling in congress. The expansion of the West into Muslim lands awakened within Muslims a shared sense of subjugation. Then steamer, rail, and telegraph made possible an animated discourse among Muslim centers linked in the past by tenuous ties. From this exchange emerged a loose network of Muslim cosmopolitans, men of common conviction who shared a critique of the West, and a vision of a revitalized Islam. After numerous failed initiatives, they finally did meet in an irregular succession of Muslim congresses between the two world wars. These were the earliest occasions on which Muslims, assembled from various parts of the Muslim world, discussed and resolved on issues of common concern. They were perhaps the broadest attempt by a group of subject peoples to ward off the West.

The uneasy first encounters made fitful progress. The earliest practical proposals, and then the congresses themselves, emerged and disappeared in rapid succession. They followed one another in no sequential order, and they bore no formal relationship to one another. Many hands were at work, often at cross-purposes, and no renowned individual made his name synonymous with the broken string of congresses. The initiative moved from continent to continent, and the action unfolded not only in Mecca, Cairo, and Jerusalem, but in the unlikely settings of Moscow, Geneva, and Tokyo. So scattered was the evidence that no attempt was made to study Muslim congresses in an integrated fashion, to weigh them against one another, and to measure their cumulative effects. Some of the leading contemporary Islamicists—Massignon, Gibb, Hartmann—believed that the advent of the congresses was a significant development in Islam, but the appreciations which they published were brief and tentative.[1] The passage of time has made possible a comprehensive study, based upon sources which were beyond the reach of contemporaries. My method has been to trace the congress idea through its early evolution, to examine the first and largely unsuccessful initiatives, and to assess the congresses convened between the two world wars. My purpose has been to establish the persistence of Muslim attachment to the political concept of a united Islam, even as Muslim empire and caliphate waned.

As the West began to divest itself of its Muslim possessions, and Muslim peoples achieved independence, the congress movement lost much of its appeal. It is here that I have drawn the account to a close, with an examination of the activities of the leading Muslim cosmopolitans during the last world war. The later revival of the congresses as diplomatic arenas for independent Muslim states occurred in a very different world, and warrants a very different approach. But here I am concerned with how an idea circulated by Muslims of radical political and religious persuasions first won general acceptance, and how it fared when first put into practice, for the most part by statesmen without states. It is a study of first encounters, of the moments when Muslims first equated the sheer expanse of Islam with political power in the modern world.

I have striven to present a cosmopolitan appraisal, as informed about the expansive world of Muslim activism as were the Muslim cosmopolitans themselves. For the congresses soon proved larger than they appeared. Their effects were felt in parts of the Muslim world far removed from the center of initiative. To study those effects, I have had to venture across the boundaries established to divide the Muslim world for the convenience of foreign scholarship. This has led me at times through unfamiliar terrain. And so I am particularly indebted to those whose own cosmopolitan knowledge of Muslim history served for me as a guide. I owe much to Professor Bernard Lewis, who supervised this study through an earlier incarnation as a Princeton University doctoral dissertation. I have never succeeded in exhausting his store of knowledge, references, and anecdotes on this or any Muslim subject. And he has given me ample opportunity to try.

Parts of the manuscript were read and commented upon by Professors Benedict Anderson, Shaul Bakhash, L. Carl Brown, William Cleveland, Charles Issawi, and Edward Lazzerini, and I thank them all. A constant companion of this work has been Professor Itamar Rabinovich, now my colleague at Tel Aviv University, who first set my sights on the Muslim congresses, and followed with countless encouragements. To the various archivists and librarians from whose collections I cite, I am most indebted. For special courtesies, I wish to offer special thanks to the Right Hon. Viscount Knebworth for permission to examine the Oriental correspondence of Wilfred Scawen Blunt, at the West Sussex County and Diocesan Record Office; to the Mohamed Ali Foundation and the Keeper of Oriental Books at the Durham University Library, for permission to consult the Abbas Hilmi II Papers; to Dr. Muhammed ᶜAmira, Chief Librarian of the Azhar Mosque Library, for permission to study the files of the Cairo caliphate congress; to Mr. Abu al-Futuh Hamid ᶜAwda, Director of the Archives of the Presidency of the Republic in Cairo, for permission to examine the Egyptian royal archives; to Mr. Daniel Bourgeois of the Swiss Federal Archives, for his kind assistance; to Mr. Yitzhak Oron, Director of Research at the Israeli Foreign Ministry, for permission to study the wartime papers of Hajj Amin al-Husayni; to the French Embassy in Cairo, for permission to consult the Embassy post records; to Dr. P. A. Alsberg, Director of the Israel State Archives, for providing Arabic documentation concerning the Jerusalem congress; and to the staff of the India Office Records, for exceptional efforts on my behalf.

The initial research was made possible through grants from the Princeton Program in Near Eastern Studies, the United States Information Service through the American Research Center in Egypt, and the Ben-Gurion Fund. For the opportunity to revise and publish the work, I acknowledge with gratitude the support of the Bronfman Program for the Study of Jewish-Arab Relations.

I am also grateful for kind acts of hospitality to Professor Shimon Shamir and the Israeli Academic Center in Cairo, and to Paulette and David Spiro of Princeton. It was my good fortune that Leslie Bialler of Columbia University Press undertook to copy-edit the manuscript. Edna Liftman guided the book past treacherous bureaucratic shoals. Then there is my wife Sandra, who learned that scholarship somehow does qualify as work, and then made the decisive contribution.

Transliteration has proved a thorny problem in a work which includes names and terms drawn from most major Muslim languages. My approach has been to avoid unsightly Arabicization in transliterating other Muslim languages, and to omit diacriticals and vowel quantities. In this manner, I hope to satisfy even readers who reach this book from opposite ends of the Muslim world, with their own conventions of transliteration. Within each Muslim language, my method has been simplified but consistent, and its principles will be readily evident to the specialist.

Islam Assembled

ONE

THE COSMOPOLITAN MILIEU
Pan-Islamic Ideals

T HE EXPANSION of the West into Muslim lands redefined for Muslim peoples the meaning of universal community. Before modern times, those conflicts which separated Muslims, whether on sectarian or political grounds, were waged by all sides with the confidence and intolerance of total conviction. The most enduring of these struggles, a contest which loomed nearly as large in Muslim historical consciousness as that between Muslim and Christian, divided Sunni and Shiʿi. From the sixteenth to eighteenth centuries, Ottoman and Crimean armies waged periodic wars against the Safavids and their successors which, for sheer ferocity, rivaled any contemporary Ottoman engagement with the Christian foe in Europe. During these confrontations, Ottoman ulama went so far as to declare that Safavid domains were not Muslim, and were legally indistinguishable from the territories of hostile Christendom. On their part, Safavid rulers actively sought alliances with Christian powers against their common Ottoman adversary. The supposed waste represented by this conflict held a great attraction for nineteenth-century Muslim moralists, familiar with a far more dynamic brand of Western military, commercial, and cultural activity. In 1881, the Young Ottoman journalist and novelist Namık Kemal (1840–1888) published a historical novel entitled *Cezmi,* set in the morass of late-sixteenth-century conflict between Safavid Iran and the Ottoman-Crimean league. The author has the brother of the Crimean Khan Mehmed Giray II fall in love with the daughter of Shah Tahmasp. Together they discuss the unity of Islam, and the joining of the three great neighboring polities against their shared Christian foe. The story reaches a climax of jealousy and murder, in the romantic style which so influenced Kemal's literary productions.[1]

The same retrospective fascination was evoked by the attempt to enforce an exchange between Sunni and Shiʿi in 1743, at the insistence of Nadir Shah. In the midst of his military campaign against the Ottomans in Iraq, the Shah summoned the Sunni scholar ʿAbdallah ibn Husayn al-Suwaydi of Baghdad, and lamented that accusations of unbelief (*kufr*) were exchanged among the Muslims of his kingdom. The ulama were to offer proofs for their mutual vilifications in an open forum. ᶜAbdallah relates that he presided at Najaf over a two-day gathering of Shiᶜi and Sunni ulama from throughout Nadir Shah's realm.[2] About seventy participants were from Iran; among the Sunnis, apparently all Hanafis, were eight Afghans and seven Uzbeks. The Iranian ulama finally signed a document in which they agreed to abandon the cursing of the first three caliphs in their Friday sermon (*khutba*), and the Afghan and Uzbek ulama affirmed in writing that they recognized the Shiᶜis as Muslims constituting one of the sects (*firaq*) of Islam. Subtle coercion was involved in the extraction of this brief reconciliation. When ᶜAbdallah went to a mosque in Kufa on Friday to hear the blessing of the caliphs in the Shiᶜi sermon, he was certain that the sermonizer meant an insult to the caliph ᶜUmar by vowelling a letter of his name incorrectly.[3] But this did not dampen the nineteenth-century Muslim impulse to romanticize the conciliatory efforts of Nadir Shah.

The modern Muslim interest in this and other attempts to moderate sectarian conflict was prompted by the continued animosity between Sunni and Shiᶜi. The orientalist E. G. Browne gave anecdotal expression to the durability of this hostility:

> The antipathy between Turk and Persian is profound, and, in my opinion, indestructable, and is both national and religious. A dervish at Khuy, in North-West Persia, boasted to me that he and some of his fellow-dervishes had accompanied the Russian army during the Russo-Turkish War, and aided the Russian arms by their prayers. I need not say that I do not ascribe the victory of the Russians entirely to this cause; and I daresay that the whole story was a figment of the dervish's fertile imagination, and that he was never near the seat of war at all; but that is neither here nor there: I merely refer to the incident as indicating how little sympathy exists between the Persians and the Turks on religious grounds.[4]

It was only the acceleration of Russian expansion at both Ottoman and Iranian expense that diminished this rooted hostility. During Iran's constitutional revolution, a period marked by Russian encroachments on Iranian territory, the Shiᶜi religious authorities resident in Iraq forged an alliance with Ottoman authorities against Muhammad ᶜAli Shah and Russian expansion. A number of the most esteemed Iranian Shiᶜi ulama met in Baghdad where they issued a proclamation calling for close cooperation between the Ottoman and Iranian states. "The complete union of Muslims, the preservation of the seed of Islam, the preservation of Islamic nations, Ottoman and Persian, against the enterprises of foreign nations and attacks of outside powers—on all these points, we are in accord. . . . We announce to the entire Persian nation that it is an obligation to have confidence in the Ottoman nation, and to offer it aid, so that it may conserve its independence, protect its territory, and preserve its frontiers from invasion by foreigners."[5] Even E.G. Browne no longer thought the old antipathy insurmountable, and chastised those who did: "Even those who think they know about the East cannot or will not believe that an *entente* between Sunnis-Shi'as is possible, whereas it is now practically a *fait accompli,* since the formal joint manifesto issued by the ulama of both parties at Baghdad. I know this not only from the Persian papers but from private letters from well-informed quarters in Kerbala too."[6]

This reconciliation, short-lived though it proved to be, represented the most striking example of the unifying potential of reaction to Western expansion. Divisions between Muslims diminished, however briefly, before the greater challenge of foreign encroachment, as the great Muslim empires lost influence, then territory, to an ascendant West. By the late nineteenth century, reformers could posit the existence of an almost universal Muslim predicament, one of subjugation to the West, and they held that discord within the community of believers was partly to blame for their own tribulations. The affective affinity of Muslims on the plane of theory was not sufficient. What was required now was effective solidarity.

The Muslim congress responded to the disorientation caused by the nineteenth-century expansion of the West into Muslim lands. The search for a remedy in the technique of assembly tapped the self-indicting conviction that Muslims had invited Western conquest and influence by their own discord, and had squandered their resources in internecine warfare while Christendom waxed.[7] But the congress was only one of several techniques that competed for the attention of those seeking to defend Muslims against the consequences of their own divisions. And the reception of this technique was affected by another response to the impact of the West: intensified attachment to the institution of the Ottoman caliphate and the person of the Ottoman sultan-caliph.

From a narrowly academic point of view, the Ottoman claim to the universal caliphate was not impeccable, and was vulnerable on the point of Qurashi descent. But the failure of the Ottomans to meet this requirement led even rigorous jurists not to a rejection of the Ottoman claim, but to suspension of the requirement, particularly within the Ottoman Empire. There, Muslim jurists and theologians, not to exclude the Arabic-speakers among them, withheld criticism and maintained the legitimacy of the Ottoman claim.[8] Dissenting voices were nearly inaudible, and were confined to a few remote provinces. The theory of the caliphate as circulated in the Ottoman Empire contained hardly an allusion to Qurashi descent and election, and substituted the enforcement of the holy law and the militant defense of Islam as valid criteria for measurement of any claim to the Muslim caliphate.[9] The Ottomans fulfilled both of these obligations to the satisfaction of many jurists among their subjects, for whom the Ottoman state and dynasty constituted the only firm bulwark against total subjugation to the rule of foreigners.

A different question was whether that caliphate was universal, whether the Ottoman caliph was the suzerain of Muslims over whom he was not sovereign. The case for the universal validity of the Ottoman caliphate was not wholly contrived, and had circulated some three hundred years before its reassertion in the nineteenth century. The great Muslim prestige enjoyed by the Ottoman state as early as the sixteenth century was a consequence of the Ottoman role as diffusor of firearms and technologies current in Europe to Muslim peoples threatened by Portuguese, Russian, or Iranian expansion.[10] This is in clearest evidence in the example of sixteenth-century Ottoman military aid to the Muslims of Atjeh, then under Portuguese pressure. Accounts in Indonesian, Turkish, and Portuguese sources establish that the Ottomans were pursuing broad recognition of their caliphate even at this early date. From these sources, it appears that Atjehnese Muslims were prepared to accept nominal Ottoman suzerainty and accord the title of universal caliph (*khalifat allah fi'l-ard*) to the Ottoman sultan, in exchange for material aid.[11]

The Ottoman admiral Seydi Ali Reis also advanced the universal claims of his sovereign at the Mughal court of Humayun, then also under Portuguese naval pressure, and these claims were received favorably. Humayun's successor Akbar also employed the title of universal caliph in addressing the Ottoman sultan.[12] A third sixteenth-century example survives in Ottoman correspondence with Malik Idris of Bornu, in which a letter to Idris from the Ottoman sultan again advanced a universal claim, along with an implicit promise of firearms.[13] Sixteenth-century recognition of this early Ottoman pretension was the consequence of a desire among Muslims elsewhere to share or benefit from superior Ottoman military technology and power. The claim to general suzerainty of the Ottoman caliphs over Muslims beyond the Ottoman Empire dates from that earlier century of crisis.

The reassertion of the Ottoman claim in the late eighteenth and early nineteenth century, and its recognition by Muslims beyond the empire, thus rested upon assumptions that were not wholly of modern manufacture.[14] What initially appeared to Muslims as a repetition of that sixteenth-century challenge evoked a response patterned along earlier precedent. Once again, Muslims in Central Asia, Sumatra, and India embraced the Ottoman sultan as their caliph. In the nineteenth century, as in the sixteenth, the Ottoman state remained the strongest Muslim power; as in the sixteenth century, Muslims threatened by an expanding West were anxious to exchange professions of allegiance for whatever military, diplomatic, or moral aid the Ottomans could spare them.

Sultan Abdülaziz (r.1861–1876) reasserted the Ottoman claim to the caliphate as a response to the entreaties of these besieged Muslims. The principal figures in this awakening were not Ottoman emissaries abroad, but Muslim political refugees who crossed Ottoman borders bearing their grievances. The impact was first felt shortly after the French conquest of Algiers, with the departure of a small number of Algerian Muslims for Syria. For the next eighty years, Algerian refugees continued to make their way east to Ottoman territories.[15] As early as 1845, during the Şamil uprising in Daghistan, Muslim refugees were issuing appeals within the Ottoman Empire for aid against Russia.[16] In 1852, Mappilla disturbances led the English to expel from Malabar the Tannal of Mambram, Sayyid Fadl ibn ʿAlawi (1830–1900), who later became an intimate advisor to Abdülhamid II, and was responsible for an attempt to assert an Ottoman claim, long in abeyance, to Dhufar.[17] From 1854, in the wake of the Crimean War, a large wave of Crimean Muslim refugees swept into Istanbul and Anatolian coastal towns, leaving an indelible impression on those who witnessed the influx.[18] Circassian Muslims also began to arrive in large numbers after the Crimean War and the consequent Russian policy of consolidation in the Caucasus. The refugees, who arrived in a series of waves over the next half a century, were resettled in the Balkans and Syria.[19] The suppression of the Great Mutiny and the Mughal dynasty in India in 1857 also brought many refugees to Ottoman territories. One, Rahmat Allah Kairanawi (1818–1890), endorsed the jihad against English rule and escaped to Mecca with a price on his head following the collapse of the Mutiny. Under the sultan-caliph's benevolent patronage, he wrote a major and enduring anti-Christian polemic.[20] Later began a stream of refugees and emissaries from Central Asia to the Ottoman capital itself, with profound effect. In the case of these territories, under growing Russian and Chinese pressure in the 1860s, the initiatives came from the endangered khanates themselves.[21] From 1873, the sultanate of Atjeh found itself at war with Holland, and turned expectantly to the sultan-caliph. The Ottomans had all but forgotten their claim to the territory, and it was the notion of a Hadrami *sayyid* in Atjehnese service, Habib ʿAbd al-Rahman al-Zahir (1833–1896), to appear in Istanbul and dramatically remind the Ottomans of alleged obligations incurred by their suzerain status.[22] One of the last important waves of refugees comprised Tunisians fleeing French rule, who played a major role in Istanbul's Muslim émigré community.[23] To accommodate this influx of refugees, the Ottoman government in 1860 established a special commission for Muslim immigration. This body continued to function for over four decades, in various forms and under various names, whenever the need arose. Renewed interest in the Ottoman caliphate began beyond the Ottoman Empire, among these besieged Muslims who thus hoped to gain Ottoman military, financial, and moral support. Its purpose was quite different from the later policy launched from Istanbul during the reign of Abdülhamid II, a policy which instead cast the Ottomans themselves as the recipients of Muslim material and moral assistance.

Abdülhamid II (r.1876–1909) continued the policy of resettling refugees and receiving delegations from territories under Western pressure, but he also sought to generate Muslim support for his caliphate in places where such support had yet to emerge spontaneously. Unable to defend his own frontiers effectively, and even less able or prepared to liberate fragments of other Muslim empires already under Western rule, he was drawn to claim a spiritual authority no longer dependent upon possession of the sinews of power. His was a policy intended to conceal weakness, to create an illusion of latent strength. The emissary, diffusing the message of the Ottoman sultan-caliph at the periphery of the empire and beyond, was the conspicuous figure in this policy of active self-assertion. In this role, he supplanted the refugee as the stimulant of solidarity.

In the doctrine associated with Abdülhamid, authority was personified in the radiant Ottoman sultan-caliph, and amplified by his possession of Mecca and Madina; around his person and his sacred possessions in Arabia revolved all Muslims. But not all were in close orbit. Most simply faced the sultan-caliph's territories in prayer; fewer cited him in their prayers; still fewer visited or resided in his domains; yet fewer bore arms in his cause. It was the task of Abdülhamid's emissaries to make Muslims aware of the sultan-caliph's prerogatives, and to ask more of those Muslims who already had acknowledged Ottoman primacy. Those emissaries gifted in speech traveled widely in the Ottoman Empire and abroad, while those prolific in the written word were maintained in Istanbul at the expense of the treasury. Together they formed a chain of transmission for the message of Ottoman primacy which, by spoken or printed word, was intended to reach the most distant Muslim enclaves.

Abdülhamid first assembled a number of Muslims from his own Arabic-speaking provinces, and in Istanbul they published works extolling the Ottoman sultan-caliph and insisting upon the absolute nature of his authority.[24] The most prolific of these authors was Abu al-Huda al-Sayyadi (1850–1909), a Rifaʿi shaykh from the vicinity of Aleppo who enjoyed the full confidence of Abdülhamid and spent his creative years writing, publishing, and intriguing in Istanbul. His most significant work, published for Arabic- and Turkish-reading audiences, argued that absolute and unqualified obedience to the Ottoman caliph was a duty incumbent upon all Muslims.[25] Abu al-Huda al-Sayyadi was one of several figures at the court who disseminated a similar message in a similar manner. Alongside him served Muhammad Zafir al-Madani (1828–1906) of Misurata in Libya. A shaykh of the Madaniyya sub-order of the predominantly North African Shadhiliyya order, he settled in Istanbul in 1875 and remained there for thirty years, enjoying an influence over Abdülhamid second only to that of Sayyid Abu al-Huda. His special sphere of activity extended to Morocco, where he sought to disseminate the message of Ottoman primacy by organizing Ottoman military missions to Mawlay Hasan and an Ottoman legation at Fez. Neither effort succeeded.[26] Also in Istanbul was Husayn al-Jisr (1845–1909), an Azhar-educated shaykh from Syrian Tripoli who titled two of his famous works in honor of Abdülhamid, although he was on the edge of that closed Arabic-speaking circle which Abdülhamid had assembled around himself.[27] Another figure in Abdülhamid's service was the aforementioned Shaykh Fadl ibn ᶜAlawi, who had arrived as a refugee from Malabar in 1852 and whose task as an emissary was to reconcile dissident sentiment in Arabia. His most accomplished student in Istanbul was the Ottoman link to the Muslims of the East African littoral. Ahmad ibn Sumayt (1861–1925), a Comorian also of Hadrami descent, had been a religious court judge in Zanzibar before fleeing to Istanbul in 1886. There he remained for two years as a guest, and returned to Zanzibar where he became an advocate of greater attachment to the Ottoman sultan-caliph.[28] That these Arabic-speaking emissaries of the Ottoman word were sorely divided by personal rivalries was established by a contemporary observer, but their work was not without effect among Arabic-speakers in the provinces and beyond.[29]

To bring the Ottoman message to Shiᶜi Muslims, the court relied in part upon Jamal al-Din al-Afghani/Asadabadi (1838–1897), an Iranian-born cosmopolitan who traveled widely in the Muslim world, teaching advanced ideas of religious reform, and jostling for a position of influence. Although his early teachings were void of pan-Islamic references, Afghani later pressed Abdülhamid to enlist him, as a roving Ottoman emissary or as an Istanbul consultant.[30] Only in 1892, after Afghani's expulsion from Iran, did Abdülhamid decide to employ him, probably to exploit his intensified hostility toward Nasir al-Din Shah. An arrangement similar to that enjoyed by Abu al-Huda al-Sayyadi was accepted by Afghani, who was given a residence and allowance in Istanbul. In return, Afghani organized a small circle of Iranians in Istanbul, who launched a letter-writing campaign directed to Shiᶜi ulama and dignitaries in Iraq, Iran, Central Asia, and India, "about the kindness and benevolence of the great Islamic Sultan toward all Muslims of whatever opinion and group they might be."[31] A short time later, however, Afghani clashed with Sayyid Abu al-Huda, fell out of favor, and died a virtual captive in 1897. The campaign to win the sympathies of Shiʿi ulama fell in part to the Ottoman ambassador in Teheran. According to a British diplomat,

> He belonged to a secret confraternity of dervishes, I think the Bektashis, cultivated a fairly long beard, and was profoundly interested in the metaphysical theology of Islam, which he used to explain and discuss with me at considerable length. He was himself, really, I think, a Sufi . . . [which] facilitated his intercourse with the more learned members of the Persian clergy, some of whom I often met and talked with at his house. I imagine, indeed, that he was chosen for this very purpose by Sultan Abdul Hamid.

The efforts of this Ottoman diplomat, continued Sir Arthur Hardinge, were not without effect: "I remember myself going with the Turkish Ambassador to hear a great Tehran Mullah preach during Moharram and being surprised at the fulsome eulogies which he heaped upon the Sultan of Turkey and on the sacred character of the latter as 'Lord of the two Continents and Seas' ('el barrein wa el bahrein')."[32]

To carry his message to points further east, the sultan-caliph relied upon other emissaries in the formal guise of diplomatic envoys and consular officials. One of the earliest of these was kazasker Ahmed Hulûsi Efendi, who in 1877 led an Ottoman mission to Kabul. There he attempted to erect a Muslim alliance against Russia by persuading the Afghan amir, Shir ʿAli, of his obligations toward the Ottoman sultan-caliph. The emissary even bore a letter from the Ottoman Şeyhülislam, who threatened to "issue a kind of excommunication" against Shir ʿAli's followers if they did not turn away from Russia.[33] Anti-Russian propagandists were always welcome in Istanbul, and the more eloquent refugees from Russian rule were encouraged to publish books and tracts against what was regarded as the perpetual enemy of the Muslims. Abdürreşid İbrahim[ov] (1857–1944), a Siberian-born Volga Tatar who studied and traveled throughout the Ottoman Empire, published a violently anti-Russian polemic in Istanbul, and later continued this work within Russia and back in Istanbul under the Young Turks.[34]

In India, the Ottomans operated a consular service, and it was to the consuls that expressions of allegiance to the Ottoman sultan-caliph were directed. These expressions were generated by that acute sense of loss evoked by the collapse of Mughal rule. Activity intensified during the Russo-Turkish war (1876–77), and centered around the Ottoman consul-general in Bombay, who channeled funds collected by Indian Muslims to Istanbul, and distributed Ottoman decorations in return. Back in the Ottoman capital, a circle of Indian Muslims operated alongside the Arab and Iranian circles. They edited and published a virulently anti-British newspaper in Urdu, done on the imperial press and with heavy subventions. The newspaper, *Payk-i Islam,* was later closed at British insistence, but its editor continued to carry on his campaign both in Istanbul and London.[35]

The techniques employed in pursuit of this policy were thoroughly traditional, and were reminiscent of those medieval methods to which Muslim emissaries had resorted at earlier times, for similar purposes. The parallel which suggests itself most insistently is Fatimid propaganda, the tools of which were similar,[36] although Ottoman propaganda certainly differed in its reliance upon some modern instruments. Among these were the printing press, the cover provided by permanent diplomacy, and the mobility afforded by the steamer and railroad. The steamer in particular figured prominently in the movements of emissaries, their printed tracts, and their correspondence. It afforded safe and speedy transport, facilitated commercial, political, and intellectual exchange among Muslims, and presented a challenge to those Western states anxious to regulate that exchange.[37] The creation of a rail network had a similar effect, most notably in the Hijaz. The construction of this railway, accomplished with Muslim financial assistance from beyond the Ottoman Empire, rendered the pilgrimage safer and cheaper.[38] These improvements certainly made the task of the emissary easier, and helped to create that cosmopolitan climate in which his message flourished.

But the aim of the emissary, despite his employment of modern methods for the speedy spread of ideas, ultimately remained as conservative as the doctrine which he was employed to propagate. For the Ottoman emissary pursued not an exchange of ideas, but the propagation of a set of fixed principles about the nature of political and religious authority in Islam. The congress idea emerged as another answer to the same challenge of Western expansion which the emissary attempted to answer, and as another response to the same technological advances from which the emissary benefited. But it drew upon two radically different assumptions: the diffusion among scattered Muslim communities of that religious and political authority claimed by the sultan-caliph, and the supremacy of a consensus of these communities to any rival source of authority. The congress idea thus surfaced beyond the wide alliance of sentiment which Ottoman emissaries were building, and often in close association with political and intellectual innovators.

TWO

A CHALLENGE TO AUTHORITY

The Congress Idea

THAT cosmopolitan awareness which made a congress feasible was formed by the contours of Western expansion into Muslim lands. The technological advances which made the theoretical convocation of a congress thinkable were of Western manufacture. But the benefits of any innovation drawn from beyond Muslim tradition were not indisputable. Like most imported institutions and techniques, this one threatened to dislodge others that were established and sanctioned by usage. So it happened that the congress idea first emerged as a challenge to the authority of the Ottoman caliphate. The transmitters of this derivative idea, to the extent that their identities can be established, were men unsympathetic to the Ottoman state, and the original association with dissent much affected the idea's subsequent reception. The congress was first advocated not to buttress established authority and enforce established belief, but to topple a perceived edifice of despotism and religious obscurantism. It began as a radical solution for those dissatisfied with the Muslim political and doctrinal order, a solution so against the prevalent grain that its first proponents were not—perhaps could not have been—Muslims.

A minor Victorian poet, Wilfrid Scawen Blunt (1840–1922), first advocated a Muslim congress in print, and first thought to disseminate the idea among influential Muslims.[1] Blunt was a social nonconformist and political romantic who later lamented having consumed the first forty years of his life preoccupied with strictly sensual pursuits. He was in quest of a cause, and eventually settled upon oppressed peoples under what he deplored as Turkish misrule. Among these he favored the inhabitants of Arabia. Between 1876 and 1879, he and his wife Anne undertook their first journeys through the Arabic-speaking provinces of the Ottoman Empire, and returned much influenced by their experiences. During these travels, Blunt acquired an appreciation of the desert Beduin Arabs that bordered on an obsession. "What Byron had done for Greece & so retrieved his soul, that I would do, I thought, for Arabia. This was my dream," wrote Blunt in his unpublished memoirs.[2] On his return to England in 1879, Blunt gave his self-imposed mission a political form. He became convinced that the Turks were responsible for the decadence of Islam, and that a great reformation of the Muslim faith could be undertaken only under Arabian auspices. In accord with this premise, he eventually advocated the transfer of the caliphate from Istanbul to Mecca, from the Ottoman house to an Arabic-speaking incumbent of Quraysh.

Blunt's recollection of his first encounter with this idea was vague, but he cited two individuals as particularly influential:

> I do not well remember whether it was from this Sabunji or from Malkum Khan that I first came to understand the historical aspect of the caliphal question and its modern aspects, but, opposed as I was to Ottoman rule, it struck me at once as one of high importance to the kind of reform I was beginning to look for.[3]

It is unlikely that Blunt learned to advocate an Arabian/Qurashi caliphate from Malkum Khan (1833/4–1908), then the Iranian minister to London, whose name became so intimately associated with the cause of Westernizing reform in Iran. It was true that Malkum, as an official Iranian representative, would have had no particular reason to insist upon the prerogatives of the Ottoman caliphate, and it has been established, on the basis of Malkum Khan's own personal papers, that his view of Islam was a strictly utilitarian one.[4] On the other hand, while Malkum's religious and political views were decidedly unconventional, one finds in his writings no mention of an Arabian caliphate, or indeed any trace of that obsession with the Arabs as a medium of reform which characterized Blunt. His two closest and most renowned correspondents, Mirza Fath ᶜAli Akhundzada and Mirza Aqa Khan Kirmani, were Arabophobes. When Malkum published at London his reformist newspaper *Qanun*, from 1890, his public views on the question of Turkish primacy were made explicit. A questioner from Herat wrote him asking where the physical center (*markaz*) of Muslim union (*ittihad*) lay; Malkum replied that "Istanbul is the first fortress of the independence of Muslim states," followed by Mecca, the Shiᶜi holy cities (ᶜatabat) in Iraq, and Kabul. But Istanbul was the "crown of the earth" which all Muslims were obliged to defend.[5] This elicited a number of letters from readers: an Indian ᶜalim insisted that Mecca was the center, on account of its holiness; a Turkistani pilgrim argued for Bukhara, as a great center of learning; an Egyptian shaykh wrote on behalf of Cairo, because of its geographic position; an Iranian prince from Khurasan cited Mashhad as equally well-placed; and so on. Malkum then retreated to the position that every Muslim land belonged to all Muslims, and that the defense of each was a collective obligation.[6] But neither in his original nor revised position was there a sign of partisanship for the Arabs, and his first reaction was immediately to cite Istanbul as the hub of Islam. At best, Malkum was probably indifferent to the whole question, and so could hardly have fired Blunt's imagination without misleading the Englishman as to his true beliefs. The possibility is not to be ruled out, but Malkum's purpose in doing so on this issue is not readily apparent.

John Louis Sabunji (1838–1931), a former priest of the Syrian Catholic Rite originally from Diyarbekir, seems the more likely source of Blunt's enlightenment on questions of the Muslim caliphate. Aside from preaching the gospel in Syria and Lebanon, Sabunji also had published newspapers in Beirut, and in 1874, having offended Maronite sensibilities, he fled to England where he remained more or less continuously for fifteen years.[7] From 1877 to 1880, Sabunji published at London the newspaper al-Nahla, which, while increasingly critical of Ottoman policies, did not yet call into question the legitimacy of the Ottoman caliphate. But upon the return of the Blunts to England in 1879, Sabunji became a tutor in Arabic to Anne, and perhaps then acquainted her husband with his changing ideas concerning the fundamental nature of the caliphate. These ideas were leading him to a violent denial of the Ottoman claim, a radical step made known through his publication of yet another newspaper in London, al-Khilafa, from January 1881.[8] The motives of his professed hostility to Ottoman primacy are obscure, for it was not a principle with him, and in 1890, after a long period as Blunt's secretary, he proceeded to Istanbul where he entered the service of Abdülhamid II as a translator of the European press.[9] This function he filled until the Young Turk revolution. Blunt saw him in 1909, and described him as "a Yildiz Palace spy, a little furtive old man dressed in black with a black skull cap on his head, a jewel in his shirt front and another jewel on his finger."[10] But all this would come later. By late 1880, the idea that "the Caliphate was not necessarily vested in the House of Othman," an idea possibly implanted by Sabunji, had carried Blunt, and he pressed it upon Gladstone at their first meeting.[11] With an Arabian caliphate, Blunt wrote in a memorandum printed for circulation in the Foreign Office, Istanbul "would cease to be of vital consequence, and the position England might assume of Protectress of the Caliphate would assure to her whatever forces Islam can still command. This is probably the only solution which could assure India permanently to her."[12]

There was yet a third possible influence upon Blunt, a series of letters to the London Times written by G.C.M. Birdwood (1832–1917), an administrator with long experience in Indian service.[13] Birdwood, who knew Sabunji as well, argued as early as 1877 that the Ottoman caliphate was a "usurpation," and that the right to the dignity belonged to the Sharif of Mecca. Birdwood insisted that "there is not the slightest authority for the claim of the Sultans of Constantinople to the Caliphate; that their assumption of the title is an illegal and heretical usurpation; and that the acceptance of their preposterous pretension to it by Mohamedans is discreditable equally to their orthodoxy, their intelligence, and their good faith."[14]

On this point, there was no room for compromise: "The Ottoman Caliphate is a usurped authority. Not even a *Plebiscitum* of the mob of Islam could possibly make the usurpation lawful and orthodox."[15] Birdwood's complaint did not just extend to the Ottoman house: "Islam has been overrun and enthralled by the Turks and Tartars for over 600 years, and there is little hope for Mahomedan Asia until the last remnants of the mouldering 'Tataric system' are swept away." Birdwood's solution was to suggest that Muslims "begin their regeneration by electing the Sheerif of Mecca Caliph of Islam."[16] The motives of this civil servant, as he made clear throughout, were considerations of imperial policy concerning the loyalty of Indian Muslims, a loyalty which could be secured for Great Britain through the transfer of the caliphate from potentially hostile to pliant hands. Blunt made no mention of Birdwood's campaign conducted on the pages of *The Times*, but he was in England at the time, and later may have overlooked this early exposure to the idea of an Arabian caliphate.

There was, however, a fourth person of hitherto unappreciated influence at work upon Blunt's Byronic imagination. In the winter of 1880–81, the Blunts set off for Jidda on what appears to have been a self-appointed political mission: "I wished to penetrate once more into Arabia, if possible through Hejaz or perhaps Yemen to Nejd. I had an idea that among the Wahhabis I might find a teacher who would give me the Arabian as opposed to the Ottoman view of Islam, and that I might devise with him a movement of reform in which I should suggest the political, he the religious elements."[17] In Jidda, Blunt met no great reformers, but did befriend the British consul, James Zohrab, appointed in 1878. Since late 1879, Zohrab had been writing to his superiors that the religious centrality of the Sharif of Mecca in the Muslim world was comparable to that of the Ottoman sultan-caliph.[18] Zohrab went so far as to advocate the separation of the Hijaz from the Ottoman Empire, and its affiliation with Great Britain, which would then be in an enviable position to influence Muslims in India and elsewhere. By January 1880, Zohrab was arguing that the Sharif of Mecca, as a direct descendant of the Prophet, carried more weight in Islam than the Ottoman caliph.[19] Blunt was already active on behalf of this notion. But Zohrab was convinced that a Muslim society, meeting in secrecy, already existed to achieve the ends which Blunt advocated. In March 1879, Zohrab reported that the Sharif informed him through Zohrab's own dragoman that "the various Mussulman nationalities are in close correspondence with each other and political events are reported to the chiefs of all. The organisation seems complete and the union perfect, and restless spirits are ever moving in search of pretexts to raise complications."[20] By August he had more details to report:

> From a Gentleman who has resided here for some years I hear, that at Mecca there exists a secret society whose object is the removal of all Mohamedans from Christian control. This Society is in communication with every Mussulman community throughout the world, and it has had a good deal to do with the revolt in Algeria. It was not intended that the revolt should commence when it did, the plan was that it should begin there when the brand of war or revolt could at the same time be applied to the other countries. Similar information has reached me from another source.
>
> The Society, which is composed of Mollahs Sheeks and Sheriffs is, I am told, so dissatisfied with the result of the late war with Russia that the question of withdrawing from the Sultan the title of Temporal Head of the Mussulman Faith is being seriously discussed. It is declared that as the Sultan is under the control of the Christian Powers, he can no longer be regarded as independent and cannot, therefore continue to be the true Representative of the Prophet and the mantle must be laid on other shoulders. This opinion, it appears, had its rise in Damascus and that city was at first decided on as the future Seat of the Head of Islam. The Society at Mecca was averse to this, it was argued that Damascus being within easy reach of European influence, it would not be a safe home; whereas Medina, which combined within itself all requirements, that is, remot[e]ness from Europe, difficulty of access, sacredness of the city and purity of the Mussulman character, indicated itself as the natural centre of the faith. Medina has, therefore, it is said, been fixed upon.[21]

Such an important decision implied the secret convening of a congress or conclave, and these Zohrab believed to be regular occurrences:

> The Province of Hedjaz is the centre to which the ideas, opinions, sentiments and aspirations of the Mussulman world are brought for discussion. The annual meeting at a fixed time ostensibly for the performance of the Pilgrimage of Representatives from every Mussulman Community affords a means without creating suspicion, to exchange opinions, to discuss plans, to criticise the actions of the European Governments and to form combinations to resist the supremacy of the Christian Powers. In the discussion in secret of political questions there is no country offering such security and facilities as the Hedjaz. A meeting of Delegates from

Mohamedan Countries at any other point could not fail of attracting Public attention but in the Hedjaz such meetings can, and it is said do annually take place and at them discussion is free without fear of betrayal.[22]

He continued to maintain his belief in the existence of this clandestine activity when Blunt was present in Arabia, reporting that "a widely extended secret society exists embracing Mussulmans of all nationalities, its object being to restore the Khalifate to the Arabs of the Hedjaz."[23] Zohrab no doubt pressed his views on the caliphate upon Blunt, who was already predisposed to accept them. But he also may well have convinced Blunt of the existence of an organized society of Muslims, meeting in secret congress, who were prepared at the opportune moment to reveal themselves and challenge the authority of the Ottoman caliphate.

Upon Blunt's return to England, he distilled his accumulated ideas into a series of articles for *The Fortnightly Review*, all of which were later published together as *The Future of Islam* (London, 1882). It was this series which most eloquently set down the argument against Turkish political predominance in Islam, and for the primacy of Arabic speakers. Here Blunt offered a critique of the Ottoman claim to the caliphate similar in all essentials to Birdwood's, and advanced the claim of Quraysh, through the Sharif of Mecca, in an identical manner: "The Sherif is already far more truly representative of spiritual rank than any Sultan or Caliph is," he wrote, echoing Zohrab's dispatches. "If no new figure should appear on the political horizon of Islam when the Ottoman empire dies, sufficiently commanding to attract the allegiance of the Mussulman world (and of such there is as yet no sign), it is certainly to the Sherifal family of Mecca that the mass of Mohammedans would look for a representative of their supreme headship, and of that Caliphate of which they stand in need." Mecca as seat of the caliphate "is, as far as I have had an opportunity of judging, the cry of the day with Mussulmans."[24]

It was in this context that Blunt first suggested the convocation of a Muslim congress, as an electoral college:

It is surely not beyond the flight of sane imagination to suppose, in the last overwhelming catastrophe of Constantinople, a council of Ulema assembling at Mecca, and according to the legal precedent of ancient days electing a Caliph. The assembly would, without doubt, witness intrigues of princes and quarrels among schoolmen and appeals to fanaticism and accusations of infidelity. Money, too, would certainly play its part there as elsewhere, and perhaps blood might be shed. But any one who remembers the history of the Christian Church in the fifteenth century, and the synods which preceded the Council of Basle, must admit that such accompaniments of intrigue and corruption are no bar to a legal solution of religious difficulties. It was above all else the rivalries of Popes and Anti-popes that precipitated the Catholic Reformation.[25]

This was only part of Blunt's vision. In his series of articles, he evidenced a profound dissatisfaction with the provisions of Islamic law on issues as diverse as slavery and marriage. "The great difficulty which, as things now stand, besets reform is this: the Sheriat, or written code of law, still stands in orthodox Islam as an *unimpeachable* authority. The law itself is an excellent law, and as such commends itself to the loyalty of honest and God-fearing men; but in certain points it is irreconcilable with the modern needs of Islam, and it cannot legally be altered."[26] Blunt sought a more flexible, utilitarian Islam, and to effect these most fundamental changes, he again anticipated a Muslim congress, this time to fill a role not unlike that of the great councils of the Church:

> Since we are imagining many things we may imagine this one too,—that our Caliph of the Koreysh, chosen by the faithful and installed at Mecca, should invite the Ulema of every land to a council at the time of the pilgrimage, and there, appointing a new Mujtaheed, should propound to them certain modifications of the Sheriat, as things necessary to the welfare of Islam, and deducible from tradition. No point of doctrine need in any way be touched, only the law. The Fakh ed din would need hardly a modification. The Fakh esh Sheriat would, in certain chapters, have to be rewritten. Who can doubt that an Omar or an Haroun, were they living at the present day, would authorize such changes, or that the faithful of their day would have accepted them as necessary and legitimate developments of Koranic teaching?[27]

Thus did Blunt prepare to realign Islam around a new political center, and radically reform the *shari⁽a*, through the medium of a series of Muslim assemblies. These would dethrone conventional authority, and establish an enlightened and responsive new orthodoxy.

Zohrab's belief in the existence of a vast secret society possibly convinced Blunt that such a forum would spring forth spontaneously upon the destruction of the Ottoman caliphate. Zohrab of course was unable to identify any members of this society, to give a detail on a single discussion among its members, or even to identify by name the sources from which he received his information. What Blunt and Zohrab had predicted was woven of the thinnest threads of evidence, and expressed their own visionary expectations.

What is first noteworthy about Blunt and those who influenced the gestation of his ideas is that they were not disinterested. They were not Muslims, but their definitive pronouncements on fundamental matters of Muslim belief were stirred by a dissatisfaction with the political and social constraints of an Islam to which they professed an informal commitment. This was certainly the case with Sabunji, who for reasons of ambition or principle identified himself with Islam as a political cause. But in Blunt and Zohrab, advocacy of an Arabian caliphate and concern for the state of Islam appeared in conjunction with highly unusual convictions about the perimeters of the faith. Blunt appreciated Islam as a cause, and even toyed with the possibility of conversion, but was unable to appreciate Islam as an intricate and varied system of belief. He could only remark on "how simple a creed Islam is compared with any form of Christianity, how easy of acceptance and how little it demands of its professors in the way of intellectual sacrifice even from minds the most sceptical in their materialism, the least prone to spiritual illusion."[28]

Zohrab held other unconventional and uninformed notions. At one moment he was writing that the Sharif of Mecca "is for Mussulmans pretty well what the Pope is for the Roman Catholic Church."[29] At the next, he maintained that the Sharif's plan to repair the Kaᶜba at Mecca would raise him "to the rank of a Prophet in the belief of Mussulmans, for as the law declares that none but a Prophet can repair the Caaba he must be a Prophet if he has been permitted to do so. The power such a belief would give him over the ignorant and fanatical would be absolute and every Mussulman would then have to obey him in every-thing."[30] One statement did violence to the Catholic papacy, the other to Muslim prophecy. The congress idea thus found its first adherents in individuals who suffered from misapprehensions about what was possible and not possible in the Islam of their time, and who entertained unsubstantiated visions of an Islam on the brink of organizational revolution.

Their Muslim conclaves also appeared in an explicitly anti-Ottoman context, thus assuring that the idea would raise defeating suspicions. If one understands the growing popularity of the Ottoman caliphate in the 1870s as a plea for help from a stronger hand, the contrived nature of agitation for an Arabian caliphate becomes clear. The province was not an independent power, and precisely at this time the central government in Istanbul had successfully reasserted Ottoman authority over the Hijaz and the right to appoint and dismiss the Sharif himself.[31] The finances of the Hijaz vilayet were also heavily dependent upon subsidies from the central government, so that once Arabia was severed from the Empire, it seemed more likely that the former, not the latter, would wither.[32] "Besides," wrote the Arabist G. P. Badger in 1877, in a response to G. C. M. Birdwood, "[the Sharif] has no influence whatever, political or spiritual, beyond his own assigned district; and the Sharifs them-selves, as well as the Arabs who are more immediately connected with him [sic], have fallen so low in the estimation of the world of Islam that few intelligent Muslims would dream of a Sharif being promoted to the Khalifate. . . . As to any solid hope of a regeneration of Islam through the elevation of the Sharif of Makkah to the Khalifate, the notion is simply preposterous."[33] The poverty of the Hijaz, and the inability of the Sharif of Mecca to project religious influence abroad, were made manifest forty years later during a brief period of Hijazi independence, and with the Saudi occupation the Hijaz again became the subsidized province of a state centered elsewhere.

Thus the congress idea, when it appeared, did so in circumstances bound to render it suspect among Sunni Muslims on religio-political grounds. The idea was intimately associated with the dismemberment of the Ottoman Empire, at a time when the Sunni Muslim world had rallied to the Ottoman caliphate. It implied radical, Westernizing reform during a period of popular reaction against the *Tanzimat* and a reassertion of fundamental religious tenets. That Blunt's ideas were anathema to many Muslims, he himself eventually recognized. Between the publication of his series in *The Fortnightly Review* and its appearance as a book, some concerned Muslim must have told Blunt that his political ideas were repugnant to believers, for in Blunt's preface, he partially recants: "Abd el Hamid Khan is still recognized as the actual Emir el Mumenin, and the restoration of a more legitimate Caliphate is deferred for the day when its fate shall have overtaken the Ottoman Empire. This is as it should be. Schism would only weaken the cause of religion, already threatened by a thousand enemies; and the premature appearance of an Anti-Caliph in Egypt or Arabia, however legitimate a candidate he might be by birth for the office, would divide the Mohammedan world into two hostile camps, and so bring scandal and injury on the general cause."[34] Then he added that the death of Abdülhamid II would signal the return of the caliphate to Cairo, so we may assume that someone respected by Blunt must have told him that his vision of Arabia as political center and Mecca as the "true metropolis" was not one shared by very many Muslims.[35]

By early 1884, he had retreated yet further. During the preparation of the Urdu translation of *The Future of Islam*, he ordered the deletion of some passages uncomplimentary to Abdülhamid: "This, I hope, will satisfy all parties; and the book, to do good, must not be condemned as unorthodox." He then told his translator "of my intention of visiting Constantinople, and trying to induce the Sultan to take up the idea of a Pan-Islamic Synod. We both agreed that, after the defeat in Egypt, Islam could not afford to wait for a more legitimate Caliph."[36] It was only with this reorientation that his approach began to fall into line the prevalent mood, to which even his most radical Muslim associates answered.

Among Muslims it remains usual to attribute the first appearance of the congress idea to Sayyid Jamal al-Din al-Afghani/Asadabadi (1838/ 9–1897), an Iranian whose posthumous veneration as the first eloquent exponent of Muslim anti-imperialism concealed a personal pattern of dissimulation, skepticism, and a consciously utilitarian vision of Islam. After Afghani's death, when the paternity of the congress idea became something of a political issue, Rashid Rida asserted unequivocally that Afghani was its father, and the attribution was often repeated in subsequent biographical accounts.[37] It must first be said that there is no evidence that Afghani ever advanced an articulate proposal for a Muslim congress. There are no more than allusions in Afghani's works, which imply that he was not unsympathetic to the idea, and may have advanced it on one or another occasion.

Afghani, at roughly the mid-point in his career, met Blunt in London (January 1883) and there also associated with Louis Sabunji, a previous acquaintance, to whose newspaper *al-Nahla* he had contributed. Whether Afghani here secretly embraced the idea of an Arabian caliphate is unknown, for he proceeded to Paris before the end of the month and began to publish his own newspaper, *al-ʿUrwa al-wuthqa*, which appealed to sentiments of Muslim unity ostensibly in support of the Ottoman caliphate. There is some evidence that *al-ʿUrwa al-wuthqa* might have been financed in part by Blunt; that an affinity of political views existed between Afghani and Blunt is well attested.[38] Yet it seems that Afghani was less sanguine about the prospects of an Arabian caliphate, having just returned from India, where enthusiasm for the Ottoman caliphate ran high; for Afghani is known to have warned Blunt in September 1883 not to raise the subject during the latter's projected trip to India. "I asked him about the language I should most prudently hold regarding the Sultan, and he advised me to say nothing against the Sultan in India or about an Arabian Caliphate; it had been spread about that the English were going to set up a sham Caliphate in Arabia, under a child, whom they would use to make themselves masters of the holy places; the Sultan's name was now venerated in India as it had not formerly been."[39]

It is thus not surprising to find no more than a hint of Blunt's idea of a Meccan Muslim congress on the pages of *al-ʿUrwa al-wuthqa*. It was first dropped in the first number of the journal, where Mecca, site of the annual pilgrimage by Muslims, was cited as "the most favorable city for the exchange of their ideas and dissemination [of those ideas] in all parts."[40] Hardly more explicit were the remarks in a subsequent article on Muslim unity, which presented a very subtle critique of the Ottoman caliphate. This piece raised questions about the ʿAbbasid claim in particular—one must remember that the Ottoman claim at this time was justified by the fiction of a testamentary designation by the last ᶜAbbasid caliph—and the author implied that the recent history of the "monarchical caliphate" was one of usurpation. The article appealed to the ulama to restore Islam's strength:

> The ulama, the sermon givers, the prayer leaders, and the preachers every-where should join together and establish centers in various lands, to advance their unity, and take the hands of the masses (al-ᶜamma), so that the revelation and true tradition will guide them. They should gather these threads into one knot, with its center in the Holy Lands [the Hijaz], the most noble of which is the House of God [Mecca].[41]

The identical idea was repeated once again in yet another issue.[42] Yet it must be concluded that if this was a presentation of Blunt's argument for a shift of the center of Islam from Istanbul to Mecca, and for the use of a congress format to effect religious reform, it was extremely subtle. The editorial thrust of al-ᶜUrwa al-wuthqa, when considered as a whole, was overwhelmingly pro-Ottoman.

By 1885, when al-ᶜUrwa al-wuthqa had ceased publication, Afghani, while still secretly voicing hostility toward the Ottoman incumbents, no longer saw in Mecca an alternative metropolis if indeed he ever had. In an October 1885 diary entry, Blunt recorded Afghani's views in this fashion:

> A long talk with Jemal-ed-Din about prospects at Constantinople and about the Caliphate. He is for the [Sudanese] Mahdi or the Mahdi's successor taking the Sultan's place, or the Sharif Own [of Mecca], or the Imam of Sanaa—any of these he thought might now take the lead. But Constantinople must remain the seat of the Caliphate, as Arabia or Africa would be mere places of exile. Amongst other things, he told me that it was he himself who had suggested to the Sherif el Huseyn [of Mecca] to claim the Caliphate, but El Huseyn had said it was impossible without armed support, and the Arabs could never unite except in the name of religion.[43]

Afghani in fact did direct his attentions increasingly to Istanbul, where he established himself at the invitation and under the patronage of Abdülhamid II in 1892. There his task was the mobilization of support among Shiᶜis in Iran, Iraq, and elsewhere, for the Ottoman claim to the universal caliphate. To this end, Afghani directed an Iranian salon in Istanbul composed principally of Azali Babis, who wrote letters to Shiᶜi ulama. But according to Afghani's nephew, Mirza Lutf Allah Asadabadi, there was a parallel plan devised by Afghani for a Muslim congress at Istanbul:

> The Sayyid [Afghani] determined that, from each of the major Islamic lands, one person would be selected by the state as an official repre-sentative, and one person from the first ranks of the ulama of [each]

people (*millet*) would be selected by the people as a true people's representative, to assemble and meet in Istanbul. In Istanbul, a great congress (*kongre*) would be founded and organized, and important problems anywhere, at any time, would be given over to the arbitration of this congress. All states and peoples of the Muslim faith would recognize the obligation to respect and follow the decisions and verdicts of the Islamic congress. . . . The purpose of the Sayyid in organizing this Islamic congress was to amass the means for progress and fulfillment of the Muslim peoples collectively, and to restore the glory and might of early Islam. Whenever a European state acted unjustly against a Muslim land, this great Islamic congress would immediately issue a proclamation to all Muslims of holy war against that state, as well as pronounce a boycott of the products and commercial agents of that state. All Muslims would rise and draw sword from sheath for battle.

The account went on to relate that the plan fell through when Abdülhamid II attempted to assert his prerogative as caliph by demanding that he serve as president of the congress, a move resisted by Afghani.[44]

There is no further confirmation that the organization of a Muslim congress was among the tasks assigned to Afghani or among the activities in which he indulged on his own initiative. Shaykh Ahmad-i Ruhi Kirmani, shortly before his extradition to Iran and secret execution for complicity in the assassination of Nasir al-Din Shah, wrote only that the task of the Iranian circle around Afghani, in which he himself participated, was the mobilization of specifically Shi^{c}i opinion.[45] Shaykh Ahmad-i Ruhi's brother, Afzal al-Mulk Kirmani, who was also in this Istanbul circle, gives precisely the same impression.[46] This is also evident in the poem by Mirza Aqa Khan Kirmani on those activities in which he was engaged.[47] It is thus not impossible that the congress account was a fiction which flourished in Iran among those reluctant to believe that Afghani was a true servant of the Ottoman sultan, and so must have had in mind some purpose or plan other than the aggrandizement of the Ottoman caliphate.

But if Afghani did propose such a congress, he might have done so in a memorandum to which he made allusion in an undated letter to Abdülhamid II:

When I received the Caliphal edict ordering me to submit and expound my humble opinion concerning the possibilities of a unification of [the world of] Islam, I felt happiness as if the eight gates of Paradise had been opened to me, and I wrote down a summary of my humble opinion on this subject in accordance with Your High Imperial order and submitted it to the Caliphal threshold. Since not a word concerning this matter has been uttered until now, I have unfortunately arrived at the conclusion that the project has been thrown into the corner of oblivion or that it has been burned by the fire of malice of partial and malicious persons,

or its contents were misinterpreted by latter-day wise men so as to diverge
from its sublime intention and it was consequently lodged among subversive literature.[48]

But as no such memorandum has yet surfaced, its precise contents
remain unknown. All that is certain is that Afghani did not advocate
such a congress in consistent fashion even when he had the opportunity
in Paris to do so without interference.

The absence of such an appeal was not incongruous with his greater
message. In this respect, one can point to parallels between Afghani and
his near-contemporaries, Theodor Herzl and W. E. B. Du Bois, who
both fashioned pan-movements analogous to that which Afghani aspired to fashion. All three shared their promotion of the revolutionary
renewal of their peoples at moments of crisis and stress; their insistence
that these widely scattered peoples, tied not by language but by religion
or race, constituted nations; and their mercurial personalities. But in one
important respect Afghani differed from both, for he sought the means
to his ends almost exclusively through close attachment to a sovereign
Muslim ruler, and approached several during the course of a long career.
All of them disappointed him.

In contrast, Herzl built an autonomous organization structured around
periodic congresses of his disciples and supporters, after the first of
which he claimed in his diary that he had founded the Jewish state.
Du Bois considered his greatest achievement that string of pan-African
congresses which he himself had organized, and through which he
claimed to have altered the course of Western policy in Africa. Herzl
and Du Bois succeeded as organizers because their peoples were without
sovereign power and without sense of political center, while Afghani
labored in Muslim capitals among Muslim rulers, with their palaces,
armies, bureaucracies, and entrenched interests. He either preferred or
was forced to work through powerful patrons, and ended his career as
a conventional Hamidian emissary.

It is not remarkable that the Ottoman state refused to entertain plans
for a congress on the grand scale envisioned by Blunt or described by
Lutf Allah Asadabadi: as a forum for election of caliphs, modification
of the *sharīᶜa*, and proclamations of jihad. But neither was the Ottoman
reaction to the proposal for a smaller Sunni-Shiᶜi forum enthusiastic.
This idea was certainly in circulation, and was repeatedly presented to
Ottoman officials by an eccentric member of the Qajar house, Abu al-
Hasan Mirza Shaykh al-Raᵓis (1846/7–1920). His background was a
privileged one. Shaykh al-Raᵓis received a thorough religious education,
and the excellent oratorical skills he exhibited in the mosque advanced

him quickly, until he was one of the foremost religious figures in Mash-had. But even then he exhibited a proclivity for enlightened thought which would later expose him to various accusations. In 1884 he quar-reled with the governor of Khurasan, and so found it expedient to leave Mashhad and proceed to Mecca, Madina, and finally Istanbul. There he remained for two years, studying and preaching, and "dressed in the customary Ottoman clerical garb." This assimilation eventually became even more pronounced, and Shaykh al-Raʾis was soon composing poems in Arabic to Abdülhamid and receiving gifts of money in return. [49] In Qajar Iran of the time, this degree of philo-Ottomanism was incon-gruous.

As part of this thorough transformation, Shaykh al-Raʾis took to the idea of a formal reconciliation between the Ottoman Empire and Qajar Iran. In August 1886, he met with Cevdet Paşa, Ottoman minister of justice, and an aide from the Ottoman commission for Muslim refugees, to suggest a seven-point plan toward this projected rapprochement. Shaykh al-Raʾis presented a general argument for reconciliation which was met with some skepticism by his hosts, and then elaborated his specific proposals. The Ottoman press would be made to revise its position toward Iran. A newspaper, "The Unity of Islam," would be published, to inform Ottoman subjects that the sultan desired Ottoman unification with the state and people of Iran. Gifts and attention would be bestowed upon the mausoleums venerated by the Twelver Shiʿa, so as to win hearts. Special consideration would be given to defending Shiʿi prerogatives in Ottoman Iraq, and the state's officials would regard Shiʿi and Sunni as equals. The Ottoman policy of discouraging marriages between Ottoman and Iranian subjects would be abandoned. Iranian pilgrims to the holy cities of Mecca and Madina would be shown every courtesy, and the Ottoman ministry of publications would censor books and articles hostile to the Shiʿa. To all this, Cevdet and his aide replied—almost brusquely—that each proposal was worthy, but that change was demanded on the Iranian side as well. [50]

At the same time, Shaykh al-Raʾis composed a short book entitled *Ittihad-i Islam,* which was not published until ten years later, in Bombay. The work effusively praised Abdülhamid for his enlightened, progres-sive rule, and his laudable efforts as caliph to unify Islam, and stressed that the Shiʿi shah could never gain comparable recognition as the *imam* of the Muslims. Shaykh al-Raʾis then made this proposal: a spiritual assembly called "The Progress of Islam" would be created to gather the great men of religion from the shrine cities in Iraq and from Mashhad. The assembly would be free from all official interference, to ensure the participation of Shiʿis from the (Russian-held) Caucasus and (British-ruled) India. The body would promote both the reconciliation of the sects (*taqrib*) and the spread of Islam (*tabligh*).[51] The nucleus of the assembly would be Shiᶜi, but Shaykh al-Raᵓis strongly implied its eventual extension to all Muslims.

The Ottomans never showed any discernible enthusiasm for these plans, although they continued to patronize Shaykh al-Raᵓis. He returned to Iran for a time, but was soon back in Istanbul, where he joined Afghani, Shaykh Ahmad-i Ruhi Kirmani, Mirza Aqa Khan Kirmani, and the circle of Iranians who wrote epistles and letters to Shiᶜis in Iraq and abroad on behalf of Abdülhamid. He also became an enthusiast of Malkum Khan's, and shared with the Istanbul Azali Babis a nearly blasphemous tone in corresponding with him.[52]

According to one account, Shaykh al-Raᵓis also stopped in Acre during a trip through the Levant, visited ᶜAbd al-Bahaᵓ, and gave the spiritual guide of the Bahaᵓi faction of Babis his unqualified allegiance.[53] Another account relates that once Shaykh al-Raᵓis had returned to Iran, Bahaᵓi missionaries were instructed by ᶜAbd al-Bahaᵓ to win him to their cause by any means, and so offered to send him to America to propagate their faith. Word was soon out that Shaykh al-Raᵓis had accepted the Bahaᵓi offer; he rushed to the pulpit at Friday prayer to deny the charge, and to remind his listeners of his lifetime of devotion to Muslim unity. Either on account of the allegation of Bahaᵓi affinities, or in retribution for the prominent role of Shaykh al-Raᵓis in the constitutional revolution of 1908, there was difficulty upon his death in having the principal *mujtahid* of Mashhad authorize his burial on the consecrated premises which Shaykh al-Raᵓis had chosen. These last episodes in his life suggest that his eccentricity met with disapproval, so that the first rudimentary suggestion of a Muslim congress reached Iran as it had reached the Ottoman Empire: through the medium of a suspected political subversive and religious nonconformist.

There is thus much evidence that the congress idea first emerged from the extreme margins of nineteenth-century Islam as a radical alternative to the established authority of the Ottoman and Qajar ruling houses and traditional religious institutions. A last example fits this pattern closely. "A group of Indian, Arab and Turkish Muslims have taken the initiative to convoke, in 1896, a pan-Islamic congress, to discuss various questions concerning the current situation in Islam." Attached to this announcement, published in the Parisian *Revue de l'Islam,* was a dissertation on the decline of Islam which ridiculed the "perfidious current" on the Bosphorus, and predicted the inevitable dismemberment of the Ottoman Empire. What would become of the secular traditions of Muslim power, speculated the article, once the caliph's realm was reduced to Asia Minor? Alongside this prophetic pessimism was a presentation of the reformist view of decline. Islam was not hostile to progress or the well-being of women, or a cause of decadence or ignorance, as the great Muslim scientific achievements of the past testified. Rather, Muslims had been overtaken by their own atrophy, criminal negligence, and impiety.

This question of education and science, it was asserted, would figure prominently in the congress, in which only Muslims would participate. And where would this event, which would "clear Islam of many unjust accusations, and establish its place in the concert of modern civilizations," take place? "There has been hesitation concerning the site of this congress, for it requires complete guarantees of independence. Some have proposed Tangier, others Cairo. Granada has been spoken of: the Spanish government would clear the Alhambra, where a large mosque would be made available for the event."[54]

Each of these proposed sites was under non-Muslim rule, a fact which would have better guaranteed the independence necessary for an attack on the Ottoman state. Nothing more was related about the authors of this plan or their efforts to effect it, but the major components remained constant: a radical reformism linked to a negation of established claims to Muslim primacy. The congress concept, innovative in a period of recrudescent conservatism, had appeared in every instance in intimate association with reputed freethinkers, rationalists, skeptics, and non-Muslim visionaries. It evoked hostility from established political and theological authority, within and beyond the Ottoman Empire and Qajar Iran, and excited more suspicion than interest before the close of the century.

THREE

AN IDEA REFINED

First Proposals from Cairo

IN THE independent Ottoman and Qajar states, the congress idea and its early advocates bore a stigma. Only in British Egypt, an occupied country whose liberation was advocated so persistently by Blunt and Afghani, was the idea allowed to flourish. From subjugated Cairo, Muhammad ⁽Abduh (1849–1905), Blunt's associate and Afghani's disciple, further propagated the congress idea. This he did in collaboration with his own student, Muhammad Rashid Rida (1865–1935), from Syrian Tripoli. Their instrument was *al-Manar*, a Cairo journal of religious and political affairs, and perhaps the most widely circulated Muslim periodical of its time. The achievement of these two men was that they took advanced notions of religious reform, tainted by association with skepticism, and through judicious recasting made them more widely palatable. Among those notions was that of a Muslim congress.

The bond linking ⁽Abduh to Afghani and Blunt was a close one. Blunt's quest for the true Islam had led him to ⁽Abduh, then a shaykh from the Delta teaching at al-Azhar, as early as 1881. The debt owed by the Englishman to the Egyptian was an acknowledged one, and Blunt found in ⁽Abduh a sympathizer with his radical ideas on religious reform and the caliphate:

> Sheykh Mohammed Abdu was strong on the point that what was needed for the Mohammedan body politic was not merely reforms but a true religious reformation. On the question of the Caliphate he looked at that time, in common with most enlightened Moslems, to its reconstruction on a more spiritual basis. He explained to me how a more legitimate exercise of its authority might be made to give new impulse to intellectual progress, and how little those who for centuries had held the title had deserved the spiritual headship of believers. The House of Othman for two hundred years had cared almost nothing for religion, and beyond the right of the sword had no claim any longer to allegiance. They were still the most powerful Mohammedan princes and so able to do most for the general advantage, but unless they could be induced to take their position seriously a new Emir el Mumenin might legitimately be looked for.[1]

In ⁽Abduh's writings, too, there was a discernible affection, if not preference, for the Arabs in this matter, although never in terms as extreme as Blunt's.[2]

More important was ᶜAbduh's relationship with Afghani. When Afghani came to Cairo, first in 1869 and again in 1871, ᶜAbduh became his fervent acolyte. Later, following ᶜAbduh's self-incriminating involvement in the ᶜUrabi revolt, he joined Afghani in that Paris room where together they wrote and edited al-ᶜUrwa al-wuthqa. Although Afghani and ᶜAbduh parted in 1884 upon the closure of the newspaper, never to meet again, an important correspondence between them survives. From it, we learn that ᶜAbduh took it upon himself to spread the word, at least during a visit to Tunis, that al-ᶜUrwa al-wuthqa was not simply a newspaper but a secret Muslim society under Afghani's guidance, with branches throughout the Muslim world. Unfortunately, only the internal regulations of the "fourth cell" of this imaginary society survive, so that it is impossible to say whether ᶜAbduh envisioned a general Muslim congress of all the cells within the secret society.[3] It seems nonetheless certain that ᶜAbduh was fully acquainted with the congress idea as it appeared in Blunt's work, and as possibly mentioned by Afghani.

In 1897, ᶜAbduh, soon to be mufti of Egypt, was joined in Cairo by Shaykh Muhammad Rashid Rida, a young enthusiast of religious reform from Syrian Tripoli. That same year, they founded al-Manar, a journal which advanced reformist ideas through Qurᵓanic exegesis and political commentary. Al-Manar was controversial from the very beginning. According to a group of ulama who asked that it be barred from Tunisia in 1904, the journal "had not ceased to undermine, at their foundations, the most essential and least debatable principles of Muslim orthodoxy."[4] Rashid Rida was often accused during his lifetime of religious nonconformism, and was the target of an ugly disturbance which followed a lesson taught by him in 1908 at the Umayyad Mosque in Damascus.[5] In ᶜAbduh and Rida, then, the congress idea remained associated with far-reaching reformism. Yet al-Manar's wide circulation, and consequent influence upon thought among Muslim readers as distant as Java and South Africa, gained for their ideas a more extensive following than in the past.[6] Through al-Manar, the rationale for a congress made inroads far afield.

Al-Manar first raised the congress issue in an article on religious reform, directed to Abdülhamid and published in 1898 in the first volume of the new journal. The article opened with explicit reference to Abdülhamid as amir al-muᵓminin, and then went on to note that the unification of creeds, teachings, and laws was the most important principle of Islamic reform.

This reform is consistent with the creation of an Islamic society, under the auspices of the caliph, which will have a branch in every Islamic land. Its greatest branch should be in Mecca, a city to which Muslims come from all over the world and where they fraternize at its holy sites. The most important meeting of this branch should be held during the pilgrimage season, when members (*a'da'*) from the rest of the branches in the rest of the world come on pilgrimage. Thus they can bring back to their own branches whatever is decided, secretly and openly, in the general assembly (*al-mujtama' al-'amm*). This is one of the advantages of establishing the great society at Mecca rather than *Dar al-Khilafa* [Istanbul]. There are other advantages, the most important among them being the distance [of Mecca] from the intrigues and suspicions of [non-Muslim] foreigners, and security from their knowing what there is no need for them to know, either in part or in whole.[7]

Here was an early expression of that radical concept of pilgrimage which set Muslim reformers apart. The traditional pilgrimage was an obligation performed usually once, by individual Muslims in search of a transcendent religious experience of communion with God. The exchange of ideas between pilgrims themselves was incidental. Shaykhs 'Abduh and Rida made that exchange central. An article in *al-Manar* lamented the attitude of returning pilgrims, who spoke much about their journey and not at all about the circumstances under which their Muslim brethren elsewhere lived. This was contrary to the meaning of the name 'Arafat, the great plain on which all pilgrims stood before God at the close of the pilgrimage: it was a place not only of ritual and prayer, but mutual acquaintance (*ta'aruf*).[8]

In Mecca itself, this exchange would be institutionalized. The proposed society would publish a religious journal in the holy city, and work to counter religious innovations and corrupt teachings. A book would be composed by the society, in which the principles of Muslim faith would be set down in conformity with the society's decisions. This work would then be translated into all Muslim languages, "and the caliph would announce that *this* is Islam, and all who believe in it are brethren in faith." The caliph would also order the society to compose books of law, drawn from all the schools (*madhahib*) and adapted to contemporary circumstances, and the resulting legislation would take effect in all Muslim states. But the caliph himself, while presiding over this unification, would be a member like all other members in the society.

The choice of Mecca as the society's center, and the relegation of the caliph to the position of an ordinary member of the society, were probably sufficient to alert Ottoman authorities to the nature of this proposal. The appeal, although couched in a deferential tone, could only offend

Ottoman sensibilities and those Muslims for whom the claims of Istanbul and the Ottoman caliphate were not open to dispute. The following year, ᶜAbduh and Rida complained that their proposal had played on the minds of these Muslims, and had taken a strange form among some writers. These had urged that the Muslim congress (al-mu ᵓtamar al-islami) be convened in Istanbul. This modification was completely detached from reality, argued an article in al-Manar: not only would a congress set in Istanbul do more harm than good, but the idea was opposed by Abdülhamid himself. The evidence for this opposition, theorized the article, could be found in the complete absence of such a proposal from the Istanbul press.[9] The proposal for an Istanbul congress had originated not in Istanbul, but in the Indian Muslim press, and al-Manar cited an Indian example calling for the creation of an Islamic association (mujtamaᶜ islami) in Istanbul, under the presidency of Abdülhamid.[10]

The poor reception which greeted al-Manar's proposal was evidenced in yet another controversy. In one of his pieces on Islam, the French historian and diplomat Gabriel Hanotaux, against whom ᶜAbduh had launched a vigorous polemic, wrote that Paris was an appropriate site for the creation of a society of ulama from all parts. Such a society, Hanotaux argued, would draw Muslims closer to France. Al-Manar launched a vigorous attack upon this suggestion, and repeated the principles of its earlier proposal.

> How did the Muslims receive this [original] proposal? The great majority are neither sensitive nor thoughtful, and as far as those assigned to write and thus guide the Muslims through the newspapers, they disfigured the proposal and turned away from its intent. They started writing articles urging an "Islamic congress" (muᵓtamar islami) in Istanbul, and so could not wait to divert the proposal into the deserts of fantasy, except to urge a switch in the venue. Among our proofs against them, by which we made them realize the error of their opinion, was to ask whether there was even one Istanbul newspaper that supported this appeal, given that all of these newspapers are virtually official, and print only what the authorities wish them to print.[11]

From al-Manar's account, it was thus clear that Abdülhamid continued to oppose the idea of a congress, not only in Mecca but under his own auspices in the Ottoman capital. The reasons for his opposition to a Meccan congress were apparent, given his concern over Arab separatism in general and Hijazi autonomy in particular.[12] The Istanbul setting probably was rejected on other grounds. It almost certainly seemed to the authorities a roundabout means for the establishment of a structurally parliamentary forum in the capital of the Empire. As the point of Hamidian pan-Islam, in the domestic sphere, was the enhancement of the absolute authority of sultan-caliph, support for such a congress would have directly contradicted established policy.

Yet while *al-Manar* was incapable of overcoming these obstacles to the organization of a congress, the journal was the perfect device for the wide dissemination of the idea through a literary piece of fiction. The congress idea was given detailed expression for the first time in ᶜAbd al-Rahman al-Kawakibi's well-known Arabic treatise, *Umm al-qura*, first published in 1900.[13] *Umm al-qura*, one of the names of Mecca, was where Kawakibi set a fictional Muslim congress the proceedings of which he ostensibly recorded but in fact composed.[14] *Umm al-qura* represented not only the most imaginative treatment, but also the most virulently anti-Ottoman elaboration, of the congress theme. For in these imaginary proceedings, Kawakibi argued at length for an end to the Ottoman caliphate, and its replacement by an Arabian Qurashi caliphate in close association with a great Muslim congress. Rashid Rida took this work and made it famous, through serialization in *al-Manar*.

Kawakibi (1854–1902) and his writings were not celebrated during his lifetime, so that important questions about his political affiliations and sincerity remain unresolved. Even the details of his public career are not clear. He was born in Aleppo to a scholarly family, and spent his youth in that city and in Antioch, receiving a solid education in Arabic, Turkish, and Persian. He showed ability, and while still in his twenties he gained a reputation as editor of Aleppo's official newspaper, *al-Furat*, and then as editor of a series of other Aleppan newspapers. His further journalistic career seems to have been one of advancement, sudden reversals, and clashes with various Ottoman governors, the reasons for which are now obscure. At the height of his Aleppan period, he filled a number of bureaucratic posts concerned with local administration. The reasons for his disaffection and fall from favor are no longer clear, but while still in Aleppo he began to compose *Umm al-qura*, an explicit repudiation of that Arabo-Turkish symbiosis in which he was formed. In 1899, at the urging of a friend, he left for Cairo, with the intention of publishing his work.[15]

Once in Cairo, he immediately published a series of implicitly anti-Ottoman articles on despotism in the Cairo daily *al-Muᵓayyad*, under the title *Tabaᵓiᶜ al-istibdad*.[16] At the same time, Kawakibi revised his draft of *Umm al-qura* six times before its clandestine publication in 1900 under the pseudonym of al-Sayyid al-Furati.[17] It seems certain that the influence upon *Umm al-qura* of Rashid Rida and perhaps Muhammad ᶜAbduh was great, for Rashid Rida later wrote that the draft first presented in Cairo by Kawakibi was only an outline, and was much expanded in consultation with himself and others. "I have the original manuscript that confirms this," wrote Rida over thirty years later.[18]

It is thus reasonable to see in *Umm al-qura* a further elaboration of ideas current in the circle of Afghani's disciples, and the theories of Wilfrid Scawen Blunt, for the familiar theme which ran through Kawakibi's work was the need for radical religious reform.[19] Like his predecessors, he insisted that there was some kernel of belief and ritual which was incontestably Islamic and indisputably valid, obscured by accretions which were neither. Kawakibi demanded a stripping away of these accretions, particularly Sufism, and urged an apologetic campaign in defense of the kernel laid bare. This attempt to reduce an integrated tradition to pristine essentials had led Afghani and ᶜAbduh to skepticism, and attracted Shaykh al-Raᵓis Qajar to Babism. Where it left Kawakibi, one cannot say, for nothing survives concerning his own convictions. During his lifetime, Kawakibi was not personally attacked for his religious views, as were Afghani, Shaykh al-Raᵓis, ᶜAbduh, and Rida, for Kawakibi published under pseudonyms and lived his creative period in relative obscurity.

Umm al-qura, then, was in great part a repetition of ideas made familiar by Kawakibi's predecessors, and on most questions, Kawakibi's views were virtually identical with the reformist opinions given currency at the same time by ᶜAbduh and Rida. Kawakibi's originality lay rather in his vivid presentation of these ideas, set down in the fictional and dramatic framework of a Muslim congress held in Mecca during the pilgrimage season of 1898. The nominal narrator, al-Sayyid al-Furati (Kawakibi himself), describes how he was moved to gather a congress and embark on a journey through the Arabic-speaking provinces of the Ottoman Empire to collect participants. Once in Mecca, he recruits another contingent from among the most notable pilgrims of more distant lands. Twenty-two Muslims, each representing a different community from Fez to China, are finally gathered together by the narrator, and Kawakibi uses their discussions as a vehicle for advancing a broad range of radical religious and social arguments.

Yet the congress setting was not only a literary device, but was itself one of those useful innovations for which *Umm al-qura* argued so forcefully. First of all, there was the congress for which *Umm al-qura* served as an account, and which Kawakibi entitled the Congress of Islamic Revival (*Muᵓtamar al-nahda al-islamiyya*). Kawakibi gave this event the character of an ad hoc and clandestine gathering of some two dozen interested participants, who met in structured sessions, elected officers, and passed a set of resolutions. The wealth of detail offered by Kawakibi for the twelve sessions of this imaginary congress can be appreciated only through a full reading of the proceedings.

The third session, devoted to the decadence which afflicted Muslims, was not untypical. A participant from Istanbul blamed Muslim rulers for interference in areas reserved for Islamic law; a Kurdish participant pointed instead to the neglect of certain natural sciences by the ulama; and an Afghan participant cited poverty and the fiscal rapacity of government as the cause. Further opinions were offered by participants from Egypt, the Najd, and China, as well as by an English Muslim from Liverpool.

Implicit in Kawakibi's presentation was the idea that such an organized exchange of ideas was instructive and worthy of frequent repetition, for Kawakibi has this small group adopt a provisional charter (*qanun*) for regulation of a permanent body entitled the Society for the Edification of the Unitarians (*Jam^{c}iyyat ta^{c}lim al-muwahhidin*). This projected society would consist of one hundred Muslims of solid reputation, whose precise method of selection was not explained. Ten of these would enjoy the rank of active members (*^{c}amilun*), another ten would serve in advisory capacities, and the remainder as honorary functionaries. The select twenty, for whom there were special language and residency requirements, would be elected in an annual general assembly of the society. The twenty then would elect a president, vice-president, first and second secretaries, and a treasurer, for limited terms. The general assembly in annual session would fill a broad supervisory role, while the select twenty, required to remain at the headquarters of the society for eight months each year, would carry on the society's daily functions. Upon the treasurer would devolve the usual responsibility for the raising and disbursement of funds. The other active and advisory members would be entrusted with carrying out a broad campaign to inform Muslims of their errors and rejuvenate religious thought through publications, educational programs, and missionary activities.[20]

Beyond these functional provisions, inspired no doubt by a foreign model, were articles in the charter which made explicit Kawakibi's theories on the primacy of the Arabs in Islam. Kawakibi made the ability to read, write, and speak Arabic a basic requirement of the society's elect. The charter designated Mecca the official center (*al-markaz al-rasmi*) of the Society for the Edification of the Unitarians. Istanbul was relegated to the status of a branch (*shu^{c}ba*), the same position enjoyed in *Umm al-qura* by Cairo, Damascus (for *al-Sham*), Aden, Hail, Tiflis, Teheran, Khiva, Kabul, Calcutta, Delhi, Singapore, Tunis, and Marrakesh. The charter further emphasized that the society would not be aligned with any Muslim state, an indication that it would not legitimize Ottoman pretensions. In the charter, then, the organizational format of the congress appeared once again in an explicitly anti-Ottoman context.

But just as the congress described in *Umm al-qura* was preparatory to a larger society, so the society was conceived by Kawakibi as preparatory to yet another organizational innovation. The dignitaries assembled under the society's auspices were to commit themselves to the convening of an even greater congress: "Three years after its inauguration, the society will endeavor to convince Muslim kings and princes to convene an official congress (*muʾtamar rasmi*) in Mecca, attended by delegates from each of them, over whom shall preside the least of these princes. The subject of the proceedings shall be religious policy (*al-siyasa al-diniyya*)."[21] The results of this great congress were anticipated by Kawakibi, through the medium of a fictional Indian Muslim prince's commentary appended to the fictional proceedings.[22] A general advisory body (*hayʾat al-shura al-ʿamma*) of one hundred members, some elected and others delegated by Muslim sultans and amirs, would meet in Mecca for one month each year, on the eve of the pilgrimage. This official body would elect an Arab caliph of Quraysh, who would serve for a period of three years, after which his term of office required renewal. His own effective reach would extend only to the Hijaz, which was to be defended by a Muslim force drawn from all Muslim states. Both the caliph and the advisory body would desist from interference in the internal affairs of Muslim states, and would concern themselves only with "religious questions." Thus was manifested Kawakibi's radical vision of the exclusively spiritual role of the caliphate, and his utter rejection of the Ottoman claim.

The book made some impression upon initial publication, although the earliest edition of the work is rare.[23] It seems to have been difficult to come by even at the turn of the century, for when the first serialized installments appeared in Rashid Rida's *al-Manar* in 1902, various Egyptian newspapers were unable to secure the full original edition. "Attempts to find this work have always been without result," reported *Les Pyramides* in 1902. "What became of it? One supposes that all the copies had been confiscated, then burnt."[24] Kawakibi thus remained unknown even to his few readers, and was led, by necessity or interest, to make his living in the service of the Khedive of Egypt, ʿAbbas Hilmi II.[25] This had some effect upon *Umm al-qura*, in which there is an incongruous passage invoking the aid of the Khedive, and placing the provisional center of the Society for the Edification of the Unitarians in Egypt. Nor was Kawakibi averse to serving the Khedive as an agent, and he went as far as Yemen to preach not an Arab caliphate of Quraysh, but a caliphate of Egypt's ruling house. In this fashion, Kawakibi managed to maintain himself in the brief period between his arrival in Cairo and his sudden death in 1902, at which time he was buried at the Khedive's expense.

Rashid Rida would not have serialized *Umm al-qura* in his widely circulated *al-Manar* had it been readily available, so that when the first installment did appear, shortly before Kawakibi's death, the effect was mildly sensational. Many believed that the Meccan congress described in *Umm al-qura* had taken place. The book itself probably let loose the rumor current in Egypt in 1901, that seventy-two delegates from all Muslim countries had met in Mecca and decided to strip Abdülhamid of the caliphate.[26] The publication of the book in *al-Manar* spread this rumor yet further, and the Arab separatist Negib Azoury, in his statement *La Réveil de la nation arabe,* alleged that Kawakibi had been unjustifiably persecuted by Abdülhamid, adding:

> Last year, a committee composed of several ulama met at Mecca to deliberate on the institution of a purely religious caliphate located at Mecca. This committee decided to confide this important dignity to a Christian foreigner, rather than leave it to the loathsome Abdul-Hamid, for it is written in the sacred books of Islam that an infidel but just prince is better than an unjust Muslim prince. The sultan learned of the existence of this committee and of some of its resolutions. To prevent this dangerous movement from spreading beyond the tomb of the Arab Prophet, he ordered the vali of the Hedjaz to provoke a massacre of pilgrims, and so render the trip perilous to all civilized Muslims.[27]

Here was not only an affirmation that the congress met, but the addition of willful distortions to Kawakibi's account. Azoury was also joined by a number of orientalists who took the proceedings of *Umm al-qura* as genuine. D. S. Margoliouth was perhaps the first of them to write about the congress as though it had occurred, and the error was often repeated.[28]

But whether mistaken for a genuine account or understood as political literature, *Umm al-qura* attracted important interest in the congress idea, for the concept henceforth was identified with a cause. *Umm al-qura* was written in Arabic, on the eve of a period in which Arabic-speakers openly challenged Turkish-speakers for primacy in Islam. Kawakibi did far more than Blunt, or even ʿAbduh and Rida, to associate the congress idea closely with one side of this incipient struggle. He also put flesh on the bones, for here were an agenda, protocols, and a rudimentary model for procedure, offered in a vivid Arabic. With the passage of time, *Umm al-qura* became widely known for its message of Arab primacy, earning for Kawakibi a posthumous fame. Modern scholarship has done much to correct the version of Kawakibi's life which emerged from his canonization by Arab nationalists, and has established his frequent resort to plagiarism. Yet *Umm al-qura,* although a collection of borrowed ideas by an author of mixed motives, was nonetheless of signal importance to the evolution of the congress idea. The book presented a detailed and imaginative construction of a gathering which hitherto had been conceived only in the most abstract sense. Kawakibi filled out the proposals of his predecessors with an engaging text that commanded the attention of reformers and their opponents alike. His influential work thus had a dual effect: it attracted to the congress idea a wide sympathy among those in the expanding reformist school; and it further assured for the concept an abiding Ottoman hostility.

FOUR

A PRACTICAL PLAN
The Gasprinskii Initiative of
1907 and Sequel

Late in October 1907, a Crimean Muslim in Western attire, speaking excellent French but little or no Arabic, disembarked from a steamer in an Egyptian port and proceeded to Cairo. He first arranged for the services of a young Kazan Tatar pursuing religious studies in Cairo, for it was essential to the visitor's purpose that he convey ideas in Arabic.[1] Within a few days, İsmail Gasprinskii [Gaspralı], and his concept of a Muslim congress in Cairo, were the subjects of widespread Egyptian comment and speculation.

Gasprinskii (1851–1914) was born in a village near Baghchesaray, to a father who had served as a translator to the Russian governor-general of the Caucasus at the time of the Şamil uprising in Daghistan.[2] Gasprinskii himself was educated in a Russian *gymnasium,* and at military lycées in Voronezh and Moscow. He then divided three formative years between Paris and Istanbul in preparation for a military career in Ottoman service allegedly denied him by Russian intervention. Disappointed, he returned to Baghchesaray to take up a career as an educator, author, and journalist. Gasprinskii's *Tercüman/Perevodchik,* a Turkish newspaper published continuously at Baghchesaray from 1883 until several years after his death, exercised a wide influence upon his own generation of Turkish-speaking Muslims under Russian rule.[3]

Tercüman developed a number of themes elaborated previously by the Tatar reformer Kayyum Nâsirî.[4] Gasprinskii similarly argued for Russo-Muslim rapprochement, the study of Russian as a key to economic and social transformation, and the emancipation of Muslim women. To achieve these aims, he advocated the reform of Muslim *mekteb* and *medrese* through the introduction of modern, essentially Russian, pedagogical approaches (*usul-ı cedid*). "They accuse me of betraying my people, almost of betraying Islam," Gasprinskii once said of those who criticized his radical reforms. "There are those who say that I am more of a Russian than is a Muscovite."[5]

Gasprinskii was indeed a conscious westernizer, resigned to a shared future with the Great Russian people. He preached not insularity and resistance, but the integration of Russian Muslims into wider Russian society through rapid Westernization. His methods were indisputably those of collaboration and adaptation: he did not flee Baghchesaray, and his military expertise, such as it was, went untested. Gasprinskii, then, shared the reformist convictions of *al-ʿUrwa al-wuthqa* and *al-Manar*, but was far more quietist, for he was subjected to all the limitations imposed by Tsarist censorship. So it was until 1905, when Gasprinskii began to seek personal atonement for past quiescence. The period of reaction that followed the collapse of the 1905 Russian revolution radicalized Muslim liberals, many of whom left the country for Turkey and Europe. Gasprinskii was not prepared to take this drastic step, but sought to compensate by adopting a less compliant tone. "My first, long period, and that of my *Perevodchik* [*Tercüman*], is finished, and a second, short, but probably more stormy period is beginning, when the old teacher and popularizer must become political. For the lack of another [newspaper], *Perevodchik* must be turned into a purely political organ and must open a cold, calculated and persistant campaign against the internal and external enemies of our Turkic people."[6] In the past, *Tercüman* had served as a vehicle for news about Muslims elsewhere, but it now began to speak in a more forward language on the subject of Muslim solidarity.

Gasprinskii proposed a congress.[7] It is impossible to say how he arrived at the idea, but several possibilities suggest themselves. As a student cadet in Moscow (1865–67), Gasprinskii was "adopted" socially by the family of the noted pan-Slavist publisher and journalist, Mikhail Katkov, who invited the young Tatar to his home each week. Here, too, Gasprinskii spent a summer vacation. At precisely this time, Katkov was a central figure in the Moscow Slavic Benevolent Committee, which organized a pan-Slavic congress in 1867; and there is evidence that Gasprinskii was impressed by the organizational concerns of the Moscow pan-Slavists.[8] Gasprinskii also had been involved in the three Russian Muslim congresses of 1905–6: he was a leading participant in each, and preparations consumed a great deal of his energy. His organizational experience was therefore considerable. Nor was it impossible that he first encountered the idea in *al-Manar*, as some of the material for *Tercüman* was drawn from the Arabic reformist press.

His own appeal for a "general Muslim congress" first appeared in *Tercüman* and was brought to Western attention by the Jewish-Hungarian orientalist Arminius Vambéry, a subscriber to the paper, in a letter from Budapest to the London *Times*. Reuters carried a synopsis of Vambéry's letter, transmitting the news to Cairo. According to Gasprinskii himself, Egyptian journalists then learned that he was already in the city, and located him after a telephone search of the major hotels.[9] The appeal, in Vambéry's translation, lamented that Muslims, "wherever and under whatever rule they be, they always remain behind their neighbors. In Algiers the Mahomedans are superseded by the Jews, in Crete by the Greeks, in Bulgaria by the Bulgarians, and in Russia by everybody." This "deplorable state" demanded study,

> but since these questions are of extraordinary interest for the cultural revival of Islam, it is preferable to discuss these matters in a common general way, instead of the hitherto used single and separate form. The first congress of the Russian Mahomedans in 1905 has greatly contributed towards the rousing and development of these thoughts, and now a much greater necessity has arisen for the convening of a general congress, the activity of which may be useful to Islam. The congress, embodying our learned clergy and literary celebrities, must not be frightened by the European clamour of Pan-Islamism, for our representatives, gathering from all parts of the world, and striving to solve many social and cultural questions, will open more than one hitherto barred way and door. We shall thus be able to sanction the unavoidably necessary reforms and innovations in Islam. . . . The world is constantly changing and progressing, and we are left behind for many miles. As this congress, owing to certain reasons, cannot meet in Constantinople, we trust to be able to unite in Cairo, which is looked upon as the second centre of Islam.[10]

The *Tercüman* appeal left a great deal unsaid. Gasprinskii no more than alluded to the purpose of his proposed congress, although he implied that the deliberations would be devoted to social and cultural rather than political affairs. Gasprinskii seems to have believed that an emphasis on this point would dissipate fears about the congress among Europeans and Egyptians alike, and he repeatedly returned to this theme once in Cairo. But in regarding the congress as an instrument for "innovations," he differed not at all from his predecessors, and there was thus no need to explain the "certain reasons" which led him to avoid Istanbul, where he had lived and had family. Gasprinskii did not know Cairo or its politics, and under other circumstances perhaps would have preferred the cockpit of Istanbul to what he described as Islam's second center. But by this time, it was doubtless apparent to him that the congress idea was anathema to Abdülhamid. No less serious was the inability of Gasprinskii, as a Russian subject, to operate freely in the Ottoman capital. In 1874, Gasprinskii had arrived in Istanbul with the intention of studying at the Ottoman War College, but the Russian ambassador, Count Nikolai Ignatiev, was able to ruin Gasprinskii's plans through representations to the Ottoman Grand Vizier. This rejection came as a great disappointment to Gasprinskii, and even long after Ignatiev's departure, Gasprinskii may have had just cause to suspect that Ottoman authorities would respond to a Russian ambassador's request to curtail his activities. The organizational ties between Muslim opponents of Russian autocracy and Ottoman opponents of Ottoman autocracy had already led to a measure of Russo-Ottoman cooperation in the suppression of seditious Muslim propaganda. Cairo was beyond Russian reach, yet was close enough to the Crimea so that, in one five-month period, Gasprinskii was able to make three round trips by steamer between his home and the seat of his proposed congress. Unspoken but ever-present was the consideration that Cairo under British occupation provided a haven for free speech which Istanbul did not.[11]

The effect in Cairo of the Reuters announcement and word of Gasprinskii's presence was electric. It is difficult now to appreciate why. The congress concept was not at all new to Egyptian readers of al-Manar, and Gasprinskii was not well known in Cairo outside a small circle of Turkish-speaking Muslim cosmopolitans and exiles who read Tercüman. That an essentially unknown Crimean Tatar could generate such excitement and anticipation was perhaps a reverberation of the Afghani legend which, no more than a decade after his death, had surrounded and then obscured his role. Afghani had appeared as a Muslim of uncertain antecedents, enveloped in a charismatic aura, who had wandered among other Muslim peoples and articulated their grievances and aspirations better than they themselves. This stranger, who stood above the mire of local politics and patronage, acted as a catalyst, opening eyes and freeing latent forces among the Muslims whom he admonished. Perhaps it was a reenactment of this drama which Cairo anticipated of Gasprinskii in the fall of 1907. On the first evening of November, three hundred Egyptian political, religious and literary figures crowded into the Continental Hotel, to be moved by Gasprinskii's oratory.[12]

It is probable that Gasprinskii's remarks on this important occasion did not meet the expectations of his audience. Gasprinskii had not the linguistic agility of Afghani, and was forced to address the assembly in Turkish, so that whatever magnification his oratorical skills lent to his ideas was lost to all but a few listeners. Even less striking was the content. The speech, of which we have Turkish, Arabic, and French versions, was not stiffened by the anti-imperialism which so often characterized Afghani's oratory.[13] Gasprinskii spoke not at all of political liberation, and very little about religious reform. Instead, he offered a dissertation on the decline of Muslim commercial acumen, to which he directly attributed the decadence of Islam. Gasprinskii's congress was to explore why the Muslims did not share equally in the distribution of wealth among nations; why they had no large steamship companies and banks; why no Muslim traders could be found in America and Europe; and how foreign and minority communities had come to control the internal markets of Muslim states. In Gasprinskii's opinion, peoples fell under foreign domination only when, by their own fault, they failed to play an efficient role in the various fields of industrious activity. "Our apathy," not their perfidy, was responsible for foreign domination, and political self-determination was possible only as a sequel to economic revitalization. Rashid Rida, in assessing Gasprinskii's remarks, agreed that public companies were the "foundations of wealth in this era." Ulama who opposed the sale and purchase of shares in enterprises like the Suez Canal, on the grounds that these transactions constituted usurious lending, left Muslims at a severe disadvantage and invited foreign financial domination.[14] It was a Muslim commonwealth in the literal sense of which Gasprinskii spoke that evening.

This commercial theme did not interest Egyptian political factions. From the Continental Hotel speech, it was clear that Gasprinskii was unprepared to voice the essentially political aspirations of Egyptians, for whom independence was a precondition for all progress.[15] Nor was he sufficiently charismatic to create his own following. Gasprinskii, unlike Afghani, soon became dependent upon more eloquent and influential Egyptian collaborators, to interpret his ideas for what was essentially a foreign audience. Both the Khedivial palace and its rivals, particularly the nationalist leader Mustafa Kamil (1874–1908), sought to play the role of intermediary, and after the Continental Hotel speech a factional struggle began among various Egyptian political groupings for possession of Gasprinskii's initiative.

Rashid Rida wrote of how the rumor spread that some who were present at the Continental Hotel speech were working behind the scenes to seize control of the congress, and suspicions began to run high. Mustafa Kamil himself had presided over a banquet for Gasprinskii at the Semiramis Hotel, and it seemed for a few days that Gasprinskii had fallen into his orbit. But Shaykh ᶜAli Yusuf (1863–1913), proprietor of the daily al-Muᵓayyad and a journalist squarely in the Khedive's camp, countered on behalf of the palace by organizing the Continental Hotel forum, and arranged a meeting to establish a congress preparatory committee. He was aided by Shaykh Muhammad Tawfiq al-Bakri (1870–1932), leader of Egyptian religious confraternities, who volunteered his home for the session. As a young man of European-style education who knew both French and English well, Shaykh al-Bakri was reported to have told Abdülhamid that "I wish for you to understand that I am not a simple mollah; I am a political man, I have general ideas, and I have read Aristotle, Montesquieu, J.-J. Rousseau, Spencer, Leroy-Beaulieu, etc."[16] "Was this fin de siècle Sheikh, this curious compound of Mecca and the Paris Boulevards, the latest development in Islamism?" Cromer asked. "I should add that the combination produced no results of any importance."[17] Shaykh al-Bakri was an irresolvable amalgam of enthusiasm for political freethinking and reluctance to reform the religious orders over which he presided.[18] He even had made his own proposal for a biennial Muslim congress in Mecca, in a short book published not long before Gasprinskii's arrival.[19] Shaykh al-Bakri naturally gravitated toward Gasprinskii, and eventually made the initiative very much his own.

Rashid Rida did not think this interest benign, and wrote that a complaint was circulating that "al-Bakri and the proprietor of *al-Mu'ayyad* had begun to tyrannize the plan, for whatever reason, and wanted to include in the congress whomsoever they chose." According to Rashid Rida, Shaykh ᶜAli Yusuf felt that he himself, Shaykh al-Bakri, Hafiz ᶜAwad (another of the Khedive's protégés), and a number of their friends, should serve on the preparatory committee, in recognition of their self-evident stature. Rashid Rida replied with a demand for the election of the committee by secret ballot. There were some outside of Shaykh ᶜAli's salon who were no less worthy, and "no one wants to contest the competence of another to his face, not publicly, so for these reasons all nations are agreed that an election of this sort should be secret."[20] No consensus could be reached on this question, and Shakyh ᶜAli Yusuf and Muhammad Tawfiq al-Bakri, along with their associates, proceeded in the coming days to act as an ad hoc preparatory committee. They scheduled the first congress for November 1908, and began to meet regularly.

It was at this point that Gasprinskii lost the initiative and its passage to the hands of a partisan faction signaled ultimate failure. Rashid Rida was soon alienated. On the pages of *al-Manar,* he wrote of the paternity of the congress idea in a manner which cast himself as its legitimate guardian. He stressed throughout that Afghani had first broached the idea, that ᶜAbduh and Kawakibi had elaborated upon it, and that Rida himself advanced it for Mecca in the very first volume of *al-Manar.*[21] Rida saw the congress idea as his own and that of his mentors, and Gasprinskii's initiative as a usurpation. Rashid Rida's resentment must have sharpened when he was excluded from the preparatory committee, and when the committee selected Salim al-Bishri, then between terms as Shaykh al-Azhar, as its president. Shaykh Salim had vigorously opposed the Azhar reforms advocated by Muhammad ᶜAbduh, and Rida criticized his equally conservative role on the congress preparatory committee.[22]

The prominent role of Shaykh al-Bakri must have been particularly disturbing to Rashid Rida, if one returns to a statement in his biography of Muhammad ᶜAbduh:

Sayyid Muhammad Tawfiq al-Bakri once told me: "I was riding with our Shaykh [Muhammad ᶜAbduh] one night during Ramadan along Darb al-

Jamamiz, and mentioned what blessings God had bestowed upon him in knowledge, wisdom, and service to Islam, and asked him: To whom should we turn for those things with which God blessed you once you are gone? [Muhammad ᶜAbduh] said: Muhammad Rashid Rida, proprietor of *al-Manar*."[23]

Rashid Rida's intention in offering this anecdote was explicit: it was Rashid Rida, not Tawfiq al-Bakri, who was the heir to ᶜAbduh, and hence Afghani. Just as annoying was the presence on the committee of Ibrahim al-Hilbawi, a lawyer who had studied under Afghani while a young Azhar student, and gained a reputation as the only one of Afghani's students daring enough to offer witticisms during his master's lectures.[24] Rashid Rida himself had done no more than write enthused letters to Afghani while a youth, and may have seen in Hilbawi a threat to his claim to represent the Afghani-ᶜAbduh tradition in his own generation. And Rashid Rida certainly must have heard disparaging things about Hilbawi from ᶜAbduh, for ᶜAbduh, in a letter to Afghani over two decades earlier, had accused Hilbawi of betraying Afghani.[25] The Gasprinskii initiative thus became a point of contention between Cairo rivals to the Afghani legacy.

The identification of Gasprinskii with Shaykh ᶜAli Yusuf attached the congress to a parochial motive, and the reservoir of support for the idea began to evaporate. There are indications that Gasprinskii, although on unfamiliar ground, was alert to this problem and tried to restore the compromised neutrality of his proposal. He first attempted to ease Ottoman anxieties, and so shift the great weight of the Empire's authority to his side. The prospects for this obviously were not good. "As for the great sultan of the Muslims," wrote Rashid Rida,

> no one doubts his displeasure with this congress and his intention to prevent it with all his power. News items from Istanbul in some of the newspapers already support this conclusion: the sultan is to write to the Ottoman special commissioner to Egypt, Gazi Ahmed Muhtar Paşa, concerning this, and will order a prohibition against the stopover for pilgrims in Egypt. Some people claim that Muhtar Paşa has written so already. The aversion of the sultan to the congress will render the project offensive to many Muslims. He fears its harm and does not anticipate its benefits, and will prevent the publication in Ottoman newspapers of any news about the congress before it is held, if indeed it is ever held.[26]

Gasprinskii nonetheless began to write to Ottoman authorities about his plan. In December 1907, during one of his shuttles between Baghchesaray and Cairo, Gasprinskii stopped in Istanbul and was granted an audience with the Grand Vizier Ferid Paşa. It was Gasprinskii's intention to reconcile the Porte to the inevitability of the congress and so assure its participation but, according to Gasprinskii, the Grand Vizier greeted his mention of the topic with silence.[27] *Al-Ahram* reported that the sultan's opposition to the congress was explicitly conveyed to Gasprinskii on this occasion, and that Gasprinskii, excusing himself to his suzerain for not abandoning the project altogether, gave assurances that nothing would be said against the Ottoman state in the congress sessions.[28]

The *Yıldız* collection in the Başbakanlık Arşivi, particularly the voluminous collection of dispatches from Ahmed Muhtar Paşa, may eventually yield details on Hamidian policy toward Gasprinskii's initiative, but the broad lines are self-evident. The Cairo political salon with which the idea was identified enjoyed a low reputation in Istanbul. Shaykh ᶜAli Yusuf was himself a subject of Abdülhamid's vivid suspicion. His newspaper, al-Muʾayyad, was banned in Syria on several occasions, most notably when it carried the original serialization of Kawakibi's indictment of tyranny, Tabaʾiᶜ al-istibdad, rightly considered a subversive tract.[29] No less objectionable to Ottoman authorities must have been the presence of two Syrians, Rafiq al-ᶜAzm and Haqqi al-ᶜAzm, on the ad hoc preparatory committee. Rafiq Bey had belonged to a Young Turk circle in Syria, and when the group established contacts with exiled Young Turks in Europe, the Ottoman police struck and Rafiq fled to Egypt. There he began to write for the newspapers, and with Rashid Rida and Abdullah Cevdet founded the "Ottoman Consultative Society," which advocated consultative government. When Abdülhamid learned of the existence of this dangerous society, he was said to have lost three nights' sleep, until his agents in Egypt told him exactly who its members were.

Rafiq's cousin, Haqqi, became the Arabic secretary of the group, and by 1907 the society was in touch with the Salonika Committee of Union and Progress. The favorable mention made of the congress plan in Abdullah Cevdet's own periodical, İçtihad, would have excited yet more Ottoman suspicion.[30] Hafiz ᶜAwad, yet another preparatory committee member, was also familiar to Ottoman authorities. He once declared that not a single Egyptian wished to see Ottoman authority reestablished in Egypt, and when Shaykh ᶜAli Yusuf published this item in al-Muʾayyad, the newspaper was banned once again in Syria.[31] As far as Ottoman authorities were concerned, Gasprinskii's proposal had fallen into the hands of conspiratorial Young Turks and Khedivial agents, who bore nothing but ill will toward the Ottoman state and the sultan-caliph.

Gasprinskii thus was forced to explore an alternative measure to restore the neutrality of his plan: the publication of his own Arabic newspaper. This was intelligible only as an attempt to dissociate the congress from Shaykh ᶜAli Yusuf's political faction, for his initiative was already receiving detailed coverage in Shaykh ᶜAli's widely circulated *al-Muᵓayyad*. Three issues of Gasprinskii's *al-Nahda* saw print in February–March 1908, and their contents are the subject of a recent article.[32] Gasprinskii announced that he intended to publish sixteen issues in Cairo before proceeding to Teheran, where he planned to publish another sixteen in Persian,[33] and then anticipated a stay in Delhi or Lucknow, where yet another sixteen numbers would appear in Urdu. This mobility would have diminished the initiative's dependence not only upon Shaykh ᶜAli Yusuf's circle but upon Egyptian politicians generally. And while Gasprinskii flattered Egyptian audiences, assuring them that Cairo had been selected as the seat of the congress for its cultural and geographic centrality and its "internationally privileged" situation, he seems to have envisioned a congress which would have met elsewhere at least occasionally. *Al-Nahda*, however, folded after only three issues, for reasons that were never adequately explained. Abdullah Battal, who edited the newspaper for Gasprinskii, wrote that *al-Nahda* had expired from a lack of public interest, and so implied that enthusiasm for the idea had dissipated quickly. In April, the French ambassador in Cairo wrote that the project had been checked. "He was too liberal for them," the ambassador wrote of Gasprinskii among the Egyptians.[34]

Following the Young Turk revolution of July 1908 and the restoration of the Ottoman constitution, there seemed to be some hope for the proposal's resuscitation. It was believed that a new regime in Istanbul might shed the obsessive opposition to the congress idea in evidence throughout the reign of Abdülhamid. Some began to speculate that the new regime might even welcome Gasprinskii's congress. Gasprinskii at first rejected this suggestion, for reasons that are no longer clear. Despite his singular lack of progress, he reiterated the centrality of Egypt and the importance of Arabic as a Muslim common language. He pointed to the arrangements already made in Cairo, argued that gathering in Cairo would raise fewer European suspicions, and stressed that half of all Muslims, like Egyptians, lived under English rule. In Cairo, he added, there was greater freedom of speech. To his mind, it was too late to change the congress site, but the second congress certainly could meet in Istanbul, the third in Teheran, and subsequent congresses elsewhere.[35]

Either Gasprinskii feared some sort of Ottoman manipulation of the congress, upon which he preferred not to elaborate, or he simply was reluctant to write off the preparatory work which he had already invested in Cairo. The self-consciously Muslim faction in Istanbul, particularly the group surrounding the newspaper *Sırat-ı müstakim*, did not relent, and gave Gasprinskii's proposal considerable coverage in 1909. A lengthy open letter from a Beirut reader was published in the newspaper, which strongly urged Gasprinskii to proceed with his work at the seat of the caliphate, and *al-Mu'ayyad* reported that Gasprinskii had finally made a decision to do so.[36] But if so, he did not act. Meanwhile, the date of the Cairo congress was repeatedly pushed back by the preparatory committee, until the event was finally set for January 1911. But these plans suffered a serious setback when Shaykh Muhammad Tawfiq al-Bakri, linchpin of the preparatory committee, succumbed to severe paranoia, abdicated all his offices, and was committed to a Beirut asylum. The foundations which Gasprinskii had constructed then disintegrated.

Gasprinskii was unprepared to attribute his failure to the vissicitudes of Egyptian politics, and insisted that the opposition of the English, Russian, and French governments had defeated the congress. But there is no evidence that Gasprinskii's efforts were impeded by British authorities on their own initiative or on behalf of any other government. The French only considered how they might plant a pliable Muslim agent in the congress.[37] And no interest in congress activities was shown in British diplomatic correspondence. It is not known whether Gasprinskii gave up his project entirely after 1911, but he seems not to have advanced it at all during a later trip to Bombay. Gasprinskii turned to other themes in the last years of his life, and although he continued to frequent Cairo and Istanbul, he dropped the congress idea from *Tercüman.*

In 1911, Rashid Rida wrote something of an obituary for the proposal in *al-Manar*:

> It seems to us that the Muslims are not yet ready to convene a general Muslim congress for discussion of their interests and how to improve their lot. Intellectuals have repeatedly advocated this step, but no one heard them, noticed them, or showed them any sympathy. It immediately occurs to anyone who studies this question that the congress must be held in Mecca or Madina; this is what Afghani first prophesized, what we proposed fourteen years ago, and what Kawakibi made vivid in his book *Umm al-qura.* We all know that Abdülhamid II did not favor such a congress in the Arabian holy cities, and neither do the Committee of Union and Progress leaders now. İsmail Gasprinskii . . . proposed a congress in Egypt a number of years ago, and his call was answered by a faction of Egyptians. They wrote a charter for the congress and published an invitation throughout [Muslim] lands, and no one answered their call. Egypt is a land that enjoys the kind of freedom that would make a congress possible here, once there is a readiness.

Rida concluded by committing himself to the eventual preparation of Muslims for such a congress.[38] This effectively marked the end of Gasprinskii's initiative.

One document does shed light on how the congress might have un-

folded had it been held: a charter drawn up by the preparatory committee and published in a number of languages, for circulation
throughout the Muslim world.[39] The charter's twenty-eight articles together constituted a rudimentary attempt to give some structure to Gasprinskii's inchoate proposal (see appendix 1). The document shared very
little with Kawakibi's idealized charter. Remarkably wide powers were
vested in the preparatory committee. It was to function as an independent body, responsible only to itself, resembling the executive and
membership committees of an exclusive society. The fifteen committee
members were self-appointed, and had the authority to add whomsoever
they chose to serve alongside them. They elected a president, two vice
presidents, a secretary and a treasurer from among their own ranks. The
committee set the date, site, hours, and duration of the general congress,
and was responsible for regulation of procedure. It was also empowered
to establish a special commission to review proposed congress agendas.

Muslims who wished to participate in the general congress organized
by the committee submitted applications. These were examined by the
committee, which admitted applicants at its discretion. Admission to
the congress, after payment of dues, assured a participant the right to
take part in the deliberations and discussions of the congress, and similarly to give advice concerning all questions within the scope of the
congress. But "as for administrative and financial questions, these are
the exclusive preserve of the organizing committee." The discussion by
congress participants of political issues was "absolutely forbidden," and
propositions of a religious character were admissible only if supported
by a Qurʾanic text, Prophetic example, the unanimous opinion of ulama,
or interpretation of sacred texts by analogy. There were no provisions
for voting within the congress, either to pass resolutions or to elect
officers. Resolutions and elections were effected by the committee
through a simple majority of its members. The congress was given no
say in the selection of the committee, whose members enjoyed an absolute authority. They, too, bore the financial burden. Each committee
member paid dues of half an Egyptian pound per month, and so supported most of the various expenses of publication and publicity. The
charter's adoption in this form by members of the preparatory committee
was probably meant to assure that the initiative was not lost by Shaykh
ʿAli Yusuf's circle to a rival group during the congress sessions.

Suspicion of motivation, the struggle among rival political factions
for control, organizational ambiguity—the Gasprinskii initiative succumbed to a combination of obstacles which Kawakibi, exploiting literary license, had avoided or ignored. But while the congress never
materialized, the press converage in Turkish and Arabic, the circulation
of invitations and the congress charter, and the attendant controversy

which spanned several years, gave the congress idea widespread currency. Gasprinskii was not the first to suggest a Muslim congress, but he was the first to pursue the idea with vigor and give it form through organization. He differed from his predecessors in moving away from strictly literary advocacy. To fill *Tercüman* with calls for a congress was not sufficient; Gasprinskii, for all his writing, recognized that success depended upon organizational effort. Gasprinskii's own organizational skills proved inadequate, but he generated newsworthy controversy and provoked thought.

Of greatest importance was the fact that Gasprinskii's initiative coincided with constitutional revolutions in the Ottoman Empire and Iran. Authoritarian regimes in both empires had reacted with hostility to congress suggestions, because the format was derived in many respects from European parliamentary models, and because it was associated so closely with advocates of decentralized government. But the constitutional revolutions brought down these barriers to an open discussion of the idea, and a congress appealed to many as constitutionalism writ large, embracing all Islam within a regional order in philosophical harmony with the new parliamentary regimes in Istanbul and Teheran. Gasprinskii's initiative rode the crest of this wave, and with him, the congress idea became popular.

A consequence of this development was that the congress idea no longer appeared in strict association with the notion of an Arabian caliphate, but became part of the intellectual baggage of Ottoman and Iranian constitutionalists and radical reformers. Of this we have three interesting examples, involving individuals in each instance marked by the imprint of sojourns in Cairo. Gasprinskii's visits to Cairo in 1907–8 briefly preceded the Cairo stay of an Iranian journalist and publisher, Mirza ᶜAli Aqa [Labib al-Mulk] Shirazi (d. 1918). ᶜAli Aqa was a man of some importance in the era before Iran's constitutional revolution, when there was hardly a Persian press within Iran. His newspaper, *Muzaffari*, published at Bushihr from about 1901, was the first to appear in southern Iran, and remained the most important of the several newspapers which flourished in the southern provinces during the first decades of this century.[40]

ᶜAli Aqa was a committed constitutionalist, and late in the reign of Muzaffar al-Din Shah he was arrested, his newspaper was closed, and he was deported to Muhammarah. The authorities eventually allowed him to return to Bushihr, where he began once again to publish *Muzaffari*. But two years later, during the disturbances that led to the collapse of the constitutional regime in Teheran, he thought himself endangered and elected to flee to India, where other constitutionalist publishers had taken refuge.[41] From there he left by steamer for the important Persian émigré center in Cairo, with the ultimate intention of reaching far more important Persian circles in Istanbul. His dealings in Cairo are difficult to reconstruct, but it seems not unlikely that he came in contact with the congress idea at the height of the Cairo congress preparatory committee's activities. He then did not proceed to Istanbul with his traveling companion, but instead left Suez by steamer for the pilgrimage, and published one issue of *Muzaffari* in Persian on a Meccan press.[42]

Muzaffari-in-exile, enjoying the freedom of press assured by the restored Ottoman constitution, called on all Muslims to set aside sectarian differences and unite. The Christian nations, divided by sectarian disputes, had always found the strength to unite against Islam. Islam could close ranks in a similar fashion, if only the ulama took the initiative, and there was no better means than the pilgrimage to realize this aim. Notable ulama and intellectuals from each Muslim country should gather for a general assembly (*majlis-i umumi*), entitled the Society (*anjuman/ hawza*) of Muslim Solidarity (*ittihad-i islamiyyan*). This would meet annually at Mecca, the greatest Muslim land and place of worship, during the pilgrimage season. It was important that the decisions taken there be carried out by Muslim rulers, but the annual assembly would not interfere in political matters, confining itself to religious questions, issues of concern to ulama, and programs for unifying the sects of Islam. The formal exclusion of politics would assure that the apprehensions of foreign powers would not be excited. The proceedings of this assembly would then be published and disseminated to pilgrims, who would carry them forth to the various lands whence they came. Thus branches would eventually be established. There then followed a lengthy discourse on the supposed testament of Peter the Great, and its insistence upon Russian rule over Istanbul; it was the duty of Iranian Shiʿis, through a great assembly, to set aside differences and come to the defense of this Ottoman city, which was the key to Asia.

The resemblance of this proposal to the Gasprinskii initiative was striking. Like Gasprinskii, and for similar reasons, ʿAli Aqa emphasized religious and social questions, and excluded partisan politics from his proposed congress. Like Gasprinskii, he sought to advance his idea through the publication of a newspaper in a country not his own. ʿAli Aqa sent copies of the Meccan *Muzaffari* to Azerbayjan and Gilan, where official censorship did not reach, and the issue is known to have arrived in Gilan, for the British vice consul at Rasht saw a copy.[43] But at this point his initiative virtually disappeared from sight. ʿAli Aqa lingered at Mecca for a time, where he reported the moving sight of Maghribi Muslims praying that God deliver Iran from the shah and afford that country liberty and peace.[44] In the summer of 1909, Teheran fell to the nationalists, the shah fled, and the second constitutional period opened; ᶜAli Aqa returned to Bushihr and began once more to publish *Muzaffari*. He was not long tolerated after the closure of the parliament in late 1911, and two officers under orders from the governor at Bushihr seized him at the baths and ultimately deported him to Ottoman Iraq. His attempts at repatriation were allegedly discouraged by the British, and he settled in Karbala, where he died. The Meccan suggestion appeared in none of the subsequent issues of *Muzaffari*, but his proposal of 1908, possibly a reaction to Gasprinskii's initiative, was further evidence for the dissemination of the congress idea.

A second instance of the impact of Gasprinskii's initiative was the growing interest in the congress idea among Ottoman Turkish reformers and Young Turk intellectuals. One faction of the Istanbul press, following the constitutional revolution of 1908, had urged Gasprinskii to transfer his enterprise to the Ottoman capital. This interest did not end with the collapse of Gasprinskii's own initiative, and 1911 saw two separate Turkish initiatives.

One appeared in the work of Mehmed Murad (1853–1912), a native of the Caucasus who, like Gasprinskii, had received his education in a Russian *gymnasium*.[45] He, too, could cite from Rousseau and Montesquieu, and was imbued with liberal ideas similar to Gasprinskii's. There was nonetheless an important difference between the two men. When Gasprinskii was a young cadet in Moscow in 1867, he had attempted to flee to the Ottoman Empire, but was stopped by the authorities at Odessa and sent home. For all his interest in the wider Muslim world, and the Ottoman Empire in particular, he lived his later life as a Russian Muslim. But Murad Bey, when sent to attend university in Moscow in 1873, succeeded in escaping and reached Istanbul. Thereafter he considered the Ottoman Empire his homeland, as did many other refugees from the Caucasus. It was as an Ottoman that he launched Young Turk societies in Europe and Egypt, and campaigned against the absolutism of Abdülhamid. His newspaper *Mizan*, launched during a period of Egyptian exile, became an important Turkish organ for the spread of liberal political concepts within the Ottoman Empire. Mehmed Murad's intellectual contribution to the 1908 revolution was prominent, although he was ambivalent about his means and, like Afghani, allowed Abdülhamid to entice him to an Istanbul post.

In 1911, shortly before his death, Murad Bey published a book in which he argued for the creation of a committee of nine Muslim notables under the direction of the Ottoman Şeyhülislam. In his committee he would include delegates from territories under British, French, Russian, and Dutch rule—by this time the great majority of Muslims—all designated by the appropriate European powers. The committee, a body fully independent of the Sublime Porte, would then deliberate in a definitive manner on the *sharīʿa*. The promise of binding resolution of the problems of Islamic law was an idea with precedents in the work of Blunt, Kawakibi, Rashid Rida, and Gasprinskii; unusual here was the emphasis upon the central role of the Ottoman Şeyhülislam, at the obvious expense of the sultan-caliph.[46] But Murad's proposal went even further in this direction. Three of the nine delegates would be entrusted with the selection of the caliph himself, a procedure in which the European powers would enjoy special privileges. This particular twist to Blunt and Kawakibi's innovative idea of an elected caliph was wholly original.[47]

Another appearance of the idea among Young Turks was registered in a secret resolution of the ruling Committee of Union and Progress, meeting in September–October 1911 in Salonika. For the first time, the idea appeared not in the work of an émigré political journalist, but among the decisions of an important political party:

> A general Congress ought to be convoked at Constantinople every year; Delegates from all the Moslem countries in the world ought to be invited to take part in this Congress which should assemble at Noury Osmanieh in Constantinople. Questions of general interest to the Moslem population of the world should be discussed and voted upon at this Congress.[48]

The appearance of these ideas in the highest deliberative body of the ruling party marked a departure from the situation of a decade earlier, when Rashid Rida cited the complete absence of such suggestions in the press of the Ottoman capital. But the resolution was a secret one, and was not published with the formal resolutions. Nor is there any evidence that the Committee of Union and Progress made an effort to organize such a congress. All that can be said is that the idea made an appearance, in a context which strongly suggested that it was intended to end the reliance of the Young Turk regime upon the Ottoman sultan-caliph as the centerpiece of pan-Islamic policy. The resolution, in neglecting to mention the caliph or caliphate, shared with Murad's more radical proposal the concept of a congress as the symbolic and functional instrument of Muslim unity. The caliphate was cast as a dependent institution of secondary importance.

The third trace of Gasprinskii's seminal influence was a proposal published in 1913 in Istanbul by Shaykh ʿAbd al-ʿAziz Shawish (1872–1929), a Muslim journalist and activist devoted to the cause of Ottoman primacy. Shaykh Shawish was born in Alexandria in Egypt, to a Maghribi family which maintained wide commercial ties across the southern coast of the Mediterranean and into the Hijaz. The effect was to impart to him a cosmopolitan vision of the Muslim world. Shaykh Shawish received a traditional education at al-Azhar and the Cairo Dar al-ᶜUlum, but then proceeded to England for some eight years, where he studied at a teachers' college, taught Arabic at Oxford, became interested in British orientalism, and met the orientalists E. G. Browne and D. S. Margoliouth. By his own account, the experience sharpened his skills as a Muslim apologist and polemicist, as it had done for Afghani.

On his return to Egypt in 1906, he drew close to the Egyptian nationalists Mustafa Kamil and Muhammad Farid, and in 1908, following Mustafa Kamil's death, Shaykh Shawish was installed by Muhammad Farid as editor of the nationalist Cairo daily al-Liwaᵓ. Shaykh Shawish now gave regular expression in print to his commitment to Muslim solidarity and Ottoman primacy. His writings and activities exposed him to repeated prosecution, so he left for Istanbul in 1912, where he founded an Arabic newspaper, al-Hilal al-ᶜuthmani. Although the Egyptian government succeeded in having him extradited later that same year on conspiracy charges, he returned to Istanbul after his acquittal. With Shakib Arslan, an eloquent Lebanese Druze, he then formed a small circle of Arab supporters of the Ottoman caliphate that functioned in Istanbul and Berlin throughout the Great War, unaffected by the growing rift between Turks and Arabs that precipitated the Arab Revolt.[49]

Among Shaykh Shawish's Istanbul literary productions was a twelve-point program for Muslim unification, centered upon an Istanbul congress:

It is essential that some of the great ulama begin to correspond with leaders of public opinion and outstanding personalities, toward the goal of a meeting to be held either in Istanbul or Mecca before the end of the current *hijri* year. How wonderful it would be were that able writer and great reformer, İsmail Bey Gasprinskii, to renew his call for an Islamic congress, which he had wanted to convene in Cairo before the proclamation of the Ottoman constitution. Its seat should now be in Istanbul, wherein flies the Islamic banner of freedom and justice, so that groups of ulama, coming from all the corners of the Islamic world, might assemble to discuss our social and religious malaise; to expose the nonsense and superstitions that have entered our *shariᶜa;* to specify each malady and prescribe a beneficial treatment for dissemination through various lands, as is possible; to restore religion's vitality and youth; to strike the hands of corrupters who falsely claim a relationship to us and are our greatest enemies. I am certain that the word of these great ulama and established personalities will be accepted by Muslims with concern, obedience, and respect, for they are the heirs of the first *imams*, and it will not be long before you see reason obliterate superstition and the road to true religion widened. This will assure us a new revival and return us to Islam as it was in its days of glory.[50]

Alongside the congress, Shaykh Shawish envisioned the creation of a number of subsidiary agencies. The first were educational. The great Nizamiyya *madrasa* in Baghdad would publish a set of journals in Arabic, Turkish, Persian, and European languages, under the editorial guidance of a committee of Islam's most renowned ulama. These authoritative journals would avoid politics and touch only on religious, social, and economic questions, so that the "Western imperialist governments" would not impede their distribution, the full cost of which would be borne by the Ottoman Inspectorate of Religious Endowments. An academy for the training of religious guides and missionary preachers would be established. Here the means to combat heinous innovations would be taught, along with the different languages and histories of the many Muslim peoples. In Istanbul itself, a free Islamic university would be established, attended by students selected by Ottoman consuls abroad from among the children of tribal leaders, ulama, and men of wealth. This would bind closely to the seat of the caliphate not only the students, but their influential fathers as well, who would be urged to visit. Arabic would be taught at the Ottoman Dar al-Funun, at Aligarh, at Orenburg, in Kazan, in the *madrasa*s of the Caucasus, Turkistan, Afghanistan, and China, in place of or in addition to European languages, so that communication between Muslims could be effected through a medium other than a European one.

Shaykh Shawish then proposed the establishment of a number of collaborative economic institutions. Muslim maritime shipping and transport companies would be established, and there would be a campaign to encourage the purchase of goods produced by Muslims instead of imports from Europe. Coordinated committees would be established in each Muslim country, to boycott the firms of states that committed injustices against Muslim peoples. Exchanges of students, officials, and ulama between Muslim countries would be promoted. An Islamic bank (*al-masraf al-islami*) would be established in Istanbul, under the auspices of the Inspectorate of Religious Endowments; it would create a public Islamic company, under an administrative committee elected by shareholders. The bank would float loans not only to the Ottoman state for military needs such as fleet construction, but would participate in a variety of commercial and industrial ventures throughout the Muslim world. Finally, the pilgrimage would be employed to promote all of these projects, and the most important pilgrims would be encouraged to proceed to Istanbul as well, to see the work achieved at the seat of the caliphate. Shaykh Shawish described the role of the pilgrimage in a separate article:

> The Muslims need not be embarrassed about calling for unity, for this is
> the greatest duty of their faith. If it is proper for Germany and England

each to boast of its solicitude for the Protestant Church, for France and Italy each to openly declare its protectorate over the Catholic Church, and for Russia to claim that it heads the Eastern (Orthodox) Church, then why should our government refrain from claiming the leadership of a religious institution similar to all the churches? Are we fanatics if we make an appeal for such a union and defend this faith at any time and place? Of course not. We are like any other nation, and will work to teach our religion and insist upon the right to defend ourselves. If other states, groups, and peoples hold congresses and establish newspapers to spread and teach their faith, then we too must convene a general Islamic congress, by which I mean the pilgrimage, and establish newspapers in all the Muslim languages.[51]

Shaykh Shawish, as editor of a major Egyptian newspaper during the Gasprinskii initiative, had absorbed Gasprinskii's themes of reform through congress, education, and economic revival. The contribution of Shaykh Shawish was that he envisioned a formidable series of subsidiary institutions: the multilingual journal, the new Muslim university, and the Islamic bank were proposals which were all to loom large in later congress initiatives. Another distinction between his vision and those of Kawakibi and Gasprinskii was his tenacious insistence that this battery of new institutions serve not some new center, but reinforce the stature of Istanbul and confirm Ottoman primacy. His was a position that soon would become untenable.

In pursuit of this plan, Shaykh Shawish enjoyed little more success than did his Crimean contemporary. He did establish a society composed of various Muslim émigrés in Istanbul, which was to raise money for the Ottoman treasury. Shaykh Shawish proceeded to Madina in 1914, where he broke ground for a new Muslim university, with the encouragement of Ottoman authorities.[52] His congress, however, did not materialize, and he spent the war years engaged in conventional Ottoman propaganda in Berlin and Istanbul. Following the Ottoman defeat, he found refuge first in Berlin, then with Mustafa Kemal [Atatürk] in Anatolia, before returning to Egypt where he finished his career in eclipse, a target of jealous Wafdist attacks. The visionary optimism of his twelve-point plan went unfulfilled, but here was certain evidence for the accelerated diffusion of the congress idea.

Innovations that emerge from the intellectual periphery often come from those who are spatially marginal. The most consistent feature of these earliest proposals is that nearly each issued from the mind of a political émigré or someone on an extended tour, passing through a land not his own. Afghani, Shaykh al-Raʾis, Rashid Rida, Gasprinskii, ʿAli Aqa Shirazi, Mehmed Murad, ʿAbd al-ʿAziz Shawish—each advanced his proposal in a place distant from that associated with his formation, and often among Muslims whose language he could not understand and whose political circumstances differed markedly from those of this own people. The travels of these forerunners, whether forced or voluntary, stirred in them a cosmopolitan awareness of the breadth of the Muslim world, and an urgent conviction that political unity would release some latent and liberating force which they believed it to possess.

Standing on the fringes of that audience which they sought to address, attempting to find a common language with which to communicate their ideas, they were literally eccentrics. But in political orders and societies under stress, when conventional thought no longer meets the demands made by rapid change and outside pressure, ideas first cultivated on the fringe excite a wider interest. The disorientation of war, and the collapse in parts of the Muslim world of a four-hundred-year-old structure of political and religious authority, finally carried the Muslim congress idea to the very center of political discourse.

FIVE

HOLY WAR
The Wartime Initiatives

O N THE EVE of the war, one or another proposal for a Muslim congress must have been familiar to the well-read Muslim who followed the Turkish, Arabic, or Persian press. Then, in November 1914, five *fatwa*s were issued in Istanbul calling upon Muslims everywhere to join a war of faith against the Entente powers. The *fatwa*s were immediately followed by a proclamation of holy war (*beyanname-i cihad*) issued over Sultan Mehmed V Reşad's imperial seal. "Gather about the lofty throne of the sultanate, as if of one heart, and cleave to the feet of the exalted throne of the caliphate. Know that the state is today at war with the governments of Russia, France and England, which are its mortal enemies. Remember that he who summons you to this great holy war is the caliph of your noble Prophet."[1] The consequence was to dampen reformist expectations of a congress before the cessation of hostilities, but also to create a fluid situation that opened new possibilities for political action.

The Committee of Union and Progress returned to an emphasis upon the intrinsic authority of the caliphate, a message transmitted through the traditional means of the emissary. A further organizational modernization was effected: The establishment of a centralized special force, the *Teşkilât-ı Mahsusa,* represented a structural improvement over the disorganized recruitment and dispatch of Hamidian emissaries. Under the general direction of Enver Paşa, one of the Committee triumvirs, *Teşkilât-ı Mahsusa* agents were sent on a series of missions to disseminate the November proclamations both in Ottoman provinces and in Muslim territories under enemy control. Most of these agents were either Turkish- or Arabic-speaking military men. Ottoman military missions organized the Sanusi resistance against the Italians in Cyrenaica, and successfully encouraged the Sanusis to launch an assault against the British in Egypt from the Western Desert. They raised and levied irregulars in the Fertile Crescent, and competed for the allegiance of tribes in Arabia. Among the more ambitious missions was one composed of an Ottoman staff colonel and an assistant, who both arrived in Afghanistan in June

1916. There, among the Afridis who controlled the Khyber Pass and exercised great influence among the neighboring frontier tribes, they unfurled a flag which they claimed had been blessed by the caliph, and drew about four hundred men to their service. On the opposite end of the Muslim world, members of an Ottoman mission based in Spain crossed into Morocco and served with Raysuni and ᶜAbd al-Malik in the resistance against the French.[2]

The primacy accorded the Ottoman state by other Sunni Muslim states from the sixteenth century was a consequence of Ottoman military superiority, related in particular to the Ottoman role as diffusor of firearms and bulwark against Europe. But the twentieth-century Ottoman military missions were not effective, and the arms which they were capable of delivering to peripheral regions were not sufficient to move men to action against modernized adversaries. Perhaps the operations against the Italians in Cyrenaica were the most successful. Those against the British from the Western Desert failed. The political work in the Arabic-speaking provinces was effective, but could not withstand the military alliance of Allied arms and the desert strike force of Arab autonomists, nationalists and brigands who joined the revolt of Husayn ibn ᶜAli, Sharif of Mecca. The Ottoman mission to Khyber was driven out when it failed to offer material assistance along with its message, and the many Arabs in the mission to Morocco began to plan flight to America when they learned of the execution of Arab nationalists by Ottoman military authorities in Syria. There were many other such missions, few of which were marked by success. The only region in which there were large-scale popular uprisings coinciding with the jihad appeal was French West Africa, in territories worked not by Ottoman missions but by Transsaharan Sanusi emissaries. These disturbances, on the order of revolts in some parts, were eventually suppressed by coordinated Anglo-French military action, and left no apparent impression in Istanbul.[3] It soon became clear that Muslims beyond the Ottoman Empire, however attached to the Ottoman caliphate, would not wage war in adverse circumstances, and without logistical support.

Yet a second approach to stirring support for the Ottoman cause was the creation of societies in Europe, where the war had thrown active Muslims of various origins and nationalities together. The exiled Egyptian nationalist Muhammad Farid described this activity at length in his political diaries. Before the war, he himself founded a Geneva-based group entitled the Society for the Progress of Islam: "During my stay in Geneva at this time, I met some Muslims, among them Turks and others, and I tried to find a bond greater than the differences in their nationalities (*ajnas*). I invited about fifteen of them to a banquet on

Muharram 10, 1331 [December 19, 1912], and we agreed to found the Society for the Progress of Islam, and to publish a newspaper on its behalf."

This Society, which included non-Muslim members, fell into abeyance along with its newspaper, but was resuscitated with Ottoman subventions upon the approach of war, through an agreement with Enver Paşa. Before and during the war, Muhammad Farid organized similar banquets of notable Muslims on the feast of ʿId al-Adha, and one year used the occasion to address Muslim prisoners of war who had fought in Russian ranks. At the banquet which followed, he advocated a more formal technique: "I spoke of the pilgrimage from a political, economic, and social perspective. Shaykh [ʿAbd al-ʿAziz] Shawish spoke on the religious and historical dimensions. . . . at the end of my speech, I spoke of the need to use the annual pilgrimage as a Muslim congress (muʾtamar islami), to strengthen the bonds of unity between Muslims, so that we might realize political unity between the Ottoman state and other Muslim peoples. . . . The event was a great success."[4]

But at no point during the war did Ottoman authorities plan something as difficult under wartime circumstances, and unprecedented under any conditions, as the organization of a Muslim congress. There was some expectation that they would. In the middle of 1916, an agent in the employ of British Intelligence overheard five or six "eminent" Egyptian ulama in conversation at the entrance to al-Azhar:

> They were maintaining that the movement of the Sherif [Husayn] is a political device arranged between the Sherif and the Turkish Government, to deceive the British, by an apparent loyalty. . . . The Allies were to be deceived, and the pilgrims were to arrive from Egypt, India and elsewhere. Mecca would then be made the meeting place of a Moslem congress, which would arrange a general union of Islam and a declaration of a Holy War in all Christian-controlled countries.[5]

The rumor was far from the mark, for the revolt of the Sharif Husayn was not a device, and the barriers which separated the Muslims of Egypt and India from Ottoman territory during wartime were nearly insurmountable.

But the unorthodox premise of this rumor was that a new fatwa, or proclamation, sanctioned by a collective body, would have a greater effect than the appeal already issued in the autumn of 1914 by the Şeyhülislam. It was this belief that had produced the inspirational proclamation to "Muslim soldiers" by ten ulama in December 1914, each of whom came from a different land.[6] And there is some evidence that, perhaps at German urging, the Committee of Union and Progress con-

sidered the reissuance of the original jihad appeal as a collective instrument. The first suggestion dates from September 1916, when a number of Muslims allegedly were assembled in Berlin at the instance of
an obscure German 'orientalist' and Enver Paşa. Named among the
participants were a number of Afghan, Iranian, Central Asian and North
African Muslims who had been involved in political work in Berlin.
Foremost among them were Muhammad Farid and Shaykh ᶜAbd al-
ᶜAziz Shawish.[7] Their principal resolution urged the Ottoman Şeyhülislam, Musa Kazım Efendi, to issue a new set of jihad *fatwas*, but this
time the documents were to be collective works. "These *fatwas*," said a
French report, "will be elaborated by the Şeyhülislam, along with a
gathering of various ulama representing those diverse religious communities bound to the caliphate. They are to be united on the occasion
of the next *mawlid*, at the imperial palace of Topkapi, wherein are preserved the relics of the Prophet, and [there] they will come to an understanding."[8] This resolution was not effected, for it was repeated in
the winter of 1916–17, by a similar assembly of Ottoman and exiled
Muslims convened in Istanbul. Among the resolutions of this gathering,
which reportedly was held at German suggestion, was an invitation to
the Ottoman Şeyhülislam to publish a new jihad *fatwa*, in the hope "that
support of an extraordinary council would produce [a] stronger impression than [did] the first such fetva."[9] And yet the Ottoman Şeyhülislam,
Musa Kazım, although widely known for his political activism, issued
no further *fatwa*, and no council or assembly was organized in his support.[10] To have followed this advice would have implied that the original
fatwa and sultan-caliph's *beyanname-i cihad* were not binding or had failed.
To have conceded that other means might have succeeded where these
had not would have been an admission with radical implications.

It was even necessary for committed Muslim sympathizers of the
Ottoman state, discouraged by the progress of the war, to pursue these
attempts to convene Muslims not in the Ottoman capital but in the
neutral capitals of Europe. There the idea was not welcomed by the
prospective hosts either. Muhammad Farid participated in such an attempt: "In early October [1917], a group representing Muslim peoples
subject to France, England, and Russia, arrived in Stockholm with the
aim of convening a Muslim congress to demand the rights of their
peoples." Participants came from the Ottoman Empire, Egypt, Tripolitania, Tunis, Algeria, Morocco, Turkistan, and India. Among them again
were ᶜAbd al-ᶜAziz Shawish and Muhammad Farid himself. "The government did not permit us to meet and speak publicly, as it was pre-
serving neutrality." Only an ad hoc gathering, under the auspices of
the Mayor of Stockholm, was permitted.[11] The war thus yielded no great

Muslim congress under Ottoman auspices, for the idea was apparently regarded as fraught with risk in the midst of a holy war waged in a conservative idiom.

Yet there were some radicals prepared to break with that conservatism. ᶜUbayd-Allah Sindhi (1872–1944) was born to Sikh parents in the district of Sialkot, northeast of Lahore.[12] He fled home to embrace Islam at the age of sixteen, and found shelter from his relations in Sindh, with the head of a Sufi order to whom he became a disciple. Two years after his conversion, ᶜUbayd-Allah entered the Deoband Dar al-ᶜUlum, then the most politicized center of traditional religious learning in Muslim India, to study under the illustrious scholar and Sarparast of Deoband, Mahmud al-Ḥasan [Shaykh al-Hind].[13] Under instructions from his mentor, ᶜUbayd-Allah began to engage in clandestine political activity. In 1915, the acolyte was ordered to proceed secretly to Afghanistan, to urge the Afghan amir to attempt to drive the British from India. In Kabul, ᶜUbayd-Allah joined forces with an Ottoman-German mission, and he became a minister in the shadow "Provisional Government of India."[14] He also engaged in a variety of political and propagandistic activities designed to arouse the Afghans to war and thwart the emergence of a German-Hindu entente inimical to Muslim interests.[15]

One of the pursuits was particularly innovative. In the summer of 1916, ᶜUbayd-Allah wrote a series of letters on yellow silk to Mahmud al-Hasan, in which he outlined a new structural approach to the unification of the Muslim world.[16] ᶜUbayd-Allah advocated a hierarchical league not unlike that attributed to Afghani and sketched by Kawakibi. "This is a special Islamic society based on military principles," ᶜUbayd-Allah wrote in one of the silk letters. "Its first object is to create an alliance among Islamic kings." ᶜUbayd-Allah then gave full details on the projected membership of this secret society, which he entitled al-Junud al-Rabbaniyya, freely rendered by British authorities as the Army of God.

The association was to have three "patrons": Mehmed V Reşad, the Ottoman sultan-caliph; Ahmad, Qajar shah of Iran; and Habiballah, amir of Afghanistan. Below them served a dozen "field marshals": Enver Paşa, the Young Turk triumvir; the Ottoman heir apparent; the Ottoman Grand Vizier; the ex-Khedive ᶜAbbas Hilmi; the Sharif of Mecca; the Naᵓib al-Saltanah at Kabul; the Muᶜin al-Saltanah at Kabul; the Nizam of Hyderabad; the Nawab of Rampur; the Nawab of Bahawalpur; and the Raᵓis al-Mujahidin, that is, the leader of the remnant of that colony established by Sayyid Ahmad Shahid [Brewli] in the previous century astride the Afghan frontier. These had continued to maintain with belligerence that India was *dar al-harb*.[17] Numerous additional officers of lesser rank followed. Named, among others, were Shaykh ᶜAbd al-ᶜAziz Shawish; Abul Kalam Azad, Meccan-born son of a charismatic pir, himself a Calcutta journalist interned by the British from 1916 to 1920; and Muhammad ᶜAli, a journalist originally from Rampur, interned from 1915 to 1919 by the British in India along with his brother, Shawkat. These later became the leading figures in the Khilafat movement. ᶜUbayd-Allah awarded himself the rank of commissioner of Kabul. The implication was that this organization would continue to function once the war was over, although ᶜUbayd-Allah proposed no specific mode of operation alongside his list of members.

The Army of God was portrayed by ᶜUbayd-Allah as though it existed. It was, in fact, nearly as fictitious as Afghani and ᶜAbduh's society, *al-ᶜUrwa al-wuthqa,* and Kawakibi's society, *Umm al-qura.* "Most of the persons designated for these high commands cannot have been consulted as to their appointments," concluded the Sedition [Rowlatt] Committee's report.[18] But the ramblings of ᶜUbayd-Allah's imagination were not random. His preference for Afghan and Indian Muslims in his selection of field marshals, an inclination even more pronounced in his choice of candidates for the lower ranks, evidenced a distortion of perspective similar to Kawakibi's, with a difference. In ᶜUbayd-Allah's lens, India and Afghanistan, rather than Arabia and the Fertile Crescent, were in clearest focus.

But of more interest was the nature of authority as understood in the silk letters. Here was a chain of command in which the arrangement of the links was uncoventional in the extreme. ᶜUbayd-Allah diminished the Ottoman caliphate's significance in his scheme. In his selection of patrons, the Ottoman caliph emerged as simply one triumvir. This shift of emphasis was made explicit when ᶜUbayd-Allah proposed the Army of God's administrative centers. "General headquarters" was located by ᶜUbayd-Allah not at the seat of the caliphate but in Madina, where Mahmud al-Hasan had established himself after the outbreak of the war. He designated three "secondary centers": Istanbul (for promoting the war in Europe and Africa), Teheran (for Central Asia), and Kabul (for India). This multiplicity of Muslim centers, and the attendant relegation of Istanbul to the second rank, reflected a dissatisfaction with the role of the Ottoman caliph and Istanbul as points of convergence and emanation, for in Kabul, ᶜUbayd-Allah was confronted with the inability of the Ottoman state to supply arms and dispatch aid for the defense of Muslims elsewhere. The silk letters of ᶜUbayd-Allah Sindhi advocated a realignment of center and periphery in Islam. They did not argue for the institutionalization of contractual authority in a congress, but did propose a diffusion, among several persons in association, of the intrinsic authority once personified in the Ottoman sultan-caliph.

Finally it must be said that the attempt to disseminate this program led only to its exposure. Once the letters fell into the hands of British Intelligence officers, those Indian Muslims listed by ᶜUbayd-Allah were compromised, and the ineffectual network was rolled up by the police in a sweep of arrests. As a consequence of the Arab rising in the Hijaz, Mahmud al-Hasan himself was arrested and interned at Malta.[19] The war closed without ᶜUbayd-Allah having fulfilled his mission, and he decided that Afghanistan was not a congenial setting for further activity. It was at this point that the syncretic strand in his religious beliefs manifested itself most clearly. He left Kabul for Moscow in late 1922, proceeded to Ankara in 1923, and then established himself in Istanbul, where he remained for some three years.[20] There he was profoundly influenced by the secularization of the Turkish state, and advocated the generalization of this process (which he called Europeanism) through all Islam, favoring such controversial reforms as the romanization of Arabic-based alphabets and the adoption of full Western attire. He arrived in Mecca three years later, and there, in the late 1930s, he dictated his Qurᵓan commentary, *Ilham al-rahman.* In this work, he advanced the uncoventional premise that all Muslims were as caliphs, and advocated the establishment of a Muslim central association (*jamᶜiyya markaziyya*), whose members would chose and depose an elected caliph of all caliphs.[21] ᶜUbayd-Allah was permitted to return to India in 1939, after a quarter of a century of exile, by which time he had embraced beliefs that earned him denunciation by certain ulama as an unbeliever. It seems not unlikely that a foretaste of his intellectual radicalization was his proposal of a Muslim alliance structured around not a caliph but an association, at a time when the primacy of the Ottoman caliphate was an article of faith among Indian Muslims.

Radical notions of religio-political authority won converts even among the ulama of Istanbul during the war. At the very epicenter of the jihad, there were those who sought not simply to issue a collective *fatwa,* but to remold the caliphate in a fashion wholly out of harmony with tradition. Here, for the first time since Kawakibi's *Umm al-qura* and Mehmed Murad's brief proposal of 1911, the idea of a congress as an electoral college for the caliphate reappeared. In the summer of 1915, a group of Istanbul ulama informed the former dragoman of the Russian embassy, just before his expulsion, that they were considering the creation of a provisional caliphate, in the event that Istanbul fell, and obtaining for him "a portion of Constantinople or the city of Damascus as a residence with independent sovereignty rights in a limited area similar to the Vatican."[22] The caliph, in the account of Sir Mark Sykes, was then to be elected:

> Their idea as to the election of the Caliph was, that after a general peace was established in the world, a body of persons composed of representatives of various schools and peoples throughout the Moslem World should be formed, and that they should proceed to elect a Caliph from among the descendants of the Prophet's family. That on a Caliph's death his successor should be elected from the same source. In this they consider that they comply with the Islamic theory of the Caliph being of the Karaysh [sic] and meeting with the approval of Islam.[23]

This proposal was identical in all essentials to Kawakibi's, with the mutation that the caliphate was to remain in Istanbul or be transferred to Damascus, a city still held by the Ottoman army in the summer of 1915. Of the precise authors of this revolutionary approach we unfortunately know nothing. Sykes simply portrayed them as representing "the views of the majority" of Istanbul ulama, but an India Office undersecretary called them "a small group . . . anxious to pick up some trifle from the wreckage of empire, but without troops or any solid party behind them."[24] Again, nothing came of the idea, but it was significant that the notion of a Vaticanized, contractual caliphate, drawn from Quraysh, had made inroads among Istanbul ulama at all, particularly so soon after the issuing of the jihad *fatwa*.

But the most forward advocates of a radically altered caliphate were at work in Cairo. There, a circle of British intelligence officers and diplomats responsible for drawing Muslim support to the prosecution of the war against the Ottoman Empire resuscitated the concept of a Meccan Qurashi counter-caliphate. Sir Mark Sykes wished "if possible to stimulate an Arab demand for the Caliphate of the Sherif [Husayn]," as part of a policy "to back the Arabic-speaking peoples against the Turkish Government on one consistent and logical plane."[25] Ronald Storrs took the same position, arguing that "it will presumably be not disagreeable to Great Britain to have the strongest spiritual in the hands of the weakest temporal power," and urged "that nothing remotely resembling an obstacle should be placed between the Sherif and his ambition."[26] In a note written in October 1914, Lord Kitchener, apparantly on no greater authority than his own, had written to the Sharif Husayn that "it may be that an Arab of true race will assume the

Khalifate at Mecca or Medina and so good may come by the help of God out of all the evil that is now occurring." Whether or not the Sharif Husayn developed an interest in the caliphate only in response to Kitchener's suggestion is the subject of a continuing debate.[27] But is seems probable that Husayn's son ᶜAbdallah, who was instrumental in the negotiations preparatory to the Arab Revolt, showed some initiative in seeking British support for his father's ascent to the caliphate.

There were two approaches by which Great Britain could pursue this objective. The first was set forth in a memorandum by Sayyid ᶜAli al-Mirghani, in response to a request by Sir Reginald Wingate, British Governor General of the Sudan. Sayyid ᶜAli was head of the Mirghaniyya/Khatmiyya religious order, one of the Sudan's two great confraternities, and he played a central role in Sudanese politics until his death. Sayyid ᶜAli earlier had written that the Sharif Husayn was "the most suitable man for this dignified position" of caliph, and added that Husayn "is a man very closely related to the Prophet and highly honoured by all Mohammedans, a fact which should give him the necessary precedence due to the honour of the position."[28]

Covert British action, not election, was the only certain means to this end: "If Great Britain was left alone to work secretly in the matter," wrote Sayyid ᶜAli, "it will not be very difficult to keep the whole scheme hidden from the general Mohammedan public, and when the result is attained the whole Mohammedan world will rejoice at having at last obtained the rightful Khalifa of Koreishite descent." This the British could effect by assuring, through their largesse, Husayn's ascendance throughout Arabia; then, "if the question of the Khalifate is decided by the majority of the Arabs in Arabia, there will be hardly any difficulty with the Mohammedans in other countries."[29] Differences of opinion were unlikely:

If the Emir becomes strong enough in the Hedjaz and other Arabian countries which will eventually come under his rule or are likely to be under his authority, this great edifice will then become complete. The new Emir will then be acknowledged by the Moslems of Egypt, India, the Sudan, the western parts, such as Algeria and Tunisia, and other parts of the World. . . . It may happen that a few of the Mohammedan places outside Arabia may refuse to acknowledge the new Khalif, but this would be of no great importance as long as he is acknowledged by the majority of the Mohammedans. A general and universal acknowledgement of the Khalif may not be forthcoming, but it is sufficient to obtain the consent of the majority of the Mohammedans.[30]

Following a series of secret measures, the Muslim world would be presented with an accomplished fact. His solution was the absolute antithesis of the congress technique, and for that reason was much favored in the Foreign Office.

From the outset, the India Office disagreed, and thought it useless if not dangerous to encourage the Sharif's ambitions. Muslims elsewhere had shown their contempt for his rebellious action against the Ottoman state, and the chances of Husayn's being acknowledged as caliph even within Arabia were not good. Through Sir Percy Cox, British Political Resident in the Persian Gulf, it was learned that Ibn Sa ud and other Arabian potentates had no intention of recognizing Husayn since, in Arabia, "no one cared in the least who called himself Caliph, and [Ibn Sa ud] reminded me that the Wahabis did not recognize any caliph after the first four."[31] The India Office had reached equally inauspicious conclusions about the state of Muslim opinion in India: "So far as can be judged by the reports received from India & by the vernacular press extracts there is no weakening whatever in the religious loyalty of Indian Moslems to the Sultan."[32] In the India Office, there then developed the idea that Britain should recognize a Meccan caliphate only upon recommendation by wider Muslim opinion. The Office urged that Husayn be told that "he must consult his co-religionists as to whether he s[houl]d proclaim himself Khalifa,"[33] although no indication was given as to how.

In the midst of this exchange, Shaykh Mustafa al-Maraghi provided an answer, in a memorandum on the caliphate written for Wingate.[34] Shaykh Maraghi (1881–1945) was a former pupil of Muhammad Abduh's from Upper Egypt, who served as chief religious judge of the Sudan from 1908 to 1919.[35] In August 1915, from his post in Khartoum, Shaykh Maraghi elaborated a detailed proposal for a Muslim congress.

He began by stating that, unless Britain took some positive step to give Muslims brighter hope concerning the caliphate, sympathy for the Ottoman caliphate would remain widespread. But were Britain to take a clear line in favor of the unification of the Muslim world on this question, the ill would find its cure.

> This done, Great Britain could then announce to the Mohammedans and declare that she expects them to unite together and hold a general meeting to discuss the question of the Khalifate. Such an announcement on the part of England will tend to create a new feeling of confidence in the hearts of the Moslems and their minds will be stimulated everywhere to consider and decide the weighty and important matter that has been thrown on their shoulders and which affects the future prospects of their existence and faith.
>
> No doubt such a new development in ideas will be, at the outstart, only local in various parts. In other words every country will start to

discuss the matter independently of the others. It is most important to explain in this declaration that Great Britain has no idea whatever of interfering in any way in the matter or of using her influence to affect the decision of the Mohammedans. Subsequently, Great Britain should facilitate the passage of delegates from one place to another with the object of uniting the Mohammedans with each other and arriving at an understanding with regard to the choice of the place where the conference should be held to choose the Khalifa.

Reliance upon Great Britain was Shaykh Maraghi's solution to the logistical problems of mobilization which had obstructed previous congress proposals. But internal organization and the congress agenda were to be the responsibility of representative Muslim delegates, who would operate in relative secrecy.

I do not mean that the conference should be open to the general public, but these delegates will prepare the minds of the public for the great event and induce every respectable community to delegate representatives to attend the conference to assist in the choice of the Khalifa and to represent them. When these delegates are assembled they will also delegate a number of them to represent every country or district in the General Conference. These are only the preliminary principles which have to be considered and worked out in detail.

The next passage revealed a number of close parallels to *Umm al-qura.* The proposal evidenced the same interest in the establishment of a modern organizational structure, and a fixed procedure for the selection of caliph. During his days at al-Azhar, Shaykh Maraghi, as one of ᶜAbduh's students, almost certainly read *Umm al-qura* as serialized in *al-Manar,* if not in book form. The influence was readily apparent. But Shaykh Maraghi went even further in the prerogatives conferred to his congress:

When the delegates are assembled from the various quarters at the appointed place for the conference, they will draw up rules which will have to be adopted by the conference—such as nominating the President, the hours of meeting, the system of collecting the votes, &c. These rules will be called the "Internal Rules of the Conference." When all this is done, the delegates will have to discuss and give their decision on the following points:—

1. The town or city which should be chosen as the seat of the Khalifa.
2. The qualities and qualifications which the Khalifa should possess.
3. The system to be invariably adopted in future in the choice of the Khalifa.
4. Whether the Khalifate should be confined to a certain family and follow the known rules of heritage or be on a strictly elective basis. Should

it be decided that the appointment should be according to the law of heredity, would it be necessary to make a permanent law which will supersede the elective system or to maintain this system in the same house and family?

5. Who shall have the right to vote.

6. What should be the system of administering the provinces which are under the rule of the Khalifa?

7. What should be the relations of the Mohammedans who are subjects to foreign and non-Moslem powers?

8. What should constitute the civil and religious rights of the Khalifa?

These are the different points which are considered to be of vital importance and which require to be discussed and decided. There is little doubt that at this conference various other matters will come up for discussion. When all these matters are decided and settled the Khalifa will then be chosen and the Mohammedans will pay homage to him and take the oath of allegiance, and thus the duty of this great and historical Mohammedan conference will come to an end.

Certainly no proposal since *Umm al-qura* was as far-reaching as this. Maraghi observed that, "if a scheme on these principles could be carried into effect, it would be the greatest event ever known in the annals of Mohammedan history and the question of the 'Khalifa' will be put on a proper and solid footing such as will never be overthrown by the tempests of ambition." Congress and caliphate were thus bound up as one by Shaykh Maraghi, as two institutions in symbiosis. But Shaykh Maraghi went further than Kawakibi, in disregarding all prior claims to intrinsic authority, unless confirmed by the contractual authority vested in the congress. It was as if the historical institution, and the vast corpus of doctrine surrounding it, had never existed.

What led him to so radical a position? Maraghi's motives in all this were never clarified, but it seems likely that, having established himself in something of an advisory capacity on Islamic issues to Wingate, he anticipated an important role in the organization of the proposed congress. There is further evidence that Shaykh Maraghi hoped at this time for the emergence of an Egyptian caliphate from Egypt's ruling house, which would explain his failure to mention the issue of Qurashi descent.[36] Were his royal patron, Sultan Husayn Kamil, to emerge as caliph from this congress, Egypt's role in Islam would be much enhanced, as would Shaykh Maraghi's. That such a man could aspire to so central a task evidenced how thoroughly the authority of the Ottoman caliphate had been eroded by war.

Unfortunately for Shaykh Maraghi, the Cairo circle of British policymakers thought the proposition unrealistic, for as early as May 1915, the British High Commissioner to Egypt, Sir Henry McMahon, had written that "any change of Caliphate in [the] immediate future is, in my opinion, more likely to come about by individual action of a candidate than through previous manifestations of Moslem opinion." He conceded that the ascent of the Sharif Husayn to the caliphate appeared desirable, but argued that "any attempt to influence Moslem opinion would be obviously harmful."[37] As was clear from the case of the Gasprinskii initiative, planned for British-controlled territory, Britain would do nothing to impede a Muslim congress, but neither was she prepared to do for the Muslims that which they had been hitherto unable to achieve themselves.

As the war drew to a close, and the Ottoman Empire was reduced piecemeal to its Turkish-speaking core, none of the specific wartime proposals appeared to have the least chance of realization. But from these initiatives, it was evident that their Muslim authors, no less than the victorious Allies, saw the possibility of gain in the collapse of Ottoman authority, and were full of ideas about alternatives to the ascendancy of the Ottoman sultan-caliph. The Ottoman obstacle was now removed. The war, in challenging the widespread veneration of the Ottoman state and the sultan-caliph as competent defenders of Islam, brought to the surface a latent struggle for succession to Muslim primacy.

In November 1918, the crisis experienced by other Muslim empires, and by the outlying provinces of the last great Muslim empire, finally overwhelmed the capital city of the Ottoman Empire. With the occupation of Istanbul by victorious Allied armies, rule at the seat of the Muslim caliphate passed to the military administration set up by the occupying powers. In a similar crisis, in an earlier era, the caliph or one of his heirs might have fled the invaders to settle on another shore, and there would have reconstituted his caliphate on firmly Muslim soil. But those few Muslim shores that were not patrolled by foreigners were unprepared to welcome so troublesome an exile, so that the Ottoman sultan-caliph chose to remain in his occupied city and, when later expelled, to select as his place of refuge a European resort. The issue of political and religious authority in Islam, already probed by unconventional thinkers, thus was thrown wide open to impassioned debate and calculated negotiation.

In these conditions of stress and disorientation, the idea of the Muslim congress shed its radical associations, and emerged transformed. For some, it appeared as an instrument to galvanize Muslim opinion for the restoration to the Ottoman sultan-caliph of his lost prerogatives. The new technique of the congress, in some relationship with the established institution of the Ottoman caliphate, might restore a semblance of the familiar order. Among those who thought the Ottoman caliphate beyond redemption, the congress idea circulated as the hammer for the forging of a new caliphate to rise from the ruins of empire, as Blunt had predicted would happen following "the last overwhelming catastrophe of Constantinople." For those who doubted the claims of any caliphate, the congress was seen as compensation for the loss of an institution once considered essential to political order, but which was no longer suited to modern circumstances and the pressing need for reform.

SIX

BETWEEN BOLSHEVISM AND ISLAM

The League of Islamic Revolutionary Societies, 1920–1921

T HE League of Islamic Revolutionary Societies represented a belated attempt to organize a Muslim congress by leaders of the Committee of Union and Progress. Their exclusive reliance upon the caliphate had failed to stir Muslim support during the war, and they had fled in disgrace. The League, under the direction of Enver Paşa (1881–1922), was the work of the Committee of Union and Progress in European exile. It led a tenuous existence for which the evidence is scant, and the efforts of its members culminated in a small Muslim congress in Moscow in 1921 which adopted an ambitious program of periodic congresses and branch associations. The League folded some time before Enver's break with Soviet authorities. This modest convention was a direct consequence of the disorientation created by the war, and emerged from the wreckage of a political order which the congress idea had served to indict and undermine.[1]

The most thorough account of the League was offered by Kazım Karabekir, who was well-positioned to observe its activities from eastern Anatolia.[2] Also informed was Ali Fuad [Cebesoy], envoy of Mustafa Kemal in Moscow.[3] Some material concerning the League and its congress seems also to survive in Cemal Paşa's papers at the Turkish Historical Society.[4]

Following the Mudros armistice of October 1918, the discredited leaders of the Committee of Union and Progress scattered and reached Germany and Switzerland. Among the refugees were all three Committee triumvirs, and Enver and Talat, probably at the suggestion of a German intermediary, went together to meet Comintern secretary Karl Radek, then in prison. During their meeting, the Comintern secretary was convinced that the disembodied remnants of the Committee of Union and Progress were of value, and that they might be redeemed to

serve the aims of Soviet policy in Muslim lands. The required task did
not differ markedly from that which the Committee of Union and
Progress had undertaken itself: the spread of anti-imperialist and particularly anti-British propaganda, conveyed in a Muslim idiom, throughout Anatolia, the Fertile Crescent, Iran, Afghanistan, and India. Few
then would have appreciated the paradox of an avowedly Muslim movement directed from Moscow under Soviet auspices. After the October
Revolution, the Bolsheviks published the secret Entente treaties dividing
the Ottoman Empire, and renounced the spoils sought by the old régime.
They attacked Anglo-French policy in the East in uncompromising
terms, and promised self-determination in those Muslim territories
which were their own imperial inheritance. The militant defense of Islam
had been one of the fundamental themes of the Ottoman claim to
Muslim primacy, and the Soviet Union's promise to continue this struggle, albeit in an altered form, attracted many Muslims in a period of
general disorientation. Radek invited his two visitors to the Soviet
Union, and while Talat declined, Enver reached Moscow in early 1920.[5]
A circle of former associates soon formed around him.[6]

In Enver's letter to Mustafa Kemal [Atatürk], written shortly after his
arrival in Moscow, he explained the move from Berlin to the Soviet
capital. It must be remembered that Enver and Mustafa Kemal had not
yet drawn apart, and still maintained a regular correspondence.

> While in Berlin, we saw that throughout the Islamic world, various local
> movements hostile to the Entente had commenced activity. These move-
> ments, deprived of organization and material means, we thought to unify,
> once the views of our friends had been ascertained. We contacted rep-
> resentatives of various Muslim countries now in Europe, especially the
> Indian [Khilafat leader] Muhammad ᶜAli, with whom a link was estab-
> lished. As a consequence, the direction of these movements will be con-
> ducted from one center (merkez), where we will create an association
> (cemiyet) composed of delegates (murahhaslar) from each country. Finally,
> I thought the work would be more fruitful if the association were located
> within Russia. On my arrival in Moscow, I spoke to the commissar of
> foreign affairs [G.V. Chicherin], who accepted my proposal, and I wrote
> to members of the association to convene here.[7]

Shortly after his arrival in the Soviet Union, Enver claimed to represent
a "union of revolutionary organizations of Morocco, Algeria, Tunisia,
Tripoli, Egypt, Arabia, and India." This was his own depiction of his
ties with leaders of various "local movements" whom he had encountered in Berlin, but there was unable to assemble in one forum. Enver
returned to Berlin a short time later to finalize the move to Moscow,
and at that time gathered together his associates to define a structure
for the League of Islamic Revolutionary Societies (İslâm İhtilâl Cemiyetleri

İttihadı). Europe had hosted the creation of various émigré Muslim societies, but this was the most ambitious, for those gathered wrote a charter (*nizamname*) to regulate a wide network of other Muslim societies.[8]

The charter (see appendix 2) provided for the establishment of a central committee to oversee centers in each Muslim country, which in turn were composed of branches. Once established, the branches in a given country would meet in periodic regional congresses (*memalik kongreleri*), where they would elect delegates to attend a general congress (*umumî kongre*), at a time and place determined by the central committee. The general congress in session would hear the report of the central committee, review finances, make any necessary changes in the charter, define a program, and finally elect members to serve on the central committee in the interim period until the next congress. The central committee then moved promptly to Moscow along with Enver, and there, with Soviet financial support, began to disburse sums for various projects. One expenditure involved the publication of a newspaper in Berlin, while most of the remaining money went to the support of individuals who directed centers in Berlin and Rome.[9]

Of the actual participants in this activity, there is little to add to the judgment of Mustafa Kemal [Atatürk]'s envoy to Moscow, Ali Fuad [Cebesoy], who wrote that the society simply gave another name to the exiled remnants of the Committee of Union and Progress.[10] When Talat, Nazım, and Halil gathered together for what was to be the last congress of the Committee of Union and Progress, in September 1921, their resolutions made it explicit that the League was the foreign-policy arm of the Committee. Through this medium, relations were to be maintained with the Soviet Union and the Third International.[11] The League was thus inseparable from the declining prospects of the Committee of Union and Progress remnant. Later in 1921, Enver finally convened a rudimentary gathering of the League in Moscow, a congress about which regrettably little is known, but about which Soviet archives one day might have much to recount. The Moscow congress was a very small gathering, of perhaps no more than a dozen persons. Among the notable participants were Fahri Paşa, the Ottoman defender of Madina against wartime Arab siege; Shakib Arslan; and Shaykh ᶜAbd al-ᶜAziz Shawish.[12] The proceedings were reportedly marked by tension between Enver and the Arabic-speaking participants, and "neither the Russians, the Turks, nor the Muslims were pleased with the result."[13]

The League of Islamic Revolutionary Societies subsequently led little more than a fictitious existence. There survives an outline of the League's

activities, presented by a Muslim spokesman to the Third Congress of
the Comintern, convened in the summer 1921 in Moscow. The chairman
of the Comintern Executive, G. Y. Zinovyev, introduced the spokesman
by noting that he represented "a revolutionary but not a communist
organization." The spokesman in turn claimed that the League maintained intimate ties with a number of religio-nationalist movements
from Morocco to Java.[14] No independent evidence confirms the existence
of such close ties. Occasional contacts maintained with various émigrés
in Europe seem more likely to have been the extent of this network.
Enver's efforts had yielded unsatisfactory results, and Radek proceeded
with an alternative plan, in which the League of Islamic Revolutionary
Societies had no role. Soviet emphasis shifted to encouragement of more
compliant Muslim national communists,[15] and the development of an
alliance of convenience with Mustafa Kemal's nascent Anatolian state.[16]
Soviet authorities soon lost their interest in the League of Islamic Revolutionary Societies, and its leader sensed an imminent fall from favor.

Enver was urged repeatedly by friends to move once again, this time
to Afghanistan, a state to which many Muslims turned following the
Ottoman collapse, and the only Muslim state that had expressed a
willingness to receive him. The Kabul invitation was declined nonetheless, for reasons which even now are unclear, but which may have
been related to Enver's vaulting ambition. While in Bukhara in the fall
of 1921, Enver, perhaps on mission for the Soviet government, went
over to the Basmachis, a Muslim movement in open resistance to Soviet
consolidation in Central Asia.[17] He was killed by Soviet troops in an
armed clash during the summer of the following year, by which time
the League of Islamic Revolutionary Societies had disappeared.[18]

SEVEN

KEMALIST TURKEY AND MUSLIM EMPIRE

The Society of Unitarians
and Aftermath, 1919–1923

T HE PROVINCIAL Anatolian town of Sivas in the fall of 1919 was the center of an embryonic military state, the creation of Mustafa Kemal [Atatürk] (1881–1938) and a circle of Ottoman military commanders for whom the terms of the Mudros armistice were unacceptable. The officers promoted their movement as an Ottoman and Muslim one. It was then impossible to know that they bore the seeds of a republican and secular state. Their declared policy was to liberate the sultan-caliph and Istanbul from foreign occupation, and so reestablish the continuum with the traditions of Ottoman primacy in Islam.

It was the promise of continuity with the Ottoman past to which Muslims elsewhere responded with expressions of sympathy for Mustafa Kemal's movement. While still in Sivas, and later in Ankara, Mustafa Kemal thought to organize this sympathy in a structured congress of Muslims. This desire culminated in the creation, near Sivas, of a secret Muslim society, known as the Society of Unitarians, and in November 1919 this society convened a Muslim congress in the presence of Mustafa Kemal and his chief aides. The Society of Unitarians continued to function under official sponsorship for some time afterward. When it ceased to exist, an attempt was made by officials of the Ankara government to convene an open Muslim congress under official Turkish auspices, an effort which was abandoned only a short time before the abolition of the Ottoman caliphate.

For the facts surrounding the first of these initiatives, conducted in absolute secrecy, there is unfortunately no corroboration in published Turkish sources, although relevant documents reached British Intelligence regularly.[1] The subsequent initiatives were discussed by a number of Turkish historians engaged in reinterpretation of this period.[2]

According to Turkish documents which came into British hands, eight unnamed "Muslim notables" met in the early fall of 1919 at an unspecified site, and drew up a charter for what they entitled the Society of [Muslim] Unitarians (*Muvahhidin*).[3] They met almost certainly at the instance of Mustafa Kemal or his close associate, Hüseyin Rauf Bey [Orbay], both of whom were quite possibly among the eight. On this occasion, they resolved to convene a congress composed of delegates and notables from all Muslim territories at a place determined by themselves, and they further agreed to operate in absolute secrecy. This self-appointed Executive Committee began to make preparations for a larger gathering, and on November 11, 1919, at a school in Zara, forty miles east-northeast of Sivas, thirty-seven named Muslims met *in camera* in the first general congress of the Society of Unitarians.

Of the method of procedure at this congress, nothing is known. Details on the participants are scant, although their names are on record. Twelve were representatives of the military movement, and reportedly among them were Mustafa Kemal and Rauf. The remaining twenty-five participants were ulama: sixteen from Anatolia, two from Trans-caucasia, two from Egypt, two from Syria, one from the Yemen, one from the Najd, and one from the Crimea. More inclusive participation was envisioned by the organizers for the future, for the opening speaker, Mustafa Kemal's colleague Bekir Sami Bey, expressed the hope that the second congress would include participants from Morocco, Algeria, Musqat, Afghanistan, India, and Bukhara, which "have been unable to send delegates to this meeting." There are grounds to doubt that invitations were ever sent abroad. It seems probable that most of the ulama who participated did not arrive especially to join the congress, but simply found themselves in the vicinity of Sivas or Zara on the appointed day. Whether from Anatolia or beyond, they were men of obscure reputations, whose names do not appear in a recent major history of ulama participation in the Anatolian events of this formative period.[4]

On the occasion of this first congress, the eighteen articles of the charter were presented to the participants for approval (see appendix 3). The purpose of the society, declared the first article, was to gather all Muslims around the besieged caliphate, for "religion must be utilised to counter every attack inspired by religion." The document was explicit on the nature of that caliphate: it was the possession of the "eldest son" of the Ottoman house, simultaneously the ruler of the Empire "by right and merit," possessing "an unshakeable right of supervision and control" over the Muslim world in its entirety. The Unitarians were determined to act on his behalf. The first congress was empowered to establish a central organization under the supervision of an executive council; to plan the establishment of branches in other Muslim countries; and to discuss methods and finance. The "preliminary duty" of the society was to secure the independence of all Muslims from foreign domination, following which a great assembly of delegates (*meclis-i muvahhidin*) from all Muslim countries would meet in Istanbul "or in any other place that may be chosen." There they would regulate their union. Each member country would take the form of a "free and independent unit," with its own president, supreme council, and ministerial council, but all would be united under the "sacred protection" of the caliphate in matters of economic, military, and foreign policies. Each member unit would then be represented on a "General Council" permanently seated in Istanbul.

In the meantime, the general congress of the Unitarians would meet annually or, if necessary, twice a year, to examine the progress of the society toward achievement of this federation of Muslim states. To better fulfill its tasks, the society's central organization would be divided into three sections. The first would deal with internal organization and finance. While funds were to be raised at first through monthly subscriptions payable by the members, and contributions from wealthy Muslims, the charter envisioned that each independent Muslim state would allocate a separate budget toward the society's activities. The task of the second section was "propaganda and publications." It was "to publish tracts, newspapers and books," and organize "special delegations" to Muslims in lands as distant as Central Africa, India, Turkistan, Sumatra, and Java. The third section was to handle "foreign policy," presumably relations with non-Muslim states. The most innovative subsidiary agency of the society was a "Supreme Court," composed of a president, four members, and two examining magistrates, whose task was the prosecution of "traitors" to the society. Since, according to article nine, the society considered all Muslims to be members *ipso facto*, the anticipated scope of this court's jurisdiction was vast.

The participants in the first congress reviewed and approved the charter, elected an eight-man Executive Council for a six-month term, and elected Mustafa Kemal president of the society. Ten resolutions were then passed, essentially strengthening the powers of the Executive Council, and most notably affirming that the Council had no fixed location but could meet in any Muslim town, as circumstances required.

The most important step taken by the congress after adjournment was its transfer, with Mustafa Kemal, to Ankara at the end of 1919. Documents concerning Ankara sessions continued to reach British Intelligence.[5] These dealt less than before with wider Muslim issues, so that one report commented that the society's tendency "to become merged in the local activities of the Nationalist movement, continues, and much of the discussion and decisions of these [most recent] two meetings are far more in the nature of Nationalist plans for local opposition to the Entente Powers than the legitimate programme, which was laid down in the proceedings of the first meeting of this society."[6] At an early date, the society did claim to have sent five delegations to the Caucasus and Azerbayjan, three to Egypt, three to Syria, two to Kurdistan, two to Iraq, one to Tunisia, one to the Yemen, one to Najd, one to Afghanistan, and one to India. Twelve active branches, all in Arabic-speaking territories, were also listed as having been established, and it was further claimed that a million copies of a proclamation of unspecified content had been distributed.[7] But by the summer of 1920, the society was reportedly "dying of inanimation," [sic] and no longer meeting.[8]

The establishment of a Muslim congress in Ankara nonetheless remained part of the early foreign policy of the new Turkish state. Mustafa Kemal himself was responsible for the form which the Society of Unitarians took, and among his aims was the continuation of the traditional Ottoman policy of solidarity, just as the Committee of Union and Progress had continued that policy. The stress upon Ottoman primacy in the charter of the Society of Unitarians was unequivocal, and the document left the caliph with nominal temporal attributes, so that it cannot be said that it foreshadowed even the limited step of the separation of caliphate and sultanate. This was Mustafa Kemal's early position: "The first goal of our struggle is to show our enemies, who intend to separate the sultanate from the caliphate, that the national will shall not permit it."[9] In this manner, he expressed his rejection of the "Vatican Proposal," by which certain British diplomats had thought "to give the Sultan-Caliph a kind of large Vatican in Constantinople, but to keep the Turkish State in Anatolia otherwise separate with a town in Asia Minor as capital for administrative purposes."[10] Any transformation of the caliphate thus threatened Istanbul itself, and on the question of Istanbul's reunification with the hinterland, the Anatolian movement was uncompromising.

Mustafa Kemal did recognize that the caliphate had not served the Ottoman war effort well, but he did not propose its abolition. He instead imagined a complementary role for the Muslim congress created by him and his associates. The society and congress would serve as intermediaries between the great reservoir of Muslims and the traditional authority of the caliph. Through such an instrument, Turkish primacy in Islam might be amplified, and the Ottoman state, through a federal solution unifying at least Turks and Arabs, might be reconstructed.[11] The creation of the society was characteristic of that distinctly Muslim and Ottoman phase through which Mustafa Kemal permitted his movement to pass, and which has, to a large extent, been obscured by subsequent Turkish nationalist historiography.[12] The idiom of discourse with other Muslims during this phase still evoked the authority of the Ottoman sultan-caliph, most vividly evident in Mustafa Kemal's proclamations (*beyannameler*) to the Muslim world, issued in the spring of 1920.[13]

This commitment lapsed when Mehmed VI Vahideddin refused to offer his patronage to the Anatolian movement conducted ostensibly on his behalf, a movement which he thought was liable to endanger what few Allied guarantees were secured through the armistice. To this we can trace the decline of the Society of Unitarians, and the secret adoption by Mustafa Kemal of a version of the British "Vatican Proposal." The British High Commissioner in Istanbul described the transformation: "There appears to be a good deal of discussion as to whether the Caliphate might not be vested in a purely spiritual personage surrounded by representatives from Islamic countries and maintaining touch with them through representatives of an ostensibly ecclesiastiç character in those countries. I find it difficult to believe that the Angora leaders would think the present moment opportune to challenge Moslem feeling in Turkey itself on so great an issue, but it would not be safe to dismiss the possibility altogether."[14]

But preparation for this transformation was in clear evidence the following month. In March 1921, an article appeared in the official Kemalist organ, over the name of Hüseyin Ragıb Bey, the Ankara government's director of publications. The article amounted to an open call for the establishment of an international Muslim society in Ankara, composed of delegates (*murahhaslar*) from throughout the Muslim world. This initiative, the article continued, was the consequence of both the "fixed resolve" of the government, and numerous representations made to Ankara by Muslims abroad. This time, however, no mention was made of the caliphate, and emphasis was placed instead upon the need to defend all Muslims against "cross and capital."[15]

The organization of the congress fell to a small committee in Ankara, which began to plan for the gathering at the home of Mehmed Âkif [Ersoy] (1873–1936), the Turkish poet who gained renown as the composer of the verses later incorporated in the modern Turkish national anthem.[16] Âkif first filled various functions on the boards of Ottoman state publications, but found his audience after the Young Turk revolution, with his original writings and translations for *Sırat-ı müstakim/ Sebilürreşad*, Istanbul's organ of Muslim cosmopolitanism. His work here established him as the Ottoman Turk most closely linked to Afghani and his disciples in the propagation of the doctrine of solidarity. The Ottoman collapse and the subjugation of Istanbul caused Mehmed Âkif to leave the capital, and he turned toward what he saw as a movement of Muslim revival in Anatolia, reaching Ankara in 1920.

His task was the organization of the Muslim congress envisioned by Hüseyin Ragıb, through a committee composed of himself; Eşref Edib

[Fergan] Bey, editor of *Sebilürreşad*, now transplanted to Ankara; and Hasan Basri [Çantay] Bey, deputy from Balıkesir. Of the work of this preparatory committee we know very little. The organizers first scheduled the congress for mid-March 1922, a year after the initial proposal, but this appeal was not well-publicized, and brought to Ankara only a handful of Muslims, about whom nothing is known. These, however, were reportedly distressed to discover upon their arrival that the congress organizers intended certain changes in connection with the caliphate, and so refused to participate in any formal gathering.[17]

Here was a subtle but significant manifestation of a new policy, for the Society of Unitarians had been unequivocal in its insistence upon a retention by the caliph of his full prerogatives. The new ambiguity was a consequence of the sultan-caliph's continued refusal to embrace the Anatolian movement as his own. While the changes in mind were unspecified, they almost certainly anticipated the punitive separation of sultanate from caliphate. In April, a month after the March failure, Eşref Edib issued a second open appeal in *Sebilürreşad*, again without reference to the caliphate. The congress was simply "to sink differences of opinion, and to join in a unanimous decision defining the attitude of Islam in connection with the great social, economic, political, and religious crisis in Europe." Anatolia, added Eşref Edib, was the best site for the gathering, since it was "far removed from European influence."[18]

In November 1922, following a series of Kemalist negotiations with the Allies, and the entry into Istanbul of a leading Kemalist representative, it became clear that the city eventually would be incorporated in the new state created by the Anatolian movement. The Istanbul government collapsed, and retribution was meeted out to the recalcitrant sultan-caliph, through the separation of the sultanate from the caliphate and the abolition of the former. The last sultan-caliph, Mehmed VI Vahideddin, fled the city, and an Ottoman successor, Abdülmecid, was installed by the Grand National Assembly as caliph alone. The Grand National Assembly lent its authority to this step, and arrogated the right to select the caliph from the Ottoman house. "On the legal side," wrote Andrew Ryan of the separation decision, "I believe a good case can be made out for the election of a Caliph by the Moslems in the immediate neighborhood of the Caliphate centre."[19] But the merits of that case were not self-evident to Muslims beyond Istanbul and Anatolia. It was thus Mustafa Kemal's hope that a broader assembly of Muslims both from his territories and from abroad would confirm the act of separation.

Early 1923 consequently saw the return of the congress idea to circulation, but this time in the proposed setting of Istanbul. While the organizers secured promises of Afghan participation,[20] a group of Syrians, Palestinians, and Egyptians began to organize delegations.[21] Over the summer, two official envoys from Ankara arrived in the Egyptian port of Alexandria, to disseminate the idea of an Istanbul caliphate congress.[22] Here one again finds the hand of Shaykh ᶜAbd al-ᶜAziz Shawish, who had arrived in Anatolia following his disappointment with Enver and the League of Islamic Revolutionary Societies. He wrote letters to Indian Muslims urging them to participate in a "Grand Conference of Muslims" at any "suitable place" in Muslim territory, and to support the establishment of a caliphate "assembly" in Istanbul.[23]

At this point, Muslims elsewhere were given to understand that the congress would simply serve the caliph in an advisory capacity (şura-yı hilafet). But in November 1923, editorials appeared in several Istanbul newspapers which made the design for an elected caliphate explicit. If the caliph were to abdicate, the articles suggested, then the institution would be refurbished through an Istanbul congress of representative Muslims. These would elect a caliph enjoying Muslim confidence, who would then be in a far better position to perform his new duties effectively. An argument ensued in the Istanbul press on this proposal, for the caliph himself protested that he had ascended to his office in a legal manner, and had received the lawful allegiance of Muslims elsewhere, through telegrams and letters. He would not consider the surrender of his prerogatives.[24]

Confronted with this refusal of the caliph and his supporters to participate voluntarily in the final transformation of the caliphate, Mustafa Kemal was driven to consider more radical methods. In light of the evidence, it seems probable that he preferred the preservation of the Ottoman caliphate in Istanbul, in a form dependent upon a Muslim congress controlled by his own organizers. But in May 1923, the British learned from the amir of Afghanistan that his government would not participate in an Istanbul caliphate congress as he, alone among Muslim rulers, had previously announced.[25] This early return must have dampened all enthusiasm for the congress, for even Afghanistan, then among Turkey's closest allies, recoiled from the changes envisioned by Mustafa Kemal. The final eclipse of the proposed Istanbul congress was one of the considerations which led Mustafa Kemal to weigh the physical expulsion of the last Ottoman caliph and his family, and so exchange the Muslim facade of his autocracy for a republican one.

In March 1924, the Turkish Grand National Assembly, acting upon the initiative of Mustafa Kemal, approved the deposition of Abdülmecid, the abolition of the caliphate, and the expulsion of all members of the Ottoman house.[26] The decision was bound to intensify the contest among Muslim régimes for primacy in Islam. But the new Turkey would not be among the rivals. The policy which began with the Society of Unitarians at Zara had run its course.

EIGHT

NEW CALIPH IN ARABIA

The Pilgrimage Congress, 1924

I N THE summer of 1916, with the outbreak of the Arab Revolt, Mecca finally passed from Ottoman hands to those of the Sharif of Mecca. For an interregnum of nearly a decade, the Sharif Husayn (1853– 1931), and briefly his son ᶜAli, were in possession of the holy premises. The Meccan sharifs had been urged to assert their claim to Muslim primacy for nearly four decades by visionaries like Blunt and Zohrab, radical Muslim reformers like Kawakibi, and finally British officials like Kitchener and Sykes. Once the war had ended in disaster for Ottoman forces, and Istanbul was overrun by Allied forces, word began to spread again of an impending Meccan congress.

A series of tentative initiatives spanned the years 1921 to 1924, none of which culminated in the anticipated congress. Then, immediately following the abolition of the Ottoman caliphate in March 1924, Husayn's followers acclaimed him caliph, and in July 1924 there met in Mecca what his organizers entitled the Pilgrimage Congress. From this long-awaited gathering, perhaps consciously imitative of Kawakibi's *Umm al-qura,* Husayn attempted to extract some sort of sanction for his new caliphate. The effort failed in the face of opposition from a bloc of unsympathetic participants, but the congress decided to reconvene annually during the pilgrimage season, and resolved to establish a permanent secretariat. By the next pilgrimage season, however, the Ikhwan of Ibn Saᶜud had overrun Mecca and opened their campaign of eradicating all traces of Hashimite rule. Husayn had fled the country.

The most important sources for the preliminary initiatives and the Pilgrimage Congress were the reports in *al-Qibla,* Mecca's official newspaper throughout the period. British and French consular reports from Jidda were also well-informed. The correspondence of Palestinian participants sheds further light on the role of Palestinian-Hijazi cooperation in the emergence of the Pilgrimage Congress.

In early 1921, a former Ottoman Şeyhülislam, Haydari-zâde İbrahim
Efendi, received a letter in Turkish from Haifa:

> In view of the fact that the congress called 'Din-i-Nahda-i-Islamiye' will
> be held at Mecca during this year's pilgrimage, distinguished and capable
> doctors of law (ulema) and philosophers from Egypt, Syria, Palestine and
> India have been invited, as well as those Moslem dignitaries who will
> assemble there in order to fulfil the sacred duty of the pilgrimage.[1]

Haydari-zâde İbrahim Efendi was asked to attend or send a capable
substitute. The invitation was signed by a certain Muhammad Adib
Ramadan al-Qudsi, an instructor at the Great Mosque in Haifa. At about
the same time, the French High Commissariat in Syria learned through
an informer that a number of Syrian notables had received similar invitations from the same source.[2] Field Marshal Lord Allenby, British
High Commissioner in Egypt, was unable to learn anything about a
Meccan congress from local Cairo sources,[3] but the British consul in
Jidda did hear rumors that Husayn's son Faysal was arranging a congress
of Arab leaders and important Muslims during the coming pilgrimage.[4]

It was difficult to determine whether this pointed to a Hashimite
congress initiative. British authorities in Palestine thought Muhammad
Adib Ramadan al-Qudsi no more than a self-important religious enthusiast, but the French in Syria considered him a Hashimite agent.
Hashimite sponsorship for a congress proposed for Hashimite territory
seemed not at all unlikely, and there was every reason for al-Qudsi to
obscure this fact. For influential Muslims held Husayn to blame for
dividing the ranks of Islam through his revolt, and for speeding the
military humiliation of Ottoman armies. Even long-standing supporters
withheld their sympathies. An important defection from his cause was
that of Rashid Rida, whose journal al-Manar had first given currency to
the idea of a Qurashi caliphate at Mecca, through the serialization of
Kawakibi's Umm al-qura. In 1916, Rida performed the pilgrimage, and
was much taken by the Sharif Husayn, who awarded him an annual
subsidy and gave him a large gift.[5] But by 1924, Rida was writing of
Husayn's movement that it was "vile and despicable."[6]

This disillusionment with Husayn was linked to the disappointment
of those like Rashid Rida who had supported his act of rebellion as an
act of liberation. Now that they apprehended the consequences of the
war—the dismemberment of the Ottoman Empire, and the Anglo-
French partition of the most populous Arabic-speaking provinces—old
supporters vented their sense of betrayal and guilt through attacks on
Husayn. Husayn invested his last years in the Hijaz in a futile attempt
to convince Muslims of his concern for his faith, and so relieve his

political isolation. The French minister in Cairo thought that rumors about a Meccan Muslim congress had been launched by Husayn himself, to test Muslim opinion.[7] Husayn, then, must have realized that his own direct invitations would probably go unanswered, and it was for this reason that the invitation was given a formal Palestinian provenance. This attempt to conceal the paternity of the proposal met with no success. Haydari-zâde İbrahim Efendi, perhaps suspecting Hashimite sponsorship, turned his invitation over to Ahmed Tevfik Paşa, the Ottoman Grand Vizier, who in turn passed on translations to the British High Commissioner in Istanbul. With this information, the British police in Palestine descended upon Muhammad Ramadan Adib al-Qudsi. He was discharged from his position in Haifa, and was put under police surveillance, while the police raided the Haifa printing firm which handled the invitations.[8] "The information which the Grand Vizier gave to [High Commissioner] Sir H. Rumbold has enabled the Palestine Gov[ernmen]t to arrest a man who might at any rate have been a nuisance as an aspiring Islamic propagandist."[9]

Husayn's supporters proceeded on a more modest scale the following year. In August 1922, Mecca was made the site of a Congress of the Arabian Peninsula (mu'tamar jazirat al-'arab). The intent was to gather only Arabic-speakers from the peninsula and the adjacent Fertile Crescent. It was even decided that, while other Muslims were permitted to attend, only Arabs had the right to speak and vote.[10] Husayn thus conceded the narrow base of his following beyond the Hijaz, and the exclusively Arab appeal of his movement. In August 1923, a second such gathering was held.[11] In both instances, participants came primarily from the Hijaz, Yemen, the Hadramawt, Syria, Palestine, and Iraq— Arabic-speaking territories in which Husayn could claim a following or a semblance of one.

But as the 1920s unfolded, Husayn increasingly began to cast himself not only as an Arab spokesman, but as a Muslim leader as well. For him, as for many Muslim Arab nationalists then and since, the two roles were not mutually exclusive. The Muslim idiom characterized his speeches and proclamations even during his rebellion against the Ottoman sultan-caliph.[12] But Husayn's Arabism was gradually sublimated when, besieged by critics, he fell back upon the vocabulary of Islam to preserve that loose confederation that had made the Arab Revolt. A new initiative for a Meccan Muslim congress was part of that transformation, which issued from political necessity.

Again, the initiative's precise origins were not clear, but once again the formal provenance was Palestinian. A fledgling alliance had been forged between Palestinian Arab nationalists and Husayn. The former urged Husayn not to sign a treaty regularizing relations with Great

Britain before securing guarantees on Palestine, and the latter, seeking to emerge from isolation, responded by actively promoting the Palestinian Arab cause.[13] In July 1922, a Palestinian "Islamic" delegation arrived in Mecca to garner support for Palestinian resistance both to Zionism and to the recently imposed League of Nations mandate for Palestine. There the delegation played a crucial role in the convening of the first Congress of the Arabian Peninsula, and ᶜAbd al-Qadir al-Muzaffar, the delegation's president, opened the first session.[14]

But the Palestinians were interested in reaching beyond the Arabs during their Meccan mission, for the delegation's activities represented the first Palestinian effort to mobilize specifically Muslim support for the Palestinian cause. Their delegation was self-avowedly Muslim, and their arrival reportedly set off demonstrations of support by Egyptian, Sudanese, Afghan, Indian, Kurdish, Turkish, Iranian, Javanese, and Arab pilgrims and residents in both Mecca and Jidda.[15] A few days later, the secretary of the delegation wrote to Jerusalem of wide Hijazi interest in a Muslim congress—a good thing indeed, "for we are in great need of a demonstration by all Muslims."[16]

This was emphasized when one member of the Palestinian delegation, at a banquet given by Husayn in their honor, rose to make a proposal. A society should be established called the Islamic Congress (al-muᵓtamar al-islami), under Husayn's presidency, and this congress should collect a sizable sum to be kept in the Hijaz for various projects. Husayn, while expressing sympathy with these aims, demurred, but the idea was not abandoned.[17] A year later, during the pilgrimage, a meeting was held in Mina in support of the Islamic Congress, and al-Qibla promised to publish its program.[18] The new society initially struck the British consul in Jidda as Arab rather than Muslim in emphasis, but within six months, the ascent of a Muslim orientation in Hijazi foreign policy was indisputable.[19]

For in early March 1924, on the heels of the abolition of the Ottoman caliphate, Husayn was acclaimed as caliph by a group of ulama and notables assembled in Transjordan.[20] The reaction in the wider Muslim world was uncompromisingly hostile, giving plain evidence that the idea of the spiritual authority of the Meccan sharifs, promoted first by Birdwood, Zohrab, and Blunt, had no foundation in Muslim consensus. Husayn attempted to overcome the unpopularity of his elevation to the caliphate by a series of steps perhaps consciously drawn from Kawakibi's Umm al-qura. He established an advisory council to the caliphate (majlis shura al-khilafa), a body of thirty-one members from various Muslim lands, but "elected" by the leading ulama and notable foreign residents of Mecca and Madina. Among the members of this council were nine Meccan notables; seven other Hijazis; three Indians; three Sudanese;

two Bukharans; two Indonesians or Malayans (*Jawa*); and one member each from the Maghrib, Syria, Turkey, Daghistan, and Afghanistan. More than half of the members of the advisory council thus represented territories under Husayn's own direct control, while those who represented other lands were drawn principally from foreign communities in the Hijaz.[21] The various tasks of this advisory council and its subcommittees were then set out in detail, and the council began to meet each Tuesday to impart its advice.[22]

Husayn finally convened the Islamic Congress in July 1924 as the Pilgrimage Congress (*mu³tamar al-hajj*), in sessions which were intended to gather prominent pilgrims from throughout the Muslim world. The method of their selection was haphazard, and the list of participants indicates that the great majority were local notables. Once assembled, they adopted a charter consisting of eight articles (see appendix 4). Few provisions were made for internal organization in this document, beyond the creation of administrative, financial, and "presidential" committees, and the call for the creation of local subcommittees (*lijan far°iyya*). The annual congress was to devote itself to the promotion of mutual awareness among Muslims, but asserted that Arab unity was to be the nucleus (*nawah*) of Muslim unity. Article eight furthermore declared the commitment of the congress to the spread of Arabic in all Muslim countries, and made Arabic the only official language of the body.[23] The Pilgrimage Congress was therefore cast from the same mold as Kawakibi's *Umm al-qura*. The primacy of the Arabs in Islam was asserted without equivocation.

Missing from the charter, however, was all mention of the caliphate. According to a Jidda source, a bloc of congress participants resisted all means of persuasion brought to bear by Husayn to extract a categorical recognition of his caliphate, and he thus saw a serious check to his candidacy in his own country.[24] The resistance was the work of Shaykh °Abd al-°Aziz al-Tha°alibi (1874–1944), a journalist and activist of Tunisian birth who reappeared often in subsequent Muslim congresses. His dissent cannot have been motivated by a religious objection, for he himself was widely suspected of harboring heterodox beliefs. The ulama of Tunis once succeeded in having him imprisoned for utterances of grossly heterodox nature, and after his release, he co-wrote with his defense lawyer, a Gallicized Tunisian Jew, a controversial book entitled *L'esprit libéral du Coran*. [25] This unconventional past was later obscured by his political activism, and his major role in the creation of the Destour party. Tha°alibi was prosecuted while in Tunisia by French authorities for his political activities, and finally left the country in 1923 for a prolonged and self-imposed exile of fourteen years, which took him through the Middle East, India, and Southeast Asia. These travels brought him also to Mecca, where Thaᶜalibi argued that the Pilgrimage Congress was not empowered by other Muslims to act on their behalf, and so enjoyed no contractual authority. The force of his personality made him much the dominant figure. His views prevailed, and the caliphate did not figure in the resolutions of the congress. The British consul in Jidda concluded that "the jejune nature of the results of the Pilgrimage Conference suggest complete failure."[26]

The council and congress therefore did little to relieve Husayn's isolation. Nor did they moderate the rapidity with which Husayn fell. Within weeks of these events, in late August 1924, his Arabian rival, ᶜAbd al-ᶜAziz Ibn Saᶜud, launched his final assault on the Hijaz, and the state built by Husayn crumbled. In October, faced with imminent Wahhabi conquest, the notables of Mecca and Jidda induced Husayn to abdicate in favor of his son ᶜAli, who renounced all Hashimite claims to the caliphate. Husayn himself fled to ᶜAqaba, and later settled in Cyprus.

The impending loss of the Hijaz prompted one last attempt by the family to convene a Muslim congress in Mecca, in the hope of precluding a Saudi conquest. In September, Husayn's son Faysal, by this time established in Iraq, proposed that ᶜAli replace Husayn, and "invite all principal Moslem countries to send deputations to Mecca and evolve [a] stable and efficient administrative council for the Hedjaz being provided for by volunteers furnished by the countries sending deputations."[27] This amounted to a Muslim internationalization of the holy city, an idea explicit in certain passages of Kawakibi's *Umm al-qura*.[28] After Husayn's abdication, Faysal pressed the idea even more desperately, with plans to appeal for the participation of King Fuʔad of Egypt, the Nawab of Rampur, the Nizam of Hyderabad, the Amir of Afghanistan, the regent of Iran, Shaykh Ahmad al-Sanusi, and Egyptian, Indian, and Southeast Asian Muslim organizations.[29] This proposal offered no respite, for in mid-October 1924, Saudi forces entered Mecca. Husayn's son and successor, ᶜAli, had no greater ambition than survival. He even promised to an Egyptian mediation mission that he would recognize King Fuʔad of Egypt as caliph, if only the Egyptians would extend to him that aid which he thought necessary to beat back Ibn Saᶜud.[30] The appeal failed, and in December 1925, Jidda fell to Ibn Saᶜud's warriors, ending the fifty-year bid by the sharifs of Mecca for Muslim primacy.

NINE

THE CALIPHATE GRAIL

The General Islamic Congress for
the Caliphate in Egypt, 1926

OVER TWO YEARS of intensive organizing effort preceded the Cairo caliphate congress of May 1926. Immediately following the abolition of the Ottoman caliphate in March 1924, the leading ulama of the mosque-university of al-Azhar met and issued a proclamation announcing their intention to convene a Muslim congress in a year's time, an event to which representatives of all Muslim peoples would be invited. The congress, convened in Egypt, "the most excellent of Islamic lands," would do no less than designate a new caliph, and so end the disarray into which the Turkish decision had cast the Muslim world.[1] In Cairo, a preparatory committee of Azhar ulama planned the agenda of the congress and the invitation of delegates from throughout the Muslim world. Elsewhere in Egypt, there emerged a string of fourteen "caliphate committees," working in support of the congress and the preparatory committee. Through additional branch committees, their reach extended to every major Egyptian population center, and their participants soon numbered in the hundreds.[2] In line with a traditional policy of religious tolerance, Great Britain had declared the restoration of the caliphate a religious problem in the solution of which Britain would not interfere. The organizers thus were able to pursue their activities in Egypt without fear of hindrance.

But despite this declaration, the caliphate congress was not strictly a religious matter, for the royal palace had a hand in the effort. Much evidence suggests that the organizers hoped not simply to solve the problem of the caliphate, but to prepare the ground for an Egyptian caliphate in the person of King Fuʾad I (r. 1920–1936). These inclinations were impossible to conceal, and the congress was shadowed by the suspicion that its conclusions were foregone. The resulting domestic criticism by opponents of the monarchy led to a postponement of the congress for a year. Then the failure of the organizers to secure wide participation led to a modification of the agenda to exclude the actual selection of a caliph. A further blow was dealt by the simultaneous preparation of a rival Muslim congress in Mecca (see following chapter).

When the Cairo congress finally met, it was only to declare that the caliphate was still possible, and that the subject demanded further examination. The participants then dispersed in the anticipation that they would elaborate upon this verdict the following year. But no effort was made toward this end, and the congress never reassembled.

The Cairo congress is the first for which extensive sources survive, among them proceedings and an archive. The Azhar preparatory committee even published a special periodical in Cairo, as a means for circulation of official proclamations and articles in support of the projected congress. The proceedings themselves were published serially in Arabic by Rashid Rida, in Urdu translation by the Indian Muslim activist and organizer ʿInayat Allah Khan Mashriqi, and in French translation by Achille Sékaly.[3] On the basis of the proceedings as translated by Sékaly, and the periodical press, a number of contemporary observers wrote secondary studies, of which Arnold Toynbee's was the most influential.[4]

In subsequent years, various relevant memoirs and published letters of participants appeared. A son of Shaykh Muhammad al-Ahmadi al-Zawahiri, who was a leading Egyptian participant and later Shaykh al-Azhar, published his father's reminiscences concerning the event.[5] Rashid Rida wrote a brief behind-the-scenes account, and in his published letters to Shakib Arslan he also discussed the congress and its antecedents.[6] Documents from several state archival collections added much more to the picture from the perspective of those foreign governments which saw themselves affected by the Cairo proceedings. Some of these sources and others were combined by Elie Kedourie in his broader study of Egypt and the caliphate question, part of which was devoted to the Cairo caliphate congress.[7] This was the first examination to press beyond the formal proceedings to arrive at another level of evidence and interpretation, and there to discover a complex web of rivalries that determined the course of the congress.

Two other archival collections then not available fully illuminate that further side of the congress. The first is the archive of the Egyptian royal palace, which contains several relevant files on preparations for the congress and the extent of palace involvement.[8] The second is a collection of 133 documents which constitute what remains of the congress papers, and which were deposited in the library of al-Azhar.[9]

The initiative was ostensibly that of the Shaykh al-Azhar, but was very much under the supervision of his personal secretary and president of the higher council of Azhar ulama, Shaykh Muhammad Faraj al-Minyawi. Planning the congress alongside him were members of an inner circle of initiates; beyond that working group was an outer circle of aides and supporters, who lent their names and time to the effort. Among the initial supporters was Rashid Rida, who only recently had described his vision of an elected caliphate in a compendium of his ideas on the subject, published in 1922. There he developed his earlier congress ideas (see chapter 3), and advocated a full-blown caliphal bureaucracy, under a caliph chosen by "those who loose and bind" and endowed with spiritual authority.[10]

For so massive an undertaking, the organizers required a budget. Although every opportunity was taken by the organizers and the king to deny any connection between them, the organizers turned to the royal palace for the necessary funds from the outset, and a solicitation letter from three of the principal congress organizers to an unnamed palace functionary gives details. The authors first dealt with the problem of creating a supportive domestic organization at the grass roots:

> We believe that the spread of the appeal within Egypt will require organizations in the capital of each district (*mudiriyya*); the creation of branch committees for those organizations in the countryside; and the selection of able preachers (*khutaba*ʾ) to spread the word, win hearts, and caress ears—all to gain approval for the idea of the congress, and then to prepare minds afterwards to accept whatever is decided, so that the appeal will be ultimately successful.

In discussing the requirements of the campaign abroad, the authors pointed to the considerable effort invested by supporters of Husayn's Meccan caliphate in the propagation of their message:

> As for spreading the word abroad, we believe that in principle this will require a special journal distributed free of charge throughout the Muslim world. The congress secretariat is prepared to edit this journal. Since we cannot count on the Egyptian press to publish the tracts of the congress secretariat, like they publish those in support of the other so-called caliphate [in the Hijaz], this requires haste in establishing a special journal at the congress secretariat. . . . it is no secret that the Hijaz, as is clear from a glance at Palestinian, Syrian, and other newspapers, is pursuing its own appeal through several means. The newspaper *al-Qibla* has been especially designated for this propaganda. And emissaries have been sent to various lands, and will try to distribute publications to the pilgrims this year. This is how the situation appears to us. The opinion of your excellency is more sublime.[11]

The answer from the palace to this entreaty does not survive, but the periodical began to appear regularly in October 1924, in a format that required a substantial outlay of money. Shaykh Muhammad Faraj al-Minyawi, the principal signatory of the solicitation, was the journal's editor, and his editorial line exactly reflected that of his letter:

A caliphate established in Mecca, among the barren rocks and amassed sands of the desert, would be an unstable caliphate parting at the seams. The beduin would plunder its strength and undermine its foundations. . . . Egypt at present is more independent than others, better fortified against the raids of Beduin (al-aᶜrab), and freer than any Muslim land in the East.[12]

The palace channeled the necessary funds through the government ministry responsible for religious endowments, which, unlike other ministries, fell under the direct supervision of the palace. The Shaykh al-Azhar wrote to the ministry requesting funds to cover an unexplained deficit, and in 1924 received £E2,500 for this purpose; the Shaykh al-Azhar accounted for the money as having been spent on the congress.[13] This financial connection was concealed until well after the conclusion of the congress, permitting the organizers to maintain that the congress was strictly the initiative of a group of disinterested ulama.

It was not without cause, then, that those Egyptians opposed to the monarchy and its aggrandizement similarly opposed the congress. First, the royal family bared their internal dissensions. ᶜUmar Tusun (1872–1944), an independently wealthy Alexandrian prince and prolific amateur historian, wrote to then-Prime Minister Saᶜd Zaghlul upon the abolition of the Ottoman caliphate, asking the government's opinion on the possibility of holding a Muslim congress in Egypt to settle the caliphate question. Tusun clearly envisioned himself as chief organizer, for he had maintained an interest in wider Muslim affairs throughout his career, and knew Turkish and Persian. Zaghlul, in his reply, deferred the decision to the king, so a short time later Tusun arrived at ᶜAbdin Palace at the head of a delegation of supportive ulama to press their request.[14] They met only the first secretary, and asked him to remind the king of their desire to organize a caliphate congress in Egypt. But the maverick prince was rightly considered less than sympathetic to the king's ambitions, and so the palace threw its weight behind the far less independent Azhar committee. Tusun, once excluded from the congress plans, began to patronize a popular Sufi shaykh, Muhammad Madi Abu al-ᶜAzaᵓim (1869–1937), who had already organized a rival congress committee of Azhar ulama disaffected with their palace-oriented colleagues. While the Tusun-Abu al-ᶜAzaᵓim committee, with its few branches, was decidedly weaker than its rival, it nonetheless complicated the task of the Azhar committee both within Egypt and abroad, and became a convenient vehicle for others hostile to the royal palace.[15]

A group of religious zealots under the leadership of the blind Shaykh Yusuf al-Dijwi (1870–1946) made the task still more difficult. Dijwi had gained renown for his leading role in the trial and persecution of Shaykh ᶜAli ᶜAbd al-Raziq, and was convinced of the necessity of an active and vital caliphate.[16] But his group, also formed immediately after the abolition of the Ottoman caliphate, opposed an Egyptian caliphate, because vice-ridden Egypt was not governed by Islamic law. Egypt as a geographic and cultural entity was certainly the Muslim land most worthy of the caliphate, wrote Shaykh Dijwi and his associates in a manifesto, but the "legal order in our country is invalid." The Afghans, who maintained the holy law of Islam, were "the single community to preserve the principles of their religion," and had succeeded the Turks to Muslim primacy. "If Afghanistan had what Egypt has, in geographic location and situation at the meeting point of east and west, and scientific and economic centrality, the Muslims from one corner of the world to another would be stirred to recognize its amir as caliph." Egypt "could yet win for herself the affection once held for the Turks and now held for the Afghans," but only if the king would enforce Islamic law, throughout the land. Shaykh Dijwi guaranteed that he and his followers then would respond by promoting the caliphate of the Egyptian royal house.[17] The palace was not enthusiastic about this suggestion, resented the unfavorable comparison of Egypt with Afghanistan, and later had the police open an investigation of Shaykh Dijwi's group. According to an official communiqué, "they were occupied with a question that did not concern them."[18]

Opposition then began to spread beyond the ulama in the Tusun-Abu al-ᶜAzaᵓim and Dijwi circles to various liberals and nationalists anxious lest the palace wield the caliphate to intimidate domestic rivals. The political struggle within Egypt had intensified in 1924, with the election and installation of a Wafdist government led by the nationalist leader Saᶜd Zaghlul (1857–1927), who had just returned from exile. It was not long before tension developed between the Wafd and the palace, and between the two central actors in the Egyptian political arena, Zaghlul and King Fuᵓad.

Zaghlul as prime minister initially wavered on the question of an Egyptian caliphate, but then decided against seeking the title for Egypt's ruler.[19] His interior minister and nephew, Fath Allah Barakat, issued orders to provincial governors that they withhold all assistance from the Azhar caliphate committees, and banned *shariᶜa* court judges from serving as members.[20] At a later date, after Zaghlul had resigned his ministry, his party went so far as to subsidize the Tusun-Abu al-ᶜAzaᵓim committees, so resolute was the Wafdist determination to thwart the palace's designs.[21] In such a charged political atmosphere, the congress plans suffered from their association with the ambitions of the Egyptian ruling house. The appearance of serious domestic opposition was thus the most probable cause of the Azhar committee's January 1925 decision to postpone the congress for one year.[22]

Domestic opposition could not forestall indefinitely a project which enjoyed the open support of Azhar ulama and the covert aid of the royal palace. The issue soon became not whether the congress would take place, but who would arrive from Muslim states and communities beyond Egypt to participate in a forum very likely to insist upon Egypt's centrality in Islam. According to Rashid Rida, who served on the preparatory subcommittee for invitations, the Azhar committee appealed to kings, sultans, princes, and heads of important religious societies throughout the Muslim world, to respond and participate. Sectarian differences were disregarded: Wahhabis, Ibadis, Zaydi and Twelver Shiᶜis, and even the Agha Khan of the Ismaᶜilis, were invited, although the question of the caliphate was not posed to these sects by the Turkish act of abolition.[23] Yet here again, the identification of the congress with the palace, and the fragmented state of Muslim opinion, worked to defeat the organizers.

One instance concerned the dissemination of the Azhar invitation in Shiᶜi Iran. On his own initiative, the Egyptian minister to Iran, ᶜAbd al-ᶜAzim Rashid Pasha, lobbied at Teheran and Qumm to convince both the government and leading Shiᶜi ulama to send authorized delegates to Cairo. The first evidence of ᶜAbd al-ᶜAzim's activity dates from October 1925, when he inserted an article in a Baghdad newspaper strongly attacking the Abu al-ᶜAzaᵓim caliphate committee.[24] By November, he had successfully planted a eulogistic front-page article about King Fuᵓad in an Iranian newspaper; the piece, printed under a portrait of Egypt's monarch, described Fuᵓad as "defender of Islam."[25] In March 1926, a Soviet radio broadcast to Iran criticized the caliphate congress, and ᶜAbd al-ᶜAzim responded by inserting counter-propaganda in two Iranian newspapers.[26] This service he paid for: "The newspaper business will do absolutely nothing without recompense," for "the state of poverty in this country has a great effect on any service in all branches." He lamented "the weak means that the foreign ministry has put in our hands—the sum of 150 pounds."[27]

In January 1926, ᶜAbd al-ᶜAzim opened a round of personal diplomacy with a visit to Qumm for meetings with religious figures. The ulama expressed their concern about the recent territorial gains of the Saudi movement in Arabia, and this gave ᶜAbd al-ᶜAzim a chance to discuss in detail Egypt's pursuit of an anti-Wahhabi policy "since the time of Muhammad ᶜAli Pasha."[28] But it was not until February that the Egyptian minister heard that the caliphate congress was scheduled definitely for May. He immediately warned his superiors that "this country has a strange belief about the caliphate," citing Twelver Shiᶜi doctrine, but this did not deter him.[29] During March, he received a batch of printed invitations to the congress from Husayn Wali, one of the Cairo organ-

izers, with a request that the Egyptian minister distribute them. This
he did, through the Iranian premier, all the while stressing that time
was short and urging speedy replies.[30]

In fact, as Sir Percy Loraine reported, the Iranian government was
"rather embarrassed" at the suggestion that Iran participate,[31] and an
elaborate game of evasion began. The Iranian premier informed ᶜAbd
al-ᶜAzim that the decision rested with the ulama, but the ulama replied
that the decision rested with the government. When ᶜAbd al-ᶜAzim
pressed Iran's minister of information, he was told that the ulama had
agreed in principle to participation, but final word was delayed because
of difficulties in contacting Shiᶜi authorities in Najaf. Could the congress
be postponed? ᶜAbd al-ᶜAzim countered that the ulama had told him
that they were in total agreement, and that the matter was in the hands
of the government. The Iranian minister replied that the ulama spoke
what they knew to be false themselves, because the real difficulty was
their inability to agree on who would represent them at Cairo.[32]

ᶜAbd al-ᶜAzim began to appreciate the futility of his efforts. An intimate of Riza Shah told him that the Shah preferred to see the congress
convened in the Hijaz, as he was certain that the ruler of any other
host country would be elected caliph. The holy cities were the *qibla* of
all Muslims, and therefore neutral sites. ᶜAbd al-ᶜAzim tried at length
to explain that Cairo was an equally neutral site, but parted discouraged.
"The circumstances which I witness here weaken any hope that Iran
will accept the invitation to the congress."[33]

A prominent ᶜalim then astonished ᶜAbd al-ᶜAzim with yet another
counter-proposal: Najaf was a more appropriate site for the congress,
since Egypt was under British influence. ᶜAbd al-ᶜAzim replied that
Najaf was located in territory under British mandate, while Egypt was
independent, and he saw in this a further sign that Iranian participation
was unlikely.[34] ᶜAbd al-ᶜAzim suggested to his own government that,
in order to secure Shiᶜi cooperation, the agenda of the congress be
expanded beyond the caliphate question to matters of general Muslim
interest.[35] But by this time, the British authorities in Egypt had become
rather annoyed with ᶜAbd al-ᶜAzim's lobbying. Unenthusiatic themselves about the congress, they thought it better that Iran abstain from
participation, and that ᶜAbd al-ᶜAzim be instructed that Iranian representation was a matter between Azhar shaykhs and Persian mullahs,
not diplomats and foreign ministers.[36] Within a month, ᶜAbd al-ᶜAzim
was sent a reprimand from the Egyptian royal diwan, informing him
that the invitation to the congress was solely the work of men of religion,
and that the Egyptian government had no official connection with the
congress.[37]

Perhaps the British insisted on the reprimand; perhaps some Egyptian authority decided that reluctant Iranian attendance was more a liability than an asset to the ultimate election of Fuʾad as caliph. ʿAbd al-ʿAzim could offer only this apology: "If I discussed the matter, it was because I saw it as my obligation toward an invitation issued from my country."[38] When the Shaykh al-Azhar finally wired an invitation, the Iranian government announced that the Shiʿi ulama had not had adequate time to study the caliphate question, and authorized Iran's diplomatic representative at Cairo to attend only as a spectator.[39]

With the establishment of Saudi control over the holy cities of Arabia, reading Saudi attitudes assumed a new urgency. In a letter to the Shaykh al-Azhar, Ibn Saʿud had promised his support for the Cairo caliphate congress provided that the participants represented the majority of Muslims. He declared himself willing to recognize the decision of such a congress as binding, and denied any personal caliphal ambition.[40] But he feared that an elected caliph—particularly a Egyptian one—might lay some claim to the holy cities only recently occupied by his forces. The Egyptians already had attempted to establish a religious protectorate over the Hijaz, shortly before the triumph of Saudi arms.[41] The Cairo organizers thus could not have been surprised when Ibn Saʿud sent no delegate to their congress, for he had little to gain from its success, and much to loose from a decisive outcome.

The Azhar committee anticipated more from Muslim India, where the fate of the caliphate had evoked profound concern among Sunni and Shiʿi alike. The Indian Khilafat Committee, under the leadership of two brothers, Muhammad ʿAli (1878–1931) and Shawkat ʿAli (1873–1938), commanded a following which reached the proportions of a mass movement in the early 1920s, and the Azhar committee regarded the participation of the organization in the Cairo caliphate congress as critical if the resolutions of the projected congress were to bind this largest Muslim community. But the Khilafat Committee leaders were wary of Egyptian intentions. When rumors reached Delhi in late March 1924 that the Azhar ulama planned to proclaim Fuʾad caliph, Shawkat ʿAli cabled Saʿd Zaghlul from Delhi expressing the hope that Egyptian ulama "do not intend any hasty action regarding future of khilafate." The Khilafat Committee was attempting to convince the Turks to appoint one of their own to the office, but should this effort fail, "future of khilafate should be left to be settled by proposed world muslim conference."[42] Shawkat ʿAli warned the Shaykh al-Azhar that "undue haste in [a] matter of such grave importance is likely to be as dangerous as undue delay or neglect."[43] Later Shawkat ʿAli asked for details about the way in which the caliph would be selected. He hoped for unanimous

agreement, but "Muslims of the far distant places would be fewer compared with local visitors who could swamp them easily. I think each
country must be assigned votes on a population basis though it may
send only fewer representative[s]." He anticipated the dispatch of a
large Indian delegation, but "there have not been wanting men who
suggested that Cairo would not be a suitable place for the Conference
as there was a chance of official interference [which] would like to
unduly influence its deliberations."[44]

An opportunity to make the Egyptian case in person was presented
to Azhar ulama in the summer of 1925, when two of the leading lights
on the Khilafat Committee, Mukhtar Ahmad Ansari (1880–1936) and
Hakim Ajmal Khan (1863–1927), reached Egypt during a trip to the
Middle East. Ansari once had been an unrestrained Turcophile, and as
a physician educated in England had led the All-India Medical Mission
to aid Ottoman war wounded during the Balkan campaign in 1913. He
was familiar with the charges leveled against the proposed congress,
and so the task of the Egyptian organizers was not an easy one. Ansari
had already made this plain. Attending a reception in his honor during
a stopover in Jerusalem, he mentioned a number of congress sites preferred by Indian Muslims, but ruled out Egypt because of the presence
there of a strong party determined to resolve the caliphate issue in favor
of King Fuʾad.[45]

In Cairo, the Azhar ulama, Shaykh Minyawi foremost among them,
encircled Ansari and Ajmal Khan from the moment they descended
from their train. The Indian Muslim envoys were polite, but seemed to
prefer the company of Shaykh Abu al-ᶜAzaʾim, with whom they met
often. By this, they gave cause to conclude that the Indian Khilafat
Committee shared in the critique of those Egyptians opposed to the
congress.[46] Later, Shawkat ᶜAli wrote to Abu al-ᶜAzaʾim in a congrat-
ulatory tone, and the Tusun-Abu al-ᶜAzaʾim committee began to speak
of itself as if in close association with the Khilafat Committee.[47] The
final decision taken in Delhi was not unexpected. Once Ajmal Khan
had returned to India and met with the ᶜAli brothers, they together
decided to formalize their abstention by declining the Azhar invitation.
Ansari, who was still in the Middle East, gave this explanation:

> The present circumstances are not propitious for holding the congress, in
> view of the political controversy and dispute over the constitutional rights
> of the [Egyptian] people, and the circulation of the rumor abroad that the
> ulama of al-Azhar are motivated in this course by a hidden force, em-
> ploying spiritual, religious influence in a struggle against the nationalist
> parties that are demanding the rights of the people. I do not credit these
> rumors with truth for a moment. But the insistence of the ulama in holding
> this congress in Cairo despite the will of all the other Muslim lands

encourages belief in these rumors and their expression as established facts. I would not want my Egyptian brethren, who deliberate and think over their every action, to damage their position of centrality in the Muslim world.

If the Egyptian ulama elected a caliph alone, Ansari warned that this figure would become "the laughingstock of the Muslim world." He instead advocated an annual Muslim congress, based upon what he described as proportional representation and so empowered to elect a truly popular caliph.[48] Muslim India was ultimately represented at the Cairo congress by a single participant, ᶜAllama ᶜInayat Allah Khan Mashriqi (1888–1963), a Cambridge-trained mathematician, teacher, and later founder of the militant pro-Axis Khaksar movement. Although later a man of influence, he was not yet well known, and the lack of an authoritative Indian Muslim voice at the congress was an unconcealed blemish.[49]

The participation of an important Indonesian delegation would also have done much to enhance the findings of a caliphate congress held in Cairo, for in the Indo-Malay periphery was a populous Muslim community which had drawn closer to Egypt, al-Azhar, and the ideas of Islamic reform as propounded by Muhammad ᶜAbduh and Rashid Rida in al-Manar.[50] An alliance of political activists and ulama in Java had succeeded in creating and directing a mass organization, the Sarekat Islam, under the leadership of Umar Sayyid Tjokroaminoto (1882–1934).[51] Rashid Rida, who had his own correspondents in Java, dispatched the congress invitations to Sarekat leaders. In December 1924, four to five hundred Sarekat activists met at Surabaja to select the movement's delegates to Cairo and to determine the policy which they were to represent. Three members from Java were selected to proceed to Cairo and convey the Sarekat plan, which argued that the powers formerly exercised by the caliph should be delegated to a council, the members of which would be chosen from various Muslim countries. The president of this council, elected by its members, would assume the title of caliph.[52]

It soon became known that the smaller but expanding Muslim reformist movement, the Muhammadijah, based both in Java and western Sumatra, had also been invited to send a delegation to Cairo, and planned to do so.[53] Now the Sarekat Islam and the Muhammadijah were then experiencing a period of heightened rivalry, so that Tjokroaminoto began to disparage the rival delegation's mission, and to insinuate that the Sarekat Islam might not participate in the Cairo congress after all. By the time of embarkation, he had hear rumors that King Fuᵓad would be declared caliph at Cairo, and this he made the pretext for possible absentation. "As matters stand," he declared once embarked, "we have heard nothing as yet from the Committee at Cairo which sent out the invitations. It is not impossible that the English may endeavor to bring their influence to bear by causing King Fuᵓad to be proclaimed Caliph. If such a thing should occur—in other words if the Caliphate is to have its seat at Cairo—then, so long as I am a representative of Dutch India, I will never give my consent to the proposal, which would be in conflict with the Koran."[54]

During a stopover in Arabia, Tjokroaminoto allowed himself to be convinced that such a development would be the inevitable outcome of a caliphate congress held in Cairo, and he did not bother to proceed to Egypt. The Azhar caliphate committee had to rest content with a two-man Muhammadijah delegation, led by the Sumatran reformer Abd al-Karim Amrullah [Hadji Rasul] (1879–1945).[55] This was a disappointment, one which assured that the decisions of the caliphate congress would become embroiled in the divisive domestic politics of one of the most populous quarters of the Muslim world.

It was also hoped to attract Muslims from another important and populous region, the Soviet Union. An invitation was extended to Musa Carullah Bigi[yev] (1875–1949), a Tatar colleague of İsmail Gasprinskii's, and a reformist publicist and theologian who had studied many years earlier in Egypt. While there, Musa Carullah had known ᶜAbduh personally, and wrote a lengthy study of Afghani and ᶜAbduh.[56] Musa Carullah had no sympathy for national communism, but chose nonetheless to remain in the Soviet Union and attempt to reconcile his faith with communism. There he received four invitations to the caliphate congress from the Azhar organizers, and he decided to attend.[57] But shortly before his departure the mufti of Ufa denounced the impending caliphate congress as under the thumb of "imperialist" (British) domination.[58] Musa Carullah almost certainly did not share this view of the congress, but Egyptian consular authorities in Istanbul did not know this; and when Musa Carullah arrived on his way to Egypt, they apparently became concerned lest a Soviet Muslim delegate appear at the congress and disturb the proceedings by making a similar accusation. The Egyptian consul refused to issue Musa Carullah a visa, leaving him much perplexed and unable to attend the proceedings.[59]

The presence in Egypt of influential North African and Syrian communities had led Egyptians to consider these regions as immediate cultural and political hinterlands.[60] The participation of Muslims from North Africa and Syria in the Cairo congress was probably regarded as a minimal requirement for success, and it was perhaps for this reason that the Azhar committee took an ususual step to assure participation. A secret appeal was made to France, which ruled Algeria, Tunisia, and Syria.

This subject was first raised in discussion with the French ambassador in Cairo, Henri Gaillard, in November 1924: "The persons who are preparing the congress have spontaneously asked me to single out, on their behalf, those Muslim figures in Algeria, Tunisia, and Syria, who seem to me the most suited for participation in the congress." In Gaillard's opinion, France stood to benefit from compliance with this request, for if French authorities did not provide a list of names, the selection "risks being guided by those Syrian and North African elements in Cairo or Alexandria who are the least favorable to France."[61]

Gaillard's argument was discussed at length by the Commission Interministèrielle des Affaires Musulmanes sitting in Paris. On the one hand, some held the view that too much was at stake for France to adopt a policy of nonintervention in a question as important as that of the caliphate. The Cairo congress might emerge as a significant political event directly affecting French interests. Critics of this opinion held that the congress, if left alone, was liable to fail to agree on the selection of a caliph and so collapse, and that France could best contribute to this result by preventing the dispatch of delegates from her Muslim possessions. Eventually the Commission settled on a compromise. If, despite all the apparent obstacles, the congress seemed about to take place, then France would communicate a list of participants to the organizers at the last minute. These participants would not really participate at all, but would act strictly as informants, for it would be hazardous to impart precise instructions to them in favor of one or another policy.[62]

The Quai notified Gaillard that he would receive a list of participants. He was instructed to use his judgment in choosing the moment for transmitting the list to the Azhar committee, and was cautioned that this moment be deferred as long as possible, to avoid the controversies likely to arise from the selection.[63] Gaillard agreed.[64] But no such lists were ever compiled. The Governor General of Algeria, when asked to supply names, expressed himself certain that the congress would not meet or would fail if it did, "the Muslims not having proven, at any time, their aptitude in the organization of a council on this scale." He therefore did not now wish to transmit such a list, for he felt that no precaution could prevent its being leaked, thus provoking an unhealthy public discussion concerning those selected. A list of qualified Algerian Muslims would be submitted if the congress seemed inevitable, but communication of a list of names from Algiers would be deferred until the last possible moment.[65] At the same time, the Governor General prevented the rise of a sympathetic movement in Algeria. ᶜAbd al-Hamid Ibn Badis (1889–1940), Algeria's leading Muslim activist, wrote to the organizers in Cairo that the French did not want Algerian notables to participate in the congress, and that he doubted whether he could represent Algeria because formation of a local committee was "impossible."[66]

The French High Commissioner in Beirut felt otherwise. He believed that Syrian Muslim participation was inevitable, and that prudent preparation was essential. From Syria he proposed to send to Cairo only religious personalities of indisputable character, chosen with discretion and uninvolved in agitation against the French. "Without imposing categorical instructions on the delegates, it would be politic to direct them toward the candidature [for the caliphate] that seems most advantageous to the interests of Syria and those of France in the East. In order that the actions of these delegates not be contested, it is essential that they appear to have escaped our direction."[67] But here again no list was prepared, for once the postponement of the congress was announced by the organizers, Gaillard wrote to Beirut that the collection of names had become "pointless."[68] The Azhar committee, despite having gone so far as to solicit the names of participants from a non-Muslim power, thus had achieved nothing, and once left to its own devices achieved no success at all in the matter of Syrian participation. The émigré Syrian activist Shakib Arslan showered advice upon the committee from his European exile, but he would not attend.[69] The self-exiled Tunisian reformist and activist ᶜAbd al-ᶜAziz al-Thaᶜalibi, then in Iraq, did accept an invitation, but he preferred to be admitted as a member of the Iraqi delegation, for reasons which he did not make clear. The caliphate committee which did function in Tunis sent no representative, for it had been deterred by Abu al-ᶜAzaʾim's campaign against the congress.[70]

Shortly after the renewal of the Azhar committee's activities, the vice-rector of al-Azhar wrote a letter to ᶜAbd al-Karim (1883–1963), leader of the Riffian resistance against the Spanish protectorate in northern Morocco and the French-supported ruling ᶜAlawi dynasty, requesting that the resistance movement send delegates to the congress.[71] Further letters from ᶜAbd al-Karim to the Azhar committee, intercepted by British postal authorities at Tangier, indicated that the correspondents were on close terms, and that funds were being dispatched secretly by the Azhar committee to ᶜAbd al-Karim.[72] By their cultivation of ᶜAbd al-Karim, the Azhar committee hoped to attract a delegation of some standing from a distant region, an aspiration still unfulfilled only three months before the rescheduled congress. In ᶜAbd al-Karim, the committee found a willing party from a major geographic periphery, one who, because of his embattled position, enjoyed a prestige in the wider Muslim world conferred by a continuing resistance to foreign encroachment.

Upon learning of this invitation, Gaillard immediately complained to his contacts at al-Azhar. "I have informed the committee that to invite or accept delegates from Abdelkerim is not admissible, for the double reason that Abdelkerim has revolted against the sovereign of his country, and because that sovereign is recognized as caliph in Morocco."[73] The committee replied to Gaillard defensively and untruthfully, claiming that ʿAbd al-Karim had solicited the invitation himself, and Gaillard did not pursue the matter further.[74]

Far more persistent, and ultimately successful, was Spain, ʿAbd al-Karim's principal battlefield adversary. A *note verbale* delivered to the Egyptian legation in Madrid by the Ministerio de Estado spoke of the "profound displeasure that would be caused in Spain by anything which would signify official or semi-official recognition of this political personality, or would demonstrate deference toward representatives of a chief in rebellion against the legitimate authority of the Spanish Protectorate of Morocco."[75] While the Egyptians considered this request, the Spanish ambassador in London pressed British authorities to make British influence in Egypt felt among the members of the Azhar committee.[76] Asked for his comments on this Spanish request, Lord Lloyd in Cairo argued that, "while realising that the presence of Riff delegates at Cairo might be inconvenient to the Spanish Government, I venture to deprecate any intervention on our part in such a delicate matter," on account of British neutrality in all that was related to the issue of the caliphate.[77] A British Foreign Office official thus informed his Spanish opposite number that "to our regret we cannot usefully take any such action as that suggested."[78]

But this exchange was overtaken by events, for the Egyptian government decided on its own accord to satisfy Spanish desiderata in a *note verbale* disclaiming all connection with the congress, and professing nonrecognition of the "rebel" ʿAbd al-Karim. "In order to bear witness to its desire to maintain the best relations with the Spanish government, the Egyptian government is disposed to refuse entry to delegates of this rebel into Egyptian territory."[79] Egyptian authorities adhered to this policy, and the interests of Morocco were defended at Cairo by a shaykh of a religious order, described explicitly in a French diplomatic source as a Spanish political agent.[80]

With the approach of the revised congress date, the organizers of the Cairo congress, in surveying the results of their campaign abroad, were bound to concede that an attempt to elect a caliph on such a narrow base would invite profound embarrassment. Yet the Azhar and the congress were far too intertwined for the committee, after nearly two years of highly publicized work, to cancel the event without even greater embarrassment. Resort to the option of another postponement would have opened the committee to intensified charges of political incompetence and organizational ineptitude. At a meeting of the preparatory committee in late April 1926, Shaykh Mustafa al-Maraghi sought an honorable exit from this impasse by suggesting a fundamental revision of the congress agenda. No longer would the congress aspire to elect a caliph. Instead, it would define the caliphate, determine whether it was necessary, determine the personal requirements of the office, and decide whether it was now possible to establish such a caliphate. If the caliphate was deemed impossible in this age, the congress would determine what measures to take. If it was deemed possible, the congress would search for the appropriate means of selection.[81] But the committee would delete from the agenda the discussion of the candidates and the selection or election of one as caliph. This probably reflected the discouragement of King Fuʾad, who told Gaillard two months before the agenda revision that the congress would be a short one and would not designate a caliph because the Muslim world was too thoroughly divided over the issue.[82]

With the opening of the congress, the extent of the defeat in the matter of participation became embarrassingly manifest. The Egyptian organizers were there in force, and a sizable delegation of notables descended from Palestine by train. Otherwise, attendance was meager. Even Rashid Rida, who actively participated in the organizing committee, and later published the proceedings, did not attend in person, and privately predicted disaster for the impending congress.[83] At an early stage, he diagnosed the faults of his fellow organizers, to which he made this allusion: "The important thing is that our colleagues, the members of the preparatory committee here, lack everything that is essential in both intelligence and initiative for this project. I cannot say more than this."[84]

To these two years of controversy and negotiation, the actual proceedings of the congress proved anticlimactic. The congress divided into three committees, which prepared reports for the plenum on various theoretical aspects of the caliphate. But the preparatory committee had set down a charter (see appendix 5) which established procedures, and the discussion of the constitutional gaps left by this document occupied much of the time of the plenary sessions. The argument revolved around the manner in which resolutions were to be adopted. The Egyptian organizers were eager to pass on to substantive questions, but other participants insisted that internal regulations be set down with greater clarity. "The congress has already held three sessions, and this is the fourth [and last]," said Shaykh Minyawi urgently, "yet we have still done nothing. We did not assemble to discuss secondary questions, but to present Muslims with useful work."[85] The constitutional problems were never fully sorted out, but were left aside at Egyptian insistence.

On substantive issues, the congress essentially divided along Egyptian and non-Egyptian lines. The former group was led by the Azhar organizers, and the latter by ᶜAbd al-ᶜAziz al-Thaᶜalibi, who had once before played this role of opposition-bloc organizer. During the Pilgrimage Congress of 1924 in Mecca he had thwarted Husayn of Mecca, and for this reason probably was invited to Cairo. But now he turned his organizing skills as spoiler on the Azhar organizers themselves. Thaᶜalibi was overheard by a police agent in his hotel lobby planning with other non-Egyptians to disturb the work of the congress, the moment it touched on the issue of candidacy for the caliphate.[86] The object of the Egyptian organizers was to avoid such a disturbance, yet prevent any decision that precluded a future caliphate of the Egyptian ruling house. To those who claimed that Qurashi descent was an essential attribute of the caliphate—a condition which would have ruled out an Egyptian caliphate—the Egyptians insisted that historical practice had invalidated the requirement. To those who claimed that the caliphate was no longer possible at all, given the sorely divided state of the Muslim world and the inability of any one Muslim ruler to defend it, Shaykh Zawahiri responded in force.[87] A candidate elected by a subsequent congress, if that congress were more representative, would meet the requirements of the *shariᶜa* by virtue of his election by a consensus of Muslims.[88]

In this manner, the congress, after only four plenary sessions held over less than a week, resolved itself into a decision to convene again the following year, in what it was hoped would be a more representative fashion. The participants, without apparent enthusiasm, committed themselves to establishing branches in their own countries, and they assented to a proposal that the next congress take place in Cairo. It seems that the agenda for the following year was then to be determined at the banquet which closed this first congress, but a reporter wrote that the participants passed the banquet in eating rather than discussion, and most went home without any idea of what the next caliphate congress would undertake.[89]

Even before the first congress, Rashid Rida had proposed that it meet a second time, and each Muslim territory would have one vote in the reconvened assembly. He even offered to write a tract on the caliphate specifically for submission to such a congress.[90] But there is no evidence that any attempt was made by the organizers to reconvene the congress the following year. For all intents and purposes, the General Islamic Congress for the Caliphate had folded.

The experience was not wholly without a sequel, for Shaykh Mustafa al-Maraghi apparently felt himself capable of achieving what the Azhar committee had not achieved. He had contributed something to the gestation of the congress idea, with his proposal of 1915 (see chapter 5). He had also participated in the preparations for the 1926 congress, although the failed event was essentially the work of others. In later years, with the elevation of a young, charismatic king in the person of Faruq I (r. 1936–1952; his former tutor Maraghi rose in stature. As Shaykh al-Azhar, he began once more to work discreetly for the emergence of an Egyptian king-caliph, and to campaign openly for a Muslim congress.

The congress suggestion this time reappeared not in the formal context of the caliphate—an invitation to certain defeat—but in the less controversial framework of Sunni–Shiᶜi reconciliation. In this initiative, Shaykh Maraghi had an active ally. "For more than a year, I have been trying to lay the foundations for an accommodation between the Sunna and the Shiᶜa." ᶜAbd al-Rahman ᶜAzzam, Egypt's minister to Iraq in 1938, justified his overtures by pure *raison d'état,* in a diplomatic dispatch to Cairo:

Al-Azhar would become the principal school of Islam in the world, in which the people of the various Islamic schools could study their *fiqh.* . . . this would strengthen Egypt's religious influence among the Shiᶜa of Iraq, Yemen, Iran, Afghanistan, and India, and naturally would be followed by an enhancement of Egypt's political centrality. Experience shows that the political influence drawn by a state from a religious appeal is a sturdy and strong one, resistant to the vicissitudes of time.[91]

ᶜAzzam Pasha reported that he already had approached influential Iraqi politicians and ulama, including three of the most prominent *mujtahid*s: Shaykh Muhammad al-Husayn Al Kashif al-Ghitaᵓ, Shaykh ᶜAbd al-Karim al-Jazaᵓiri, and the *marjaᶜ al-taqlid,* Ayat Allah Abu al-Hasan Isfahani. To them, he spoke of Muslim unity, the need for a Muslim congress to examine religious issues, and the role of al-Azhar as a university for all the sects of Islam.

Where had these ideas originated? A year earlier in Egypt, ᶜAzzam had raised these issues with Shaykh Maraghi, who had been in full agreement. The diplomat now asked his foreign ministry to present three concrete proposals to the Shaykh al-Azhar. ᶜAzzam suggested first that Maraghi visit Najaf and Karbala, an act which ᶜAzzam expected would have a tremendous effect; second, that al-Azhar accept students from *madhahib* other than the Sunni four, and allow these students to study *fiqh* from ulama of their own *madhahib*; and last, that Shaykh Maraghi "call for a general Islamic congress among the ulama, whose purpose will be religious," and whose task would be the reconciliation of the various sects (*al-taqrib bayna al-madhahib*).[92] The foreign ministry acceded, and sent a copy of ᶜAzzam's dispatch to Shaykh Maraghi.[93]

But the initiative had already been taken. In late October 1936, ᶜAbd al-Karim al-Zanjani, a Najafi ᶜalim, arrived in Egypt for a stay which lasted nearly two months. Shaykh Maraghi held a tea party for him, and the Shiᶜi rapidly became a popular speaker around Cairo's Muslim activist circuit.[94] Zanjani's theme was the identity of Sunni and Shiᶜi interests, and his biographer devotes a chapter to a comparison of Zanjani and Jamal al-Din al-Afghani.[95]

After Zanjani's return to Iraq, Shaykh Maraghi began to correspond with him. Maraghi's hope, he once confided to Lord Lloyd, was that Muslim countries would send delegates "to sit on a permanent sort of Supreme Islamic Council, eventually to be established at Cairo, where all questions affecting any one of them as a member of the Islamic Union, would be considered and a common policy formulated."[96] To this end, Shaykh Maraghi began to speak openly of a reconciliation of the sects,[97] and decided to involve the Shiᶜi Twelver community of Iraq in this plan through his new acquaintance. Zanjani does not appear to have counted for much at Najaf, and certainly there were ulama of far higher standing and distinction to whom Shaykh Maraghi might have turned. That the Shaykh al-Azhar chose to cultivate Zanjani was perhaps related to the Iraqi ᶜalim's past flexibility in matters concerning the caliphate. In 1924, Zanjani offered his allegiance to Husayn of Mecca as caliph.[98] This act, unconventional by any Twelver Shiᶜi standard, set Zanjani squarely on the side of political expediency in matters of the caliphate.

And to Shaykh Maraghi this was essential. For at exactly the same time, he had won over the leader of Ismaᶜili Shiᶜism to a radical proposition: "Before his departure [from Egypt]," wrote Lampson in Cairo, "the Aga Khan enformed me on February 11th of the gist of his conversation with Sheikh el Maraghi. He said that the Sheikh had quoted historical precedents for local rulers assuming local Caliphate titles in the past. Sheikh el Maraghi had urged that the same thing could properly be done in Egypt today, and if done by one Muslim ruler, it would doubtless be done by others."[99]

Shaykh Maraghi first asked Zanjani's opinion of the proposed Muslim council in February 1938.[100] Zanjani replied favorably, but then added two reservations. He first stressed that the Shiᶜi public believed that government appointees were removed from divine favor, and so representation on the council had best be nongovernmental. His second point was that a site free from foreign influence was essential to the success of the plan.[101] Maraghi answered that he too preferred men of religion as delegates, but saw no reason not to include some prominent figures who were not ulama. He avoided the question of the proposed site by not mentioning it, and went to some pains to assure Zanjani that he had not made an attempt through official channels to transform Najafi religious institutes into appendages of al-Azhar, although he did hope for closer ties.[102]

Just below the surface of the correspondence was an evident tension. Zanjani had successfully conveyed to Maraghi that he understood the Shaykh al-Azhar's centralizing aim, and was not much in sympathy with an Egyptian bid for ascendancy. Another source reported that Zanjani "did not commit himself to any opinion regarding the suggestion that King Faruq should be proclaimed caliph."[103] Zanjani had drawn his line on the wrong side of Shaykh Maraghi's plans; with the collapse of his scheme for a Muslim council, Maraghi severed his Najaf connection.[104] The Shaykh al-Azhar did not visit that city, and appears to have made no further initiative to secure a Shiʿi constituency. During the subsequent six years until his death, Shaykh Maraghi occasionally returned to the congress theme, but did not pursue it actively, and no serious attempt was ever again made in Egypt's era of constitutional monarchy to convene a Muslim congress in Cairo. There were those in the palace who continued to covet the caliphate for Egypt, but they sought to win their prize by guile, as in January 1939, when a palace-inspired crowd acclaimed Faruq caliph as he departed from Friday prayers.[105]

This expressed the loss of self-assurance caused al-Azhar by the Cairo caliphate congress. Much of the argument for Egyptian primacy rested on the claim that Cairo, as the cradle of al-Azhar and modern Muslim reform, was entitled to the deference accorded the capital city of a faith. This assertion substituted theological preeminence for military prowess as the principal attribute of centrality in Islam, and then insisted upon the absolute supremacy of Egypt in the field of Muslim learning. Neither assumption had made much headway beyond Egypt. Military prowess still counted for a great deal, and made for the continued prestige among Muslims enjoyed by republican and secular Turkey. And even those who recognized the importance of cultural and theological primacy were not bound necessarily to Egypt. At the turn of the century, al-Azhar, underminded by self-imposed isolation and state neglect, was still roughly equal in stature to institutions of Muslim learning in Tunis, Damascus, and Deoband. The subsequent transformation in the Egyptian preception of Egypt's relative standing in Islam owed much to the extensive reform of al-Azhar. It was also tied to the emergence of the

Shaykh al-Azhar as the preeminent religious dignitary within Egypt, finally superseding the leaders of the two great Egyptian religious confraternities.[106]

But the effects of these changes had not been felt beyond Egypt when the Cairo caliphate congress put them to a rigorous test. The results were unfortunate, for al-Azhar's preeminence was not widely acknowledged, a fact which the congress exposed but could not rectify. The impact in Cairo, both in al-Azhar and the royal palace, was chastening. Egypt's bid for the caliphate and primacy in Islam survived the setback of 1926. But the technique of the Muslim congress was shed in favor of outright self-assertion, in what one diplomat called Egypt's "pursuit of the Caliphate Grail."[107]

TEN

THE FATE OF MECCA

The Congress of the
Islamic World, 1926

T HE MECCAN CONGRESS of June–July 1926 was convened in response to several invitations from ʿAbd al-ʿAziz Ibn Saʿud (1880–1953), issued over a period of two years. Ibn Saʿud made his initial appeal in the midst of his controversial Hijazi campaign of conquest, at a time when he was still regarded by many Muslims beyond Arabia as an intolerant sectarian. Hence the response of those invited—Muslim states and associations—was slow in coming and eventually incomplete.

The congress, as described in the earlier versions of the invitation, was to have determined the future form of government for the Hijaz, and in this manner Ibn Saʿud aspired to case himself as trustee rather than conqueror. But following the fall of Mecca, Madina, and Jidda to Ibn Saʿud's arms, his acclamation as King of the Hijaz by the notables of the province left little to be determined in the matter of government. The projected agenda thus was reduced to discussion of means to improve the conditions of the pilgrimage, with the transparent aim of securing formal Muslim acquiescence in the newly installed régime.

Resistance to such acquiescence was fairly widespread. The war that raged in the holy cities and their vicinity had generated much talk in India of an international régime for the Hijaz similar to that proposed by Kawakibi in his *Umm al-qura*; the disorder in Arabia had encouraged the revival of latent Egyptian territorial ambitions directed toward the Hijaz. The tensions which lay beneath the preparation, proceedings, and aftermath of the congress thus stemmed from the dispute among Muslims over Saudi measures to assure permanence of rule over the province and the cities of pilgrimage. The congress met once, adopted a charter and a set of resolutions, and dispersed with the intention of reconvening the following year. But the participants were never summoned back.

The Meccan congress was planned as a public event, and evoked much contemporary interest and comment. The most important Egyptian daily newspapers sent their own correspondents to Mecca to cover the proceedings. Through their accounts or those which appeared in the semi-official newspaper *Umm al-qura* of Mecca, the wider Muslim world was kept informed of the daily proceedings of the congress. These found their way to the West through a study by Achille Sékaly, who published a generally reliable French summary of the sessions as they were reported in the Egyptian Arabic press, along with his own introduction.[1] A number of studies later were written by orientalists and journalists who drew upon these two sources. Of this group of contemporary secondary sources, Arnold Toynbee's account, in the annual political survey of the Royal Institute of International Affairs, wielded the most influence.[2]

But over the years, reminiscences and letters of participants were published, revealing more thoroughly an inner dimension of the congress. The posthumously published "memoirs" of Shaykh Muhammad al-Ahmadi al-Zawahiri, chief of the Egyptian delegation to the congress and later rector of al-Azhar, represented a major corrective to accounts based on the public record, for they reflected the depth of conflict in the congress sessions.[3] An important retrospective appraisal of the congress from a Saudi point of view was provided by Hafiz Wahba, adviser to Ibn Saᶜud and principal organizer of the congress, who also conceded that the congress was marked by intense controversy.[4] Also revealing were Rashid Rida's letters to Shakib Arslan, compiled in Mecca during the congress.[5] Written from another perspective were the recollections of ᶜAjaj Nuwayhid, a Lebanese Druze from Palestine, who acted both as participant and interpreter at the congress.[6] Of limited use were the odd accounts of Iqbal ᶜAli Shah, an Indo-Afghan publicist of uncertain allegiance and the father of Sufi proselytizer Idries Shah. He attended the congress as an observer and spied on the Russian Muslim delegation for the British vice consul in Jidda.[7]

Governments with an interest in the congress also collected informed accounts, and the dispatches of the British vice consul in Jidda, S. R. Jordan, contained much confidential information on the factions within the congress.[8] More candid than any previous accounts of these factions were undoubtedly the secret reports to King Fuᵓad of Egypt, written by members of the Egyptian delegation immediately upon their return from Mecca, and by the Egyptian consul in Jidda.[9]

On April 28, 1926, Ibn Saᶜud telegraphed invitations to various Muslim rulers and associations, urging them to attend a Meccan Muslim congress

for the service of the two holy sanctuaries and their inhabitants, to secure their future, to increase the means of comfort for pilgrims and visitors,

to improve the holy lands in all respects which all the Muslims in general
care for, to fulfill our promises we made and with a view to our wish to
see the Muslims cooperating in serving these holy lands.[10]

This was a reiteration of long-standing invitation which only one Indian
Muslim society had accepted.[11] But the congress proposal had taken on
a new urgency for Ibn Saᶜud, because in January 1926 he had been
acclaimed king by the notables of the subjugated province. The step
had betrayed his ambition, and had abrogated the pledge which he had
given in the past to involve the wider Muslim world in determining the
political future of the Hijaz. Now he sought recognition of the accomplished fact of his kingship.

He and his advisers thus opened a campaign to secure participants
for a Muslim congress under Saudi auspices, scheduled for June 1926.
This time the invitations had a much greater effect, for Ibn Saᶜud was
now ruler of the holy cities, recognized by the Western powers and
responsible for the conduct of the pilgrimage. So began the modern
transformation by which the Saudis were to shed their association with
schismatic fanaticism, and become for many Muslims the sole keepers
of the orthodox flame.

The stages of preparation and deliberation overlapped, for the organizers continued to draw delegations and reiterate invitations even
after the opening of the congress. Ibn Saᶜud had originally hoped that
the official representatives of Muslim states would predominate in the
congress. But when the first session opened, in a former Turkish barrack,
not one official delegation was present from beyond Arabia. Participants
represented a number of Muslim associations, some more important
than others, or attended in their personal capacities. Only a week later
did an official Yemeni delegation arrive, and after the congress recessed
for the pilgrimage rites, three other official delegations arrived, from
Egypt, Turkey, and Afghanistan. The organizers welcomed the presence
of these delegations as an achievement, although the combination of
official and unofficial delegations proved unwieldy. "In political questions, the congress was divided into two halves," wrote Shaykh Zawahiri
in his secret report. "In the first were the representatives of independent
governments, of conservative disposition, and in the second were representatives of peoples, of hotheaded disposition."[12]

The animated judgments of Shaykh Zawahiri throw much new light
on the composition of the congress. Of the unofficial participants, he
was most impressed by the representatives of the Indian Khilafat Committee. The delegation was led by two brothers, Muhammad and Shawkat ᶜAli, who once had spoken for the largest and best organized of
Muslim political associations.[13] They were originally supportive of Ibn

Saʿud in his war against Husayn of Mecca, whose Arab rebellion against the Ottoman caliph they had regarded as treasonable. But as the Saudi occupation of the Hijaz wore on, a reaction set in.

> They were collectively opposed to the government of Ibn Saʿud and the Wahhabis in the Hijaz, although an unheeded minority among them sided with the Wahhabis. The most noticeable leaders among the Indians were Muhammad ʿAli; Shawkat ʿAli; and Shuʿayb Qurashi, a lawyer educated in England and a moving speaker. Shaykh [Sulayman] al-Nadwi is a calm and self-possessed ʿalim. . . . The first three carried out harsh and relentless assaults against the government of Ibn Saʿud and criticized his administrative and religious policy. They are generally men of emotion more than men of thought, and their religious emotion is like steampower which, when controlled by someone wise, will generate great things. They hold affection for Egypt, but detest the English occupation. Were it not for this, they would have bound all their hopes to Egypt. I spoke with Muhammad ʿAli about the hopes of the Indians and the Islamic revival, and he said that all their hopes were riding on the Turks, but that the Turks had frustrated them. When Ibn Saʿud's movement had arisen, they turned their hopes toward him, but when they came to Mecca and saw what they saw, he let them down also.[14]

One of the delegates, Shuʿayb Qurashi, had been present in the Hijaz as representative of the Indian Khilafat Committee when Ibn Saʿud had been proclaimed king. In his wounded reaction to this sudden development, confided to an Indian friend in an intercepted letter, Qurashi vented the resentment which later animated the Committee's delegation: "friend Ibne Saud got himself proclaimed King of Hedjaz yesterday. Of course it was at the repeated request of Hejazis. There was a bayat, a promise to act according to the book and the Sunnah. There may also be created a Legislative Assembly for Hedjaz. But all this is bunkum. The whole show was got up. It was a prearranged plan. The Hejazis do not want him. I have ascertained their views first hand. . . . Of course we can protest, but the real decision will have to be taken by the Committee in India."[15] The Khilafat Committee eventually agreed to join the congress despite the failure of Ibn Saʿud to respond to their concerns, but the delegation was determined to cause a stir and perhaps win the Khilafat Committee some say in the administration of the Hijaz.

The Javanese delegation was also of considerable importance, led as it was by Umar Sayyid Tjokroaminoto (1882–1934), a scion of an aristocratic Javanese family and a former native administrator. Leader of the Sarekat Islam, a large movement that claimed a membership in the millions, he had declined an invitation to the Cairo caliphate congress in favor of the Meccan congress. But the Javanese did not impress Zawahiri: "They are a weak people in every matter. They were like a grasping, drowning person, wishing to find something to support them, and able to move neither hand nor tongue. They did not say a word, and avoided any commitment." That they were silent was born out by the record.[16] Of the Syrians and Palestinians, foremost among them the mufti of Jerusalem, Amin al-Husayni, Zawahiri had this to say: "They caused a great stir with their immature opinions. All that interested them was, first, to appear on the stage in any possible manner, and second, to protest what was happening in their own country and ask for aid." No more constructive were the Soviet Muslim delegates, who lacked self-confidence. They "had the feeling that the other nations accused them of atheism and Bolshevism. They proclaimed their innocence on every occasion, and it seemed that they were not among the leaders of their country, because they tried to avoid any commitment."[17] From the Sudan came two persons who frankly admitted to the Egyptian delegation that they had arrived as simple pilgrims, and never claimed to represent anybody.[18]

The Arabian delegations, whether from Najd, ᶜAsir, or the Hijaz, were Saudi-controlled. Of the Hijazis, Zawahiri wrote that "they are simple souls. There were those among them who did not hide their moaning about the Najdis; then there were Beduin shaykhs who did not understand what was going on, and they assembled with a group of Najdis as representatives of the Hijaz." Before the arrival of the official Egyptian delegation, Egypt was spoken for by Shaykh Muhammad Madi Abu al-ᶜAzaʾim, who played a leading role in the domestic opposition to the Cairo caliphate congress that had just drawn to a close (see previous chapter). Abu al-ᶜAzaʾim had acted in Egypt as a Saudi apologist and went so far as to claim the caliphate for Ibn Saᶜud.[19]

The most prominent delegate present in a private capacity was Rashid Rida, editor of al-Manar, who long had advocated precisely this sort of congress. Zawahiri wrote of him that

> he supports Ibn Saᶜud with the pen, so that one Hijazi said: Ibn Saᶜud claims that he took the Hijaz with his sword, but Shaykh Rashid claims that it was taken by the pen. He was the object of suspicion among the Indians and others, and Muhammad ᶜAli told me that Shaykh Rashid took from Ibn Saᶜud about £6,000. When I mentioned this to Shaykh Hafiz [Wahba], he said: There is money in this affair. Muhammad ᶜAli said to Rashid Rida in jest: Be quiet and I will pay you.[20]

In a private letter, Rida himself put Ibn Saᶜud's contribution to his work at £4,000.[21] The Egyptian consul and British vice consul both put the sum at £2,000.[22] When open rumors began to circulate about this connection a year later, Rida wrote a lengthy defensive polemic on patronage.[23]

Such was the composition of the congress during the pre-pilgrimage stage. The Saudi-controlled delegations, enjoying the active support of Rashid Rida, soon clashed with the Indian Khilafat Committee delegation. The former were at an advantage owing to the composition of the remaining delegations, in which their own chosen sympathizers predominated.

In the post-pilgrimage stage of the congress, following the arrival of the official delegations, the balance shifted only slightly. The Turkish delegation, according to Zawahiri, remained aloof: "I learned from another quarter that the Turks had decided to participate in the congress before the settlement of the Mosul question, to execute a political maneuver. When they came to an agreement [with the British] over Mosul, they refused to turn back in disorder, and so sent a token delegation. This was clear from the work of the delegation. It avoided all political or financial commitment."[24] The Turkish delegate told the British vice consul that "he had been sent by the Ghazi Mustafa Kemal Pasha with a watching brief only."[25] The Afghan delegate, a diplomat posted to Ankara, was "like the shadow" of the Turkish delegate.[26] For the Yemeni delegate, a relative of the Imam Yahya who arrived in Mecca with a large retinue of retainers and slaves, the congress was apparently an opportunity to settle bilateral issues with Ibn Saᶜud, and he played no role in the congress. "It seems improbable that a Governor of a coastal town in Arabia [Hudayda] would travel with twenty or more armed retainers and make so much show for the pleasure of proceeding to Mecca ostensibly to take part in a conference for which he might easily have been too late."[27] Only the official Egyptian delegation, headed by Zawahiri, added its voice to that of the Indian Khilafat Committee's delegation, in constituting a rudimentary bloc of opposition. As a precondition of entry into the hall, the Egyptians insisted on the expulsion of Abu al-ᶜAzaᵓim, and he was forced out despite his protests.

Ibn Saᶜud's more vociferous opponents were absent from the congress altogether. Iraq's King Faysal was invited, but would not take part in any gathering organized by the Saudi archrival. More telling was Iran's refusal to send a representative, a decision rooted in the legacy of Wahhabi-Shiᶜi animosity. An Iranian delegation, led by Iran's consul-general in Damascus, did arrive in Cairo in order to proceed to the congress by Red Sea steamer. But they paused in Egypt as higher consultations took place between Teheran and Iran's minister to Cairo. Finally the Iranian government decided against any participation; Iran's prime minister pronounced that "the Persian Government is unable to stand by and view unconcernedly the actions of a small band of bigots who are engaged in endeavouring to force their opinions on the Mohammadan world." Iran demanded the creation of a general assembly of Muslims to regulate the holy shrines, and called on all Muslims "not [to] permit any further humiliating insults to be heaped on their sanctuaries and their faith."[28] This was the most important abstention.

To avoid any charge of interference, Ibn Saᶜud himself did not attend the congress, aside from an initial appearance to the salute of twenty-one guns. "The explosions were so loud and so shook the building that several delegates became panicky and left the building, fearing it was about to collapse."[29] But on this occasion, Ibn Saᶜud did inform the participants that they were not to discuss the domestic or international policies of any state, a constraint that several of his listeners regarded as insufferable and were prepared to ignore.[30]

For the evidence categorically contradicts Toynbee's assertion that political and religious controversy "was not the outstanding feature of the Mecca congress," and that the issues of improved public administration and pilgrimage arrangements were "non-contentious."[31] Zawahiri's published memoirs bring out the conflicts quite clearly, while in his secret report, he provides an even more candid version:

> The first days of the congress passed, and the organizers were in sweet dreams (*ahlam ladhidha*), and they imagined that everything was going in their favor. But this did not last long. The congress especially took up issues of their pretended leadership, like the question of religious tolerance, and the question of criticism of the government's administration and organization. It became clear that the congress was moving toward the creation of an international body which would oversee the government of the Hijaz and hold it to account. At the same time, they were not getting from the congress a single *dirham*, nor recognition of the legality of their rule in the Hijaz. To the contrary, they heard debate which held that they were not fit to rule the Hijaz. Not one of the Indians called Ibn Saᶜud anything but sultan [of Najd, i.e., not king of the Hijaz], to the point where one of their speakers—brother Shawkat ᶜAli—said: I am not ready to bear good witness to the government of this country.[32]

Hafiz Wahba later confessed that there "was a radical difference in mentality and outlook between Nejdis and Moslems in other countries," and "on this rock the Conference foundered, the dispute continuing to rage without hope of reconciliation."[33]

The course of these seventy-eight hours of debates can be followed through sources long available, but a few new points suggest themselves. It has not been appreciated how the opposing parties first clashed over control of the congress itself, before substantive issues were raised for debate. At the outset, the officers were elected by a straight vote of those participants present in the hall; and right away the Indian Khilafat Committee delegation challenged this procedure. First they questioned the credentials of certain other delegations: "Before any work, we must know which members have the right to vote." Then they favored a proportional form of representation, and demanded that each delegation enjoy voting power roughly commensurate with the size of the population it purported to represent.

As the election of officers was necessary even before such issues could be decided, these objections were temporarily put aside.[34] But when discussion of permanent statutes began (see appendix 6), entitlement to participation and mode of voting were central. Rashid Rida, who drew up a preliminary charter for the congress, made membership a simple function of Ibn Sa‛ud's personal invitation.[35] This was resisted by many delegates, who eventually prevailed in establishing a system of three-tiered representation: by Muslim states, by branches of the congress, and wherever appropriate by delegates of Muslim peoples chosen in the most representative manner possible. Each territory (qutr) was then to be accorded a certain number of votes, based on a rough estimate of its importance, the degree of its independence, and the size of its Muslim population. By this agreement, India was awarded the largest number of votes (four of a total of fifty), stirring a protest from another delegation which claimed that each Muslim territory should be entitled to an equal say. Shawkat ‛Ali replied that "we in India are seventy million Muslims out of three hundred million, and if we wanted to, we could demand a fourth of the votes of the congress. But we are willing to settle for four votes and not more."[36]

This was the first and only appearance of the idea of proportional representation in a Muslim congress. There was no attempt to actually apply the provision during the sessions, and late-arriving Egyptian delegates noted that each participant present in the hall had one vote regardless of how many other participants were in attendance from his own country.[37] The participants apparently thought to postpone the implementation of proportional representation until a subsequent and fuller congress, for many of the regions which were accorded votes in this system were not represented at all in this first congress.

In their arrangements for procedural order, the participants and delegates exhibited little evidence of experience, and this expanded the possibilities for conflict. They knew enough to provide for the formation of committees, but these failed for a time to function for lack of participants. The result was that the general sessions were not preceded by adequate preparation. "I see no great benefit in our meeting here," said the Turkish delegate, "because the committees answerable to this session are unable to work. After noon prayer, part of their time is wasted waiting for those who do not show up, and more time passes drinking coffee without result. After evening prayer, they adjourn for dinner, so that the committees do nothing."[38] Well into the congress, the proposals committee had yet to assemble because a sufficient number

of its members had yet to appear for a gathering. A quorum was therefore set for this committee of only one-fourth of its members.[39]

The situation in the plenum was not better, and participants were
often absent or drifted in late. On at least two occasions, the president
of the congress failed to appear at all. After waiting in one instance for
forty minutes, those present appointed another chairman in his place.[40]
According to the semi-official *Umm al-qura*, average attendance at the
general sessions was 49 of the 66 participants,[41] and this rate of absen-
teeism did not reflect the extent and effects of tardiness. "It is unrea-
sonable that we should order the affairs of the people," said one delegate
commenting on tardiness, "when we cannot order our own."[42]

At the same time, certain delegates made a concerted effort to insert
political items in the agenda. In private meetings held during the first
stage of the congress, the ᶜAli brothers and Rashid Rida had pressed
Ibn Saᶜud to consent to a collective oath of congress delegates in the
Kaᶜba. There they would pledge to do everything possible to rid the
Arabian peninsula of all foreign influence. The oath's advocates again
raised the subject during a banquet held for them by Ibn Saᶜud. "The
King then invited me to speak," wrote Hafiz Wahba.

> After complimenting them on their zeal and brotherly interest, I asked
> them to define the words 'Arabian Peninsula'. They said they had meant
> the Peninsula proper and Iraq, Syria, Palestine, Akaba, and Maan as well.
> I said that we must be practical; a statement of this kind might well
> involve the Hejaz in difficulties. Those present could not honestly say
> that they represented the entire Moslem world, and if in any way they
> were instrumental in putting the Hejaz into a diplomatically awkward
> position, they might not be able to give all the help they should. So there
> seemed no point in pursuing a fantasy. Delegates from Turkey, Afghan-
> istan, Egypt and Yemen were even then on the way, and the least they
> could do would be to wait until these delegates arrived before making
> such a pledge, for if the latter agreed to it, it would be their governments
> who would be able to do something to carry it out. Nothing, I concluded,
> could be lost by waiting for a few days.

As Wahba had expected, none of the official delegations would have
anything to do with the proposed pledge and its implicit condemnation
of British and French rule over areas bordering the peninsula proper.
The oath was never taken.[43]

A similar atmosphere prevailed in the deliberations of the proposals
committee. Reminiscences of the committee's proceedings, which were
conducted in private and did not figure in any contemporary account,
were published by ᶜAjaj Nuwayhid. From these it is clear that Ibn Saᶜud's
insistence that the delegates exclude wider politics from their deliberations met with considerable resistance. For example, French and Span-

ish forces were then in the last stages of crushing ᶜAbd al-Karim's Rif rebellion in Morocco, and although the cause was lost, Muhammad ᶜAli proposed to the committee that the congress issue an urgent appeal to all Muslims for money to sustain the uprising. According to Nuwayhid, the proposal won the assent of all but the official Turkish delegate, who maintained that such issues were beyond the scope of the congress. "Listen, my brother," pleaded Muhammad ᶜAli, "what is the difference between our appeal on behalf of ᶜAbd al-Karim, and our appeals on your behalf when you fought the Greeks?" This was a transparent attempt to alter the purposes for which the congress had been convened. But the appeal was never launched, for while in the Kaᶜba at prayer, Muhammad ᶜAli and Amin al-Husayni belatedly learned that ᶜAbd al-Karim already had surrendered himself to the French.[44]

Rashid Rida provoked still more controversy when he proposed an Islamic pact (mithaq islami) to be concluded among Muslim governments. According to this plan, disputes between Muslim states would be referred to the Meccan congress for arbitration. Rida thus envisioned the evolution of the congress from a symposium on the narrow issues of the Hijaz, to the founding session of a league of Muslim states. The official Egyptian delegation maintained that such a proposal far exceeded the terms of reference set down for the congress by Ibn Saᶜud. Rida was advocating a political pact—so the wider world would perceive it— and the Egyptians could not enter into such an agreement. This opposition could not be overcome.[45]

In a subtler manner, Muhammed ᶜAli suggested in the proposals committee that a resolution be passed calling upon Muslims not to spill Muslim blood. According to Nuwayhid, the real motive behind this seemingly right-spirited resolution was to influence West African Muslim soldiers in French service. These Muslim forces had played a prominent role in the suppression of Syrian unrest over the past several years.[46] The Saudis, however, may have thought the proposed resolution to be directed against them, as they had taken the Hijaz by sword, and Wahhabi forces had committed some unfortunate atrocities against other Muslims during the campaign. The resolution was defeated in a plenary vote by a majority of two to one, its opponents arguing again that it was not directly related to affairs of the Hijaz.[47] Only the constant vigilance of the official delegations assured that the congress was not plunged into political controversy by such motions.

Yet there were also serious disputes over the specifically Hijazi issues related to the welfare of pilgrims, matters within the formal purview of the congress. The lengthy debates over sanitary conditions, taxation of pilgrims, proposed railway construction, and the Hijaz railway, are outlined by Sékaly and the accounts derived from his work.[48] In general, the host delegations resisted the many proposals which meant outside Muslim regulation of Hijazi affairs, while participants from beyond tended to withhold commitments of support and promises of funds which the organizers pressed them to make. For proposed railway construction, the Egyptian delegation called for the creation of an international Muslim company, accountable to its stockholders; the host delegations insisted that the money be raised through unrestricted contributions. All agreed that the pilgrims should be taxed to raise money for general improvements; no one wished to bear the onus of collecting such taxes. The Khilafat delegation demanded that the Hijazi government's books be opened to international Muslim inspection; the host delegations regarded accountability as an infringement of sovereignty.

But more contentious than all of these questions was the issue of Muslim religious freedom and pluralism in the holy cities. The pilgrimage brought together believers from widely scattered parts, with their own traditional rituals and formula of prayer. Yet part of the puritan Wahhabi vision had been to purify the holy cities of all practices not in accord with their rigorous fundamentalism. Shaykh Zawahiri described the consequences, as he witnessed them in the Grand Mosque in Mecca. In this scene, the incident revolved around the Wahhabi doctrine that Muslim supplicants address only God in prayer, and not his prophets.

> I saw here with my own two eyes a thing that pained my soul. I was in the mosque yesterday, lingering after I had performed my circumambulations, and I saw a group of people surround an Egyptian. They castigated him vehemently, saying: "You prayed 'Oh, Prophet of God'!" This frightened the Egyptian to his very soul. He disavowed having so prayed, shrank back, and was so terrified that it opened my eyes. He came to me after that, along with many of the Egyptians, saying to us: "You saw how they reproach us." I calmed them down, told them not to be afraid, and to be patient until the truth becomes known by the guidance of God. I will not deny to you that I concealed in my heart that I, too, open my prayers with "Oh, Prophet of God."[49]

An Indian delegate, with the support of other participants from India and Russia and the official Egyptian, Yemeni, and Afghan delegations, introduced a resolution that led to a heated exchange. He essentially proposed noninterference by the Hijazi authorities in the pilgrimage rites. Ibn Sa^ud's delegations united to decry the heretical "innovations" which had flourished in the holy cities before the Saudi conquest, and soundly defeated the resolution in a show of hands. An uproar followed, with Muhammed ^Ali demanding a secret vote, and the Afghan delegate threatening that a Hijaz without religious freedom would loose the sympathy of all Islam. The same majority which defeated the resolution hurriedly passed another, which established a theological committee of ulama to examine the issue further. The session was adjourned in the midst of protestations.⁵⁰ The outbreak led Ibn Saᶜud to issue what was essentially a reprimand to the congress, in which he spelled out his personal point of view. No pilgrim would be questioned about his beliefs; but no practices which contradicted the Muslim consensus could be permitted.⁵¹ This served only to excite further controversy.

According to Shaykh Zawahiri, "it became clear to the organizers that their best plan was at least to be rid of the congress this year. The secretary of the congress told me during its last days that the congress had dashed their hopes, and that the only thing important to them now was that it end in peace."⁵² The organizers secured from the unofficial delegations a last-minute resolution, introduced by Rashid Rida, favoring the inclusion of Maᶜan and ᶜAqaba in Hijazi and hence Saudi territory. They then succeeded in having the congress adjourned. The departing participants were given to understand that the congress would meet for a second time during the next pilgrimage season.⁵³ Upon this last resolution on Maᶜan and ᶜAqaba, and the promise of an annual congress, hinged those appraisals of the congress which saw it as an unmitigated Saudi success.

"I have gone closely into the proceedings of the Pan-islamic Congress held at Mecca in June," wrote George Antonius to Sir Gilbert Clayton. "I am inclined to believe that for the first time in many years, perhaps in the whole course of modern history, HMG find themselves faced with the problem of a, if not united, at any rate uniting, Islam; and . . . . you know how little I possess the temperament of an Islamophile alarmist."⁵⁴ Yet the Turkish delegate confided to the British vice consul that the results of the congress could be summed up in one word—"nil"—for "the Arabs can only agree on one thing, and that is, to disagree on everything."⁵⁵ And British Foreign Office minutes on the vice consul's dispatches were no more sanguine. The congress evidenced "how hopelessly disunited Islam is and how little a pan-islamic conference can hope to achieve."⁵⁶ The congress had ended in an ambiguous fashion which at first lent support to utterly contradictory readings of its significance.

There were three major provisions made for the establishment of a permanent organization. First, it was determined that the congress would meet annually in Mecca. The participants even went so far as to debate, at some length, the proper policy in the event that war made a Meccan congress impossible in any given year. Second, the congress adopted an annual estimated budget of approximately £6,000 to £10,000, and it was agreed that each territory would contribute £300 per annum for each voting delegate permitted it by the proportional voting provision of the charter. From these dues, the expenses of convening the congress would be met, and the salaries of a permanent staff paid. Third, the election of an executive committee was made the task of the annual congress in session, and it was clearly intended that this committee be international in composition.[57] But the requirement of residence in the Hijaz left this task, as before, to Ibn Saᶜud's own organizers, since nearly all of the participants planned to return home at the conclusion of the congress. In this first congress, the election of the executive committee was therefore deferred, and a temporary committee of Saudi organizers was entrusted with interim administration.

But Rashid Rida did succeed, after some debate, in having his close friend Shakib Arslan, then in Geneva, elected to the post of secretary general. Rida evidently hoped to enjoy a preponderant influence over an institution, the creation of which he had advocated for over twenty-five years. With the election of Shakib Arslan, one of his closest associates, the goal was within reach. But there were participants who doubted that Arslan would leave a moderate clime to live in the Hijaz, so Rashid Rida wrote to him at length to assure him that the weather in Taᵓif would suit him, particularly in the winter, and Rida even relayed daytime and nighttime temperatures.[58] In a second letter, Rida told Arslan that he would write to Ibn Saᶜud to arrange for Arslan's travel, and told the reluctant secretary general that his stay in Mecca would involve no expense, as Ibn Saᶜud had covered all the costs incurred by the participants during the congress.[59] Arslan had plans to travel to America and so put off leaving for the Hijaz, but there seemed to be an understanding that he would in fact arrive at his post before the second congress.[60]

The irrepressible Iqbal ᶜAli Shah was also sure that the congress would meet again: "The Conference will be held yearly and is destined to grow in importance. It is bound to exercise a tremendous influence upon the minds and thoughts of the two hundred and fifty million followers of the Prophet, a power which none can afford to ignore."[61] In his quest for the limelight, he again offered his services to the British, seeking their aid in securing an appointment from Ibn Saᶜud as a delegate from Great Britain to the second congress. "He was prepared at the conclusion of his visit to place at the disposal of Government a report, to be handed to His Majesty's Consul, embodying such information as he might have recorded during his journey."[62]

Tjokroaminoto, upon his return to Java, convened at Surabaja the sixth local Al-Islam conference, and had this broad organization transform itself formally into a branch of the Meccan organization. Seven separate provisions were made to collect £900, the sum which would be required of the three voting delegates whom the Muslims of the Netherlands East Indies were entitled to dispatch the following year.[63]

But Rida was already receiving signals that there would not be a second congress. "The temporary committee has done nothing; indeed, it has not even met, as I had believed. The proceedings of the sessions are to be published by me, and I told the King [Ibn Saᶜud], the president of the congress, and the [temporary] secretary, that publication was impossible because of the many Arabic errors in the text. Editing is essential. In the first place, I have not heard that they edited it. . . . I will mention to the King all that is necessary for the upcoming congress, by the next post."[64] By early March 1927, the generally reliable 'Oriental correspondent' of al-Muqattam was already expressing his belief that the second congress would not be held. He noted that the members of the temporary committee had yet to meet, and that the resolutions of the congress remained no more than ink on paper.[65] As the members of the temporary committee were those very same advisers to Ibn Saᶜud who had convened the first congress, it can only be concluded that the lack of any action represented a conscious decision to discourage the convening of a second congress.

One reason for this decision was the fact that the congress had served as an open channel for uncensored criticism. Friends certainly were won to the Saudi cause at the congress, and most of the resolutions served in one way or another to legitimize Saudi policies. But the domestic costs of an open congress in a rapidly closing political system were high. The lone Meccan newspaper could not selectively suppress the contents of speeches in its almost daily account of the proceedings, accounts which were checked by the participants themselves and read by the inhabitants of what was still a newly subjugated province. With consolidation of Saudi rule in the Hijaz not yet complete, the prospect of published criticism by even a single congress participant from abroad was a cause for concern. Rashid Rida had almost certainly identified a similar obsession in the Ottoman opposition to a Meccan congress nearly thirty years earlier. He misunderstood the identical Saudi dilemma in believing that Ibn Saᶜud favored the publication of the congress proceedings. In the form of a slim Arabic volume, these proceedings would have taken on new life as subversive literature, as insidious as Kawakibi's Umm al-qura. They were never published.

The presence of foreign Muslim delegations perhaps also had an unhealthy effect upon Ibn Saᶜud's advisers, most of whom were foreign as well. This was in clearest evidence in the case of Hafiz Wahba, his Egyptian-born confidant, whose personal diplomacy had secured Egypt's participation in the congress. A few months after the Egyptian delegation had returned home, Hafiz Wahba wrote an ingratiating letter to the Egyptian consul in Jidda, inspired by "my obligations as an Egyptian."

> The idea of the Islamic congress, and the goal which I sought to achieve through the participation of the Egyptian government, have already had the desired effect. Many of the ideas which the Egyptian delegation advocated, especially the idea of religious freedom, have had a great effect in India. My principal aim was to found a great bloc of Muslims who would involve themselves in this issue, until these people here would alter their behavior and their way of rule. Freedom of religion is among the most important matters sought by all Islamic governments.
>   Personal correspondence from India informs me that there is a great movement afoot over there, against Ibn Saᶜud. The reasons for the movement go back in truth to the bad behavior exhibited by the people of his religious administration. I have always tried to ease the situation as much as possible, and the Indians in the rest of their speeches stand behind Egypt's policy in the congress. I hope that Egypt takes a firm position which will raise her head in the Islamic world, and will render her the axis of Islam.

Ibn Saᶜud's mentality, continued Wahba, now approximated that of the detested ex-Sharif Husayn, and Wahba praised the young Prince Saᶜud, "for disagreeing with his father in the conduct of administration."[66] This dispatch gave evidence of just one of many possibilities for anti-Saudi intrigue among Ibn Saᶜud's advisers opened by the congress and its delegations.

Expense was also a major consideration. The unofficial delegations probably arrived under their own steam, but were then maintained, in some instances for several months, at Ibn Saᶜud's expense.[67] According to Rashid Rida, Ibn Saᶜud paid for accommodation, board, and local transportation.[68] Aside from Rida, who received a large sum mentioned earlier, other sympathetic delegates also received sums of money from Ibn Saᶜud. Amin al-Husayni was awarded £1,000, "and many of the others received amounts varying from £200 to £600. It is calculated that, with presents, bribes, and other incidental expenditure, the conference cost Ibn Saud £20,000."[69] By all accounts, the affair was expensive, and for this reason the burden had been shifted to the participants. But it was one which they were unlikely to bear, and the small Saudi treasury had to face the prospect of heavy subventions to a forum of dubious utility.

Perhaps the most important disincentive to the reconvening of the congress was the behavior of the Indian Khilafat Committee delegation upon their return home. Muhammad ᶜAli opened an unrestrained campaign of speeches and articles severely critical of Saudi policy and the conduct of the congress.[70] In his own newspaper, the Urdu *Hamdard* of Delhi, he expressed no hope for the success of the projected congress executive committee ("seven more paid servants" for Ibn Saᶜud), and suggested that the congress would be used by crowds of Syrian, Hijazi, and Najdi hangers-on to embezzle *awqaf* funds.[71] Once he and his brother began to urge Indian Muslims to forego the pilgrimage, Ibn Saᶜud grew concerned. With the occupation of the Hijaz, income from the pilgrimage quickly had become the principal source of Saudi state revenue, and Indian Muslims represented a large portion of the annual influx. Ibn Saᶜud sent an emissary to India with the express purpose of refuting the charges of the Khilafat leaders, and the ulama of Madina, presented with an inquiry especially mentioning the ᶜAli brothers and Shuᶜayb Qurashi, issued a *fatwa* reiterating the obligatory nature of the pilgrimage. "Whosoever denies that it is such a duty is an infidel."[72] The congress thus had all the attributes of a domestic political and economic liability, and so was allowed to expire.

In 1927 Ahmad Shafiq, a close associate of Rashid Rida's, arrived in Mecca and met with Tawfiq al-Sharif, who had been the congress secretary during sessions and Ibn Saᶜud's emissary to India, and was now on the temporary committee. Sharif blamed the inactivity on the unwillingness of those states which had sent official delegations to send them again, and the attitude adopted by the ᶜAli brothers. In a meeting with Ibn Saᶜud, Shafiq urged a new Muslim congress to end sectarian differences, and Ibn Saᶜud ordered three of his advisers—Hafiz Wahba, Yusuf Yasin, and Fuʾad Hamza—to assist Shafiq in the task. But then Shafiq was told not to spread word of the congress until the opinions of the various Muslim states had been determined.[73] The appeal was never made public. By 1928, Iqbal ᶜAli Shah's enthusiasm for the Saudi-sponsored congress had also waned, and he was busy approaching the Foreign Office about his own plan for a "Grand Moslem Conference for the Cultural Regeneration of Islam," a scheme which was rebuffed.[74]

In 1929, the elected secretary general of the congress, Shakib Arslan, performed the pilgrimage. He later wrote an effusive tract on the visit, in which he lavished praise on the administration and character of Ibn Saᶜud.[75] But, as one of Arslan's Arab biographers notes, there was a striking omission from this account. "He does not discuss with us the organization of the great pilgrimage congress (*muʾtamar al-hajj al-akbar*), and putting it to use for the benefit of Islam and the welfare of the Muslims; yet he expands upon matters far less weighty than this great issue, as in his discussion of the kindness of the pilgrims' guides."[76] Arslan's presence in the Hijaz would have been a suitable opportunity for Ibn Saᶜud to have reconvened the congress had he sought to do so, but obviously he did not, and so Arslan avoided the issue entirely in his book.

Ibn Saᶜud instead went his own way, and adopted an unequivocal
policy as rigid as that of the Ottomans, prohibiting all activity that
could be construed as political during the pilgrimage. To convey his
own message at that season, he developed an alternative to the banned
congress that continues in an altered form, as an annual tradition. In
1928 he reopened the congress building for a tea party of prominent
pilgrims, and within a few years the event had evolved into the pilgrimage banquet, usually held at one of the royal palaces near Mecca.[77]
On this annual occasion, before the most distinguished pilgrims, Ibn
Saᶜud delivered a monologue on the theme of Muslim solidarity. Once
his speech had been rendered into Urdu, other selected speakers offered
supplementary remarks. The forum was formally social, enjoyed no
authority to debate and resolve, and was suited to Ibn Saᶜud's authoritarian requirements and disposition. Until his death in 1953, there remained in effect an inviolable prohibition against any more formal
demonstration of Muslim solidarity at Mecca.

ELEVEN

IN DEFENSE OF JERUSALEM

The General Islamic Congress, 1931

T HROUGH THE Jerusalem Muslim congress of December 1931, that faction of Palestine's Arabs under the leadership of Amin al-Husayni (1897–1974) attempted to commit wider Muslim opinion to support for the cause of Muslim Palestine. The aim was to challenge the Western sanction accorded the League of Nations mandate and the projected establishment of a Jewish national home. The proposed congress, devoted ostensibly to the preservation of the Muslim holy places in Jerusalem, was ruled by British authorities to be of a religious nature, and while the mandatory power was out of sympathy with the aims of the congress, it thus did little to impede the efforts of the organizers. These were left to surmount only those obstacles raised by Muslim opponents at home and abroad. Such opposition, which was considerable, was either overcome or ignored, and the congress, once convened, endorsed a series of resolutions for the defense of the holy places against encroachment, and the preservation of the Muslim-Arab character of Palestine.

Because these resolutions entailed a number of ambitious and costly projects, such as the building of a Muslim university and the purchase of land, the participants went further, establishing a permanent secretariat and scheduling future congresses at two-year intervals. The permanent secretariat functioned for perhaps as long as five years, but with steadily diminishing results, and the congress was not reconvened. The failure of the secretariat to raise funds to effect the congress resolutions appears to have been the principal cause of the withering of this initiative. In 1937, with the flight of Amin al-Husayni from Palestine to an exile abroad, the organization finally ceased to function, although the network of political and personal ties which it created continued for years afterward to work on behalf of the Palestine Arab cause.

Because of the widespread interest in the conflict over Palestine and the conscious efforts of the organizers to seize the limelight, the congress won coverage more extensive than that accorded any of its predecessors. In addition to the Palestinian press, which was consumed with the event, the Western and foreign Arab press showed a sustained interest in the proceedings. The prelude, proceedings, and aftermath of the congress were therefore amply covered in the open press, and it was a participating journalist, Muhammad ᶜAli al-Tahir, who left one of the fullest accounts of events behind the scenes, written only six months after the congress.[1]

As was to be expected, Rashid Rida's *al-Manar* also covered the congress, but from the narrow vantage point of his own contribution to its proceedings.[2] A fairly straightforward account in Arabic was written by the Palestinian Arab historian Muhammad ᶜIzzat Darwaza, who had served as recording secretary to the congress.[3] Later came other memoirs, the most interesting of these by ᶜAjaj Nuwayhid.[4]

The desire to write about the Jerusalem proceedings while they were still fresh was also great for Western scholars and publicists. H. A. R. Gibb's account was the most influential of these several studies,[5] all of which were superseded once British, French, Palestinian Arab, Zionist, and Egyptian archival materials became available. A number of documented historical studies then appeared, some more thorough than others.[6]

There remains an important source which has yet to reappear and fully illuminate the congress: the archive of the congress itself. The location of these documents was known as recently as 1955, when the papers were searched by an Azhar historian for a manuscript autobiography of Shakib Arslan. The material was then stored in a disorganized fashion in a room near al-Aqsa, but now cannot be located.[7]

The Palestinian Arab initiative for a general Muslim congress dated in a sense from the dispatch of an Islamic mission to the Hijaz in 1922. At that time, the delegation prevailed upon Husayn of Mecca to convene precisely this sort of gathering, and then actively participated (see chapter 8). Large Palestinian Muslim delegations also figured in the subsequent congress of 1926, organized under Saudi auspices (see previous chapter). Personal ties were forged at these encounters with the Indian Khilafat Committee leaders Muhammad and Shawkat ᶜAli. Upon their disappointment with Ibn Saᶜud's policies, these brothers were in search of an alternative Arab alliance, and in early 1929 Muhammad ᶜAli first suggested the creation of a Supreme Islamic Council in Jerusalem composed of representatives drawn from throughout the Muslim world.[8] The bond was sealed in early 1931 upon Muhammad ᶜAli's death, when Amin al-Husayni wired Shawkat ᶜAli asking him to inter his deceased brother in Jerusalem.[9]

From the interaction of Amin al-Husayni and Shawkat ᶜAli on this occasion, the idea of a general Muslim congress in Jerusalem was reborn. Earlier, in 1928, when it became evident that the congress organizations established in Cairo and Mecca two years before had collapsed, Amin al-Husayni had convened in Jerusalem a "general" Muslim congress in defense of the holy places, but it had been attended only by delegates from neighboring territories.[10] With the promise of cooperation from the Indian Khilafat Committee, a new Jerusalem congress was sure to attract far wider participation and attention. The Khilafat leaders, in turn, would then perhaps be in a position to forge that Muslim alliance which had repeatedly eluded them, most recently in their falling out with Ibn Saᶜud.

A preparatory committee was established, which entered into widespread correspondence with influential Muslims abroad, while Amin al-Husayni and Shawkat ᶜAli began to lobby in public and private on behalf of the projected congress.[11] Their themes were the defense of the holy places, and their concrete project was the establishment of a new Muslim university in Jerusalem. A third theme, the restoration of the Hijaz railroad to Muslim control, emerged with the sudden seizure of the Damascus station's premises by French authorities while the congress was in preparation. But the prelude to the congress was a round of confrontations with those who opposed the organizers personally or the idea of a Jerusalem Muslim congress generally. Both forms of opposition were either reconciled or defeated, but not without influence upon the congress itself.

Because Palestine was a territory under British mandate, it was first necessary to secure British acquiescence in the congress plans. There was much concern at the Foreign Office over the possible effects of the congress on British relations with certain states, and the banning of the congress was briefly entertained. The most worrisome of these considerations, to judge from the official correspondence, concerned Italian apprehensions about the congress. Italian forces had just crushed the last vestiges of Muslim resistance in Libya, and in September 1931 had captured and executed its leader, ᶜUmar al-Mukhtar. A wave of revulsion had swept the Muslim world, and the Italian government greatly feared that it would be made the butt of the resolutions of any such congress. The Foreign Office was given to understand that were this to happen in Jerusalem, Anglo-Italian relations would suffer.[12]

But there were weightier considerations. It was the view of the Colonial Office that any step to ban the congress "might be so much resented [within Palestine] as to precipitate disorder possibly even on the scale of an Arab rebellion."[13] A similar threat was seen by the India Office, which was informed by the Government of India that "Muhammadan feeling [in India] is very unsettled and disturbed," that "causes of discontent to Muslims should be avoided so far as this is possible," and that "the proposal to prohibit the Conference be definitely abandoned."[14] In the face of these reiterated appeals, the Foreign Office relented in its opposition, and the strength of these purely pragmatic arguments was then linked to a principle by a Foreign Office official: "I think there is so much to be said for maintaining our traditional attitude of non-intervention in such quasi-religious matters, that we had better adopt the line the C.O. [Colonial Office] suggest."[15] That line finally prevailed.

The subsequent efforts of British authorities concentrated upon extracting various assurances from Amin al-Husayni, to the effect that issues liable to embarrass Great Britain or disturb public order would not be raised at the congress. Such assurances were readily given by Amin al-Husayni to the new British High Commissioner in Palestine, Sir Arthur Wauchope, who wrote advising that "prohibition of the congress should not be contemplated. It would cause deep resentment and would, in addition, be impossible to enforce, since even if Shawkat Ali and other intending participants were to be refused entrance into Palestine, local adherents of the Mufti would probably meet in [the] Haram area and go through [the] agenda of [the] congress."[16] In any case, "I believe he will carry out his pledges and so he will go far to make me feel that we can work together when his word has once been given in the cause of law and order."[17] The Secretary of State for Colonies replied to a pointed parliamentary question on the congress in this fashion: "As a result of inquiries made of the High Commissioner for Palestine, I am convinced that the Mufti [Amin al-Husayni], who has issued invitations for the congress, realises his responsibilities and is anxious to conduct the congress in such a manner as to cause no embarrassment to His Majesty's or the Palestine administration."[18] At various stages, British authorities thus brought pressure to bear upon the organizers, but there was never any serious doubt that the congress would be permitted.

There were two parties in Palestine who were disquieted by British policy. The Zionists first had hoped that the congress would be banned outright.[19] Once the British decision was made, they concentrated their efforts upon diminishing participation in the congress. Publicly it was declared the policy of the Jewish Agency to maintain "absolute silence with regard to the preparations for this conference. We consider this in the present case the more wholesome, I may say only useful, tactics, and I am glad that we have succeeded in winning the Hebrew press over to a similar attitude. Any interference on our part would have immensely strengthened the Mufti's position both in Palestine and abroad."[20] But the Agency did go so far as to secretly employ a minor

Arab journalist to conduct a covert campaign against the congress in Palestine, Syria, and Egypt, a service for which he was paid. The results of this effort were negligible.[21]

Another opposition group was that faction of Palestinian Arabs personally opposed to Amin al-Husayni. Their challenge was somewhat more effective.[22] They suspected that Amin al-Husayni would use the congress as a tool for self-aggrandizement from which they, his rivals, were likely to suffer most. This faction, headed by the Nashashibi and Khalidi families of Jerusalem, first attacked the congress and its preparatory committee in a manifesto that claimed the entire effort to be unrepresentative of Palestinian Muslims on account of their own exclusion. They then called for a restructuring of the preparatory committee to include them.[23] The Husayni faction's newspaper retorted with a refutation, as did Amin al-Husayni himself, in a counter-manifesto to the Muslim world.[24] As a gesture, the preparatory committee then unilaterally announced that several new members—among them two Nashashibis—would be added to its ranks,[25] an offer that the opposition rejected. A last-minute mediation effort by Shawkat ʿAli and the president of the Young Men's Muslim Association in Egypt, ʿAbd al-Hamid Saʿid, then failed, and the Palestinian opposition opened a relentless campaign against the congress throughout its deliberations.[26] They went so far as to convene a counter-congress, attended by about 1,000 local notables and shaykhs, under the presidency of Raghib al-Nashashibi.[27]

The presence of so vocal an opposition to the congress among so many Muslims just beyond the congress hall not only made for bad press, but split the failed negotiators Shawkat ʿAli and ʿAbd al-Hamid Saʿid from Amin al-Husayni. "The *mufti* and his party would not allow the others to share in the planning of the Conference and the invitations to it," Shawkat ʿAli wrote to a friend. "I protested, and I must say that the opposition behaved nobly; they made it known that they were in sympathy with the Conference and willing to support the university-to-be, but they could not but oppose the *mufti*'s directing the whole affair. If the *mufti* would have followed my advice we should have obtained even better results."[28]

Different results perhaps would have been obtained if Shawkat ʿAli himself had not spoken of the caliphate during the preparatory stages of the congress. To the distress of the Palestinian organizers, he made no secret of his continued allegiance to the deposed Ottoman caliph Abdülmecid, then in exile in France. "Do the Muslims now have a caliph?" he was asked in an interview. "Yes," replied Shawkat ʿAli, "and he is an exile in Nice. In my heart and mind, he remains caliph; I accepted him and swore allegiance to him already in the past, and I cannot go back on what I have done."[29]

The exiled Ottoman pretender apparently believed that the caliphate indeed would figure in the congress agenda, and through his secretary he reminded the Muslim world and the impending congress that the allegiance pledged to him upon his ascension in 1922 was still binding.[30] There were parties who made a connection and immediately feared that Shawkat ᶜAli envisioned a restoration of Abdülmecid to the caliphate at the Jerusalem congress.

Egyptian circles were the first to respond with suspicion, since the Azhar committee which convened the Cairo caliphate congress of 1926 had expressly repudiated Abdülmecid's claim.[31] The Azhar journal reminded Amin al-Husayni of the conclusions of this congress, in which delegates of his own faction had participated.[32] Amin al-Husayni, who hoped for full Egyptian participation and had written King Fuᵓad requesting the dispatch of official delegates,[33] was thus forced to deny to Egyptian authorities that the congress had anything to do with the caliphate, and maintained that rumors to the contrary were fabrications manufactured by the Zionists.[34] Finally, in an attempt to undo the damage Shawkat ᶜAli had done, Amin al-Husayni traveled to Egypt a month before the congress, to reassure the king and other worried parties that the caliphate was not on the agenda.

Shawkat ᶜAli's detailed comments on the role of the projected Muslim university in Jerusalem also had direct repercussions in Egypt. The university, as he imagined it, would have fulfilled many of those tasks coveted by al-Azhar.[35] Naturally the Shaykh al-Azhar, then Muhammad al-Ahmadi al-Zawahiri, was distressed, and told Amin al-Husayni so.[36] Rashid Rida believed that this response was unjustified, and that the proposed new university would not detract from al-Azhar's central role.[37] But the concern drew upon the justified sense of insecurity engendered by the Azhar-sponsored caliphate congress of 1926. This had revealed the frailty of al-Azhar's claim to primacy among Islamic institutions, which no reassurance could alleviate. Amin al-Husayni first retaliated, and his paper published a scathing attack on Zawahiri.[38] But Amin al-Husayni later apologized, and offered his assurances. He declared that the new Muslim university, planned on a modest scale, was intended only to counter the Hebrew University of Jerusalem, and not to challenge al-Azhar.[39]

These assurances, on both the issues of the caliphate and the university, were embodied in a letter from Amin al-Husayni to the Egyptian premier Sidqi Pasha, but King Fuᵓad remained unconvinced of Amin al-Husayni's sincerity.[40] The fact that several members of the Wafd party, rivals to the palace, had accepted their invitations to Jerusalem further concerned Egyptian authorities, who asked that British consular authorities issue visas to these opponents only with the warning that they behave themselves.[41] All this had so unnerving an effect in official Cairo that no official delegation was dispatched from Egypt, although care was taken to covertly finance an unofficial delegation that would defend the royal palace's interests against the Wafd in the congress sessions.

The sons of Husayn of Mecca—ᶜAbdallah, Faysal, and ᶜAli—also required assurances on the question of the caliphate, for they too had an interest here, and while they now advanced no claim, it was certainly undesirable that some act of the congress exclude the possibility of a future claim on their behalf. Husayn himself had died earlier in the year, and Amin al-Husayni had been permitted by the sons to arrange for his burial in Jerusalem near Muhammad ᶜAli. The Egyptian consul in Jerusalem felt certain that part of this understanding was a secret agreement with Amin al-Husayni to secure the caliphate, probably for Faysal of Iraq, at a future congress. For the existence of such a deal there is no other evidence, but Amman and Baghdad certainly did insist on guarantees similar to those given to Cairo, and these Amin al-Husayni made during a trip to Amman.[42]

Saudi suspicions, on the other hand, could not be alleviated. There remained a profound distrust of Shawkat ᶜAli, who had so incensed the organizers of the 1926 Meccan Muslim congress. And there was a general reluctance to see others succeed where ᶜAbd al-ᶜAziz Ibn Saᶜud had not. Saudi annoyance was expressed to British diplomats,[43] and while Ibn Saᶜud pleaded that the congress invitation sent to him by Amin al-Husayni simply had arrived too late, it is certain that a decision was taken against sending a representative to Jerusalem.[44] The Saudis furthermore threatened the Palestinian project by encouraging the circulation of a rumor that the Meccan congress first held in 1926 was about to be reconvened.[45]

Among those consumed by rumors of a resurrected Ottoman caliphate were Turkish diplomats. They were particularly concerned lest Abdülmecid be admitted to Palestine as a participant in the congress, a possibility raised by Shawkat ᶜAli. The deposed caliph resided at Nice, and so the Turkish ambassador to France personally applied to the Quai d'Orsay. Münir Bey explained that a new caliph inevitably would group around him all of the forces hostile to the Turkish republic, and that European powers with Muslim interests, including France, could not afford this permanent menace to their tranquility. The ambassador hoped that the French government would offer new proof to the Turkish government of its amicable disposition, and would abstain from facilitating the departure of the deposed caliph for Palestine. The French government was unreceptive. Münir Bey was told that Abdülmecid had always exhibited reserve and correct demeanor in France; the French government neither could encourage nor impede his ambitions. The Turks were advised to take their problem to the British who, after all, held the mandate for Palestine.[46]

This the Turkish foreign minister did. Tevfik Rüştü [Aras] informed the British ambassador at Ankara that a revived caliphate would constitute a "subversive force," a "focus of intrigue and rebellion" against the British Empire, and an instrument of reaction within Turkey. The Turkish government did not find Abdülmecid alarming; he was a harmless old gentleman. It was the institution, not the figurehead, which disturbed Tevfik Rüştü's government.[47] This time, the Turkish appeal struck a responsive chord. The Colonial Office asked Sir Arthur Wauchope, British High Commissioner in Palestine, whether "it would be practicable to refuse [Abdülmecid's] visa on grounds of public order should an application for one be received."[48] While awaiting Wauchope's reply, an interdepartmental meeting held at the Colonial Office agreed that once Abdülmecid was admitted to Palestine, it would be impossible to get him out, and so it was best to bar his entry. Until Wauchope's reply was received, passport authorities were asked not to issue Palestine visas to the deposed caliph or any of his entourage.[49] The eventual answer from Jerusalem was unequivocal: a visit to Palestine by Abdülmecid was undesirable, and any visa application should be refused.[50] On this recommendation, consular and passport control officers were instructed not to grant the deposed caliph a visa for Palestine without first consulting the Foreign Office.[51] Amin al-Husayni himself was not unaware of the discomfort experienced by the Turks, distraught over the rumor of the Ottoman caliphate's revival, and announced that Abdülmecid would not be invited to the congress.

Having thus fulfilled the desiderata of the Turkish government on this point, Amin al-Husayni attempted to invite an official Turkish delegation, and approached the Turkish consul in Jerusalem with a request that the consulate forward an invitation to Ankara. The consul refused to accept any communication, and Amin al-Husayni was forced to send his message by ordinary post. Tevfik Rüştü did not intend to reply: the mufti held no representative office in Palestine which qualified him to invite the head of a foreign state to send official delegates to an unofficial gathering.[52] At the same time, the Turkish foreign minister had hoped that the congress would be prohibited altogether, and "was distinctly disconcerted and somewhat cross and resentful" upon learning that British authorities intended to permit the gathering. "He thought it an easy matter to prohibit what purported to be a pan-Moslem conference summoned by a minor religious dignitary of a town of secondary sacred importance who had no standing for issuing invitations to Governments, and that the anti-British and anti-Jewish character of the mufti's invitation would have afforded sufficient cause for suppression of the congress."[53] But as the congress was to be held, Turkey would ensure that the Republic was not alone in declining the invitation. This was the decision of Mustafa Kemal himself, who told a French diplomat that the congress was contrary to the principles which he himself had championed, and that he was determined that no independent Muslim country participate.[54] To this end, Turkey approached Iran, Afghanistan, Albania, Egypt, and Iraq, while the Turkish consul in Jerusalem acted personally to defeat the congress. Not only did he decline his invitation to a reception for the delegates; he discouraged the Egyptian consul from attending as well.[55] When the Turkish consul learned that the Turkish flag flew among the flags of Muslim states in the assembly hall of the congress, he successfully insisted upon the banner's removal. Tevfik Rüştü made Turkish policy a matter of public record in his reply to a question from a member of the National Assembly:

It is true that we also received invitations from the promoters of the congress, but republican Turkey can have nothing to do with undertakings of this kind, which aim at holding peoples back on the way of progress, and which have, undeniably, deplorable consequences. We are especially opposed to the use of religion as a political instrument in internal and foreign policy. We are watching developments closely. As long as it shows no near or distant connexion with our national affairs, this undertaking will remain a matter of local importance for the regions represented by those assembled there, but immaterial to us.[56]

Among the results of the Turkish diplomacy of opposition was the reluctance of other states to send official delegations, for fear of harming relations with Turkey. Following the congress, Shakib Arslan wrote a lengthy indictment of Turkish policy toward the congress, in which he focused on the activity of Tevfik Rüştü. To oppose the Jerusalem congress, he wrote, was not the business of a state that considered itself secular; and he pointed to the discrepancy between Turkish participation in the Meccan Muslim congress of 1926, and hostility to the Jerusalem congress of 1931. In Arslan's opinion, Turkish policy was directly responsible for the absence of Muslims from Afghanistan, the Soviet Union, Rumania, Bulgaria, and Greece. In particular he cited Turkish pressure brought to bear on Greece, which prevented the participation of the former Ottoman Şeyhülislam Mustafa Sabri, then in Greek exile.[57]

Thus the Jerusalem congress was reduced to a gathering of unofficial participants, some important and others self-important.[58] From Egypt, Rashid Rida came once again. ʿAbd al-Rahman ʿAzzam, later secretary general of the Arab League, was also in attendance, on behalf of the Wafd. From Syria came Riyad al-Sulh (1894–1951), later prime minister;

Shukri al-Quwwatli (1891–1967), later president; and Saʿid al-Jazaʾiri, grandson of the Algerian resistance leader ʿAbd al-Qadir and president of the Damascus Society for the Defense of the Hijaz Railway.[59] The Tunisian reformist ʿAbd al-ʿAziz al-Thaʿalibi, a participant in two previous Muslim congresses, contributed much to the organization and deliberations of this congress. And for the first time, an important Moroccan delegation attended, led by Muhammad al-Makki al-Nasiri and Muhammad al-Kattani, two leading activists from Rabat and Fez respectively. A large delegation of Bosnian Muslims also participated, and they established ties with Amin al-Husayni which became important during the mufti's subsequent wartime exile (see chapter 13). From India came Sir Muhammad Iqbal (1876–1938), the noted Urdu and Persian poet-philosopher.[60] A number of important expatriates purported to speak for Soviet-ruled Muslim territories. Among them was the Volga Tatar author and journalist Ayaz İshaki [İdilli] (1878–1954), at this time in European exile. İshaki had been a friend of Gasprinskii's.[61] Also present was yet another Tatar activist, Musa Carullah Bigi (1875–1949), who had been invited to the Cairo congress and had participated in the Meccan congress. He had now opted for exile. The organizers made much of the presence of a grandson of the Imam Şamil, Said Şamil, who conducted a vigorous campaign from exile against Soviet rule in the Caucasus.[62] Also in attendance was Ziyaʾ al-Din Tabatabaʾi, former prime minister of Iran then in exile in Switzerland.

Of particular interest to many contemporary observers was the presence of Shaykh Muhammad al-Husayn Al Kashif al-Ghitaʾ (1877/8–1954), the first noted Twelver Shiʿi cleric to participate in a Muslim congress. His father, Shaykh ʿAli Al Kashif al-Ghitaʾ, had been very much a Muslim cosmopolitan in the nineteenth-century tradition, having lived both in Iran and Iraq, and having traveled in the Hijaz, Syria, Turkey, and India.[63] His son had also traveled widely as a youth, spending several years in Syria and Lebanon after a pilgrimage to the Hijaz. During a short stay in Cairo, he lectured at al-Azhar, and impressed a number of noted Egyptian ulama.[64] Shaykh Muhammad al-Husayn first gained fame for his published correspondence with the Maronite man of letters, Amin al-Rayhani,[65] and attracted further attention upon his return to Iraq in 1914, when he joined a group of Shiʿi ulama to fight in the Ottoman jihad. He then embarked upon a period of great literary productivity, and nearly all of his theological works appeared in both Arabic and Persian.[66]

It was this *mujtahid* of standing whom Amin al-Husayni invited to attend the Jerusalem Muslim congress of 1931, and Shaykh Muhammad al-Husayn accepted. That he agreed to participate was almost certainly due to the repeated assurances of Amin al-Husayni that the caliphate would not figure in the agenda of the congress. Shaykh Muhammad al-Husayn's departure for Jerusalem was made the occasion of a celebration in Najaf, and a motorcade of more than thirty cars accompanied him to Baghdad, the first leg of his journey.[67] Once in Jerusalem, he met the many assembled delegates, and led them all in prayer at the opening celebrations in the Aqsa mosque.[68] Shaykh Muhammad al-Husayn also addressed the congress, and later visited Haifa, Jaffa, Nablus, Jenin, Tyre, Sidon, and Beirut.[69] Much was made of the *mujtahid's* presence by the congress organizers and by outside observers.[70] There was no Sunni–Shi'i dialogue on religious questions at Jerusalem, nor were there advances in the moderation of doctrinal differences. But a political understanding was reached that had important implications later, for Shaykh Muhammad al-Husayn remained for many years the most consistent critic of Zionism in Shi'i clerical circles. The pattern of participation at Jerusalem, then, did not differ from that of the earlier congresses. Known figures with reputations that spanned Africa and Asia mingled with obscure local notables. Yet the participants from distant parts were overwhelmed numerically by what were essentially local delegations of Palestinians, Transjordanians, Lebanese, and Syrians. As soon became clear, these were nearly all supportive of Amin al-Husayni's view of how the congress should unfold, and were poised to sweep all opposition aside.

By all reports, the opening of the congress stirrea the participants. Accounts relate that the choice of Muhammad al-Husayn Al Kashif al-Ghita⁾ to lead in prayer had a marked effect on the participants, and another noteworthy innovation at the opening of the congress was a collective oath-taking "to defend the holy places with every bit of strength." These opening exercises seemed auspicious, although even the first evening's ceremonies were marred by a verbal altercation between two Egyptians, one of whom was beaten by the assembled crowd and had to be extricated by the police.[71]

But more serious differences soon surfaced. Once convened, the congress divided into committees, and then split in the plenum along lines anticipated by the controversies that raged in the preparatory period. On the issue of the Muslim holy places of Jerusalem, a broad general consensus obtained. All agreed that some action was necessary to protect these sites from possible encroachments. But a heated debate arose as to whether the defense of the holy places required an end to the British mandate, and Palestinian Arab independence. All recognized the value of the proposed Muslim university, but a dispute erupted over whether Arabic should predominate on campus, which subjects should be taught, and the general spirit which would prevail in the institution. On all of these central issues, Shawkat ᶜAli found himself opposed by a bloc that had drawn closer to Amin al-Husayni as he himself had drawn away during the preparations. He warned the congress of the possible reaction by Great Britain to any broad condemnation of the mandate for Palestine, and insisted that the university be multilingual and teach law and medicine, thus assuring its essentially liberal and cosmopolitan character. These positions perhaps owed less to principled conviction than to a lingering ambition to lead or at least define the themes of the congress.

But Shawkat ᶜAli and his supporters were simply outnumbered. Only two days into the congress, he made these angry remarks to his own small bloc, the leadership of which he shared with fellow mediator ᶜAbd al-Hamid Saᶜid:

> Shame them, gentlemen, by your greatness; the greatness which I expected from Haj Amin eff[endi] I have found in you. You have behaved remarkably. Wallah "my friends" have hurt me. You have shamed them. I know it is very hard for you, but I want more sacrifice from you. I swear by God that the whole Moslem world will be at your feet. I beg you in the name of Islam to sacrifice. You have done greatness—do more. And "those people," they talk in the name of God!
>
> In two days I have heard things which have staggered me. Mad people do not talk like them.[72]

Amin al-Husayni's publicist, Muhammad ᶜAli al-Tahir, wrote at some length of the obstructionist activities of the Shawkat ᶜAli-ᶜAbd al-Hamid Saᶜid faction, which he identified as a bloc (*kutla*) seated separately.[73] But this group was too small, and resolutions were carried by the plenum over their objections. Another faction, also described as a separate bloc by Tahir, disrupted the proceedings on occasion, perhaps in cooperation with an official of the Jewish Agency, but this had little effect on the proceedings.[74] On the whole, the success of Amin al-Husayni in keeping his personal opponents outside the congress hall left little doubt as to the outcome of the deliberations.

The policy which he chose was to make the congress memorable for its militant posturing. This called for delicate maneuvering, for he had drawn up an agenda for approval by the authorities that shunned all issues of possible embarrassment to the mandatory government, and was confined to the theme of Muslim holy places in Jerusalem and their welfare. Framed in narrow religious terms, this was not a controversial or exciting issue; to charge the atmosphere of the congress, the discussion of more overtly political subjects was necessary. This Amin al-Husayni encouraged by never explicitly informing the participants themselves of those assurances which he had given to British authorities. As a result, the deliberations were punctuated by moments of overexuberance, and by speeches and resolutions which went far beyond the scope of the approved agenda.

The impassioned speech by the Egyptian participant ᶜAbd al-Rahman ᶜAzzam, on the subject of Italian "atrocities" in Libya, so contradicted the organizers' prior assurances that the British High Commissioner did not wait for the inevitable Italian representations, but immediately ordered the offender's expulsion from Palestine.[75] ᶜAwni ᶜAbd al-Hadi, a Palestinian Istiqlalist and a pillar of the congress, made a speech on Zionist aspirations considered by the authorities to have exceeded all acceptable bounds, but which went unpunished. A general resolution against colonialism (istiᶜmar) was also carried, and colonialism's various manifestations in different Muslim lands were attacked by many participants in their plenary speeches. When reproached by a distraught British High Commissioner over the course of the deliberations, Amin al-Husayni pleaded that he had been unable to restrain the participants involved, and so had not violated his prior pledge.[76] In fact, he had made no effort to inform even those participants with whom he was closely allied of the assurances which he had given. In public, he was reluctant to admit that he had even discussed such assurances at all. By this tactic, Amin al-Husayni had assured the transformation of the congress from a forum devoted to one issue in its narrowest religious sense, to a general assembly concerned with the political causes of Muslims everywhere.

When the organizers made provisions for a permanent bureau and subsequent congresses (see appendix 7), this was done with a very real anticipation of success, and a desire not to allow the congress to expire on any account. This zeal was conveyed to participants and observers. The optimistic note upon which the final session concluded, in such marked contrast to the disillusionment in which past congresses had disbanded, excited much optimism in H. A. R. Gibb. He attributed the change to the development of an organizational aptitude in Islam. The congress, he wrote, "undoubtedly achieved a very substantial measure of success." Of the proposals, he concluded that "there is every likelihood that they will have practical results of some kind. If this should be so, we may regard it as certain that the congress movement will steadily gain in strength, and that its work for the maintenance of cultural unity will assume decisive importance."[77] "It deserves to rank as an epoch-making conference for this reason," wrote George Antonius, "that for the first time in centuries Moslem effort has at last found its expression in a systematic and business-like organization. . . . I have no hesitation in regarding this as potentially the most important constructive effort among Moslems in recent years, and one which is fraught with far-reaching possibilities."[78]

Less sympathetic observers were less sanguine, but were disturbed nonetheless by the potential of the congress. As a Zionist leader pointed out in internal correspondence, "a conference which is almost a failure may become the starting point of a development which in the future leads to a conference which is a success."[79] British High Commissioner Wauchope felt strongly that "a second Moslem Congress might arouse great excitement in Palestine; that, owing to the position of the Jews in Palestine, it is an unsuitable country in which to hold further Moslem Congresses." But he was "loath to suggest at this moment that a decision should now be taken to prohibit the holding of any Moslem Congress in the future," on account of "legal difficulties" and Muslim opinion.[80] In the view of the French consul in Jerusalem, "a dangerous instrument of propaganda and agitation has been put in Hadj Amin's hands which, if he uses it skillfully, could complicate the task of those powers in authority in Muslim lands."[81]

Early in the congress, the question of an executive committee was raised.[82] Shawkat ᶜAli argued for a large committee of fifty members from forty-one Muslim regions. India would be entitled to three members; Turkey, Iran, Afghanistan, Egypt, China, Java, and Sumatra would each have two members on the committee; and the rest would have one. These members would be selected not by the congress then assembled but by the regions which they were to represent. And this division would also serve as the basis of voting in future congresses. Precisely such a method had been instituted, at least formally, at the Meccan congress of 1926, where votes were reserved even for territories from which no participants were in attendance.

But the idea did not carry at Jerusalem six years later. "Let us not grasp at fantasies," retorted one participant. ᶜAbd al-Rahman ᶜAzzam argued that Shawkat ᶜAli's proposal demanded a measure of local organization that was exceptional in the Muslim world:

> We ask for a logical, democratic way to give the congress the right to elect the executive committee. If some of you fear that the congress will fall under a clique of people, this will never happen. We will be obedient and we will represent freedom. No one will tyrannize another. The election of the committee is the prerogative of the congress. Our Indian brethren are right in that, in their country, there is an organized Islamic movement, and we hope it will become so in our country. [But] they speak for their country, whereas we are factions and parties, and are unable to agree on one view and send representatives to the executive committee.[83]

Ziyaᵓ al-Din Tabatabaᵓi argued in his turn that a large executive committee opposed all conventional norms of congresses and assemblies. A smaller administrative arm for the congress would be far more efficient, and he argued for a maximum of five members. In the end, the congress adopted a compromise figure of twenty-five, all of whom were elected by the participants in a secret ballot.[84] Few of those elected had any intention of immersing themselves in the work of the congress after its adjournment, so that a position on the executive committee became an honorary distinction. The real work was left to a seven-man permanent bureau with wide powers, which was to function in Jerusalem between congresses. Shawkat ᶜAli responded to this course of events by resigning the seat to which he was elected on the executive committee:

> During the conference I tried to counteract the disagreement, when it appeared, but I did not succeed, so one of the leading Egyptians [ᶜAbd al-Hamid Saᶜid] was kept out of the Standing Committee that is to carry into practice the resolutions of the conference. Only those whom the majority wished were elected to the Committee. I myself was elected nearly unanimously, but when I saw how things were, I said I wanted to be an ordinary member of the Conference only.—This is rather sad, but don't lose heart; the good people in Palestine understand this, and later on our efforts will no doubt bring about a reconciliation. We are sure of success and victory, but the leaders must understand that they are to sacrifice. Next summer I shall return to Palestine, then we shall try again to bring about peace.[85]

Shawkat ᶜAli's resignation in protest signaled his break with the congress and its passage completely into the hands of his opponents. The participants furthermore agreed that Amin al-Husayni, as president of the congress in session, would also be president of the executive committee, and that future congresses would meet at two-year intervals. There had been a debate on all of these issues. Some were afraid of losing momentum during an interregnum of two years, and Shawkat ᶜAli strongly favored not only an annual congress, but its meeting in India the following year. But ᶜAbd al-ᶜAziz al-Thaᶜalibi pointed out that those participants who came from afar could not bear the repeated expense, and the resolutions were too ambitious for execution in one year. Rashid Rida pointed out that the congress had been convened specifically in defense of Palestine, and so should always be held in Jerusalem. In the end, it was decided to meet every two years, and to recognize Jerusalem as the seat of the congress.[86]

The members of the executive committee, on the day after the congress and before dispersing, elected a series of officers to the permanent bureau. They chose as secretary general the former prime minister of Iran, Ziyaᵓ al-Din Tabatabaᵓi, who had been among the more active participants at the congress. Ziyaᵓ al-Din was famous for his crucial role in the ascent of Riza Shah.[87] At that time, he was prime minister, but was later exiled, took up residence in Geneva, and befriended Amin al-

Husayni, Shakib Arslan, and other activists. An able organizer, he was urged by many delegates to supervise the permanent secretariat of the congress. Ziyaᵓ al-Din finally agreed, and upon his shoulders fell the burden of administration and fundraising after the close of the congress.[88] It was theorized by some that his selection was made in the hope that Iran might be drawn into the congress in the future. But in Iran, Ziyaᵓ al-Din had ceased to count for much, according to an American observer:

> After being Prime Minister for a few months he was forced to leave the country and had long since been almost forgotten. It is astonishing, in this land of bazaar rumours, how little is known by usually well informed persons as to his subsequent movements. "He appears to have lived by his pen, principally in Scandinavia" is about all the Legation has been able to ascertain through casual informal inquiry.[89]

To dispel any doubt, *Iran* and other Iranian newspapers denied the rumor that Tabatabaᵓi represented his country at the Jerusalem congress, and affirmed that the government had not appointed any representative.[90] In fact, Ziyaᵓ al-Din then played an elusive role in Muslim émigré circles in Europe that has yet to be clarified. Shakib Arslan relates that Ziyaᵓ al-Din was in fact the instrument of the ex-Khedive ᶜAbbas Hilmi, who had promised to finance a Muslim information center in Geneva under Ziyaᵓ al-Din's directorship. According to Shakib, the Geneva plan fell through when ᶜAbbas Hilmi decided that the idea would be opposed by Mustafa Kemal, who had promised the Syrian throne to the ex-Khedive.[91]

But another more complex Geneva plan tied ᶜAbbas Hilmi to Tabatabaᵓi. In November 1931, the ex-Khedive announced the creation in Geneva of an Alliance Musulmane Internationale. The charter of this organization dictated that it would compete directly with the Jerusalem congress. The Alliance, according to this document, would organize a world Muslim congress every three years, attended by a hierarchy of dues-paying and honorary members. From this congress, too, would emerge a supreme council and an executive committee.[92] To this initiative he had attracted no organizer of stature. The space left for "founding members" in his own copy of the charter was blank. Rashid Rida described what was then learned about this initiative:

> It was rumoured that H. E. Prince ᶜAbbas Hilmi Pasha, former Khedive of Egypt, had created a society in Geneva called the Alliance Musulmane, which would hold periodic Muslim congresses. Then we learned that he had made Sayyid Ziyaᵓ al-Din Tabatabaᵓi secretary general of this organization. Now the executive committee of the first General Muslim Congress [in Jerusalem] also had chosen this Tabatabaᵓi to be their sec-

retary general, and he hesitated to accept the post. He travelled to Europe, promising the president of the congress [Amin al-Husayni] that he would write to him as to whether or not he would accept. When it became clear that he worked for ᶜAbbas Hilmi, his acceptance became problematic. He nonetheless wrote to Amin al-Husayni accepting, and asked Amin al-Husayni to consult with the other members of the executive committee in this matter. From what we understand of the Alliance Musulmane, he will have to work to annex the executive committee of the Jerusalem congress to the European Alliance Musulmane, and entrust the matter of a second congress to the latter, to expand the Alliance's breadth, on account of the wealth of the Alliance and the freedom that prevails at the site of its headquarters [Geneva]. This contradicts an official decision of the executive committee of the congress, and the president of the first congress [Amin al-Husayni] cannot decide the issue alone.

Rashid Rida obviously disapproved, claiming that Tabatabaᵓi could not serve both these masters at once, nor could he absorb one organization into the other.[93]

Two possibilities thus suggest themselves. Ziyaᵓ al-Din may have continued his close relationship with ᶜAbbas Hilmi even after accepting his new position, with the ultimate intention of making the Jerusalem congress an avenue for the ex-Khedive's return to Muslim politics. Or perhaps he was offered the office of secretary general as an inducement to abandon the Geneva congress plan which he had drawn up with ᶜAbbas Hilmi, and which was liable to compete with the Jerusalem congress. Following the adjournment of the congress, Ziyaᵓ al-Din returned to Geneva to wrap up his affairs and arrange to move his family. According to an intelligence source, his return to Palestine was "delayed for various reasons, one of which was the proposed formation at Geneva of the International Islamic Association. The policy of the proposed Association in relation to the Islamic Congress of Jerusalem was not definitely decided and it was suggested that the persons who were interested in the Association had agreed to dispense with the services of Dia el Din in order to secure through him control of the Islamic Congress. It, however, appears that the proposed Association at Geneva failed to materialize."[94]

What is certain is that he took to his office with an unrestrained zeal.[95] He immediately drew up a fourteen-point list of aims and procedures for the permanent bureau.[96] The resolutions of the congress on the Hijaz railway, and protests against Jewish encroachments on Muslim holy places, Italian atrocities in Libya, and the Berber dahir, were all formally conveyed to the mandatory power, various governments, and the League of Nations.[97] The formation of branch committees within and beyond Palestine proceeded apace. Ziyaᵓ al-Din completed a detailed set of regulations for these branches, outlining the dues structure and the division of revenues between the central treasury and the branches.[98] Nearly all the branches were located in Palestine, Transjordan, and Syria, and in a speech to an assembly of representatives of local branches, Ziya⊃ al-Din set a target of 50,000 members for Palestine.[99]

By late 1932, however, the crucial issue had become one of money, for Ziya⊃ al-Din wished to show real progress in the construction of the Muslim university before the next congress, scheduled for 1933. The development of the three faculties planned by Ziya⊃ al-Din—theology and religious law, medicine and pharmacy, and engineering—required substantial sums for the hiring of faculty, the construction of a building, and the purchase of equipment.[100] Ziya⊃ al-Din hoped to raise the starting expenses within Palestine, and the figure he gave in an open appeal was £P5,000.[101] Amin al-Husayni explained to an American visitor that £P4,000 per annum would be raised by subscriptions, and a slightly larger sum, the annual revenue of a valuable *waqf* building, would be dedicated in perpetuity to the university.[102] An appeal was simultaneously issued to Muslim kings, amirs, and influential persons.[103]

But it proved difficult to raise money strictly through postal appeals, so Amin al-Husayni, Ziya⊃ al-Din, and treasurer Muhammad ᶜAli ᶜAlluba planned a fund-raising tour to Iraq and India. The party set out in May 1933 for Iraq, where they remained for two weeks, and visited the Shiᶜi shrine cities as the guests of Muhammad al-Husayn Al Kashif al-Ghita⊃.[104] The delegation then proceeded to India. The outcome of this trip, both financial and political, was unsatisfactory. Antonius wrote that no announcement was made concerning the sums collected, "but I have been given privately to understand that they fell far short of expectations."[105]

Unable to carry forth the university plan, the permanent bureau began gradually to sink into inactivity. A respite was offered by the outbreak of war between Ibn Saᶜud and the Imam Yahya of Yemen, and this opportunity was seized to send a mediation delegation to Arabia consisting of Amin al-Husayni, Muhammad ᶜAli ᶜAlluba, and Shakib Arslan. For a time, the mission captured headlines, and was not without effect. But in settling that dispute, a different breach widened, this time between Amin al-Husayni and Muhammad ᶜAli ᶜAlluba. ᶜAlluba, on his return to Egypt, attempted to have the permanent secretariat transferred to Cairo, a move which Amin al-Husayni resisted successfully.[106] This case for moving the headquarters to some site outside of Palestine, and hence away from Amin al-Husayni, was enhanced by the failure of negotiations between Amin al-Husayni and his Palestinian opposition over the delayed second congress. Many of those from beyond Palestine who participated in the first congress urged Amin al-Husayni to arrive at some kind of accord, so that a second congress would not be accompanied again by a counter-congress of his own opponents across town. Shawkat ᶜAli briefly tried his hand as mediator in these negotiations in 1933, and two Syrians made a similar attempt in early 1935.[107] Later that year the congress had virtually ceased to function, and Ziyaᵓ al-Din again spent the better part of his time in Europe.[108] Amin al-Husayni continued to employ his title of congress president on occasion, and did so in 1936 when issuing a *fatwa* declaring the ᶜAlawis of Syria to be true Muslims.[109] But before the year was out, an Arab rebellion had spread throughout Palestine, and a Jerusalem Muslim congress would never again be convened in Palestine under mandate.

Amin al-Husayni may have considered the reconvening of the congress in Mecca once it was no longer possible to do so in Jerusalem, and his pilgrimage planned for February 1937 gave rise to much talk about the possibility. But Ibn Saᶜud, consistent with his policy, informed Amin al-Husayni that no such congress could be permitted.[110] Amin al-Husayni was forced to declare that his visit was "solely for religious purposes" and that no congress would take place.[111] When a number of pilgrims met informally to discuss various issues, Amin al-Husayni addressed them only reluctantly, and was careful to avoid all political references, never once mentioning even Palestine.[112]

Amin al-Husayni later settled upon Berlin as his chosen place of exile, and he passed the war years there (see chapter 13). Much of his time was spent attempting to convince the German Foreign Office that he exercised greater influence than other Arab exiles in Berlin, leading him to make this assertion:

> There is a supranational association, the "Muslim Congress," under his—the Grand Mufti's—leadership. Delegates of all Muslim countries belong to this congress. The congress, he said, still exists and functions today. The political possibilities for Germany which might stem from cooperation with the congress are, he says, undoubtedly significant. The Grand Mufti repeatedly expressed his regret that the existing possibilities for working together are not being fully exploited. He and his collaborators could do much more for the German cause if closer cooperation could exist between the German authorities and himself.[113]

Like Kawakibi's fiction, the Jerusalem congress finally became a figment of one man's imagination.

TWELVE

SWISS EXILE

The European Muslim Congress,
1935

S INCE THE late nineteenth century, Muslim political activists had
worked to defend their causes in European capitals. Afghani's publication of al-ʿUrwa al-wuthqa in Paris, and his diplomatic forays in London,
had set a personal precedent. In later years, émigrés and converts formed
societies which gathered Muslims from very different parts, and promoted a cosmopolitan sense of Muslim solidarity. The European Muslim
Congress, held in Geneva in September 1935, represented a first attempt
to gather these activists from throughout the continent under one roof.
A circle around the Geneva-based Lebanese émigré Shakib Arslan (1869–
1946) promoted and organized the event. In addition to his literary
activities, Arslan had been involved in past congress initiatives, but
never before had played a leading role.

The organization of the congress proved a severe test of Arslan's
influence. Preparations took two years, and the congress was postponed
twice. There were impediments created by the general lack of coordi-
nation among the various societies and communities in Europe, but
Arslan's own controversial politics also were at issue. When the congress
finally met, not all of these obstacles had been overcome, diminishing
participation. The deliberations were for the most part of an informative
nature, but Arslan allowed the occasional mention of political causes
which enjoyed his support. These intrusions had divisive effects and
exposed the congress to criticism from Arslan's numerous personal opponents. Although it was resolved that the congress meet annually, this
detrimental controversy and the decline of Geneva as a center of Muslim
activism assured that the congress did not meet again.

Important details concerning early preparations for the congress appeared in Arslan's published letters to Rashid Rida, but as Rida died
shortly before the congress met, this correspondence includes nothing
about the deliberations.[1] The principal published accounts of the congress were written by the organizers and participants themselves. Arslan's own periodical, La Nation arabe, carried an authorized account of

the deliberations, as did the émigré newspaper *La Tribune d'Orient* of Geneva.[2] The Damascus newspaper *al-Ayyam* happened to have a correspondent in Geneva, and it alone offered a first-hand report in a Muslim language. These accounts inspired two brief reports which appeared in contemporary orientalist journals.[3] The ubiquitous Iqbal ᶜAli Shah, a participant, left an account which inevitably emphasized his own contribution, but also mentioned some otherwise unreported dissensions within the congress.[4] Swiss official files shed some further light on the preparations, but have yet to illuminate the deliberations.[5] The voluminous but inaccessible private papers of Arslan, in family possession, are likely one day to answer outstanding questions about the Geneva congress, and the several earlier congresses which involved Arslan.

The initiative for a European Muslim congress first belonged to Mahmud Salim, an Egyptian journalist and lawyer long resident in Paris. He had been among the lesser participants in the 1931 Jerusalem Muslim congress, where the idea of a European Muslim congress was first mooted. The concept fired his imagination. The following year, Mahmud Salim embarked on a journey which took him through the Middle East and Europe to stir Muslim interest in the idea, and he then published a pamphlet on the subject. The pamphlet indicated that he had won the support of Amin al-Husayni and Ziyaᵓ al-Din Tabatabaᵓi, and Salim began to formulate detailed plans in frequent séances with the members of a Paris-based society, La Fraternité Musulmane. This circle declared the projected European Muslim congress an emanation of the earlier Jerusalem Muslim congress, a formal claim advanced to legitimize the scheme. But in practice, this was an independent initiative in its own right.[6]

Mahmud Salim's group envisioned the aims of the projected congress to be intellectual, social, and educational. According to one of Salim's Paris collaborators, "questions of current politics, which often lead to acerbic conflicts without palpable results, will be left aside."[7] The Paris salon around Salim also resolved that the congress should be open to all interested participants: "All Muslims living in Europe will be invited to participate, whether they are of European nationality, or are foreigners residing on this continent: industrialists, men of commerce, professors, students, officials, diplomats, artists, scholars, artisans—in a word, people of intellect from every walk of life." According to this plan, the congress was to be convened in Geneva the following August.[8] There was little to excite controversy in this preliminary statement of aims. But with their choice of Geneva, the Paris group appealed to Shakib

Arslan for support. Since the end of the war, Arslan had waged a campaign to gain the endorsement of enlightened world opinion for Muslim and Arab claims to independence. At the same time, Arslan corresponded extensively with noted Muslim activists such as Rashid Rida and Amin al-Husyani, who involved him in their politics. Around Arslan in Geneva revolved a great deal of Muslim political activity, for, like Afghani, whose circle he had attended many years earlier in Istanbul, Arslan combined an undeniable charisma with a certain capacity for dissimulation and intrigue.[9]

Now Mahmud Salim needed Arslan's broad network of affiliations. Salim's own influence was limited, and he was so unlikely a source for so ambitious an initiative that many assumed that the ex-Khedive ʿAbbas Hilmi stood behind his endeavors.[10] The suspicion was understandable, for the ex-Khedive only recently had sought to convene his own Muslim congress in Geneva (see previous chapter). But it was to Shakib Arslan that Salim finally turned for support when he found his own efforts inadequate. Arslan wrote to Rashid Rida relating that

> Mahmud Bey Salim originated this idea, and published a pamphlet about it. He came to Geneva and spoke with us, and we had no objection. But we indicated to him that he should proceed slowly and not rush into convening the congress, because a Muslim congress held in Europe must be worthy of the honor of Islam. We did not want it to be a simple meeting, where words are exchanged and the participants disagree.

Arslan and his associates insisted that Salim postpone the congress until 1934, and they undertook to raise the £300 to £400 which they deemed necessary for funding a respectable congress. Mahmud Salim expressed his satisfaction with this decision.[11] "I had no intention of presiding over this congress because of my many other preoccupations," wrote Arslan, "but Mahmud Salim and other friends convinced me, despite myself, to accept the presidency."[12] Now the initiative belonged to Arslan, a political activist and polemicist.

The promotion of the congress fell to a Geneva committee over which Arslan presided, and for which his Syrian colleague Ihsan al-Jabiri acted as treasurer. By this time, Ziyaʾ al-Din Tabatabaʾi, secretary general of the Jerusalem congress, had ceased to fill his functions in Jerusalem and had returned to Geneva. Arslan made him secretary general of the Geneva preparatory committee, and so established a formal link of continuity with the Jerusalem congress. Ihsan Sami Haqqi, a Palestinian journalist appointed assistant secretary general, laid most of the groundwork for the congress. Another key member of the committee from its inception was ʿAli al-Ghayati, an Egyptian émigré in Geneva since 1910, and editor of *La Tribune d'Orient*. Ghayati's ostensible aim in his career had been to defend the rights of Eastern peoples at the seat of the League of Nations, and the rallying of his established journal to the side of the congress put an additional means of propagation at the disposal of the preparatory committee.[13] Also on the committee was Zaki ᶜAli, an Egyptian physician resident in Geneva who served as Arslan's secretary, and who was close to the ex-Khedive.[14] The congress was scheduled for September 1934, and the preparatory committee began to meet and plan a policy for invitations. They determined that the event was to gather not only notables from the indigenous Muslim minorities of Europe, but also Muslim political activists in European exile.

At an early stage, the organizers even hoped that the representatives of Muslim governments to the League of Nations would attend, but only one Muslim government showed any interest in the plan. During a stopover in Turkey, Mahmud Salim put his proposal to Receb Bey [Peker] (1880–1950), secretary general of the ruling Republican People's Party, who approved the congress idea provided that the caliphate did not figure in the agenda.[15] After the initiative passed to Arslan's hands, the Turkish government took an even greater interest in the congress. During a Geneva banquet, Arslan was approached by Cemal Husni, Turkish ambassador to Switzerland, and Necmeddin Sadak, a newspaper editor, deputy from Sivas, and later foreign minister.

> Then [the Turkish ambassador] asked me whether I intended to invite Turkey. I said no. He asked why not; were not the province of Edirne and even Istanbul part of Europe? I told him that we had seen Turkey refrain from involvement in Islamic questions. But we attach importance to this congress from the social aspect, said Necmeddin Sadak.
> He took my hand and reiterated this. I told him amicably but to the point: In a word, we have excluded you from our activities.[16]

The Turkish ambassador did not relent. He arranged to meet with Ihsan al-Jabiri, insisted that Turkey receive an invitation, and assured Jabiri that the Muslims of Edirne would be permitted by the Turkish government to send representatives. Jabiri promised the Turkish ambassador that an invitation would be sent, explaining to Arslan that no harm had been done: If the Turks came, fine; if not, the loss was their own. But Arslan remained adamant: "It is impossible for me to support the sending of an invitation card to the Ankara government. We can send an invitation card to the mufti of Edirne; he is free to send a delegation, or not to send one." In justifying his position, Arslan cited the campaign waged by the Turkish government against the 1931 Jerusalem Muslim congress, a campaign which La Nation arabe had criticized (see previous chapter). The Geneva congress was a direct sequel to that earlier gathering; how did Turkey now dare to solicit an invitation?[17] Rashid Rida agreed, adding that there was no point in inviting the mufti of Edirne either.[18]

Arslan chose instead to devote his efforts to securing the participation of unofficial delegations, and began with a round of personal diplomacy among Balkan Muslims. He spent much of the winter of 1933–34 in Yugoslavia as the guest of the organized Bosnian Muslim community, strengthening ties established during the 1931 Jerusalem congress and spreading word of the forthcoming Geneva congress.

But in April 1934, he joined the Jerusalem congress mission to mediate in the war between Saudi Arabia and Yemen, and did not return to Geneva until September, the month for which the congress had been scheduled. Only upon Arslan's return did he begin to issue proper invitations. Thus, Great Britain's leading Muslim and president of the British Muslim Association, Lord Headley (1855–1935), received Arslan's telegraphed invitation only a week before the scheduled opening of the congress. Without time to weigh his reply, he turned for advice to officials in the Foreign and India Offices, who persuaded him not to attend.[19] With so little advance notice, most of the invited participants must have sent their regrets, and the congress was postponed again. A short time later, Arslan rescheduled the event for September 1935, to coincide with the regular meeting of the League of Nations Assembly. The preparatory committee, chastened by failure, planned its moves more deliberately in a campaign to assure broad participation in the congress.

The first challenge was posed by Swiss authorities, who hitherto had shown little interest in the projected congress. In March 1935, congress organizer Ihsan Sami Haqqi requested a *permis de séjour* for one year to enable him to reside in Geneva. Swiss federal authorities thought that this provided a rare opportunity to secure detailed information on the congress plans, and Haqqi Bey was summoned before the police in Geneva to make a statement.[20] There he drew a wholly innocuous sketch of the purposes of the congress, which he defined as the reform of Muslim education in Europe. The congress had no political aim, and while some of the leading organizers were known for their political activism, the congress itself would not take up their causes.[21] In view of this forswearing of politics, and the estimate of the Swiss Division of Foreign Affairs that the congress would not have important political repercussions, Haqqi Bey was granted his *permis de séjour*. An attached condition stipulated that he abstain from all political activity which might disturb Swiss relations with other states.[22]

Arslan had an identical condition attached to his *permis de séjour*, and in light of Haqqi Bey's police interrogation, Arslan now thought it prudent to request official authorization for the congress. "Political discussions are excluded from our program," he emphasized,[23] and the Swiss Division of Foreign Affairs concluded that

we do not have sufficient grounds for barring the convening of the European Muslim Congress in Switzerland. It would be preferable that deliberations of this sort not coincide with the regular session of the League of Nations Assembly, but in Chekib Arslan's letter addressed to Genevan authorities, he expressly declared that "political discussions are excluded" from the program of this congress. We do not wish to cast doubt on the value of a commitment assumed spontaneously by the organizers.[24]

So long as there were no "tempestuous political demonstrations" during the congress, there was no reason to ban it, a formal reservation conveyed to Arslan.[25] And so Arslan, wary lest he be accused of abusing Swiss hospitality, announced repeatedly in public that the congress had no political purpose, although he and his associates all were known for their committed political activism. The congress proceedings soon would test Arslan's undertaking.

A second challenge cast a lengthier shadow over the preparatory work. Arslan had known Mussolini personally since 1922, when the Italian dictator was still editor-in-chief of the party newspaper *Popolo d'Italia.* According to Arslan,

Mussolini wrote articles in the *Popolo d'Italia* which demanded Syrian independence with such ardor as we had never seen in any European. A short time later, Mussolini became head of state, and—strange thing for a revolutionary turned head of state—did not change his attitude toward our cause. The Italian delegation at the League of Nations always demanded the abolition of British and French mandates over Iraq, Palestine, Syria and Lebanon, and supported the complete independence of those countries.[26]

Arslan had withdrawn his hand of friendship when Italian forces ruthlessly suppressed a movement of Muslim resistance in Libya in 1931. The conduct of this military campaign had elicited condemnations of Italian policy from the Jerusalem Muslim congress, and from Arslan himself on the pages of *La Nation arabe.* But on the very eve of the congress came purported evidence that Arslan's always discreet Italian liaison had been renewed. In April 1935, two Palestinian Arab newspapers reproduced what appeared to be a damaging letter sent by Arslan to Amin al-Husayni, president of the Jerusalem Muslim congress. In it, Arslan wrote that he was "satisfied with the last parley and with the assurances which Mussolini has given personally. I am confident that Italy will not treat us as England and France have treated us." In the purported letter, Arslan said that he would open a campaign in favor

of Italy on the pages of *La Nation arabe*, and asked Amin al-Husayni to
adopt a similar policy. Arslan denied authorship of the published letter,
and Amin al-Husayni's camp claimed that it had been forged by their
Palestinian Arab opponents.[27]

But to his correspondent Rashid Rida, Arslan admitted that he had
come to a renewed understanding with Mussolini during a recent visit
to Rome. "I will not become an Italian propagandist, and Mussolini will
not ask me to become one," but Arslan had made certain "demands of
Mussolini concerning Syria, Palestine, and Tripolitania, and I wrote
things about Eritrea which would gladden Mussolini, so that he would
meet my demands. After all, if we only said what we had been saying
before, then he doubtless never would act [on our behalf]. But he has
already fulfilled part, and I am asking him to fulfill the rest."[28] By his
understanding with the Duce, Arslan would overlook aspects of Italian
colonization in Libya, and apologize for Italian policies in Eritrea, while
Mussolini would support the independence of the far more numerous
Muslim peoples under French and British rule. Arslan believed without
doubt that he thus served the best interests of his cause as a whole.
Yet the suspicion inevitably gained ground that the European Muslim
Congress was meant to serve Italian political interests, an insinuation
which dogged the congress and warded off potential participants.[29]

In the end, about sixty invited participants did arrive in Geneva. A
minority were Muslim nationals of European states, while most were
Muslims from predominantly Muslim countries then residing in Europe.
The indigenous Muslim communities of Eastern and Southeastern Europe met few of the organizers' expectations. The Muslim population
of Yugoslavia, the continent's largest, was represented by an acknowledged leader, Salim Muftic, the president of the Council of Ulama seated
at Sarajevo. Muftic had attended the Jerusalem congress four years
earlier, and headed a large delegation to the Geneva sequel. Also in
attendance was Huszein Hilmi Durics (1889–1940), a Bosnian residing
in Hungary who for some years had been involved in an attempt to
construct a mosque in Budapest. He had visited Amin al-Husayni in
Palestine the previous year, and for several years had been in close
correspondence with Arslan. Durics had secured informal recognition
as mufti of Budapest from the city's Bosnian residents.[30] One of the
most articulate participants was the mufti of Poland, Jakub Szynkiewicz,
who had taken his doctorate in old Turkish syntax, and had attended
the Cairo caliphate congress in 1926. He, too, was involved in a plan
to build a mosque, in Warsaw.[31] But there were no noteworthy participants from the sizable Muslim communities of Albania, Bulgaria, Ro-
mania, and Greece.[32]

None of the participants could speak with authority on behalf of the heterogeneous and largely émigré Muslim populations of Western Europe. The venerable Lord Headley had died earlier in the year, and the organized British Muslim community was represented by Sir Hubert Omar Stewart Rankin, a Scot who did not enjoy a comparable reputation. France's Muslim population, swollen by waves of proletarian immigration from North Africa, was represented by Misali al-Hajj, an Algerian activist and orator based in Paris, and the commanding spirit behind the maximalist society Etoile Nord-Africaine. It was Arslan who led Misali to discard his earlier Communist sympathies, and to embrace Muslim pan-nationalist precepts. The relationship between the two men was one of master to disciple.[33] Most of the other participants from Western Europe attended in their private capacities or on behalf of minor associations.

One participant was ready to claim that the conferees were "fully representative" and "fully accredited" by nine million Muslims in Europe.[34] But a Muslim member of the League of Nations secretariat judged the delegates "distinctly third-rate."[35] The truth fell somewhere between these extremes, and this uneven turnout was due principally to the suspicions attached to Arslan's political affinities among Muslims who thought him driven by disguised motives. These persons for the most part simply stayed away from the congress, so setting the stage for Arslan's unchallenged reign throughout its sessions. Only in one instance did any other impediment discourage participants. Some of the members of Misali al-Hajj's party in Paris complained that they had been detained en route by French police in the border town of Bellegarde for thirty hours. Although they had protested to the chief of police that the congress was of an exclusively religious character, he held the opinion that "when Muslims meet to speak about religion, they occupy themselves instead with politics." Aspiring participants from Lyon were returned home under escort; those from Paris were admonished to turn back, but managed to board a train for Annemasse, and there crossed the Swiss border.[36]

"As I entered the lofty hall," wrote one participant, "the Imam of the Paris Mosque was already reciting the verses of the Quran at the opening of the meeting."[37] Thereafter the deliberations were punctuated by theatrical demonstrations which served to charge the atmosphere in the Geneva hotel where the participants had gathered. Arslan himself later led his guests in Friday congregational prayer, an act of conscious ecumenical significance in view of his Druze origin. In another dramatic episode, the director of the Istituto Superiore Orientale di Napoli, Count Bernardo Barbiellini Amidei, appeared before the congress to ask that it formally recognize his adherence to Islam. At the demand of Jakub Szynkiewicz, he pronounced the profession of faith (shahada) three times before congress participants who had risen as one to their feet, and chose for himself an Arabic name.[38] Some time also was consumed in the practical arrangement of an internal regime for the duration of the sessions. Arslan was acclaimed president without debate. With the help of his fellow organizers, named in corpore to a permanent committee, he dictated the agenda of the congress and determined rudimentary rules of procedure.

But that matter which occupied the far larger part of the proceedings concerned the conditions which prevailed in various Muslim communities throughout Europe. This provided the theme for the numerous informative speeches which filled the agenda. The representatives of the indigenous East and Southeast European Muslim communities were lavish in their praise of their governments, under which they claimed to have prospered. In contrast, the remarks of some participants from the émigré communities of Western Europe evidenced that the rule of their host countries over their coreligionists had left them embittered. There were even accounts which had émigré and indigenous Muslim spokesmen at odds. According to one participant, discussion after the opening prayer "assumed a high degree of passionate exposition on the part of certain Algerians and Palestinians resident in Europe, and in spite of the earnest pleadings of the Bosnian delegation for a calmer atmosphere, the discussion got more and more heated."[39]

But Arslan carefully controlled the political signals which emanated from the sessions. In his inaugural speech, he stressed that the aims of the congress were not political, and thanked the Swiss and Genevan authorities for their hospitality, which they had made contingent upon his avoidance of political controversy. Later he maintained that "every time an orator attempted to deviate even slightly from the line which we ourselves had drawn, he was called to order."[40] Yet from the outset, Arslan held that the issue of Zionist settlement in Palestine involved the fate of Muslim holy places. This was properly speaking a religious question and so had a place in the deliberations.

When Ihsan al-Jabiri mounted the podium to speak on Palestine, he prefaced his address with this caveat: "I am not dealing with a colonial problem. I make no allusion, favorable or detrimental, to the conquering powers who have created this deplorable situation. I touch only upon a religious question, vital to Islam." This ritual pronouncement accomplished, Jabiri then proceeded to deliver a severe indictment of Jewish settlement and British policy in Palestine.[41] His address proved to be the centerpiece of the deliberations. The participants unanimously decided to communicate their opposition to the creation of a Jewish national home to the League of Nations and the British government, stressing in their resolutions that the question of Palestine, while "purely a political one for both the Jews and the mandatory power, is a strictly religious one from the Muslim point of view."[42] Through reiteration of this problematic distinction, Arslan was able to maintain, if need be, that he had not violated his assurances to Swiss authorities. At the same time, he imagined that the Swiss would show less indulgence toward a similar assault on French policy in North Africa and Syria, and none was made. All that Misali al-Hajj could do in his public remarks was to draw a dismal picture of the state of Algerian workers in France.[43]

It was obvious that any reference made to Italian colonial policy during the congress would draw particular attention, since Arslan's detractors had labeled him an apologist for Mussolini's imperial quest. On the grounds that the congress excluded political questions, Arslan refused two intentionally provocative appeals demanding that the congress condemn Italian designs against Ethiopia, which Italian forces were to invade the following month. Were the congress to have taken a stand on this issue, he later wrote, then would it not have had a duty to protest the British occupation of Egypt and the Sudan, and French policy in Morocco, Algeria, Tunisia, and Syria?[44]

Yet the proceedings left one foreign diplomat with the distinct impression that the organizers had gone still further, and sought "to present Italy to the delegates in a favorable light."[45] A still stronger impression was left by an address delivered in Arabic to the congress by the Italian orientalist Laura Veccia Vaglieri. Arslan later explained that she had come to assist Count Barbiellini, and so although she was not a Muslim, she had been allowed to attend the sessions.[46] She also had been shown special consideration because she was then writing a book which supposedly bore on questions raised during the congress. But according to a British memorandum, Veccia Vaglieri wrote reports on each day's proceedings and passed them to the Italian consul general in Geneva.[47]

Although Count Barbiellini departed from the congress early, she remained in attendance, and even addressed the congress on the beneficial reforms instituted by Italy in its Muslim possessions. Arslan responded in turn by welcoming those reforms, with a single reservation concerning the confiscation of certain Muslim lands in Tripolitania.[48] Nothing could have been further from the spirit of the 1931 Jerusalem Muslim congress, during which one speaker had delivered so vitriolic an attack on Italian colonial policy that British authorities had no choice but to expel him from Palestine. The Italian presence at the 1935 Geneva Muslim congress gave an early indication that leading Muslim activists were slipping into Axis orbit; Arslan was but the first of many to do so.

With cries of "Vive l'Islam!" the congress dispersed after four days
of deliberations. There had been no attempt to elaborate detailed provisions for the perpetuation of the congress as an organization. The
participants merely agreed in principle to meet annually, and elected
members to a permanent committee led by Arslan and Jabiri. The members of this body were the same persons who had organized the congress.
During the following months, ᶜAli al-Ghayati's *Tribune d'Orient* published
occasional items on the activities of this committee, since Ghayati served
as its secretary.

But Arslan's principal work on behalf of the congress was not to plan
for the next year's meeting, but to refute accusations leveled against
the proceedings just concluded. As an emanation of the Jerusalem Muslim congress, the Geneva congress excited those same political factions
in Palestine and Egypt which opposed Amin al-Husayni's ambitions.
Critics in both countries maintained that the congress had been a blunt
instrument of propaganda on behalf of Italian colonialism, and much
was made of the presence and remarks of Veccia Vaglieri at the congress.[49] All that Arslan could do from remote Geneva was to publish a
rebuttal to these charges in an Egyptian newspaper weeks after they
had appeared.[50]

This spate of polemics combined with the decline of Geneva as an
émigré center, to defeat all prospects for subsequent congresses envisioned by the organizers. In 1936, Anglo-Egyptian, Franco-Syrian, and
Franco-Lebanese treaties were signed, leading Arslan and others to plan
ends to their exiles. ᶜAli al-Ghayati closed his newspaper, and returned
to Egypt in 1937. Arslan and Jabiri departed for Syria the same year,
Arslan to serve as elder statesman, Jabiri to serve as a provincial governor. In the event, Arslan's appointed role did not satisfy him, and he
returned to Geneva in 1938, but he made no apparent effort to revive
the congress.

For there had been a marked change in the attitude of Swiss authorities, who were led by the deteriorating situation in Europe to become strict with Arslan. Shortly after his return to Geneva, Arslan was
summoned for a series of difficult interrogations by the police, concerning the full range of his political affiliations. A misstep here might
have meant deportation. "I have always respected the law," he protested.
"I have never done anything to compromise Switzerland or which was
illegal."[51] Arslan's responses to his interrogators were brilliant exercises
in dissimulation, and he was not expelled. But the restrictions governing
political activity in his *permis de séjour* acquired new force. The European
Muslim Congress, the consequence of a lost combination of opportunity
and will, would not meet again.

In the meantime, the Italians, lacking Arslan's subtlety, barged ahead with their claim to Muslim allegiances. In March 1937, Mussolini visited Tripolitania, and there was girded with the 'sword of Islam' by Muslim notables. In fact, the sword, a Yemeni relic, had been purchased in Florence with official Italian funds, and the notables were pressed into bestowing the exalted title upon the blade. "Muslims may rest assured," declared Mussolini, "that Italy will always be the friend and protector of Islam throughout the world." Commenting upon the girding, Italian foreign minister Count Ciano asserted that "every day there reaches us from the most distant lands evidence of the impression produced by that event in the whole boundless Islamic world, which, in accordance with its traditions, loves in the Duce the wisdom of the statesman united to the action of the warrior."[52] This claim was perhaps the ultimate yield of the European Muslim Congress.

THIRTEEN

CONGRESSES OF COLLABORATION

Islam and the Axis,
1938–1945

"F OR THE PRESENT, every Moslem nation must sink into her own deeper self, temporarily focus her vision on herself alone, until all are strong and powerful to form a living family of republics." So admonished Sir Muhammad Iqbal, Indian Muslim poet, philosopher, and a participant in the 1931 Jerusalem Muslim congress.[1] None could challenge Iqbal's commitment to the cause of independence for all Muslim peoples. He still maintained that Islam "recognizes artificial boundaries and racial distinctions for facility of reference only, and not for restricting the social horizons of its members." But a sinking into "deeper self" was essential if the various parts of the whole were to gain or preserve independence from foreign rule, and then garner strength.[2]

One of the aims of Muslim activists through their congresses had been to deny legitimacy to the division of Muslim lands by foreigners, and to affirm that Muslims alone would define the scale of their allegiances. Now Iqbal argued that it was pointless to resist this division. Independence still could be won and preserved, but only within the boundaries recognized as legitimate by those foreign powers which decided the destinies of Muslims. Iqbal thus called upon each Muslim people to make a separate calculation, and to go its separate way, if only for a time. His was a denial of a shared Muslim predicament.

Not all Indian Muslims heeded Iqbal's admonition. As late as October 1938, an Indian Muslim delegation appeared in Cairo, to participate in an Interparliamentary Congress of Arab and Muslim Lands for the Defense of Palestine. This event was the handiwork of Muhammad ᶜAli ᶜAlluba, the former treasurer of the Jerusalem Muslim congress, who had participated in Amin al-Husayni's unsuccessful 1933 fundraising tour through India. ᶜAlluba nonetheless invited a delegation of Muhammad ᶜAli Jinnah's All-India Muslim League to Cairo, and that delegation played a major role in what was otherwise an Arab congress, attended by leading Christian Arab nationalists. Muslims "ought to treat Muslim questions from a Muslim point of view without distinction of nationality," declared the leader of the delegation.[3] But seven years earlier it had been sufficient to convene what was formally a Muslim congress on this same issue, restricted to Muslim participants and insistent on the Muslim attachment to Palestine. Now Muhammad ʿAli ʿAlluba did not seek to reconvene that congress, but created an entirely new forum, in which the Arab nationalist emphasis was predominant and the Muslim content ambiguous. His confidence had been shaken in the effectiveness of an exclusively Muslim approach to the defense of Palestine.[4]

This narrowing of allegiance thinned the ranks of the Muslim committed. Then came the choice of leading Muslim activists to side with the Axis powers, and attempts to organize wider Muslim opinion in support of Axis war aims. Disciples of Afghani and heirs of Rashid Rida cast in their lots with the rising forces of totalitarianism, in the conviction that it would rid the Muslim world of two seemingly greater evils, colonialism and imperialism.

Of the warring powers, Japan gave the fullest credit to Muslim allegiances, and made the greatest effort to win them. This determined policy was designed to secure the sympathies of important Muslim populations in regions marked for possible Japanese expansion, in China, the Soviet Union, the Netherlands Indies, and British Malaya and India.[5] To advance these aims, Japanese authorities encouraged the establishment of numerous Muslim societies and institutions throughout the 1930s, not only in Japan, but in Manchukuo and later in occupied China. In 1938, all of these bodies were made subordinate to the Greater Japan Muslim League (*Dai Nippon Kaikyo Kyokai*), under the presidency of Abdürreşid İbrahim[ov], a Siberian-born Volga Tatar.

Abdürreşid İbrahim (1852–1944) was a Muslim activist in the most cosmopolitan tradition. He had traveled extensively in Muslim lands and in Europe, and at various times had joined forces with Abdülhamid II and Afghani. But his particular obsession had been the liberation of Muslims subjected to Russian rule, an aim which he sought to realize through association with Japan. During a period spent in Japan in 1908–9, İbrahim concluded a written pact of Muslim-Japanese cooperation against Russia with Toyama Mitsuru, the influential patron of the expansionist Black Dragon Society. These and similar patriotic societies— with their vision of a Japanese-dominated Asia and their close ties to the political and military elite—provided consistent support for a policy of embracing Muslim causes.[6] So too did Japan's growing community of Tatar Muslim refugees who had escaped from Russian rule and revolution, and who soon began to organize themselves.[7]

In 1933, İbrahim left Istanbul to return to Tokyo at the invitation of the Japanese Foreign Ministry, in the midst of renewed Japanese efforts to cultivate Muslim sympathies. He immediately rose to a position of prominence in the local community, which in 1938 celebrated the opening of a great central mosque in Tokyo, in the presence of many visiting Muslim dignitaries from abroad.[8] That event signaled a doubling of Japanese efforts in the field. Upon the opening of the mosque, a Greater Japan Muslim League was established in Tokyo, under the presidency of a former minister of war and prime minister, who then vacated the position for İbrahim. The purpose of the League was to coordinate the work of the numerous Japanese-inspired Muslim associations, and to inform the wider Muslim world of Japan's determination to defend Muslim interests. The League was a governmental creation, and in its first year of operation, the Japanese Foreign Ministry, Army, and Navy provided ¥100,000 of the League's total budget of ¥112,000.[9]

In November 1939, the new League sponsored an Islamic Exhibition in Tokyo and Osaka, to which it invited Muslims from within Japan's sphere of influence and beyond. The response to this appeal was modest, for the invitations preceded the exhibition by less than two months. From Manchukuo came delegations from Japanese-initiated associations, foremost among them the Manchukuo Muslim Peoples' League, which had been established to unite and thus control the Muslims of the puppet-state.[10] From Japanese-occupied China came representatives of the All China Muslim League, a Peking-based association financed by the Japanese Army.[11] But the most celebrated participants arrived from Indonesia, for theirs was the only major delegation from beyond the Japanese sphere. In 1937, the principal Indonesian Muslim organizations—Muhammadijah, Sarekat Islam, and Nadhatul Ulama—formed a federative front, the Madjlis Islam A'laa Indonesia (MIAI). It was the MIAI which dispatched a four-man delegation to Tokyo that included Muhammadijah youth leader and Jerusalem congress delegate Abdul Kahar Muzakkir (1907–1973); student organizer Ahmad Kasmat; and Azhar graduate Farid Ma'ruf.[12]

The exhibition, once opened, thus gathered a cosmopolitan collection of Muslims from the Soviet Union, China, Indonesia, and Japan. The foreign guests were shown evidence of Japan's impressive military and industrial achievements, and learned of Japan's interest in the Muslim cause. The organizers then took advantage of the presence of these delegations, to convene them in a session which the participants audaciously named the First World Muslim Congress. One of the resolutions passed by this unexpected meeting provided for an annual Muslim congress in Tokyo, under the auspices of the Greater Japan Muslim League, a decision made at the explicit request of those government ministries which sponsored the League. The resolutions also called for the publication of a periodical, and officers were elected.[13] For a power so far removed from the central Muslim lands, Japan's decision to patronize such an organization represented a bold bid, commensurate with its ambitions.

But the spread of war thwarted plans for further congresses. In April 1940, the Greater Japan Muslim League informed its sponsoring government ministries that war conditions in the Near East, Central Asia, Africa, and India made the convening of a second congress impractical. Representatives from Indonesia were particularly hesitant to participate because of the worsening of Japanese-Dutch relations, and the League anticipated that none of them would arrive. This meant that only Muslims from Manchuria and China would attend, and under these circumstances, the purposes of the congress could not be served. The League proposed to postpone the congress, and the authorities concurred.[14] İbrahim had to rest satisfied with conventional means of propaganda for conveyance of his message to the wider Muslim world, principally by radio broadcasts: "Every Wednesday I address the world of Islam on radio, sometimes in Turkish and sometimes in Arabic."[15]

The importance of the first congress lay in the strengthening of ties with Indonesian Muslims, who in 1942 fell under direct Japanese rule. The congress had set an exemplary precedent for the collaboration of Indonesian Muslim activists with Japanese occupation authorities. It was true that the Indonesian Muslim delegates to the congress had told Dutch interrogators on their return that the Japanese had struck them as insincere in their solicitude for Islam.[16] But Abdul Kahar Muzakkir, a delegate, eventually served for a time as head of the Religious Affairs Office in the military occupation administration. The other participants were also notable collaborators. In that respect, the congress had served the purpose of projecting an image of Japan compatible with Indonesian Muslim aspirations.[17] But by the time of İbrahim's death in 1944, the policy of cultivating Muslim sympathies had yielded few other appreciable results.

Hitler's early statement, *Mein Kampf,* dismissed any German appeal to Muslim sentiment as delusory and dangerous. "The 'Holy War' can produce in our German muttonheads the pleasant thrill that now others are ready to shed their blood for us, because this cowardly speculation has, to speak bluntly, been the silent father of all such hopes—but in reality it will meet a ghastly end under the fire of English machinegun companies and the hail of explosive bombs."[18] So it was most prudent for the German diplomat Fritz Grobba, in a memorandum on the Arab question written in March 1941, to determine that "the Islamic idea (Holy War) is impracticable under the present grouping of powers. Arab nationality and Islam are not identical. The Arabs to be brought into our plans are fighting not for religious, but for political aims."[19]

But Amin al-Husayni arrived in Berlin exile in November 1941, and began to advance his claim to a wider Muslim authority.[20] For this was world war, and involved political destinies of Muslims everywhere. Amin al-Husayni's expansive approach received important encouragement from Shakib Arslan, who had played so prominent a role in earlier Muslim congresses. Arslan remained in Switzerland throughout the war, as a result of a Swiss decision not to readmit him if he visited Italy or Germany. But Arslan conducted a continuous correspondence with Amin al-Husayni, relentlessly pressing him to intervene in wider Muslim affairs. In one turbulent letter, Arslan called upon his correspondent to demand independence for the Muslims of the Caucasus: "Perhaps the Germans will tell us that we Arabs should mind our own business, that we should not interfere in non-Arab questions, that we should confine ourselves to our national demands and think of no one but ourselves. It is this view that I want to completely refute. We Arabs are at the vanguard of the Islamic nation which numbers 400 million people worldwide. We are united with this nation by bonds of solidarity and mutual responsibility, from the furthest reaches of China to the shores of the Atlantic Ocean. Our aims and the aims of all Islamic peoples are identical."[21]

In another letter, in which he asked Amin al-Husayni to press Japan to formulate an "Islamic policy," Arslan insisted that "we must work for the general wellbeing of Islam, for the aims of Islam and Arabism are identical."[22] In still another letter, appealing to Amin al-Husayni to act on behalf of Bosnian Muslims, Arslan predicted that "the entire Muslim world will learn who Amin al-Husayni is, and what he has done in the service of Islam and the Muslims, wherever and whoever they may be. They will realize that his struggle is not limited to his homeland of Palestine or to the Arab nation. All of Europe will learn that the Muslims are brethren regardless of nationality, and that we do not distinguish between Arab and non-Arab."[23] At the very foundation of "our demands" must be the conviction that "behind the Arab world is the even larger Islamic world, comprising 400 million persons. . . . this Islamic world is completely bound to the Arab world, as the body is to the head." It was the duty of the Arabs to seek the liberation of all Muslims subjected to British, French, Russian, and Dutch rule.[24] This flood of letters stimulated and sanctioned Amin al-Husayni's bid to widen his claims.

In Berlin, Amin al-Husayni put forth a detailed proposal along identical lines. The Muslims, he wrote in a memorandum, were the true friends of Germany, engaged in a common struggle against the Jews, the British, and the Communists. But that cooperation needed more organized expression. First, Amin al-Husayni proposed the creation of a special department for Muslim affairs within the German Foreign Office, responsible for the broad sweep of Muslim concerns from East Asia to West Africa. Second, he proposed the recruitment of an "Islamic army, drawn from among the many North African Muslims resident in France, and from the Muslims of the Balkans and Soviet Russia, to join the struggle alongside the German troops. Better use should also be made of the numerous Muslim prisoners of war than has been made so far, and Muslim emissaries should be dispatched to visit the prisoner camps in an organized fashion." Third, Germany should issue a declaration of true intentions "to the Muslims in general and the Arabs in particular," concerning their future independence. And last, he proposed "an Islamic-Arab congress, to be attended by Muslims residing in Europe. This would constitute a splendid demonstration of Arab and Muslim cooperation with Germany, in which official German statements and speeches can be delivered. These would find a powerful echo and wide dissemination in the Arab and Islamic worlds."[25] The last proposal immediately evoked the European Muslim Congress convened in Geneva by Arslan in 1935 (see previous chapter).

But, as in the past, Indian Muslims stood in Amin al-Husayni's way, refusing to recognize what they regarded as his unsubstantiated claim to wider Muslim authority. The Berlin in which Amin al-Husayni now found himself was a city with a lengthy history of Muslim émigré activism, boasting numerous Muslim publications and established Muslim institutions. Foremost among these was the Islamische Gemeinde, a society founded twenty years earlier by Indian Muslims. This association structured Muslim life in Berlin, and directed the administration of Berlin's great central mosque.[26] The attitude of the mosque and the association to Amin al-Husayni soon became a source of controversy, for they would not admit the newcomer's claim to primacy.

The German Foreign Office provided Amin al-Husayni with the base from which he made that claim, the Islamische Zentralinstitut. This was a minor association established in 1927, which had been inactive for many years. An Arab circle revived it in September 1941 at the prompting of the German Foreign Office for purposes of propaganda. Amin al-Husayni assumed the leadership of the Islamische Zentralinstitut during his first year in Berlin, and with the approach of the festival of ⁀Id *al-Adha* in December 1942, led a maneuver to gain control of the central mosque.[27]

Amin al-Husayni proposed to mark the reestablishment of the Islamische Zentralinstitut during the festival prayers in the central mosque. He argued that this would assure a more political tone in the central mosque's ceremonies, so that they could be broadcast overseas with the same alleged effect as the proceedings of the rival London mosque.[28] But one of Amin al-Husayni's secretaries, Mustafa al-Wakil, set forth more expansive claims in a letter to Ernst Woermann, the undersecretary who would decide the issue at the German Foreign Office:

> How can it happen, with the presence of His Eminence [Amin al-Husayni] in Germany, where there is only a small number of Moslems, that the responsibility in such religious matters is not referred to His Eminence, while His Eminence is the first authority in religious and other questions concerning Moslems and Arabs, and while His Eminence is president of the All Moslem Conference of which Moslem leaders from the whole world have been members? It is curious to find that it is forgotten here that the natural course is to put the questions of the Moslems in Germany under the high supervision of His Eminence.

Wakil wished that "the orders of the German Foreign Ministry would be clear and decisive," namely, to leave to Amin al-Husayni all authority over the Islamische Zentralinstitut, the Islamische Gemeinde, the mosque, festival prayers, and the *ᶜId al-Adha* celebrations.[29] There was no doubt that the officers of the Islamische Zentralinstitut viewed supervision of the upcoming celebrations as a decisive step toward the unification of all Muslim institutions in Berlin under their own auspices.[30]

These proposals met with stiff opposition from the officers of the Islamische Gemeinde responsible for administration of the mosque, and who were for the most part Indian Muslims. As Woermann noted, they had directed the affairs of the central mosque on their own for many years. Yet now Amin al-Husayni sought to make himself the sole spokesman of all the city's Muslims, without even consulting Subhas Chandra Bose, his Indian opposite in Berlin.[31] Bose already was resentful of Amin al-Husayni's claim to influence over Indian Muslims, whom Bose maintained were within his own jurisdiction. Once, after Amin al-Husayni had issued an appeal to Indian Muslims, Bose complained to German foreign minister Ribbentrop about the encroachment, and insinuated that Amin al-Husayni's Muslim propaganda constituted "religious imperialism."[32] This placed the Islamische Gemeinde and Bose on the same side of an acrimonious dispute between Amin al-Husayni and his principal Arab rival in Berlin, Rashid ᶜAli al-Kaylani; so that when the Islamische Gemeinde sponsored a major gathering to affirm Indian-Arab unity, the invited speakers were Bose and Kaylani.[33] The Islamische Gemeinde had some influential supporters in its resistance to Amin al-Husayni's bid, and Woermann wondered whether the time was ripe for the Islamische Zentralinstitut to attempt to dislodge the Islamische Gemeinde.[34]

Ultimately, the director of the Islamische Gemeinde allowed that Amin al-Husayni, as an esteemed religious dignitary, might conduct the festival prayers, but this could not constitute a service to mark the reestablishment of the Islamische Zentralinstitut. The compromise meant that the Islamische Gemeinde and the Islamische Zentralinstitut would remain distinct, and that the central mosque would continue to function as it had in the past, under the supervision of its founders.[35] The address with which Amin al-Husayni inaugurated the Islamische Zentralinstitut was delivered not in the mosque, but in a hall. There he spoke on the obligatory character of the war against the Allies and Zionism.[36] In a letter marking the event, he assured Hitler the friendship, cooperation, and sympathy of the 400 million Muslims throughout the world, in support of the Axis struggle against the Judeo–Bolshevik–Anglo-Saxon alliance.[37] But those involved in this episode had learned something of the limits of Amin al-Husayni's influence. Having failed to establish its authority over the Muslim community of Berlin, the Islamische Zentralinstitut did not emerge as an important center of activism, and its functions essentially were restricted to the field of publishing.[38]

Henceforth, Amin al-Husayni's wider claims remained for the most part unacknowledged by the German Foreign Office. First, there was no German willingness to impose his authority upon those Muslims unprepared to accept it. Second, Germany's future plans for the various Muslim peoples were not uniform. Not only were there restraining obligations to Italy and Japan in the Mediterranean, South, and Southeast Asia; but the Muslim-populated and oil-producing areas of the Soviet Union were slated for German exploitation and possible colonization. A German declaration in favor of Muslim independence everywhere was unthinkable. And while Amin al-Husayni offered to convene a Muslim congress to amplify Muslim support for Germany, he was just as likely to use a gathered assembly to attempt to extract new commitments from his hosts. The congress, then, was undesirable from the German point of view, and the German Foreign Office checked Amin al-Husayni's every attempt to establish his wider Muslim authority. In November 1944, he complained that the German Foreign Office official responsible for his affairs had obstructed the work of the Islamische Zentralinstitut, and:

frequently even demands of me that I desist from addressing appeals to Muslims, even though I am president of the Islamic World Congress, and even though I occupy a leading position in the Islamic world. As against this, however, we see that our common enemy, the English and the Russians, are trying to conduct propaganda in the Islamic world by approaching personalities not competent in Islamic matters, who are but loosely linked with the Islamic world. These they promote to be muftis and place in positions of Muslim leadership. The enemies convene Muslim congresses, establish institutes, publish newspapers and periodicals, and strive by all means to make the desired impact upon the Islamic world.[39]

These were all possibilities for collaboration—among them a Muslim congress—which the German Foreign Office had thwarted.

But Amin al-Husayni made a far deeper impression upon the SS-Hauptamt and the Ostministerium. Both were responsible for political mobilization and military recruitment of Muslims in German-occupied territories, and offered Amin al-Husayni another opportunity to fill the role of Muslim spiritual leader. It was on behalf of the SS-Hauptamt that he embarked upon a recruitment campaign among Bosnian Muslims in 1943, a success which owed much to ties forged in earlier Muslim congresses with leaders of the Bosnian Muslim community.[40] He also visited Turkic Muslim prisoners of war who were being recruited in large numbers to SS ranks, and helped to found a school for Turkic Muslim SS chaplains in Dresden in 1944, where he preached his doctrine of Muslim solidarity.[41] At the same time, Amin al-Husayni conducted his own private diplomacy, invoking his authority as president of the Muslim congress established in Jerusalem over a decade earlier. In the boldest of these initiatives, he wrote to the Japanese foreign minister sometime in 1943, offering to employ the Jerusalem congress network to raise an "Islamic army" of Asian Muslim volunteers, to fight alongside Japanese forces.[42] In June 1944, in the wake of a letter from Arslan, he proposed a still more elaborate program of Japanese-Muslim cooperation, again in a communication to the Japanese foreign minister. This time he offered to send a personal representative whose task would be the organization of an "Islamic liberation army" composed of Asian Muslims, and proposed a pact between Japan and the "Islamic leadership"—a transparent reference to himself.[43] This constituted an obvious attempt to circumvent the German Foreign Office in his pursuit of a decisive say in wider Muslim affairs, but, like his demand for a wartime Muslim congress, the proposal came to nothing.

"It is a characteristic of the Moslem world, from the shores of the Atlantic to those of the Pacific, that what affects one, for good or evil, affects all." This was the revised judgment of Hitler, made during the last months of war in besieged Berlin. "We had a great chance of pursuing a splendid policy with regard to Islam. But we missed the bus, as we missed it on several other occasions, thanks to our loyalty to the Italian alliance." The Italians, still remembered for their "barbarous reprisals" against Muslim resistance in Libya, "created a feeling of *malaise* among our Islamic friends, who inevitably saw in us accomplices, willing or unwilling, of their oppressors." Alone, Germany could have "aroused the enthusiasm of the whole of Islam."[44] On the brink of defeat, the ridicule expressed in *Mein Kampf* of such "cowardly speculation" was forgotten. But while the "whole of Islam" did remain uncommitted, the leading Muslim cosmopolitans had openly embraced the German cause, and now could not escape the humiliation of defeat.

Not one figure who had organized a past Muslim congress now came forward to declare a Muslim preference for the Allied cause. The proposal that a new Muslim congress be organized to elicit such a declaration received but brief consideration, prompted by a cable from Lord Linlithgow, Viceroy of India, to the Secretary of State at the India Office. In this awkwardly worded communication of July 1940, the Viceroy suggested that a British-inspired Muslim congress might serve an important war aim:

> I have wondered once or twice whether it was worth suggesting that you might consider whether His Majesty's Government ought not to try to encourage and strengthen the obvious feeling among Moslems that Axis expansion in Mohamedan regions was against the interests of Islam, and possibly even to consider the practicability and desirability (as to which His Majesty's Government are in a much better position to reach any conclusion than we can possibly be here) of promoting somewhere a Pan-Islamic conference which might voice these feelings.

The Viceroy offered no clear solution to the immediate problems of venue and sponsor raised by his proposal, except to point out that the congress could not be held in his own domain:

> There are I think very obvious objections to choosing India which is a follower rather than a leader in Islamic activities, but it is just conceivable that if you thought there was anything in the idea at all it might be worth sounding [British ambassador to Egypt Miles] Lampson as to whether Cairo or Egypt might not be a useful venue. I seem to have seen recently a speech by the Rector of Al Azhar University [Mustafa al-Maraghi] in which he referred to Cairo as centre of Islam, though I am of course well aware that Ibn Saud or the King of the Yemen would be likely to take a very different view of any such claim, and that full weight would have to be given to risk of any stressing of it giving rise to dissensions between

various Islamic countries rather than promoting a single front against Axis expansion, which we should be anxious to see.[45]

But commentators at the India and Foreign Offices did not discern this "obvious feeling" among Muslims against Axis expansion. Roland Peel, political secretary at the India Office, thought that "the objections to any kind of Pan-Islamic Conference are overwhelming." No Muslim leader had the uncontested authority necessary to convene such an assembly, and the choice of a venue was bound to result in unwholesome controversy. Cairo was arguably the best setting, but "even if the Conference were successfully assembled, how are you to insure that the right kind of feelings will be voiced? It is much more likely that they would get on to awkward questions like Palestine and Syria. I am afraid that the risk of promoting dissension between the Islamic countries, rather than a united front against Axis expansion is a real one, and I feel sure that the F[oreign] O[ffice] would be firmly opposed to any idea of a Conference."[46]

This conservative conjecture proved sound. The Foreign Office held that such a forum would be difficult to convene and control, for "it might degenerate into an anti-British meeting . . . anyone disposed to criticise our measures for the defence against Axis expansion of British territory inhabited by Moslems might take the opportunity to voice his views at the Conference."[47] The Viceroy was informed of this verdict, and he withdrew his suggestion.[48]

Nor was there a single Muslim cosmopolitan prepared to lend of his personal prestige to the war effort. Shaykh Mustafa al-Maraghi, whom Lord Linlithgow had mentioned as an interested party, perhaps did have a stake, for he held Amin al-Husayni in low regard, and lost no opportunity to question this rival's Muslim credentials.[49] But early in the conflict, Shaykh Maraghi made it known that he saw no point in Egypt's declaring war against the Axis powers.[50] The first Axis bombings of Egyptian cities led him to take to the pulpit to charge that Egypt had been dragged into a war against its will, and that the only reward the country had reaped for allowing the British to base their armies there had been the killing of innocent men, women, and children.[51]

Unable to secure a convincing Muslim endorsement of the Allied cause, Great Britain developed Muslim propaganda along other lines. The theme of this bid was Great Britain's record of demonstrated respect for Muslim religious freedom, and as further proof of this solicitude, British officials actively encouraged the establishment of a central mosque in London. The new edifice figured prominently in news and information provided to Muslims through various Allied media.[52] But with the leading Muslim cosmopolitans arrayed on the side of the enemy, the principal avenues of propaganda led necessarily in different directions.

The Axis defeat dealt a serious blow to the Muslim cosmopolitans and the congresses they had championed. They had lost none of their moral authority, accumulated during years of struggle against foreign rule. In the eyes of their followers, they lost no credibility for having collaborated with totalitarian states. They had made a wrong choice, but not an evil one. Yet through their exertions on behalf of the Axis cause, they had identified activist Islam with collaboration in the mind of the West, and the Allied powers which stood to remake the Muslim world were no longer prepared to indulge them or treat with them. This denial of recognition proved an insurmountable handicap. Muslim peoples, anxious to gain some advantage from the war, turned to leaders whom the victorious powers were prepared to recognize — to the secular nationalists who had supported the Allies during the war, and who demanded and got as their reward not the liberation of the Muslim world, but freedom and independence for their individual peoples.

FOURTEEN

CONCLUSIONS

T HE GREAT disappointment of the Muslim congresses was that they failed to merge in a single organization. The establishment of a permanent organization was the professed aim of every initiative. Each one made some provision for a permanent secretariat entrusted with the convening of periodic congresses. Yet none of the congresses succeeded in perpetuating itself long beyond adjournment. Was there a fundamental flaw in the very premise of the congresses, some chronic weakness in the Muslim body politic which thwarted every attempt to organize the sentiment of Muslim solidarity?

The congresses were grounded in the belief that the vastness of the Muslim world constituted a strength. In their numbers, and in their broad geographic dispersal, the Muslims represented a potentially formidable force. Were Muslims to express themselves as one, were they to define their political priorities, resolve their own disputes, and even mend doctrine, then their collective determination would serve to ward off their enemies. "If the Muslims were to organize themselves," wrote one congress sponsor, "all of the difficulties which afflict them would disappear immediately. Those [non-Muslim] states having Muslim populations could no longer permit themselves to treat their Muslim subjects as some of them do today."[1]

Yet the flaw lay in that same vastness of the Muslim world which the Muslim cosmopolitans counted as a strength, for it gave rise to sharp differences of perspective among them. A sense of subjugation to the West was the binding force of the congresses, yet the political conditions under which Muslims lived varied widely. It made some difference whether one submitted to British, French, Russian, or Dutch rule. It made still more difference whether one's land was occupied for strategic, economic, or colonizing purposes. It made a great deal of difference whether one was subjected directly to foreign rule, or enjoyed a measure of independence as part of the balance of foreign power. The calculations made separately by Muslims in different predicaments ruled out an unambiguous consensus.

The Muslims, then, did not constitute an effective political community, for their differences were too profound. These might have been transcended by a visionary and charismatic leader, obsessed with the details of organization, and aware of the paramount importance of continuity and periodicity. But the Muslim congresses found no one prepared to work so methodically to bring Muslims together. The triumvirate of Rashid Rida, Shakib Arslan, and Amin al-Husayni did figure over the years in many of the initiatives and congresses. They shared a profound commitment to the cause of Muslim unity, and inspired others with the considerable force of their personalities. But as organizers, they lacked persistence, and were too deeply involved in political and literary controversies to serve as menders of Muslim divisions.

Had the congresses been convened near the seats of government of those foreign powers which ruled Muslim destinies, their participants might have felt compelled to display greater singleness of purpose. Under watchful foreign eyes, the moral compulsion to stem controversy might have fortified the congresses, and made a deeper impression upon world opinion. But with few exceptions, Muslim congresses met in Muslim settings, often removed from outside scrutiny. This preference stemmed from a conception of the congress as an essentially conspiratorial event, the proceedings of which had to be kept in confidence from the West. The avowed purpose was not to impress foreigners, but to plan common action against foreign oppressors; and was this aim not served best by secrecy? The notion was expressed perfectly by Kawakibi in *Umm al-qura*, the story of a Muslim congress that unfolded as a plot (see chapter 3). But the atmosphere in these settings was laden with Muslim rivalries and Muslim intrigues, and these permeated the congress preparations and proceedings. Divisive controversy was exacerbated by the lack of one great center in Islam. There was no single city, state, or body of theologians which enjoyed undisputed primacy in determination of Muslim priorities. Instead there were many figures who claimed to speak on behalf of authentic Islam, and who organized rival congresses in rival settings to demonstrate their authority.

Muslim cosmopolitans also failed to define a theme powerful enough to wilt the pretensions and pride which congress participants brought to the proceedings. The broad cause of Muslim independence was complicated by the fact that the aims and methods of foreign control differed widely across the expansive world of Islam. And so the congresses instead delved indecisively in religious reform, the caliphate, and the fate of the holy cities of Arabia. When these issues also failed to provide the foundation of a Muslim consensus, the Muslim congresses turned to the winning of Palestine. This purpose did concern all Muslims for religious reasons, but still failed to move them to spend their political energies and material resources. The Muslim congresses lacked a well-defined cause for which Muslims were prepared to make sacrifices, and a vast chasm opened up between pledges and deeds.

Without inspiring leadership, ambiance, and purpose, Muslims in congress could not rise above their differences, hence the emergence of a broken pattern of congresses. The movement for unity was disunited, and failed to yield a single series of congresses and one representative organization. Instead, the congresses rivaled one another, and became arenas for other Muslim rivalries. The West was not intimidated by the alleged unity of Muslim purpose, and on no occasion did any foreign power yield to the demands of assembled Muslims. As an instrument for the liberation of Muslim peoples, the congresses proved utterly ineffective.

But the congresses did intensify the exchange of views among Muslims themselves. Congress organizers and congress participants boarded steamers and trains, then aircraft, for distant destinations, to establish a network of ties far more extensive than that which had prevailed in the Ottoman period. Some of the Muslim cosmopolitans even attended several of the congresses, compensating in some measure for the organizational discontinuity of the congresses themselves.

The simplest function of this network was to inform. In the previous century, much of the information which reached Muslims about the situation, opinions, and concerns of other Muslims came from suspect sources. Word of events in distant Muslim lands often reached other Muslim centers through non-Muslim media, censored publications, and plain rumor. The congresses, in providing opportunities for personal encounters, gave Muslims a much more vivid sense of the challenges faced by Muslims elsewhere. Participants returned home with more accurate impressions of developments in the wider Muslim world, and then were able to disseminate that information with more authority and conviction.

Yet the congresses did more than inform. The deliberations, and the network they created, demonstrated the tenacity of Muslim adherence to the concept of a united world of Islam. Despite the disintegration of the last great Muslim empire and the demise of the universal caliphate, the ideal of Muslim unity continued to move Muslims. This Muslim political allegiance was unwieldy in scope and in some respects anachronistic. Its adherents did not or could not articulate a clear and compelling program for its implementation. Yet Muslim nationalism had the singular quality of authenticity. It was not a modern contrivance, but drew on the traditional concept of the *umma,* the universal and indivisible nation of Islam. The congresses represented a standing protest by Muslim cosmopolitans against the arbitrary division of the Muslim world by foreign powers, a division accepted so readily by pragmatic secular nationalists.

Buffeted by winds of change, that ideal of unity found shelter in the deliberations and doings of the Muslim congresses. There it reposed, a latent challenge to narrower nationalism and the breaking up of the Muslim world into dozens of states. For an interlude, the congresses were halted by a world war, and the leading Muslim cosmopolitans were discredited. But then followed the momentous partitions of India and Palestine, and a new and very different congress movement arose from these ordeals. This time its purpose was the establishment of an organization of Muslim states, many of which had just achieved their independence. That effort, drawn out over two decades, and deserving of separate study, ultimately succeeded. Thus was realized, in form if not in substance, the visions of those Muslims who had proposed and organized the first congresses, in the shadow of the West.

STATUTES OF THE ISLAMIC CONGRESS

SECTION I

First Article. —An Organizing Committee has been established in the city of Cairo to convene a General Islamic Congress. This Committee is composed of members whose names are affixed to these statutes, among whom are a President, two Vice Presidents, a Secretary, and a Treasurer.

Art. 2. —The Organizing Committee is empowered to include any Muslim resident of Egypt, whose assistance and participation are deemed useful to it, as a founding member.

Art. 3. —Should a vacancy occur on the Committee for the offices of president, vice-president, treasurer, or secretary, the Committee will proceed in its next session to choose successors, who will be elected from among the members of the Committee by secret ballot and simple majority.

Art. 4. —The deliberations and decisions of the Committee will be valid regardless of the number of members present, provided that the session has been convened in conformity with the provisions of article 6 of these Statutes. A simple majority will suffice to validate decisions.

Art. 5. —The Committee will meet on the first Tuesday of each lunar month. The President nevertheless may convene the Committee at his discretion more frequently than once a month, and he also must convene it at any time upon the request of three members of the Committee.

Art. 6. —Notifications of sessions of the Committee will be addressed by the President to all members, giving detailed information as to the agenda, the place, and the hour of the reunion. These notifications will be sent at least three days before the date set for the session.

SOURCE: French pamphlet issued by the preparatory committee and included in the Oppenheim (Cairo) dispatch of May 20, 1908, Archiv des Auswärtigen Amts as filmed by the University of California, *NA* microcopy T-139, reel 399, frames 510–15.

Art. 7. —The members of the Organizing Committee will pay the Treasurer monthly dues of half an Egyptian pound, payable monthly.

Art. 8. —The income from dues will be used to prepare the reception of congress participants as well as to defray the costs of printing, publicity, and other expenses incurred by the work of the Congress.

Art. 9. —The members of the Organizing Committee will be jointly responsible for the expenses of administering the Committee, as well as the costs of correspondence, publication, and distribution.

Art. 10. —As soon as the date for the convening of the Congress has been set, the Organizing Committee will nominate a sub-commission to establish the budget.
The members of the Committee will bear the costs of all deficits, in a manner to be determined by the sub-commission for the budget. This sub-commission will be composed of the Treasurer of the Committee, and four other members elected by a simple majority through secret ballot.

Art. 11. The decisions of the sub-commission for the budget will be implemented upon approval of the Organizing Committee.

Art. 12. —The Organizing Committee may appoint necessary personnel such as clerks, translators, and other agents. It also may set down internal regulations to assure the smooth progress of its operations.

Art. 13. —At the conclusion of the Congress, the Committee will proceed to liquidate its own administrative and financial affairs. The balance of its accounts, as well as books, documents, and other assets, will be put to such use as the Committee may determine upon the close of the Congress.

SECTION II
AIM OF THE CONGRESS

Art. 14. —First, the Congress is to examine the causes behind the decadence of the Muslims from the social point of view, as well as innovations which superstition has introduced into their religious system; and second, it is to study the means for eliminating these causes of decadence, and prepare the uplifting of the Muslims.

Art. 15. —No proposition having a religious character will be admitted unless it is supported by a text of the Koran, the tradition (*Sounna*), the unanimous opinion of doctors of the faith, or interpretation of the sacred texts through analogy.

Art. 16 —Political questions of any kind are absolutely forbidden in the Congress.

SECTION III
MEMBERS OF THE CONGRESS

Art. 17. —Any enlightened Muslim who might be of assistance in the success of the Congress is eligible for membership.

Art. 18. —Requests for admission are to be addressed to the President of the Organizing Committee. This Committee must consider such requests within fifteen days of their submission.

Art. 19. —The admission fee is set at one hundred piastres.

Art. 20. —Requests for admission must be received no later than fifteen days before the date of the reunion of the Congress from persons resident in Egypt, and at least two months in advance from persons residing abroad.

Art. 21. —Members of the Organizing Committee are members of the Congress by right. Persons also may take part who are nominated by the Committee either as members or honorary presidents.

Art. 22. —All members have the right to take part in the deliberations and discussions of the Congress, as well as to give their views on all the questions which might be raised by the Congress. As for administrative and financial questions, these are the exclusive preserve of the Organizing Committee.

SECTION IV
CONVENING OF THE CONGRESS

Art. 23. —Six months before the convening of the Congress, the Organizing Committee will fix the date and place of meeting.

Art. 24. —The admissible languages of the deliberations are Arabic, Turkish, Persian and Urdu.

Art. 25. —Three months before the convening of the Congress, a special commission will be formed, to which will be submitted all communications, and which will choose those that are to be submitted to the Congress. This commission will also choose the documents to be released for publication at the close of the Congress.

Art. 26. —The Organizing Committee may divide the Congress into various sections, each of which will consider a specific matter.

Art. 27. —At least sixty days before the opening of the Congress, the Organizing Committee will determine the duration and hours of the Congress. It may likewise regulate the length of sessions, etc.

Art. 28. —On the day set for the closure of the Congress, the members will meet in plenary session to determine the date of the next Islamic Congress.

These Statutes have been approved by the Organizing Committee of the Islamic Congress in its session of Tuesday, Zul Hegat 17, 1325 (January 21, 1908).

Signatures:

SELIM EL BECHIRI, MOHAMAD TEWFIK EL BAKRI, HUSSEIN WASSEF, ALY YOUSSEF, HASSAN BEFKI, MOUSSA GHALEB, IBRAHIM EL HELBAOUI, OMAR LOUTFY, MOHAMAD HASSANEIN, YOUSSEF SADDIK, RAFIK EL AZM, HAKI EL AZM, HASSAN BAKRI, AHMAD HAFEZ AWAD, MOHAMAD AHMAD EL CHERIF.

THE LEAGUE OF ISLAMIC REVOLUTIONARY SOCIETIES CHARTER

A. THE AIMS OF THE SOCIETY

The aim of the Society is to make the Muslims—who are used like slaves, enslaved and dominated by the imperialists and capitalists—masters of their own fate under the leadership of Turkey; to ensure their free and independent organization within their national culture; and to liberate them from captivity. The aim of the Society is to create the organization necessary to realize the aforementioned goal, by uplifting and uniting the Muslims spiritually. In places where Muslims are in the minority, the Society shall try to safeguard their civil rights.

B. ORGANIZATION

1. The Society shall be composed of a central committee; one autonomous committee in each land; and branches, as many as required, which shall be linked to the autonomous committees.

2. The central committee shall be composed of 3–7 founding members, and one representative of every autonomous committee affiliated with the Society. Every year, there shall be elected a president, secretary, and treasurer, and these three shall be responsible for presenting specific subjects for discussion in the meetings of the central committee. In the event that any of the three offices becomes vacant, substitute members elected in advance by a majority vote shall immediately fill them. The president and the secretary, or the president and the treasurer, must sign all documents of the Society, alongside the seal.

3. The duties of the central committee shall be to ensure the establishment of the Society in every land; to supervise the Society; to ensure the unity of the autonomous committees; to cooperate with other non-Muslim nations and classes which are struggling for their freedom; and to organize regular contact with them. The central committee shall also

SOURCE: Karabekir, *İstiklâl Harbimizde: Enver Paşa*, 123-25. I am indebted to Ared Misirliyan for his translation of this document.

be responsible for convening the general congress, and for implementing its resolutions. All activities and public functions shall be carried out with the approval of the central committee.

4. One-third of the members of the central committee shall be replaced at each congress, and new members shall be elected in their place. The reelection of former members shall be permitted.

5. Autonomous committees: Within the geographic confines of each land, there shall be an autonomous committee. Each autonomous committee shall consist of 3–7 members. Their periodic replacement shall follow the example of the central committee, and the responsibilities shall also be distributed in the same fashion as in the central committee.

6. The duties of the autonomous committees: The autonomous committees shall establish and independently direct all kinds of [subordinate] organizations, within their geographic regions, in accord with the principles defined by the central committee, and adopted by the congresses.

7. Branches: Each land shall be divided according to regions [which shall be served by] branches. Each branch shall be administered by a council composed of 3–7 members. These shall be appointed by either the autonomous committee or the central committee. The members shall fulfill their duties in the same fashion as in the autonomous committees. These branches shall receive orders and instructions from the autonomous committees, or from the central committee.

C. CONGRESSES

8. Congresses convened by the autonomous committee: Each year, each autonomous committee shall convene at an appointed time, a congress of representatives of the branches, in order to discuss various problems related to its organization, and to pass resolutions. They shall also prepare a report on the general situation and the activities undertaken during the year, as well as a financial report, both of which shall be presented to the general congress. In addition, they shall elect new members to the autonomous committee, and delegates to be sent to the general congress.

[Article 9 omitted in source.]

10. General congress: The central committee shall convene, at a time and place which it shall fix, a general congress of delegates from the various lands. Each autonomous committee shall be entitled to one vote, regardless of how many delegates it sends.

11. Upon the conclusion of the general congress, the central committee and the autonomous committees shall be responsible for implementing

its resolutions, and have the right to [discuss the particulars in] smaller meetings.

12. The general congress shall hear the report of the central committee; shall review the financial accounts and activities carried out by the Society; shall approve the budget; shall make changes in the Charter if necessary; shall determine the general outline of the program of political action; and shall elect the members of the central committee.

D. MEMBERS

13. Every person who works on behalf of the Society is accepted as a member. There are no differences of rank and prestige among members; all are brothers and equal.

14. In order for a person to be accepted as a member by the Society, two present members must nominate and give assurances regarding him. After the nomination has been studied, and approved in the branch, the procedure of initiation by oath takes place, according to the prescribed formula. Every person who joins the Society shall be bound to it for the rest of his life, and is not permitted to leave it.

15. Every brother must carry out the task appointed to him by the Society, to the best of his capabilities, and must assist the Society by all the material and physical means at his disposal.

E. FORMULA OF THE OATH

"I swear before God and give my word of honor, that I will offer even my soul and property, in order to save our oppressed brothers from captivity, and to raise them spiritually and materially. I swear likewise to preserve the secrecy of the Society. So help me God."

THE CONSTITUTION OF THE SOCIETY OF 'MOUVAHIDIN'

Art. 1. —In recognition of the fact that, in spite of the progress of civilisation, fanaticism still predominates in the world and that in consequence religion must be utilised to counter every attack inspired by religion, an organisation, at present secret, entitled the Society of 'Mouvahidin' has been established by the assistance of eight Muslim notables whose names are known.

The principal aim of this Society is to gather together all the Musulmans of the world around the Khalifate and to establish among them union and solidarity, respecting at the same time their autonomy and their territorial and cultural independence.

Art. 2. —In order to attain its object the Society will first hold a Congress composed of delegates and notables from all Musulman territories. This Congress will deal with the following questions:—

a) the establishment of the methods which will be adopted by the Society to obtain its objects.

b) to settle how the funds necessary to the Society are to be collected.

c) to settle the lines of action to be adopted by the organisations which are to be formed in the various centres.

d) to elect members of the Central organisation and of the Executive council.

Art. 3. —The Khalifate is the possession of the eldest son of the Osman Dynasty, who, at the same time, is by right and merit ruler of the Ottoman Empire. This sublime office holds an unshakeable right of supervision and control throughout the Musulman world.

Art. 4. —It is the preliminary duty of the Society to make efforts to obtain, in accordance with the principle of Nationality recognised also by Europe, independence for those of the Musulman peoples who are not in actual fact independent or who are, in the status of colonies or dominions, under the domination of Foreign Powers. When their in-

SOURCE: FO371/4162, E177629/521/44.

dependence has been secured, Pan-Islamism will be established in accordance with decisions to be arrived at by an Assembly of the 'Mouvahidin' (Majlis-i-Mouvahidin) which will be composed of delegates from all countries and will meet at the seat of the Khalifate or in any other place that may be chosen.

Art 5. —Although the Society completely abstains from the useless shedding of blood, it will nevertheless retaliate should it meet with armed opposition to the accomplishment of its legitimate objects.

Art. 6. —The funds of the Society will be composed at present of monthly subscriptions payable by the members and of contributions from rich Musulmans. Later, each country gaining its independence will open a separate head in its budget in connection with the above-mentioned funds.

Art. 7. —The actions and accounts of the Society will be examined by a General Congress to be convened once a year or, if found necessary, half-yearly.

Art. 8. —Until the convocation of the first Congress the founders of the Society will form an Executive Council and all business will be conducted in complete secrecy.

Art. 9. —Since, in accordance with a particular chapter of Koran, all the faithful must in principle rally to the rescue and assistance of their brethren, all Musulmans are ipso facto considered members of this Society.

Art. 10. —The Society will have a Supreme Court, composed of a President, four members and two Examining Magistrates. This Court will decide the fate of traitors to the Society.

Art. 11. —Every member is absolutely bound to obey the orders of the Society even at the cost of his life. Those who fail to obey orders will be charged with tre[a]son and their cases will be referred to the Supreme Court.

Art. 12. —It is the duty of the Executive Council to settle, in accordance with political requirements, the locality for the convocation of the First Congress and the despatch of delegates to different Musulman countries.

Art. 13. —The Society will commence work without loss of time. Since the religion of Islam ordains that the liberty and the religious integrity, the life and honour, of the various peoples residing in Muslim countries should be respected, those non-Muslims who have not acted in opposition to the objects of the Society will be placed under protection and in perfect security.

Art. 14. —It is the duty of the Society to organise in mosques classes for the purpose of explaining in suitable language the wishes of the Society; to publish tracts, newspapers and books; to organise special delegations for the purpose of propaganda; and to send, defraying all expenses, special delegates to Turkestan, to the Caucasus, to Asiatic Russia, to India, Afghanistan, Baluchistan, Persia, Java, Muscat, Syria, Sumatra, Iraq, and North and Central Africa.

Art. 15. —The Society will be composed of three sections of which the first will deal with organisation and interior economy, the second with propaganda and publications, and the third with foreign policy.

Art. 16. —The Supreme Court and the members of the headquarters Delegation will frame special rules dealing with the instructions which the above-mentioned sections will follow.

Art. 17. —Every country joining the Union shall form in itself a free and independent unit. These countries will be united together under the sacred protection of the Khalifate only so far as economic, military and foreign policies are concerned. Every independent country will have its own President, a Supreme Council and a Ministerial Council. In addition a General Council of 'Mouvahidin' in which all Moslem countries will be represented, will be established at the seat of the Khalifate.

Art. 18. —The Congress at its first meeting will be free to modify and to alter the articles of this constitution on condition that its fundamental objects are not affected.

PROGRAM OF THE PILGRIMAGE CONGRESS

The aims of the Congress shall be:

1. To find means for promoting mutual understanding among Muslim peoples, through their ulama and thinkers.

2. To consider Arab unity the nucleus of Islamic unity, and a model which will stimulate other Muslim peoples to establish their unity, and so be linked with one another.

3. To create an executive committee to compose a program for the general congress, and to establish branch committees in the various Islamic lands which will be linked to the main committee of the Congress.

4. To create a financial committee whose task will be to consider devising the best instruments for raising funds for the purpose of effectively carrying out the resolutions of the Congress.

5. To find means for disseminating and defending the idea of the Congress among Muslim peoples, while noting that the fundamental aim of the Congress is strictly to deal with religious questions affecting the material and spiritual well-being of the Muslims.

6. To appeal to Muslim peoples to take an interest in the education and instruction of youth according to the true precepts of religion, so that in future there will be men who understand religious thought, as it relates to this world and the next, and who will work together to defend it; and to deter Muslims from sending their children to foreign schools, as these schools proselytize, promote atheism, and weaken the national spirit, under the pretext of diffusing science and civilization. The Muslims should replace such schools with their own indigenous, purely Islamic schools, and secure the best available teachers.

7. To use the most efficacious means to educate a group of young Muslims in each Islamic country in the technical and life sciences, such as industry, engineering, medicine, pharmacology, agriculture, chemistry, military technology, transportation and communications, in accordance with the divine prescription: "And ready against them what force you can."

SOURCE: *Al-Qibla,* July 7, 1924.

8. To disseminate the Arabic language and promote its instruction in all the Islamic countries, for this language is the one in which religion was revealed, and religion is the only bond which links the Muslims. Through this language, mutual understanding among them will be possible, despite differences of race and tongue, and Arabic must be the official language of the Congress.

THE GENERAL ISLAMIC CONGRESS FOR THE CALIPHATE IN CAIRO

Charter adopted by the preparatory committee of the Congress in its session of Sunday, Shawwal 12, 1344/April 25, 1926.

Art. 1. —The Congress shall be presided over by His Eminence, the Shaykh al-Azhar.

Art. 2. —The Congress shall have a vice president, who shall be named by the administrative committee of the Congress, and who shall carry out the duties of the president in the event of his absence.

Art. 3. —The president of the Congress shall preside over the sessions, give the floor, direct questions, announce the resolutions, and speak in the name of the Congress.

Art. 4. —The maintenance of order shall be the responsibility of the Congress participants, under the supervision of the president on behalf of the Congress.

Art. 5. —The Congress secretariat shall consist of the secretary general and his assistants, who must know the languages of the participants in order to make the necessary translations, should circumstances require this.

Art. 6. —The secretary general shall examine the credentials of the delegates, in conformity with the invitations issued by the Congress. He shall record their names, and their addresses in Egypt and in their own countries, in a special register. He shall issue each delegate with a pass indicating his name, title, and country.

Art. 7. —The secretariat shall establish the agenda of each of the sessions of the Congress, shall transcribe the proceedings, record the

SOURCE: Sékaly, *Le Congrès du Khalifat,* 42–45.

resolutions, take attendance, and keep a list of those delegates who desire the floor.

Art. 8. —The secretariat shall edit the proceedings and the resolutions of the commissions, and submit reports to the president of the Congress.

Art. 9. —The president shall open and close the sessions, and set the date of the next meeting at the close of each session.

Art. 10. —Arabic shall be the official language of the Congress. Those who do not know it well may speak and comment in their own languages, after the secretariat has translated and distributed their speeches and papers to the other members. As for ordinary remarks, they shall be translated during the sessions themselves.

Art. 11. —The first meeting of the Congress shall be an inaugural session for the presentation of members. At that time, a commission shall be named, chosen from among the members, to examine the speeches, proposals, and papers before they are read to the Congress. This Commission shall submit the results of its examination to the Congress president, indicating which communications may be delivered to the Congress, and a schedule for their presentation.

Art. 12. —In its second session, the Congress shall examine the agenda, and determine the number of sessions as well as the agenda of each session. The Congress may form commissions to study certain questions, should it so choose.

Art. 13. —The commissions shall examine the matters submitted to them, and each shall separately submit a report containing the results of their deliberations. Each commission shall appoint one of its members as rapporteur, and his report shall be presented to the Congress at a predetermined time.

Art. 14. —The president shall transmit proposals and other communications received by him to the relevant commissions.

Art. 15. —Every member of the Congress has the right to speak during a session, after having requested and obtained the permission of the president, on a first-come, first-served basis, following the scheduled speakers.

Art. 16. —Remarks shall only be addressed to the president or the Congress assembly.

Art. 17. —The speaker shall not stray from his subject, repeat something that has already been said, or speak twice on the same subject.

Art. 18. —Interruption of the speaker shall not be permitted, except to call him to order, which is the prerogative of the president.

Art. 19. —The president shall conclude the discussion if no member desires the floor to present a new point of view.

Art. 20. —Should a group of members request that discussion be closed, the president shall solicit the advice of the Congress.

Art. 21. —Votes shall be conducted by alphabetical roll call.

Art. 22. —Resolutions regarding the questions on the agenda and specific propositions shall be passed by a majority of those members present. In the event of a tie, the president's vote shall be decisive.

Art. 23. —The secretariat, under the supervision of the president, shall count the votes and determine the results, which shall be announced by the president.

Art. 24. —The secretariat shall edit the minutes of each session's deliberations, and shall read them at the beginning of the following session. If there are no objections, the text shall be considered approved. It shall be signed by the president of the session and the secretary general or his representative, then transcribed in a register and signed again.

Art. 25. —The president shall communicate letters and correspondence of any importance to the Congress.

Art. 26. —The sessions of the Congress shall be public, and admission shall be by personal pass.

CONSTITUTION OF THE CONGRESS OF THE ISLAMIC WORLD

In the name of God, the All-Merciful, the Compassionate

In response to the invitation of His Excellency ᶜAbd al-ᶜAziz ibn ᶜAbd al-Rahman al-Faysal Al Saᶜud, the Congress of the Islamic World met on Monday, Dhu al-Hijja 26, 1344, and set down the following constitution for this and subsequent congresses:

Art. 1. —This congress will be known as the Congress of the Islamic World.

Art. 2. —The aims of the Congress are:
a). to promote mutual understanding and unity among Muslims, in realization of God's words, "verily, the believers are brethren";
b). to examine and advance the religious, social, cultural, and economic development of the Muslims;
c). to examine and promote the improvement of security in the holy precincts of the Hijaz; to better the facilities for transportation, health, communications; to facilitate the pilgrimage, and to remove all obstacles which impede the fulfillment of this religious duty; to guarantee the integrity of the Hijaz, and to safeguard its rights.

Art. 3. —The Congress will meet in Mecca each year during the pilgrimage season. Should that prove impossible, the Congress will convene in another independent Muslim land. Should that, too, prove impossible, guidance will be sought in God's admonition, "and serve God as you are best able."

Art. 4. —These are the lands of the Islamic world, in [Arabic] alphabetical order: South and West Africa; East Africa; Afghanistan; South America; North America; Europe (its Muslim population); Iran; Turkey; Tunisia; Java and Sumatra; Algeria; Ethiopia; the Hijaz; the Persian Gulf; Russia; the Rif; Zanzibar; the Sudan; Syria; Transjordan; China; Tri-

SOURCE: *Al-Ahram,* June 23, 30, 1926.

politania; Iraq; Asir; Palestine; the Philippines; the Congo; Morocco; Egypt; Malaya and Ceylon; the Najd; India; and Yemen.

Each of these countries shall have one vote, with certain modifications. The Hijaz, as it contains the site which all Muslims face in prayer, shall have three votes; Afghanistan, Iran, Turkey, Egypt, the Najd, and Yemen, since they are independent countries, shall each have two votes; India, since it is the most populous Muslim land, shall have four votes; and for the same reason, China shall have three votes, Java together with Sumatra shall also have three, and Russia shall have two votes.

Art. 5. —The Congress shall be comprised of:
a). delegates of independent governments;
b). delegates of branch committees of this Congress in lands where such committees exist;
c). representatives of Muslim peoples, selected in the most representative manner possible in every Muslim land.

Art. 6. —The direction of the Congress shall be entrusted to a president, first vice president, second vice president, and a secretary general. In some lands, branches of the secretariat general shall be established, and these will be linked to the central secretariat general.

Art. 7. —The Congress shall establish an executive committee, including the president of the Congress and the two vice presidents to be elected at the opening session, as well as six additional members and a secretary general, to be elected at the closing session. One of the six shall be the treasurer. These members and the secretary general shall always reside at the headquarters of the Congress. In the absence of the president, the sessions of the executive committee will be presided over by one of the two vice presidents, or the secretary general.

Art. 8. —If the presidency should become vacant, either of the vice presidents or the secretary general shall fill the office. If the secretariat or one of the six positions on the executive committee should become vacant, then the executive committee shall select a replacement.

Art. 9. —The executive committee shall set the date for convening the second congress during the next pilgrimage season, and will issue the invitations.

Art. 10. —At the opening of the Congress, the session shall be presided over by the previous president, one of the vice presidents, or the eldest member of the executive committee. A new president shall then immediately be elected by secret ballot. The secretary general, the secretaries of congress branches (as provided by article 6), and the six members of the executive committee (mentioned in article 7), shall be elected during the closing session of the congress. Some or all of these office holders may be reelected.

Art. 11. —Prior to the opening session, every delegate must present his credentials to the secretary general, or to a body designated to examine them.

Art. 12. —The duties of the president are to preside over the Congress sessions, to convene them at the appointed times, to keep order, to give the floor and address questions, to order votes, to adjourn the sessions at their close, to set the time of subsequent sessions, and to supervise the implementation of the Congress resolutions and the activities of the secretariats general in various countries.

Art. 13. —The duties of the two vice presidents are to exercise all the functions of the president during his absence, and to assist the president if necessary.

Art. 14. —The duties of the secretary general are to handle executive and administrative affairs under the guidance of the president, to see to the implementation of the Congress resolutions, to direct the activities of the central secretariat general, to conduct correspondence and send invitations to the meetings, to prepare the annual budget with the approval of the executive committee, to keep accounts, to issue an annual report on Congress activities, to maintain constant contact with the secretaries general abroad and with branches of the congress, and to carry out any other tasks delegated by the president.

Art. 15. —The duty of the secretaries general abroad is to fulfill tasks like those of the Congress secretary general, each in his own country. They will maintain contact with the central secretariat general, which will assign various duties to them.

Art. 16. —All of the members of the executive committee shall be entrusted with carrying out those activities assigned to them by the congress, under the supervision of the president and secretary general. They shall be individually and collectively responsible for their actions.

Art. 17. —The president, the vice presidents, the remaining secretaries, and the other members of the executive committee, shall be responsible for their actions before the Congress.

Art. 18. —The central secretary general, the secretaries general in the various countries, and members of the executive committee, shall receive salaries fixed for them by the Congress.

Art. 19. —The duties of the treasurer are to collect revenues and issue receipts, and to authorize expenditures in return for receipts. He shall register all income and expenses in his books immediately, and he shall be responsible for the accounting and financial activities.

Art. 20. —From time to time, the Congress shall issue instructions as to the use of its funds and the amounts to be held by the treasurer.

Art. 21. —The fiscal year of the Congress shall terminate at the end of the lunar month of Sha'ban, and shall begin at the start of the lunar month of Ramadan.

Art. 22. —Each year the Congress shall appoint a competent accountant to study its books, and he shall submit a report to the Congress by the first day of the lunar month of Dhu al-Qa'da.

Art. 23. —The Congress shall issue instructions to authorize the withdrawal of funds from their place of deposit, and their disbursement by the treasurer.

Art. 24. —Every member of the agenda committee who has a proposal shall submit it in writing to the secretary general of the Congress three days before the opening of the Congress, signed by the initiator and at least one other sponsor. Every delegation from the countries listed in article 4 shall be entitled to appoint one member to this committee, or more, depending upon its voting strength. These members, as well as the president and the two vice presidents elected on the first day (as stipulated in article 10), and the secretary general, shall constitute the agenda committee.

As for late-arriving delegations, they shall appoint their member to the committee on the day of their arrival. On the opening day of the Congress, the secretary general shall present the received proposals to this committee for its consideration. The committee shall then issue them in the form of the Congress agenda. Late proposals shall not be accepted unless there are extenuating circumstances, in which case the committee may consider them as appendices to the agenda.

Art. 25. —Unwritten proposals shall not be accepted. Should a non-member wish to submit a proposal, he must do so to the secretary general at least three days in advance. Should the initiator be a member, no time limit on submission shall apply. The secretary general shall submit all such proposals to the agenda committee, and the committee shall determine what is acceptable for submission to the Congress.

Art. 26. —All questions discussed by the Congress shall be decided by an absolute majority of the votes. In the event of a tie, the president's vote shall be decisive. A quorum shall consist of delegations from six of those countries listed in article 4, unless a modification of this Charter is envisioned, in which case the quorum specified in article 27 shall be required.

Art. 27. —No amendment, addition, or deletion shall be made to the text of this Constitution without a two-thirds majority of attending members, in the presence of delegations from at least ten of the countries listed in article 4.

Art. 28. —The executive committee shall legally represent the Congress when out of session. The secretary general shall hold power of attorney for the committee, and may retain whomsoever he wishes as the committee's legal counsel.

Art. 29. —Each year, the secretary general, with the assent of the executive committee, shall present a detailed report on the income and expenditures of the Congress for the fiscal year ending in the month of Sha ban prior to the Congress. He shall also present a budget for the coming year, as provided in article 14. The Congress may revise and amend this budget before approving it.

Art. 30. —The sum comprising the annual budget of the Congress shall be provided by all the Islamic countries which are members, in proportion to their voting strength. The contribution of each country must be paid before its delegates may exercise the prerogatives of membership.

Art. 31. —The permanent expenses of the Congress shall consist of:

£   300   Expenses of convening the Congress.
     500   Postage, telegrams, publications, etc.
    1000   Furnishings.

360–600	Yearly salary of the secretary general.
6 × 20–40	Monthly salaries of six members of the executive committee.
6 × 20–40	Monthly salaries of six regional secretaries general.
6 × 8–12	Monthly salaries of six clerks at secretariat general.
3 × 3	Monthly salaries of three servants.
200	Miscellaneous

Equals a minimum total of £6224, and a maximum of £9632.

Every country listed in article 4 shall provide the Congress with dues of £ 300 annually per vote. A country's delegation shall not be admitted to the Congress until such dues are paid.

Art. 32. —Resolutions related to the Hijaz shall be submitted by the Congress president to the government of the Hijaz for examination and, if possible, implementation.

CHARTER OF THE GENERAL ISLAMIC CONGRESS

*Adopted by the Congress in its fourteenth session
held on Tuesday, Shaᶜban 6, 1350/December 10, 1931*

Art. 1. —A periodic, general congress of Muslims from throughout the world shall be held and known as the General Islamic Congress.

Art. 2. —The aims of the Congress are:
a). to promote cooperation among Muslims of whatever origin or sect, to spread Islamic culture and virtues, and to promote the spirit of general Islamic brotherhood;
b). to defend Muslim interests and preserve the holy places and lands from any intervention;
c). to combat Christian missionary efforts and campaigns among the Muslims;
d). to establish universities and scholarly institutions to work for unification of Islamic culture and the instruction of the Arabic language to Islamic youth, through the founding of a university in Jerusalem to be known as the al-Aqsa Mosque University;
e). to examine other Islamic matters of importance to the Muslims.

Art. 3. —Future congresses shall be composed of the following persons:
a). those who were present at the first congress;
b). those invited by the preparatory committee to future congresses, whether as individuals or as representatives of Islamic organizations;
c). those Muslims whom the Congress itself invites to participate during its sessions.

Art. 4. —The Congress may regard any individual as a member, even though he may be absent from its sessions, provided he has rendered notable cultural or material services to the Muslims.

Art. 5. —The Congress shall meet once every two years. The ex-

SOURCE: *Al-Jamiᶜa al-ᶜarabiyya*, December 18, 1931.

ecutive committee, by a three-fourths majority, may convene the Congress in the interim should unforseen circumstances warrant it.

Art. 6. —The seat of the Congress shall be Jerusalem. The Congress may choose another seat for its activities, and each session may choose the site of the following session. The executive committee shall determine the site of extraordinary sessions.

Art. 7. —The Congress, while in session, shall be directed by a board composed of the president, four deputies, four observers, and four secretaries, to be elected by the Congress in accordance with its internal statutes.

Art. 8. —The Congress, while in session, shall establish such committees as it deems necessary, to study projects and submit reports.

Art. 9. —The Congress shall elect an executive committee from among its members, to be composed of twenty-five members representing as many Islamic peoples as possible. The executive committee's special tasks will be:
   a). to implement the resolutions of the Congress, and supervise its committees and bureaus;
   b). to take measures to convene the next Congress and define its agenda;
   c). to establish branches throughout Islamic lands, and send delegations abroad to explain the aims of the Congress.
The executive committee shall set down internal statutes to regulate its work, sessions, and finances, and these statutes shall be presented to the next meeting of the Congress.

Art. 10. —The executive committee shall elect a bureau of seven persons from among the Congress members, among them a secretary general, an assistant secretary general, and a treasurer, with these responsibilities:
   a). to implement the decisions of the executive committee;
   b). to conduct the secretarial and accounting tasks.
The secretary general shall organize the meetings of the bureau and implement its decisions. The bureau shall be collectively responsible to the executive committee.

Art. 11. —The president of the Congress shall preside over meetings of the executive committee.

Art. 12. —The executive committee and the bureau shall continue their work until the next congress, at which time a new executive committee shall be elected, which shall in turn elect a new bureau. Members of the executive committee and bureau may be reelected.

Art. 13. —The finances of the Congress shall be drawn from subscriptions, contributions, and other sources.

Art. 14. —The treasurer shall be responsible for the funds, accounting, and financial transactions of the Congress. These shall be examined annually by a certified accountant.

Art. 15. —All funds received on behalf of the Congress by any of its members or committees must be turned over to the treasurer. Expenditures shall be authorized only upon the approval of the bureau, and in accordance with the resolutions of the executive committee and the Congress. The funds of the Congress are to be kept in accounts opened by the bureau, in the name of the General Islamic Congress. No funds may be withdrawn without the signatures of two members of the bureau, one of whom must be the treasurer.

Art. 16. —The Congress may decide by a two-thirds majority of those present to expel a member, if it is established that he has conspired against the Congress or has worked to frustrate it. The accused shall have the right to defend himself in person or through a representative.

Art. 17. —This Charter may be altered only by a two-thirds majority decision of Congress members in attendance, provided that the change and its purpose are presented to members of the Congress at least two days before debate over the matter.

ABBREVIATIONS

AFC	Archives of the French Embassy, Cairo.
AHP	Abbas Hilmi II Papers, Durham University Library, Durham.
Antonius-Oxford	Papers of George Antonius in the Library of St. Antony's College, Oxford.
Azhar File	Records of the General Islamic Congress for the Caliphate in Egypt, Azhar Mosque Library, Cairo.
Blunt-Chichester	Papers of Wilfrid Scawen Blunt in the West Sussex County and Diocesan Record Office, Chichester.
Blunt-Fitzwilliam	Papers of Wilfrid Scawen Blunt in the Fitzwilliam Museum, Cambridge.
CO	Colonial Office Archives, Public Record Office, London.
CZA	Central Zionist Archives, Jerusalem.
DWQ	Dar al-Watha²iq al-Qawmiyya (Egyptian National Archives), Cairo.
EI²	*Encyclopaedia of Islam*, 2d edition, Leiden.
FO	Foreign Office Archives, Public Record Office, London.
GFO	Political Archives of the German Foreign Office, Microcopy T-120, National Archives, Washington.
ISA	Israel State Archives, Jerusalem.
JMFA	Japanese Ministry of Foreign Affairs Archives, Microforms Division, Library of Congress, Washington.
L/P&J	Public and Judicial Department Archives, India Office Records, London.
L/P&S	Political and Secret Department Archives, India Office Records, London.

MRJ	Mahfuzat Ri^ʾasat al-Jumhuriyya (Archives of the Presidency of the Republic), Cairo.
Mufti Files	Wartime Papers of Hajj Amin al-Husayni, Israeli Foreign Ministry, Jerusalem.
NA	National Archives, Washington.
SFA	Records of the Ministère Public Fédéral, Swiss Federal Archives, Bern.

NOTES

INTRODUCTION

1. Louis Massignon, "L'entente islamique internationale et les deux congrès musulmans de 1926"; H. A. R. Gibb, *Whither Islam?* 354–64; Richard Hartmann, "Zum Gedanken des 'Kongresses' in den Reformbestrebungen des islamischen Orients."

1. THE COSMOPOLITAN MILIEU

1. The novel went through many editions. It is summarized by F. A. Tansel, ed. *Namık Kemal'in mektupları*, 2: 177–79. For more details on the publication of the book, see Ömer Faruk Akün, "Nâmık Kemal'in Kitap Halindeki Eserlerinin İlk Neşirleri." For Namık Kemal's appeal for Muslim solidarity in his own era, see Mustafa Özön, *Namık Kemal ve İbret Gazetesi,* 74–78.
2. The gathering was called a *majlis;* the dialogue, *muhawara.*
3. ʿAbdallah Efendi ibn Husayn al-Suwaydi, *al-Hujjaj al-qatʿiyya li-ittifaq al-firaq al-islamiyya,* 22–27. Cf. L. Lockhart, *Nadir Shah,* 233; and Hamid Algar, "Shiʿism and Iran in the Eighteenth Century," 294–96.
4. E. G. Browne, "Pan-Islamism," 323.
5. Text of proclamation in *Revue du monde musulman* (1911), 13: 385–86. Details on the attitudes of Iraq's Shiʿi scholars to the Ottoman state are provided by Abdul-Hadi Hairi, *Shiʿism and Constitutionalism in Iran.*
6. E. G. Browne (Cambridge) to Wilfrid Scawen Blunt, February 16, 1911, in Blunt-Chichester, file 9, "Edward G. Browne."
7. On the origins of this current of thought, see Dwight E. Lee, "The Origins of Pan-Islamism," and Nikki R. Keddie, "Pan-Islam as Proto-Nationalism."
8. H. A. R. Gibb, "Luṭfi Paşa on the Ottoman Caliphate," and Fritz Steppat, "Khalifat, Dār al-Islām und die loyalität der Araber zum osmanischen Reich bei Hanafitischen Juristen des 19. Jahrhunderts."
9. See Gibb, *Studies on the Civilization of Islam,* 141–50.
10. Halil İnalcık, "The Socio-Political Effects of the Diffusion of Fire-arms in the Middle East," 202–10.
11. Anthony Reid, "Sixteenth Century Turkish Influence in Western Indonesia"; Seljuk Affan, "Relations Between the Ottoman Empire and the Muslim Kingdoms in the Malay-Indonesian Archipelago"; and documents published by Razaulhak Şah, "Açi Padişahı Sultan Alâeddin'in Kanunî Sultan Süleyman'a Mektubu."
12. Aziz Ahmad, *Studies in Islamic Culture in the Indian Environment,* 27–28.
13. B. G. Martin, "Maî Idrîs of Bornu and the Ottoman Turks, 1576–78," 478–79. A more complete set of documents was published by Cengiz Orhonlu, "Osmanlı-Bornu münasebetine âid belgeler."
14. This reassertion is described by Bernard Lewis, "Ottoman Empire in the Mid-Nineteenth Century: A Review," 290–94.
15. For Algerian immigration see Charles-Robert Ageron, *Les Algériens musulmans et la France (1871–1919),* 2: 1079–92; see also J. Desparmet, "La turcophilie en Algérie," citing

extensively from folklore and poems. On the émigrés, see Pierre Bardin, *Algériens et Tunisiens dans l'Empire Ottoman de 1848 à 1914.*

16. Pertev Boratav, "La Russie dans les Archives ottomanes. Un dossier ottoman sur l'*imâm* Chamil."

17. On the events which led to his expulsion, and the prestige which he continued to enjoy in Malabar, see Stephen F. Dale, "The Mappilla Outbreaks: Ideology and Social Conflict in Nineteenth-Century Kerala," 90–93; and his *Islamic Society on the South Asian Frontier,* 113–18, 127–37, 164–69. For Sayyid Fadl's activities in Dhofar, see J. G. Lorimer, *Gazetteer of the Persian Gulf, Oman, and Central Arabia,* 1: 591–92, 595–97, 599; and J. B. Kelly, *Britain and the Persian Gulf,* 772–75.

18. Marc Pinson, "Russian Policy and the Emigration of the Crimean Tatars to the Ottoman Empire, 1854–1862."

19. Marc Pinson, "Ottoman Colonization of the Circassians in Rumili After the Crimean War," and Kemal H. Karpat, "The Status of the Muslim under European Rule: The Eviction and Settlement of the Cerkes."

20. A. A. Powell, "Maulānā Raḥmat Allāh Kairānawī and Muslim-Christian Controversy in India in the Mid-19th Century." The polemic, entitled *Izhar al-haqq,* has seen many translations and editions, and in the past decade has enjoyed a renewed popularity, if one is to judge from the appearance of several new editions in Arabic and Urdu.

21. Roderic H. Davison, *Reform in the Ottoman Empire, 1856–1876,* 272–74. For an approach that might yield much on this subject, see Grace Martin Smith, "The Özbek Tekkes of Istanbul."

22. See the following works by Anthony Reid: "Nineteenth Century Pan-Islam in Indonesia and Malaysia"; "Indonesian Diplomacy. A Documentary Study of Atjehnese Foreign Policy in the Reign of Sultan Mahmud, 1870–4"; "Habib Abdur-Rahman az-Zahir (1833–1896)"; and *The Contest for North Sumatra: Atjeh, the Netherlands, and Britain, 1858–1898,* 81–85, 119–29, 145–46.

23. ʿAli al-Shanufi, "Fasl min al-rihla al-hijaziyya li-Muhammad al-Sanusi." On Muhammad al-Sanusi, see Ali Chenoufi, *Un savant tunisien du XIXᵐᵉ siècle: Muhammad as-Sanusi, sa vie et son oeuvre.*

24. This circle was first described by C. Snouck Hurgronje, "Eenige Arabische strijdschriften besproken" (originally published in 1897), and in summarized form in his review entitled "Les confréries religieuses, la Mecque, et le Panislamisme" (originally written in 1900).

25. On this figure, see the bibliographical article by Werner Ende, "Sayyid Abū al-Hudā, ein Vertrauter Abdülhamid's II. Notwendigkeit und Probleme einer kritischen Biographie," and B. Abu-Manneh, "Sultan Abdulhamid II and Shaikh Abulhuda Al-Sayyadi."

26. On Shaykh Zafir, see A. Le Chatelier, *Les Confréries musulmanes du Hedjaz,* 112–24; Jean-Louis Miège, *Le Maroc et l'Europe,* 4: 173–79; and Wali al-Din Yakan, *al-Maʿlum waʾl-majhul,* 100–101, 169–77. Real Ottoman progress was made in Morocco only at the end of Abdülhamid's reign, and under the Young Turk regime. See Jean Deny, "Instructeurs militaires turcs au Maroc sous Moulay Hafidh," and Edmund Burke, "Pan-Islam and Moroccan Resistance to French Colonial Penetration, 1900–1912."

27. On his life, see the biographical preface by his son to an edition of his tract entitled *al-Risala al-hamidiyya;* and Ahmad al-Sharabasi, *Rashid Rida, sahib al-Manar,* 231–46 (Husayn al-Jisr was Rashid Rida's teacher).

28. On Ahmad ibn Sumayt, see B. G. Martin, "Notes on Some Members of the Learned Classes of Zanzibar and East Africa in the Nineteenth Century," 541–45; Randall Lee Pouwels, "Islam and Islamic Leadership in the Coastal Communities of Eastern Africa, 1700 to 1914," 492–501; and their sources. On the growth of pro-Ottoman sympathies

among the Muslims of East Africa, see K. Axenfeld, "Geistige Kämpfe in der Eingeborenenbevölkerung an der Küste Ostafrikas," especially 654f.

29. It was the thesis of Hurgronje, in his "Eenige Arabische strijdschriften besproken," that this circle was too torn by rivalries to constitute an efficient bureau of propaganda.

30. For his approach of 1879, see Nikki R. Keddie, *Sayyid Jamāl ad-Dīn "al-Afghānī": A Political Biography*, 129–42, translating and analyzing the appeal in Iraj Afshar and Asghar Mahdavi, *Majmūʿa-yi asnad ve-madarik-i chap nashuda dar bara-yi Sayyid Jamal al-Din mashhur bih-Afghani*, photos 26–27. For his approach of 1885, see Keddie, 246–68. For Afghani's last appeal, of 1892, see Jacob M. Landau, "Al-Afghāni's Pan-Islamic Project."

31. Keddie, *Sayyid Jamāl ad-Dīn*, 380–81.

32. Arthur H. Hardinge, *A Diplomatist in the East*, 273–74.

33. There are at least three studies of this mission. See Dwight E. Lee, "A Turkish Mission to Afghanistan, 1877"; D. P. Singhal, "A Turkish Mission to Kabul—A Forgotten Chapter of History"; and M. Cavid Baysun, "Şirvanî-zade Ahmed Hulûsi Efendi'nin Efganistan elçiliğine âid vesikalar," where the diary of the mission is published.

34. On this figure, see Eşref Edib, "Meşhur İslâm seyyahı Abdürreşid İbrahim Efendi"; Azade-Ayse Rorlich, "Transition into the Twentieth Century: Reform and Secularization among the Volga Tatars," 233–35, 267–68; and Edward J. Lazzerini, "Abdurreşid Ibragimov (Ibrahimov)."

35. On nineteenth-century Indian Muslim attachment to the Ottoman Empire, see R. M. Shukla, *Britain, India and the Turkish Empire 1853–1882*, 94–120; Y. B. Mathur, *Muslims and Changing India*, 120–34; and A. Halim, "Russo-Turkish War of 1876–77 and the Muslims of Bengal." The activities of the Indian Muslim circle in Istanbul are detailed by Shukla, 155–85.

36. Compare the Ottoman campaign to that described by M. Canard, "L'Impérialisme des Fātimides et leur propagande," and W. Ivanow, "The Organisation of the Fatimid Propaganda."

37. For one example of a reaction to this problem, as it arose in Algeria, see Pierre Boyer, "L'Administration française et la règlementation du pèlerinage à la Mecque (1830–1894)."

38. See William Ochsenwald, *The Hijaz Railroad*; and Jacob M. Landau, *The Hejaz Railway and the Muslim Pilgrimage: A Case of Ottoman Political Propaganda*.

2. A CHALLENGE TO AUTHORITY

1. On Blunt, see Elizabeth Longford, *A Pilgrimage of Passion: The Life of Wilfrid Scawen Blunt*; Albert Hourani, "Wilfrid Scawen Blunt and the Revival of the East"; and Kathryn Tidrick, *Heart-beguiling Araby*, 107–35.

2. "Alms to Oblivion," part 4, chapter 5, in Blunt-Fitzwilliam, MS. 323–1975.

3. Wilfrid Scawen Blunt, *Secret History of the English Occupation of Egypt*, 66.

4. Hamid Algar, *Mīrzā Malkum Khān. A Study in the History of Iranian Nationalism.*

5. *Qanun*, no. 17 (issue not dated).

6. *Qanun*, no. 18 (issue not dated).

7. On Sabunji's English period, see L. Zolondek, "Sabunji in England 1876–91: His Role in Arabic Journalism."

8. Philippe de Tarrazi, *Taʾrikh al-sahafa al-ʿarabiyya*, 2: 251–52. The newspaper itself does not appear to have survived.

9. Tarrazi, *Taʾrikh al-sahafa*, 2:94, where his salary and position are described.

10. Wilfrid Scawen Blunt, *My Diaries*, 2: 260.

11. Blunt, *Secret History*, 67.

12. "Memoir on the Position of the Ottoman Sultans towards Islam," confidential print dated July 24, 1880, in a volume of newspaper cuttings compiled by W.S.B., 1878–1882, Blunt-Chichester. Fragment also in Blunt-Fitzwilliam, MS. 1511–1977. Blunt went public that summer with a similar though not yet developed argument. See W. S. Blunt, "The Sultan's Heirs in Asia," and his letter to *The Spectator*, June 5, 1880.

13. *Dictionary of National Biography, 1912–1921*, 46–47.

14. *The Times*, June 25, 1877.

15. *The Times*, October 15, 1877.

16. *The Times*, July 9, 1877.

17. Blunt, *Secret History*, 65.

18. Blunt later counted Zohrab among his "rather intimate friends," in Blunt, *Secret History*, 121. Zohrab received the Blunts in Jidda and tried to arrange for their safe passage, as described by Zohrab (Jidda), dispatch of December 23, 1880, FO78/3131. A small file of four letters from Zohrab to Blunt and his wife, all written during the first half of 1881, is preserved in Blunt-Chichester, file 61, "J. W. Zohrab."

19. Zohrab (Cairo), dispatch of January 9, 1880, FO78/3131.

20. Zohrab (Jidda), dispatch of March 12, 1879, FO78/2988.

21. Ibid., August 6, 1879.

22. Consul Zohrab's Letter Book, vol. 2, "Report on the Establishment required to carry on the duties of Her Majesty's Consulate at Jeddah" [September 1879], FO685/1.

23. Zohrab (Jidda), dispatch of February 8, 1881, FO78/3314.

24. Blunt, *The Future of Islam*, 128-9.

25. Ibid., 131.

26. Ibid., 161.

27. Ibid., 166.

28. "Alms to Oblivion," part 4, in Blunt-Fitzwilliam, MS. 324–1975; also in MS. 44–1975. "I have been many times on the point of making my public declaration of faith, if only as a protest and proof of my standing on the side of Eastern right against Western wrong. What has deterred me has been the impossibility of bringing myself to believe in a future life, and lacking this, the uselessness of any religious creed other than a creed political."

29. Zohrab (Cairo) to Alston, January 12, 1880, FO78/3131.

30. Zohrab (Jidda), dispatch of May 19, 1881, FO78/3314.

31. Butrus Abu-Manneh, "Sultan Abdülhamid II and the Sharifs of Mecca (1880–1900)."

32. William L. Ochsenwald, "Ottoman Subsidies to the Hijaz, 1877–1886."

33. George Percy Badger, "The Precedents and Usages Regulating the Muslim Khalifate," 280–81.

34. Blunt, *The Future of Islam*, viii.

35. Ibid., ix.

36. Blunt, *India Under Ripon*, 124–25.

37. See, for example, Sadr Vasiqi, *Sayyid Jamal al-Din Husayni*, 111–15.

38. Elie Kedourie, "Afghani in Paris: A Note"; and Keddie, *Sayyid Jamāl ad-Dīn*, 215–19, for a full account of what is known about the newspaper's finances. To this evidence can be added yet another letter from ᶜAbduh (Paris) to Blunt, April 2, 1884, Blunt-Chichester, file 1, "Sheykh Mohammed Abduh." ᶜAbduh, Afghani's co-editor, writes that "we beg of your generosity that you will assist this newspaper with as much as you can of material help, & as much as your liberality permits." ᶜAbduh asked Blunt to send his views for publication, but not to do so through the medium of "rabbis" or "priests"— the latter an apparent reference to Sabunji.

39. Blunt, *India under Ripon*, 13.

40. *Al-ᶜUrwa al-wuthqa*, March 13, 1884.

41. Ibid., April 10, 1884.

42. Ibid., June 5, 1884.

43. Blunt, *Gordon at Khartoum*, 492.

44. Mirza Lutf Allah Khan Asadabadi, *Sharh-i hal ve asar-i Sayyid Jamal al-Din Asadabadi maʿruf bih Afghani*, 56.

45. Shaykh Ahmad-i Ruhi (Trabzon) to his mother (Kirman), Ramadan 22, 1312/March 19, 1895, in Faridun Adamiyat, *Andishehha-yi Mirza Aqa Khan Kirmani*, 280–81.

46. In his preface to the Azali Babi text *Hasht Bihisht*, as translated by Nikki Keddie, "Religion and Irreligion in Early Iranian Nationalism," 292–95.

47. For Persian text and translation, see Edward G. Browne, *The Persian Revolution of 1905–1909*, 409–15, especially 412.

48. Keddie, *Sayyid Jamāl ad-Dīn*, 445.

49. The most thorough account of Shaykh al-Raʾis is offered by Ibrahim Safaʾi, *Rahbaran-i mashruteh*, 1: 563–91. Other biographical sources are not as frank. See Javahir Kalam, "Hujjat al-Islam vala Shahzada Abu al-Hasan Shaykh al-Raʾis Qajar," and Muhammad Nasir Mirza Fursat, *Kitab-i asar-i ʿajam*, 529–30.

50. Minutes of the meeting, in Abu al-Hasan Shaykh al-Raʾis, *Muntakhab-i nafis az asar-i hazrat-i Shaykh al-Raʾis*, 117–23.

51. Abu al-Hasan Shaykh al-Raʾis, *Ittihad-i Islam*, 83–84.

52. Algar, *Malkum Khān*, 225–27.

53. H. M. Balyuzi, *Edward Granville Browne and the Bahá ʾí Faith*, 90.

54. H. O'Mahoney, "Le Congrès Panislamique," 17–18.

3. An Idea Refined

1. Blunt, *Secret History*, 106.

2. For when Blunt consulted him about the fitness of the Arabs for such a central role in Islam, ʿAbduh replied that they were indeed fit, but the Turks would never permit them to exercise authority, and the Turks were militarily stronger. Furthermore, if one of these two peoples fell under European domination as a consequence of internecine strife, all Islam would suffer. With this argument, ʿAbduh claimed to have dissuaded Blunt from pursuing the idea of an Arabian caliphate. Muhammad ʿAmara, *al-Aʿmal al-kamila li ʾl-imam Muhammad ʿAbduh*, 1: 735.

3. For the text, see Rashid Rida, *Taʾrikh al-ustadh al-imam al-shaykh Muhammad ʿAbduh*, 1: 283–87. According to Rida, the basic charter (*qanun asasi*) of this organization was not put to paper, lest it fall into the wrong hands. But it is obvious that the society never existed. What is certain is that ʿAbduh organized a "branch" during a visit to Tunis in 1884–85. See M. Chenoufi, "Les deux séjours de Muhammad ʿAbduh en Tunisie." On that occasion, he claimed that the society was founded by Afghani in India, but no evidence exists for the creation of a formal society there; see Aziz Ahmad, "Afghānī's Indian Contacts." For alleged correspondence of the society's members—their names deleted to protect them— see Rida, *Taʾrikh al-ustadh al-imam*, 2: 553 ff.

4. Mustapha Kraiem, "Au sujet des incidences des deux séjours de Muhammad ʿAbduh en Tunisie," 92.

5. Al-Munsif al-Shanufi, " ʿAlaʾiq Rashid Rida, sahib al-Manar, maʿa al-tunisiyyin," 133–37.

6. On the school identified with their thought, see Henri Laoust, "Le réformisme orthodoxe des 'Salafiyya' et les caractères généraux de son orientation actuelle."

7. *Al-Manar* (December 17, 1898), 1(39): 765–66.

8. *Al-Manar* (August 5, 1899), 2(21): 325.

9. *Al-Manar* (September 23, 1899), 2(28): 433–34.

10. *Al-Manar* (December 31, 1898), 1(41): 807.

11. *Al-Manar* (April 30, 1900), 3(7): 153–54.

12. See Abu-Manneh, "Sultan Abdülhamid II and the Sharifs of Mecca." This was also a period of Ottoman apprehension over revolt in Yemen. See John Baldry, "Al-Yaman and the Turkish Occupation, 1849–1914."

13. Kawakibi has been the subject of several biographies. Among them are Norbert Tapiero, *Les idées réformistes d'al-Kawākibī, 1265-1320–1849-1902*; Sylvia G. Haim, "The Ideas of a Precursor, ᶜAbd al-Raḥmān al-Kawākibī (1849–1902)"; Sami al-Dahhan, *ᶜAbd al-Rahman al-Kawakibi*; and ᶜAbbas Mahmud al-ᶜAqqad, *al-Rahhala "Kaf": ᶜAbd al-Rahman al-Kawakibi*.

14. Al-Sayyid al-Furati [ᶜAbd al-Rahman al-Kawakibi], *Umm al-qura*. I have used a copy of the rare early edition, which belongs to the Princeton University Library. The Princeton copy is bound with *Tabāᵖiᶜ al-istibdad*, and the binding bears the name of the former owner, ᶜAbd al-Hamid al-Bakri (1876–1940), Shaykh al-Sajjada al-Bakriyya from 1911.

15. Aleppans reported having seen drafts of *Umm al-qura* before Kawakibi's departure. See Kamil al-Ghazzi, " ᶜAbd al-Rahman al-Kawakibi," 448–49; and the preface to the edition of *Umm al-qura* published in Aleppo in 1959. On the survival of that symbiosis through Kawakibi's formative years, see Shimon Shamir, "Midhat Pasha and the Anti-Turkish Agitation in Syria."

16. A work since shown to have been much influenced by Vittorio Alfieri's *Della Tirannide*, in Sylvia Haim, "Alfieri and al-Kawākibī."

17. According to Rashid Rida's obituary for Kawakibi, in *al-Manar* (July 1902), 5(7): 279.

18. *Al-Manar* (February 1932), 33(2): 114.

19. On the possible influence of Blunt, see Sylvia G. Haim, "Blunt and al-Kawākibī." Here it is noted that Blunt's *Future of Islam* was not translated into Arabic (p. 137), although Blunt himself wrote that the essays in *The Fortnightly Review* "found their way, to some extent, in translation to Egypt." Blunt, *Secret History*, 122. I have found no translation in Blunt's own papers.

20. For the charter, see Kawakibi, *Umm al-qura*, 169–88; Tapiero, *Les idées réformistes*, 48–56.

21. Ibid., 186.

22. Ibid., 211–12.

23. Something on the appearance of the book can be learned from the reports to the Khedive ᶜAbbas Hilmi from one of his informants, Muhammad ᶜUrfi. At first, ᶜUrfi believed the congress to have been genuine, and related that the book had surfaced in the possession of pilgrims arriving in Egypt from Mecca. For his first report on the book, see Muhammad ᶜUrfi to Khedive ᶜAbbas Hilmi, October 4, 1900, in *AHP*, 32:7. In a subsequent undated letter, which obviously accompanied a copy of the book, he summarized *Umm al-qura*'s contents; see *AHP*, 32:72–73. ᶜUrfi, in reporting an encounter with Kawakibi, knew to identify him as "one of the authors of *Umm al-qura*," in a letter to the Khedive of March 11, 1901, *AHP*, 32:38, 41.

24. *Les Pyramides*, March 19, 1902.

25. For a summary of the evidence, see Sylvia G. Haim, *Arab Nationalism: An Anthology*, 28–29; Elie Kedourie, "The Politics of Political Literature: Kawakibi, Azoury and Jung," 109–11; Dahhan, *ᶜAbd al-Rahman al-Kawakibi*, 29–30; ᶜAqqad, *al-Rahhala "Kaf": ᶜAbd al-Rahman al-Kawakibi*, 101 ff. But I found no correspondence between Kawakibi and the Khedive in the latter's papers.

26. L. Hirszowicz, "The Sultan and the Khedive, 1892–1908," 304–5, citing a Russian diplomatic dispatch.

27. Negib Azoury, *Le Réveil de la nation arabe*, 229.

28. D. S. Margoliouth, "Mohammedan Explanations of the Failure of Mohammedanism: A Conference at Meccah."

4. A PRACTICAL PLAN

1. See A. Battal-Taymas, "Ben Onu gördüm (İsmail Gaspıralı hakkında notlar)," 649–50.

2. On Gasprinskii, see Edward James Lazzerini, "Ismail Bey Gasprinskii and Muslim Modernism in Russia, 1878–1914"; Cafer Seydahmet, *Gaspıralı İsmail Bey*; Z. V. Togan, "Ismāᶜīl Gasprali (Gasprinski)"; and Gerhard von Mende, *Der nationale Kampf der Russlandtürken*, 44–61.

3. For an assessment of this newspaper's significance, see Alexandre Bennigsen and Chantal Lemercier-Quelquejay, *La presse et le mouvement national chez les musulmans de Russie avant 1920*, 35–42.

4. Ch. Lemercier-Quelquejay, "Un réformateur tatar au XIXᵉ siècle: ᶜAbdul Qajjum al-Nasyri."

5. Lazzerini, "Ismail Bey Gasprinskii," 24.

6. Ibid., 104–5.

7. For general accounts of his proposal, see Martin Hartmann, "Der Islam 1907/1908," 11(2): 212–15; 12(2): 34–37; Thomas Kuttner, "Russian *Jadidism* and the Islamic World: Ismail Gasprinskii in Cairo—1908," concerning the Arabic newspaper *al-Nahda* which Gasprinskii published in Cairo; and Lazzerini, "Ismail Bey Gasprinskii," 108–27.

8. See Charles Hostler, *Turkism and the Soviets*, 128. Katkov appears to have viewed the cultivation of selected Muslims as an important activity; he later invited Afghani to Petrograd. See Keddie, *Sayyid Jamāl ad-Dīn*, 282.

9. Gasprinskii described his reception in Cairo and the effect of the Reuter dispatch in *Tercüman*, November 2, 1907. I am indebted to Edward Lazzerini, who provided me with his microfilms of *Tercüman*.

10. Vambéry letter of October 12, 1907, in *The Times*, October 22, 1907. The relevant issue of *Tercüman* is missing from the collection at my disposal.

11. On several occasions, Gasprinskii dismissed the suggestion of a European city, such as Geneva, as a site for the congress. He may have feared that a Muslim congress in Europe would inevitably deteriorate into a forum for Ottoman exiles seeking to vent their hostility toward the Hamidian regime.

12. The more noteworthy Egyptian participants are listed in *Tercüman*, November 20, 1907.

13. For versions of the text, see *Revue du monde musulman* (November–December 1907), 3(11–12): 497–500; *Sırat-ı müstakim* (Cemazi II, 6, 1327), 1(42): 248–50; *Tercüman*, November 20, 1907; *al-Manar* (November 1907), 10(9): 658–73; *al-Muqtataf* (December 1907), 32(2): 968–81.

14. *Al-Manar* (November 1907), 10(9): 677–78.

15. For the climate in Egypt, see Arthur J. Goldschmidt, "The Egyptian Nationalist Party: 1892–1919"; Fritz Steppat, "Nationalismus und Islam bei Muṣṭafā Kāmil"; Abbas Kelidar, "Shaykh ᶜAli Yusuf"; and Ann Elizabeth Mayer, " ᶜAbbās Hilmī II."

16. Cambon (Constantinople), dispatch of September 1, 1892, *Documents diplomatiques français, 1891–1914*, ser. 1, 10: 23.

17. Lord Cromer, *Modern Egypt*, 2: 177.

18. On his modernist critics, see F. de Jong, "Turuq and turuq-opposition in 20th century Egypt," 84–86. For an account of his career, see F. de Jong, "Muhammad Tawfīk b. ᶜAlī b. Muḥammad al-Bakrī."

19. Muhammad Tawfiq al-Bakri, *al-Mustaqbal lᶦʔl-islam,* 46.

20. *Al-Manar* (November 1907), 10(9): 706–7.

21. Ibid., 673–77, 708.

22. *Al-Manar* (May 1908), 11(3): 181–84.

23. Rashid Rida, *Taʔrikh al-ustadh al-imam,* 1: 1024.

24. ᶜAbbas Mahmud al-ᶜAqqad, *Rijal ᶜaraftuhum,* 183–84.

25. Afshar and Mahdavi, *Majmuᶜa-yi asnad va-madarik,* photo 135.

26. *Al-Manar* (November 1907), 10(9): 682.

27. *Sırat-ı müstakim* (August 6, 1909), 1(48): 339–40.

28. *Revue du monde musulman* (January 1908), 4(1): 136.

29. ᶜAli Yusuf, *Bayan fi khitat al-Muʔayyad tujaha al-dawla al-ᶜaliyya al-ᶜuthmaniyya,* 18.

30. *Içtihad* (Cairo) (September 1907), 2(4): 287.

31. J. Alexander, *The Truth about Egypt,* 126.

32. Kuttner, "Russian *Jadïdism* and the Islamic World." See also *Revue du monde musulman* (May 1908), 5(5): 173–77, for summaries of each of the three issues. I again am indebted to Edward Lazzerini, who provided me with photographs of *al-Nahda.*

33. Gasprinskii wrote that the Persian ambassador at Istanbul, with whom he had an audience, took a great interest in the congress plan; see *Sırat-ı müstakim* (August 6, 1909), 1(48): 339. A laudatory article on the ambassador (Mirza Riza Khan) appears in *Tercüman,* January 2, 1909.

34. Chevandier de Valdrôme (Cairo), dispatch of April 7, 1908, *AFC,* carton 64, file 12/1.

35. *Revue du monde musulman* (October 1908), 6(10): 284; Lazzerini, "Ismail Bey Gasprinskii," 122; *Tercüman,* September 14, 1908.

36. *Sırat-ı müstakim* (September 3, 1909), 1(52): 409–11; Mahir Hasan Fahmi, *Muhammad Tawfiq al-Bakri,* 87.

37. For the exchange on this subject, see Picquart, Ministry of War (Paris) to Foreign Ministry, March 12, 1908; Foreign Ministry to de Valdrôme (Cairo), March 18, 1908; de Valdrôme (Cairo), dispatch of April 20/28, 1908; all in *AFC,* carton 64, file 12/2.

38. *Al-Manar* (October 1911), 14(10): 737–38.

39. I have used the French pamphlet issued by the preparatory committee and included in the Oppenheim (Cairo) dispatch of May 20, 1908, Archiv des Auswärtigen Amts as filmed by the University of California, *NA* microcopy T-139, reel 399, frames 510–15. A French translation of the Arabic version appeared in *Revue du monde musulman* (February 1908), 4(2): 399–403.

40. On the newspaper's early years, see *Revue du monde musulman* (May 1907), 2(7): 414–15; Muhammad Sadr Hashimi, *Tarikh-i jaraʔid va majallat-i Iran,* 4: 211–13. E. G. Browne acquired a large collection of the paper, now preserved in the Cambridge University Library.

41. *Revue du monde musulman* (September 1908), 6(9): 191; Sadr Hashimi, *Tarikh-i jaraʔid,* 4: 214.

42. *Muzaffari* (Mecca), Dhu al-Hijja 1326 [December–January 1908–9]. The special issue was not numbered. Edward G. Browne, *The Press and Poetry in Modern Persia,* 141, wrote that he had not seen this issue, but a copy is preserved in the Cambridge collection, although it is bound out of sequence. A summary was made by L. Bouvet, "Un Projet de Parlement musulman international."

43. *Revue du monde musulman* (June 1910), 11(6): 336; Browne, *Press and Poetry,* 141. It was probably Vice Consul Rabino who supplied E. G. Browne with the copy now in Cambridge. See Rabino's letters to Browne in Cambridge University Library, add. MS. 7604.

44. *Revue du monde musulman* (May 1909), 8(5): 91.

45. On Mehmed Murad, see F. A. Tansel, "Mizancı Murad Bey"; E. E. Ramsaur, *The*

Young Turks: Prelude to Revolution, 27–28, 38–51; Şerif Mardin, *Jön Türklerin siyasi fikirleri 1895–1908,* 49–92.

46. This was a reflection of Young Turk policy by which the appointed Şeyhülislam was used to offset the traditional authority of the dynastic sultan-caliph. For a Muslim critique of this policy, see Henri Laoust, *Le califat dans la doctrine de Rashīd Riḍā,* 236-7.

47. Mehmed Murad, *Tatlı Emeller·Acı Hakikatler,* 19.

48. "Secret Decisions of the Annual Congress of the Central Committee of Union and Progress," FO371/1263, file 51124. A virtually identical text appeared in *The Times,* December 27, 1911. This was not among the public resolutions of the congress as given by X, "Doctrines et programmes des partis politiques ottomans," 152–58; and Tarık Z. Tunaya, *Türkiyede siyasi·partiler, 1859–1952,* 212–14.

49. See the biographies of Shaykh Shawish by Anwar al-Jindi, *ᶜAbd al-ᶜAziz Jawish,* and Salim ᶜAbd al-Nabi Qunaybir, *ᶜAbd al-ᶜAziz Jawish, 1872–1929.*

50. ᶜAbd al-ᶜAziz Shawish, *al-ᶜAlam al-islami,* 11–16, quote on p. 12.

51. Ibid., 19–20.

52. He was accompanied by Shakib Arslan, who described the opening of the *Dar al-Funun* at Madina in his *Sira dhatiyya,* 112–15.

5. HOLY WAR

1. *Ceride-i ilmiyye* (Istanbul) (Muharrem 1333), 1(7): 462. The text of the *fatwa*s, in Turkish, Arabic, Persian, Tatar, and Urdu, appears here on pp. 437–53; that of the *beyanname,* in all five languages, on pp. 454–80. For the surrounding circumstances, see Geoffrey Lewis, "The Ottoman Proclamation of Jihād in 1914," 164; Philip H. Stoddard, "The Ottoman Government and the Arabs, 1911 to 1918," 23–31; and Hikmet Bayur, *Türk inkılâbı tarihi,* 3(1): 317–34. For the many issues surrounding the jihad theme in modern times, see Rudolf Peters, *Islam and Colonialism: The Doctrine of Jihād in Modern History.*

2. On efforts in the Ottoman provinces, see Stoddard, "Ottoman Government." On the special efforts devoted to winning the support of Shiʿi ulama, see Werner Ende, "Iraq in World War I: The Turks, the Germans, and the Shiʿite Mujtahids' Call for Jihād." For the mission to Khyber, see Lal Baha, "Activities of Turkish Agents in Khyber during World War I," and Ludwig W. Adamec, *Afghanistan, 1900–1923: A Diplomatic History,* 96–100. For the mission to Morocco, see Edmund Burke, "Moroccan Resistance, Pan-Islam and German War Strategy, 1914–1918," 457–61.

3. See Jide Osuntokun, "Nigeria's Colonial Government and the Islamic Insurgency in French West Africa, 1914–1918." On the role of the Sanusi order in the Tuareg uprising of 1916–17, see Finn Fuglestad, "Les révoltes des Touareg du Niger (1916–17)." For a view of the Tuareg revolt as an autonomous development, see André Bourgeot, "Les échanges transsahariens, la Senusiya et les revoltes twareg de 1916–17."

4. For accounts of these endeavors, see Muhammad Farid, *Awraq Muhammad Farid,* 85, 101, 117–18, 147, 219–20, 232–33, 261. In 1915, Farid published a pamphlet in which he made explicit the aims of the Society for the Progress of Islam. An Ottoman victory would "truly be complete only upon the liberation not merely of Egypt, but of the Nile Valley as far as the equator, in order to drive England from the Red Sea and prepare, if not accomplish, the ruin of her Indian empire." Egypt and the Sudan would form the first pillar of an "Islamic confederation." The various Muslim peoples within the confederation would enjoy autonomy, on the pattern of multilingual and multinational Switzerland. See Marc Trefzger, *Die nationale Bewegung Ägyptens vor 1928 im Spiegel der Schweizerischen Öffentlichkeit,* 56–57.

5. *Arab Bulletin* (Cairo) (June 30, 1916), no. 7, p. 5, in L/P&S/10/657.

6. Tunis, Egypt, Algeria, Marrakesh, the Sudan, India, the Caucasus, Bukhara, Teheran, and Afghanistan. For a translation of the Arabic text, see *Welt des Islams*, o.s. 3(2): 121–25.

7. On their activities in Berlin during the war years, see Muhammad Farid, *Awraq Muhammad Farid*, passim; and Lothar Rathmann, "Ägypten im Exil (1914–1918)—Patrioten oder Kollaborateure des deutschen Imperialismus?" On the North Africans in Berlin during the same period, see Béchir Tlili, "La Grande Guerre et les questions tunisiennes: le groupement de la *Revue du Maghreb* (1916–1918)"; and Peter Heine, "Ṣaliḥ ash-Sharif at-Tunisi, a North African Nationalist in Berlin during the First World War."

8. Foreign Ministry to Defrance (Cairo), October 28 and November 8, 1916, in *AFC*, carton 536, file 166/5.

9. Sir George Buchanan (Petrograd), telegram of January 30, 1917, in FO371/3048, 23979/23979/W44. Based on information supplied by the Russian government.

10. On Musa Kazım, see Abdülkadir Altunsu, *Osmanlı Şeyhülislâmları*, 233–37. For his pan-Islamic activities, see Bayur, *Türk inkılâbı tarihi*, 2(4): 377:84.

11. Farid, *Awraq Muhammad Farid*, 379; Thiebaut (Stockholm), dispatch of October 6, 1917, *AFC*, carton 533, file 166/1.

13. Ziya-ul-Hasan Faruqi, *The Deoband School and the Demand for Pakistan*, 56–60. For the background, see Barbara Daly Metcalf, *Islamic Renewal in British India: Deoband, 1860–1900*.

14. The Niedermayer-Hentig expedition. For two accounts based on German archival sources, see Renate Vogel, *Die Persien- und Afghanistanexpedition Oskar Ritter v. Niedermayers 1915/16*; and Adamec, *Afghanistan, 1900–1923*, 83–96.

15. See Zafer Hasan Aybek, "Ubayd-Allah Sindhi in Afghanistan"; Mohammed Fahim, "Afghanistan and World War I"; and ᶜUbayd-Allah's own memoirs, *Kabul min sat sal*.

16. I have used the transliterated and translated texts of the Urdu letters which appear in C. E. W. Sands, *Report on the Silk Letter Conspiracy Case*, appendix A (composed by the Criminal Intelligence Office). A copy of this report is in L/P&S/10/663.

17. On the revival of the Mujahidin during the war, see Lal Baha, "The Activities of the Mujāhidīn, 1900–1936," 99–110.

18. Government of India, *Sedition Committee Report, 1918,* 178.

19. Husayn Ahmad Madani, *Safarnama-yi Shaykh al-Hind*. This account, which covers Mahmud al-Hasan's arrest in the Hijaz and his deportation to Malta via Cairo, is one of several Urdu sources that have much to say about the Ottoman conduct of the war, and have yet to be studied systematically for that purpose.

20. Detlev H. Khalid, " ᶜUbayd-Allāh Sindhi in Turkey."

21. ᶜUbayd-Allah Sindi, *Ilham al-rahman fi tafsir al-Qurʾan*, 298–300.

22. British Minister (Sofia) to Director of Military Operations, June 28, 1915, L/P&S/10/523, item 2433.

23. Sykes (Nish) telegram to Directory of Military Operations, June 29, 1915, L/P&S/10/523, item 2673.

24. T. Holderness, minute of July 3, 1915, L/P&S/10/523, item 2433.

25. Sykes memorandum on Policy in the Middle East, part one, October 28, 1915, in L/P&S/10/525, reg. no. 4524.

26. Ronald Storrs, "Note on Khalifate," May 20, 1915, in FO141/587, 545/2.

27. See the exchange in *International Journal of Middle East Studies* (August 1979), 10(3): 420–26.

28. Translation of Ali Morghani memorandum on the Caliphate, Khartoum, May 6, 1915, in Hardinge Papers, Cambridge University Library, 72: 58.

29. Translation of Sidi Ali Morghani memorandum on the Caliphate, August 12, 1915, in Wingate (Khartoum) dispatch of August 14, 1915, L/P&S/10/523, item 3225.

30. Translation of Ali Morghani's memorandum on the Caliphate, Khartoum, May 6, 1915, in Hardinge Papers, Cambridge University Library, 72: 58.

31. Percy Cox (at sea) to A. H. Grant, December 27, 1915, L/P&S/10/525, item 754.

32. Minute of A. Hirtzel, January 4, 1915, to letter from Under-Secretary of State, Foreign Office, January 4, 1915, L/P&S/10/523.

33. For the debate on the need for "consent of his co-religionists," see minute by A. Hirtzel, October 27, 1915, L/P&S/10/523, no. 3935.

34. Translation of a note addressed to Wingate, by Shaykh Mohammed Mustafa [al-Maraghi], Grand Kadi of the Sudan, Khartoum, August 18, 1915, in Hardinge Papers, Cambridge University Library, 72: 387–89.

35. On ᶜAbduh and Maraghi, see Anwar al-Jindi, al-Imam al-Maraghi, 38–47.

36. Elie Kedourie, "Egypt and the Caliphate, 1915–52," 179–81; although for a brief time, Shaykh Maraghi had favored the Sharif Husayn's candidacy. See Kedourie, In the Anglo-Arab Labyrinth, 23.

37. McMahon (Cairo), dispatch of May 14, 1915, L/P&S/10/523, item 2074.

6. BETWEEN BOLSHEVISM AND ISLAM

1. On Enver and this period of his career, see D. A. Rustow, "Enwer Pasha"; Paul Dumont, "La fascination du bolchevisme: Enver pacha et le parti des soviets populaires"; A. A. Cruickshank, "The Young Turk Challenge in Postwar Turkey"; and Azade-Ayse Rorlich, "Fellow Travellers: Enver Pasha and the Bolshevik Government 1918–1920."

2. Kâzım Karabekir, İstiklâl Harbimizde: Enver Paşa ve İttihat Terakki Erkânı.

3. Ali Fuat Cebesoy, Moskova Hatıraları.

4. As studied by Şevket Süreyya Aydemir, Makedonya'dan ortaasya'ya: Enver Paşa, 1914–1922.

5. For Radek's description of the meeting, see E. H. Carr, "Radek's 'Political Salon' in Berlin 1919," 419–20.

6. There he joined Cemal Paşa, the other triumvir, who had commanded the Ottoman armies in Syria and Palestine, and Halil Paşa, Enver's uncle, former commander of Ottoman forces in Iraq, and victor of Kut. Enver was also met in Moscow by Hacı Sami, the most renowned wartime Ottoman agent. Hacı Sami spent the war years under cover in India and Central Asia, and Enver came to rely increasingly upon his advice. For one of Hacı Sami's reports, see Karabekir, İstiklâl Harbimizde: Enver Paşa, 57–64.

7. Enver to Mustafa Kemal, August 26, 1920, in Karabekir, İstiklâl Harbimizde: Enver Paşa, 22–23; Dumont, "La fascination du bolchevisme," 148. On August 6, 1920, Indian Khilafat leader Muhammad ᶜAli met Talat in Switzerland.

8. The text of the charter is provided by Karabekir, İstiklâl Harbimizde: Enver Paşa, 123–25. The resolutions of the Berlin gathering are given in a summary form by Cebesoy, Moskova Hatıralari, 224–25.

9. For a list of expenditures, see Aydemir, Makedonya'dan ortaasya'ya, 551–52.

10. Cebesoy, Moskova Hatıralari, 230.

11. Karabekir, İstiklâl Harbimizde: Enver Paşa, 151, 153, for texts.

12. A photograph of eleven assembled Muslim delegates at Moscow, including Enver, Fahri, and Shakib, appears in Aydemir, Makedonya'dan ortaasya'ya, 587.

13. Ibid., 586–88. Shakib Arslan makes no mention of the congress in his recollection of this visit, but simply writes that he joined Enver in Moscow for a month to satisfy his curiosity about the Soviet Union. See Arslan, Sira dhatiyya, 265.

14. Protokoll des III. Kongresses der Kommunistischen Internationale, 103–10.

15. For this development, see Stephen White, "Communism and the East: The Baku Congress, 1920."

16. On this early chapter in Soviet-Turkish relations, see Paul Dumont, "L'axe Moscou-

Ankara. Les relations turco-soviétiques de 1919 à 1922," and Gotthard Jäschke, "Le rôle du communisme dans les relations russo-turques de 1919 à 1922."

17. On Enver's decision to break his Soviet ties, and his role of leadership in the Basmachi movement, see "The Basmachis: The Central Asian Resistance Movement," 242–46.

18. A 1939 survey of Muslim associations active in Berlin made reference to a certain "Union for the Liberation of Islam, a Bolshevik creation originally concerned with Central Europe but now rallied to Nazism. It is now devoted to the Near East." Bernard Vernier, *La politique islamique de l'Allemagne,* 33. Whether this refers to some remnant of the Berlin branch of Enver's society is not clear.

7. KEMALIST TURKEY AND MUSLIM EMPIRE

1. This account of the first Kemalist initiative is drawn from a set of Turkish documents secured through "Agent T.20/10," who apparently had penetrated not the Anatolian movement but the Sublime Porte. These are translated in FO371/4162, E177629/521/44. The cover dispatches, but not the translations themselves, were published in *Documents on British Foreign Policy, 1919–1939,* ser. 1, 4: 1028–31.

2. Particularly by Cemal Kutay, *Kurtuluşun ve cumhuriyetin manevi mimarları.*

3. A Turkish circular which appeared in Aleppo in October 1919, entitled "Mustafa Kemal's Proclamation to the Syrians," reported that the "Unitarians" would "soon be the visitors of their Arab brethren, and will scatter the enemy." Text of proclamation in *Documents on British Foreign Policy, 1919–1939,* ser. 1, 4: 478.

4. Kutay, *Kurtuluşun,* passim.

5. For example, see the report on the society dated February 6, 1920, in L/P&S/11/169.

6. Weekly summary of intelligence reports from Constantinople branch of Military Intelligence, for week ending February 21, 1920, L/P&S/11/170, p. 2109.

7. Branches in the following cities or locales: Damascus, Homs, Aleppo, Tyre, Baalbek, Haifa, Baghdad, Najaf, Kuwayt, Cairo, Tanta, Rosetta. On November 10, 1919, Meinertz-hagen wrote of Syria that "Turkish influence is gradually creeping back, and signs are not wanting of a rejuvenated popularity of Turkish rule with all its forgotten disadvantages. . . . This is not confined to Syria alone, but has recently been traced in Jerusalem and other Palestinian centres." Clayton wrote on October 15, 1919, that "it is safe to say that the majority of the Moslems in Aleppo vilayet, and a very large number in the vilayet of Damascus, are in sympathy with Turkish aspirations, and would prefer union with Turkey to being under an unpopular European power." *Documents on British Foreign Policy, 1919–1939,* ser. 1, 4: 522–23, 566.

8. S. I. S. secret police report on Asia Minor, August 12, 1920, in FO371/5178, E11702/345/44.

9. Speech of April 24, 1920, *Atatürk 'ün Söylev ve Demeçleri,* 59.

10. Ryan (Constantinople) to Forbes Adam, October 26, 1919, in Andrew Ryan Papers, FO800/240. On the "Vatican Proposal," see A. L. Macfie, "The British Decision regarding the Future of Constantinople (November 1918–January 1920)," 395–97.

11. For a history of federal solutions built around a Turco-Arab core, see Gotthard Jäschke, "Ein scherifisches Bündnisangebot an Mustafa Kemal." Alongside this effort was an attempt to work through the exiled Sanusi chief, Ahmad al-Sharif. On his arrival and activity in Ankara, see Hüsameddin Ertürk, *İki devrin perde arkası,* 476–81.

12. Although it was documented early, on the basis of then-available published sources, by Gotthard Jäschke, "Nationalismus und Religion im türkischen Befreiungskriege." For

another treatment, see Dankwart Rustow, "Politics and Islam in Turkey, 1920–1955," 70–79.

13. For the text of the first *Alem-i Islâma Beyanname*, of March 17, 1920, see Karabekir, *İstiklâl Harbimiz*, 549; *Atatürk'ün Tamim, Telegraf ve Beyannameleri*, 258–59. For the May proclamation, see 319–26.

14. Sir Horace Rumbold (Constantinople), dispatch of February 7, 1921, in *Documents on British Foreign Policy, 1919–1939*, ser. 1, 17: 48–49.

15. *Hakimiyet-i milliye*, March 11, 1921; translation in FO371/6470, E5714/1/44. See also Kutay, *Kurtuluşun*, 253–63, for the fullest Turkish discussion of the initiative.

16. See Fevziye Abdullah Tansel, *Mehmed Akif: Hayatı ve Eserleri*, especially 51–96.

17. Eastern Summary (SIS) no. 709, June 8, 1922, FO371/7883, E5949/27/44.

18. *Sebilürreşad*, April 13, 1922; Eastern Summary (SIS) no. 709, June 8, 1922, FO371/7883, E5949/27/44.

19. Ryan (Lausanne) to Nevile Henderson (Constantinople), November 28, 1922, Andrew Ryan Papers, FO800/240.

20. Interview with Abdul Hadi, Afghan minister in London, *Sunday Times*, November 12, 1922; also L/P&S/10/895, P.4618.

21. SIS report of January 10, 1923, FO371/8967, E520/85/16.

22. Unattributed draft dispatch (Alexandria), August 23, 1923, *AFC*, carton 18, file 6.

23. Appendix to a memorandum entitled "Pan-Islamism and the Caliphate, July 1923–March 1924," dated April 28, 1924, FO371/10110, E3657/2029/65.

24. *Tevhid-i efkâr*, November 9, 1923; *Akşam*, November 9, 1923; *Oriente Moderno* (1923), 3: 409.

25. Humphrys (Kabul), dispatch of May 5, 1923, FO371/9130, E4616/199/44.

26. C. A. Nallino, "La Fine del così detto califfato ottomano," and Sylvia G. Haim, "The Abolition of the Caliphate and its Aftermath."

8. NEW CALIPH IN ARABIA

1. Translation of letter dated Receb 27, 1339, FO371/6470, E6447/1/44. Identical information on this initiative appears in FO141/816, f. 13327. On Haydari-zâde İbrahim, see Altunsu, *Osmanlı Şeyhülislâmları*, 252–53.

2. "Renseignements d'un informateur," Beyrut, April 6, 1921, *AFC*, carton 131, file 26/3.

3. Allenby (Cairo), telegram of June 19, 1921, FO371/6471, E7001/1/44.

4. W. E. Marshall (Jidda), dispatch of June 10, 1921, L/P&S/10/926, P. 3281 (E7445/455/91).

5. Sharabasi, *Rashid Rida*, 47.

6. *Al-Manar* (July 1924), 25(5): 390.

7. H. Gaillard (Cairo), dispatch of September 9, 1921, *AFC*, carton 66, file 12/1.

8. W. H. Deedes, Civil Secretary (Jerusalem) to Sir Horace Rumbold, British High Commissioner (Constantinople), August 30, 1921, FO371/6475, E10577/1/44.

9. W. S. Edmonds, minute of September 22, 1921, to dispatch cited in previous note.

10. *Al-Muqattam*, August 23, 1922; *Oriente Moderno* (1922), 2: 291–92.

11. *Al-Qibla*, August 6, 1923.

12. See C. Ernest Dawn, "Ideological Influences in the Arab Revolt."

13. Yehoshua Porath, "The Palestinians and the Negotiations for the British-Hijazi Treaty, 1920–1925." For another view, see Suleiman Mousa, "A Matter of Principle: King Hussein of the Hijaz and the Arabs of Palestine."

14. A role acknowledged by Muhammad al-Sasi, secretary general of the Conference

of the Arabian Peninsula and editor of *al-Qibla*, in a letter to Jamal al-Husayni, secretary of the Arab Executive Committee (Jerusalem), October 11, 1922, *ISA*, division 65, file 15.

15. *Al-Qibla*, July 17, 1922.

16. Adib Abu al-Diba (Mecca) to Jamal al-Husayni (Jerusalem), July 18, 1922, *ISA*, division 65, file 7.

17. W. E. Marshall (Jidda), dispatch of August 30, 1922, L/P&S/10/926, P. 4048.

18. R. W. Bullard (Jidda), dispatch of August 29, 1923, L/P&S/10/926, P. 3841 (E9280/653/91).

19. R. W. Bullard (Jidda), dispatch of October 31, 1923, L/P&S/10/926, P. 4682 (E1151/653/91).

20. A hostile but well-documented account of the various pledges of allegiance offered to Husayn appears in *al-Manar* (July 1924), 25(5): 390–400. For a collection of similar materials, see *Oriente Moderno* (1924), 4: 226–39. The Meccan *al-Qibla* for March and April carried many professions of allegiance from widely scattered parts.

21. R. W. Bullard (Jidda), dispatch of April 30, 1924, L/P&S/10/1115, P. 2434 (E4379/424/91). One of the two "Javanese" members was a pilgrims' guide. See R. W. Bullard, dispatch of May 29, 1924, L/P&S/10/1115, P. 2798 (E5217/424/91).

22. *Oriente Moderno* (1924), 4: 295–96; *al-Qibla*, April 3, 1924.

23. For the congress and its proceedings, see *Oriente Moderno* (1924), 4: 600–602; and *al-Qibla* for the month of July 1924. The text of the charter appears in *al-Qibla*, July 7, 1924. The insistence upon Arabic as the official language did not prevent the use of unofficial languages at the congress, and *al-Qibla*, July 17, 1924, reports that the proceedings were translated into Turkish, Persian, and Indonesian.

24. Kellar El Menouar, Algerian subject and Gérant du consulat de France (Jidda), dispatch of August 4, 1924, *AFC*, carton 71, file 13/4.

25. On these incidents, see Arnold Green, *The Tunisian Ulama, 1873–1915*, 185–87; and Nicola Ziadeh, *Origins of Nationalism in Tunisia*, 98–102. On the opinions current in Tunisia on wider Muslim affairs, just before Thaᶜalibi's departure, see Béchir Tlili, "Au seuil du nationalisme tunisien. Documents inédits sur le panislamisme au Maghreb (1919–1923)."

26. R. W. Bullard (Jidda), dispatch of August 30, 1924, L/P&S/10/1115, P. 3971 (E7907/424/91).

27. Sir Henry Dobbs, British High Commissioner (Baghdad), telegram to Secretary of State for Colonies, September 24, 1924, L/P&S/10/1124, P. 3884.

28. Kawakibi suggested that security in the Hijaz be provided by a mixed military force under the command of the caliph's advisory council. Kawakibi, *Umm al-qura*, 211–12.

29. Sir Henry Dobbs (Baghdad), telegram to Secretary of State for Colonies, October 26, 1924, FO371/10015, E9441/7624/91. Wrote Dobbs of Faysal: "I consider that he will probably receive considerable number of rebuffs. These may enlighten (him?) more than any of my arguments can do as to the true attitude of Moslems in other countries toward the Hashimite family and the Hedjaz question. I trust therefore that I may be given early instructions to inform him that there is no objection to his proposals."

30. On this episode, see Martin Kramer, "Shaykh Marāghī's Mission to the Hijāz, 1925."

9. The Caliphate Grail

1. For the text of the proclamation, see *Majallat al-muʾtamar al-islami al-ᶜamm liʾl-khilafa bi-Misr* (October 1924), no. 1, 20–23; Achille Sékaly, *Le Congrès du Khalifat et le Congrès du Monde Musulman*, 29–33; and Arnold J. Toynbee, *Survey of International Affairs 1925*, 1: 576–78.

2. There exists in ᶜAbdin Palace an exhaustive list, nearly sixty pages long, of the names

of all the members of the principal and branch committees; see *MRJ*, file 761, "Lijan al-khilafa al-islamiyya bi-Misr." On the organization of committees in Upper Egypt, see Fakhr al-Din al-Ahmadi al-Zawahiri, *al-Siyasa waʾl-Azhar, min mudhakkirat Shaykh al-Islam al-Zawahiri*, 210.

3. Rashid Rida, "Mudhakkirat muʾtamar al-khilafa al-islamiyya"; ʿInayat Allah Khan Mashriqi, *Khitab-i muʾtamar-i khilafat*; Sékaly, *Congrès du Khalifat*, 4–11, 29–122. For complaints about the integrity of the official proceedings, which are the basis for all these published versions, see *al-Siyasa*, June 21, 1926.

4. Toynbee, *Survey 1925*, 81–91; and also F. Taillardat, "Les congrès interislamiques de 1926."

5. Zawahiri, *al-Siyasa waʾl-Azhar*, 207–17.

6. *Al-Manar* (March 14, 1926), 26(10): 789–91; Shakib Arslan, *Sayyid Rashid Rida aw ikhaʾ arbaʿin sanna*, 335 ff.

7. Elie Kedourie, "Egypt and the Caliphate, 1915–52," 183–89, 193–95.

8. On this archive, see Martin Kramer, "Egypt's Royal Archives, 1922–52."

9. These papers had been kept by Husayn Wali, the congress secretary, and were presented to the library of al-Azhar mosque in 1967 by one of his nephews. The correspondence concerning the file itself gives cause to doubt that the collection is complete. For a preliminary study of the material, see Mahmud Sharqawi, "Dirasat wathaʾiq ʿan muʾtamar al-khilafa al-islamiyya 1926."

10. These ideas are discussed by Malcolm H. Kerr, *Islamic Reform: The Political and Legal Theories of Muhammad ʿAbduh and Rashīd Ridā*, 183–85.

11. Muhammad Faraj al-Minyawi and ʿAbd al-Baqi Surrur Naʿim to unnamed addressee, May 20, 1924, *DWQ*, ʿAbdin: al-khilafa al-islamiyya, uncatalogued box.

12. *Majallat al-muʾtamar* (1925), no. 7, 167–68.

13. According to the minister, as quoted in *al-Manar* (May 31, 1927), 28(4): 316. Further details in *al-Manar* (May 2, 1927), 28(2): 156–57.

14. Text of Tusun's letter and Zaghlul's reply in *al-Muqattam*, March 20, 1924. On Tusun, see Gaston Weit, "Son altesse le Prince Omar Toussoun."

15. The meeting which ended in the creation of this committee is described in *al-Muqattam*, March 22, 1924. A thorough account of Abu al-ʿAzaʾim's campaign, with extensive citations from his personal correspondence, is given by ʿAbd al-Munʿim Muhammad Shuqruf, *al-Imam Muhammad Madi Abu al-ʿAzaʾim*, 219–46. On his career, see F. de Jong, "Muḥammad Māḍī Abuʾl-ʿAzāʾim."

16. See Yusuf al-Dijwi, *al-Islam wa-usul al-hukm waʾl-radd ʿalayhi.*

17. Handwritten Arabic text of manifesto, undated, signatories Yusuf al-Dijwi, et al., in *MRJ*, file 763.

18. Details on the investigation in Ahmad Shafiq, *Hawliyyat Misr al-siyasiyya*, 4(3): 40; Gaillard (Cairo), dispatch of February 9, 1926, *AFC*, carton 71, file 13/4.

19. According to diplomatic sources, Zaghlul, immediately following the decision of the Turks to abolish the caliphate, urged Fuʾad to declare himself caliph, and to use this caliphate as a lever against the British. See H. Gaillard (Cairo), dispatch of March 12, 1924, *AFC*, carton 71, file 13/4; High Commissioner (Cairo), dispatch of March 29, 1924, FO141/587, file 545. According to another account, Zaghlul did no more than ask Fuʾad about his intentions; see Shafiq, *Hawliyyat*, 4(3): 149–50.

20. *Al-Siyasa*, September 15, 1925.

21. Gaillard (Cairo) to High Commisioner (Beirut), March 26, 1926, *AFC*, carton 71, file 13/4.

22. Text of January 17, 1925 decision in Arabic, Turkish, Persian, French, and English, in *Majallat al-muʾtamar* (January 1925), no. 4.

23. *Al-Manar* (March 14, 1926), 26(10): 789–90.

24. ᶜAbd al-ᶜAzim Rashid (Teheran), dispatch of October 12, 1925, *MRJ*, file 763. All correspondence from and to ᶜAbd al-ᶜAzim is from this file, unless another reference is given.

25. ᶜAbd al-ᶜAzim dispatch, November 16, 1925. The dispatch includes the relevant issue of the newspaper, dated November 16, 1925.

26. French translations from the Persian newspapers, in *MRJ*, file 763.

27. ᶜAbd al-ᶜAzim dispatch, March 16, 1926, *DWQ*, ᶜAbdin: al-khilafa al-islamiyyà, uncatalogued box.

28. ᶜAbd al-ᶜAzim dispatch, January 11, 1926.

29. ᶜAbd al-ᶜAzim dispatch, February 18, 1926.

30. ᶜAbd al-ᶜAzim dispatch, March 25, 1926.

31. Sir Percy Loraine (Teheran), telegram of March 4, 1926, FO371/11476, E1511/1511/65.

32. ᶜAbd al-ᶜAzim dispatch, April 13, 1926.

33. ᶜAbd al-ᶜAzim dispatch, March 25, 1926.

34. ᶜAbd al-ᶜAzim dispatch, April 13, 1926.

35. Unattributed note, n.d., L/P&S/11/261, P. 838 (in file 3125).

36. Minute (author's name illegible), March 5, 1926, FO141/587, file 545.

37. Tawfiq Nasim (Cairo) to ᶜAbd al-ᶜAzim (Teheran), April 4, 1926.

38. ᶜAbd al-ᶜAzim dispatch, April 22, 1926.

39. *Oriente Moderno* (1926), 6: 268.

40. ᶜAbd al-ᶜAziz Ibn Saᶜud to the Shaykh al-Azhar, December 9, 1925, Azhar File, document 111.

41. On this attempt, see Kramer, "Shaykh Marāghī's Mission to the Hijāz."

42. Shawkat ᶜAli and Kifayat Allah (Delhi), telegram to Saᶜd Zaghlul (Cairo), March 27, 1924, *DWQ*, Prime Ministry: al-khilafa al-islamiyya, uncatalogued box.

43. Shawkat ᶜAli (Aligarh) to Shaykh al-Azhar (Cairo), March 14, 1924, Azhar File, document 4.

44. Shawkat ᶜAli (Bombay) to Husayn Wali (Cairo), January 15, 1925, Azhar File, document 117.

45. District Commisioner (Jerusalem) to Chief Secretary, August 21, 1925, L/P&S/10/1155, P. 3908.

46. See the note on the visit, "described by Police as coming form a usually reliable source," in G. Lloyd (Cairo), dispatch of October 25, 1925, L/P&S/11/261, P. 3921.

47. Text of letter from Shawkat ᶜAli to Abu al-ᶜAzaˀim, in *al-Watan*, October 8, 1925. See also the report on a meeting of the committee under Abu al-ᶜAzaˀim in *al-Akhbar*, October 17, 1925.

48. *Al-Liwaˀ al-misri*, March 31, 1926. On the failure of the Azhar organizers to sway Hakim Ajmal Khan as well, see Arslan (Lausanne) to ᶜAbbas Hilmi, October 3, 1925, *AHP*, 118:160.

49. On Mashriqi and the Khaksars, see Shan Muhammad, *The Khaksar Movement in India*.

50. See William R. Roff, "Indonesian and Malay Students in Cairo in the 1920's."

51. On Tjokroaminoto, see Almez, *H. O. S. Tjokroaminoto*; on the Sarekat Islam, see Deliar Noer, *The Modernist Muslim Movement in Indonesia, 1900–1942*, 101–53.

52. Crosby (Batavia), "Note on the Native Movement and on the Political Situation in the Netherlands East Indies Generally," January 3, 1925, FO371/11084, W1038/156/29; Tjokroaminoto (Jogjakarta) to Husayn Wali (Cairo), January 2, 1925, Azhar File, document 78.

53. On the Muhammadijah, see Noer, *Modernist Muslim Movement*, 73–83.

54. *Java Bode*, March 24, 1926, as translated in Crosby (Batavia), dispatch of March 25, 1926, FO371/11476, E623/1511/65.

55. On Hadji Rasul, see Noer, *Modernist Muslim Movement*, 37–38. On the delegation and its role in Cairo, there is an account in Hadji Rasul's biography by his son, Hamka (Hadji

Abdul Malik Karim Amrullah), *Ajahku. Riwayat hidup Dr. Abd. Karim Amrullah dan perdjuangan kaum agama*, 91–101.

56. On Musa Carullah, see Abdallah [Battal-] Taymas, *Musa Carullah Bigi*; Rorlich, "Transition Into the Twentieth Century," 58–62.

57. Interview in Istanbul with Musa Carullah, in *al-Liwaᵓ al-misri*, May 25, 1926.

58. Text of letter from mufti to Kalinin, *Izvestia*, March 18, 1926.

59. Musa Carullah sent a lengthy letter of protest to the Azhar committee, which apparently is preserved in Shaykh Zawahiri's papers; see Zawahiri, *al-Siyasa waᵓl-Azhar*, 214.

60. See André Raymond, "Tunisiens et Maghrebins au Caire au dix-huitième siècle," and Albert Hourani, "The Syrians in Egypt in the Eighteenth and Nineteenth Centuries."

61. Gaillard (Cairo), dispatch of December 12, 1924, *AFC*, carton 71, file 13/4.

62. Minutes of meeting of November 7, 1924, *AFC*, carton 71, file 13/4.

63. Ministry (Paris) to Gaillard (Cairo), January 13, 1925, *AFC*, carton 71, file 13/4.

64. Gaillard (Cairo), dispatch of January 31, 1925, *AFC*, carton 71, file 13/4.

65. Governor General Steeg (Algiers) to Foreign Ministry, November 19, 1924, *AFC*, carton 71, file 13/4.

66. ᶜAbd al-Hamid Ibn Badis (Constantine) to Husayn Wali (Cairo), October 4, 1924, Azhar File, document 37. On Ibn Badis, see Ali Merad, *Ibn Bādis, commentateur du Coran*, 23–51. For his attitude toward the congress, and his demand that Algerian Muslims participate, see *al-Shihab*, April 22, 1926.

67. General Sarrail (Beirut), dispatch of January 7, 1925, *AFC*, carton 71, file 13/4.

68. Gaillard (Cairo) to Sarrail (Beirut), February 24, 1925, *AFC*, carton 71, file 13/4.

69. Arslan (Berlin) to Shaykh Faraj al-Minyawi (Cairo), November 29, 1924, Azhar File, document 71; memorandum by Minyawi, January 27, 1926, quoting letter from Arslan dated January 6, 1926, Azhar File, document 127.

70. This is implied by the sort of questions submitted in a letter by the committee chairman Ahmad Tawfiq al-Madani (Tunis) to Husayn Wali (Cairo), Rabiᶜ II, 3, 1343, Azhar File, document 48.

71. Letter from Husayn Wali (Cairo) to ᶜAbd al-Karim, February 18, 1926, in *al-Muqattam*, February 20, 1926.

72. Correspondence, translations, in *AFC*, carton 71, file 13/4.

73. Gaillard (Cairo), telegram of February 20, 1926, in *AFC*, carton 71, file 13/4.

74. Gaillard dispatch of February 22, 1926, *AFC*, carton 71, file 13/4.

75. *Note verbale*, March 12, 1926, *MRJ*, file 763.

76. Marquis de Merry del Val to Sir William Tyrrell, March 17, 1926, FO371/11920, W2249/2249/28.

77. Lloyd (Cairo), dispatch of April 10, 1926, FO371/11920, W3227/2449/28.

78. R. H. Campbell to Manuel de Ynclan, April 28, 1926, FO371/11920, W3227/2449/28.

79. Foreign Ministry (Cairo) to Legation (Madrid), March 28, 1926, *MRJ*, file 763.

80. Urbain Blanc (Rabat), dispatch of April 23, 1926, *AFC*, carton 71, file 13/4.

81. Lloyd (Cairo), dispatch of May 25, 1926, FO371/11476, E3178/1511/65.

82. Gaillard (Cairo), dispatch of February 28, 1926, *AFC*, carton 71, file 13/4.

83. Rida to Arslan (n.p., n.d.), in Arslan, *Sayyid Rashid Rida*, 367.

84. Rida (Cairo) to Arslan, January 1, 1925, in Arslan, *Sayyid Rashid Rida*, 352.

85. Sékaly, *Congrès du Khalifat*, 96.

86. Cairo City Police report of May 16, 1926, in FO141/587, file 545.

87. The argument against the possibility of the caliphate belonged to that committee on which the Egyptian presence was negligible. The assumptions of its report were proven largely accurate. For texts, see *al-Manar* (August 18, 1926), 27(5): 370–77; Sékaly, *Congrès du Khalifat*, 102–10; Toynbee, *Survey 1925*, 578–81.

88. For his response to the committee report mentioned in the previous note, see *al-Manar* (September 7, 1926), 27(6): 449–53; Sékaly, *Congrès du Khalifat,* 110–15. For his logic in pursuing this approach, which essentially adjourned the congress, see Zawahiri, *al-Siyasa waʾl-Azhar,* 216–17.

89. *Al-Siyasa,* June 21, 1926.

90. *Al-Manar* (May 13, 1926), 27(2): 143.

91. ʿAbd al-Rahman ʿAzzam (Baghdad), dispatch of April 10, 1938, *MRJ,* file 1243.

92. Ibid.

93. Foreign Minister to Chief of the Royal Diwan, May 5, 1938, *MRJ,* file 1243.

94. His stay in Egypt is chronicled exhaustively by Muhammad Hadi al-Daftar, *Safha min rihlat al-imam al-Zanjani wa-khutabuhu fiʾl-aqtar al-ʿarabiyya waʾl-ʿawasim al-islamiyya,* 1: 41–88, 293–488.

95. Ibid., 190–260. In contrast, a British diplomat at Baghdad with whom the shaykh sometimes conferred found him "an oily creature and not at all trustworthy." V. Holt (Baghdad) to J. A. de C. Hamilton (Alexandria), June 28, 1938, FO371/22004, J3026/2014/16.

96. Sir Miles Lampson (Cairo), dispatch of March 25, 1938, FO371/21838, E1114/1034/65.

97. For an example from April 1938, see Ahmad Shafiq, *Aʿmali baʿda mudhakkirati,* 289.

98. *Al-Qibla,* July 7, 1924, for text of pledge.

99. Lampson (Cairo), dispatch of February 17, 1938, FO371/21838, E1114/1034/65.

100. Maraghi (Cairo) to Zanjani (Najaf), February 26, 1938, reproduced by Muhammad Saʿid Al Thabit, *al-Wahda al-islamiyya aw al-taqrib bayna madhahib al-muslimin,* 68–71.

101. Zanjani (Najaf) to Maraghi (Cairo), April 9, 1938, in Thabit, *al-Wahda,* 72–76.

102. Maraghi (Cairo) to Zanjani (Najaf), May 3, 1938, in Thabit, *al-Wahda,* 77–79.

103. V. Holt (Baghdad) to J. A. de C. Hamilton (Alexandria), June 28, 1938, FO371/22004, J3026/2014/16.

104. Zanjani did appear at a Damascus congress of ulama later in 1938. There he successfully proposed a resolution endorsing cooperation between *madhahib,* and the congress decided to create a committee to consider a more general congress of ulama devoted to the sectarian problem. The Damascus congress, a local affair, was never reconvened. See *Muqarrarat muʾtamar al-ʿulamaʾ al-awwal,* 14; *Oriente Moderno* (1938), 18: 552–53.

105. On this incident and the events surrouding it, see Kedourie, "Egypt and the Caliphate," 204–5; and *DWQ,* ʿAbdin: al-khilafa al-islamiyya, uncatalogued box, file on the "supposed oath of allegiance."

106. See Daniel Crecelius, "The Emergence of the Shaykh al-Azhar as the pre-eminent Religious Leader in Egypt."

107. In comments on Egyptian aspirations by Sir Percy Loraine (Ankara) to Ronald Campbell, March 11, 1938, FO371/21838, E1527/1034/65.

10. THE FATE OF MECCA

1. Sékaly, *Le Congrès du Khalifat et le Congrès du Monde Musulman,* 11–25, 125–219.

2. See Toynbee, *Survey 1925,* 308–19. Writing in other languages but relying upon the same sources were Taillardat, "Les congrès interislamiques," and Hadsch Moh. Nāfiʿ Tschelebi, "Die Bruderschaft Arabiens und der islamische Weltkongress zu Mekka 1926."

3. Material related to the Meccan congress was culled by Shaykh Zawahiri's son from some papers that remained in his father's possession. Zawahiri, *al-Siyasa waʾl-Azhar,* 229–63.

4. Hafiz Wahba, *Jazirat al-ʿarab fiʾl-qarn al-ʿishrin,* 267–75; this work was translated as

Sheikh Hafiz Wahba, *Arabian Days.*

5. Arslan, *Sayyid Rashid Rida,* 443 ff.

6. ᶜAjaj Nuwayhid, "Al-Hajj Amin al-Husayni fiᵓl-muᵓtamar al-islami al-ᶜamm fi Makka."

7. Sirdar Ikbal Ali Shah, "First Moslem Congress," and "The Meccan Conference." On his visit to the Muslim delegation from the Soviet Union, "at the instigation of this agency," see enclosure in Jordan (Jidda), dispatch of July 3, 1926, FO371/11446, E4319/1426/91.

8. Although the value of this is diminished by his occasional reliance upon Iqbal ᶜAli Shah for certain details. See these two principal reports: Jordan (Jidda), enclosure in dispatch of June 23, 1926; and enclosure in dispatch of July 15, 1926, FO371/11433, E4186/4677/20/91.

9. Report by Shaykh Muhammad al-Ahmadi al-Zawahiri, undated MS. (hereafter: Zawahiri Report, and not to be confused with the report which Zawahiri's son essentially reproduces in his book, which is less candid); report by Egyptian consul Amin Tawfiq (Jidda), enclosed in his dispatch of September 1, 1926 (hereafter: Tawfiq Report); both in *MRJ,* file 1477, "Muᵓtamar Makka al-islami."

10. Text of Ibn Saᶜud's telegram to invited participants, enclosed in Jordan (Jidda), dispatch of May 1, 1926, L/P&S/10/1115, P. 1939 (E3198/367/91).

11. Ibn Saᶜud's proclamation on the day of his acclamation as king of the Hijaz, in *Umm al-qura,* January 8, 1926.

12. Zawahiri Report.

13. On the movement, see Gail Minault, *The Khilafat Movement: Religious Symbolism and Political Mobilization in India.* The study ends with the convening of the Meccan congress, by which time, it is argued, the ᶜAli brothers were in eclipse. For other accounts, see A. C. Niemeijer, *The Khilafat Movement in India, 1919–1924;* and Francis Robinson, *Separatism Among Indian Muslims: The Politics of the United Provinces' Muslims 1860–1923.*

14. Zawahiri Report.

15. Qurashi (Mecca) to ᶜAbd al-Rahman Siddiqi, January 9, 1926, translated in secret report of February 19, 1926, L/P&S/10/1165, P&J (S) 258. The rebuff of this delegation is described by Jordan (Jidda), dispatch of January 29, 1926, FO406/57.

16. On Tjokroaminoto in Mecca, see Almez, *H. O. S. Tjokroaminoto,* 171–73.

17. Zawahiri Report.

18. Ibid.

19. Charles Hertopp (Cairo) to Jordan (Jidda), May 29, 1926, FO371/11433, E3505/20/91. Abu al-ᶜAzaᵓim's role at the Meccan congress is described by Shuqruf, *al-Imam Muhammad Madi Abu al-ᶜAzaᵓim,* 246–52.

20. Zawahiri Report.

21. Rida (Mecca) to Arslan, June 19, 1926, in Arslan, *Sayyid Rashid Rida,* 445.

22. Tawfiq Report; and Jordan (Jidda), enclosure in dispatch of July 31, 1926, L/P&S/10/1115, E4937/367/91.

23. *Al-Manar* (August 27, 1927), 28(6): 465–73.

24. Zawahiri Report.

25. Jordan (Jidda), enclosure in dispatch of July 15, 1926, FO371/11433, E4677/20/91.

26. Zawahiri Report.

27. Jordan (Jidda), enclosure in dispatch of June 23, 1926, FO371/11433, E4186/20/91.

28. On the delegation's wait in Cairo, see *al-Muqattam,* June 1, 20, 1926. On the Iranian prime minister's statement, see *Iran,* June 25, 1926, as quoted in FO371/11433, E4327/20/91.

29. Jordan (Jidda), enclosure in dispatch of June 23, 1926, FO371/11433, E4186/20/91.

30. For Ibn Saᶜud's remarks, see Sékaly, *Congrès du Khalifat,* 128–31.

31. Toynbee, *Survey 1925,* 315.

32. Zawahiri Report.
33. Wahba, *Arabian Days*, 156–57.
34. *Umm al-qura*, June 11, 1926; *Wadi al-Nil*, June 16, 1926.
35. Rashid Rida's proposed charter in *Umm al-qura*, June 11, 1926.
36. *Al-Siyasa*, June 24, 1926; Sékaly, *Congrès du Khalifat*, 137.
37. Zawahiri Report.
38. *Umm al-qura*, July 2, 1926.
39. Ibid.
40. *Al-Ahram*, June 16, 30, 1926.
41. *Umm al-qura*, July 14, 1926.
42. Ibid., June 18, 1926.
43. Wahba, *Arabian Days*, 157–58. For the plenary discussion of the proposal to rid Arabia of foreign influence, see Sékaly, *Congrès du Khalifat*, 163–66. Only in light of Wahba's account does Sékaly's report of Arabian opposition to the proposal make sense.
44. Nuwayhid, "al-Hajj Amin al-Husayni fi'l-mu'tamar al-islami," 36–37.
45. Zawahiri Report.
46. Nuwayhid, "al-Hajj Amin al-Husayni fi'l-mu'tamar al-islami," 35.
47. *Umm al-qura*, July 9, 14, 1926.
48. See in particular Sékaly's introduction, *Congrès du Khalifat*, 16–24. The issue of slavery (Sékaly, 201) was raised by a participant only at the urging of the British vice consul at Jidda, and would otherwise not have figured in the proceedings. See Jordan (Jidda), dispatch of July 20, 1926, FO371/11446, E4678/900/91. The restoration of the Hijaz railway to Muslim control (Sékaly, 155–62) was a constant subject of Muslim discussion. For the background to this controversy, see W. L. Ochsenwald, "A Modern *Waqf*: The Hijaz Railway, 1900–48."
49. Zawahiri Report.
50. Sékaly, *Congrès du Khalifat*, 183–86.
51. Text in Sékaly, *Congrès du Khalifat*, 189–92; *Umm al-qura*, July 6, 1926; Arabic text also in Georg Kampffmeyer, "Urkunden und Berichte zur Gegenwartsgeschichte des arabischen Orients."
52. Zawahiri Report.
53. For these resolutions, see *Umm al-qura*, July 23, 1926; Sékaly, *Congrès du Khalifat*, 207–9.
54. Antonius (Jerusalem) to Clayton, September 11, 1926, in Clayton Papers, Sudan Archive, Durham University Library.
55. Jordan (Jidda), enclosure no. 1 in dispatch of August 9, 1926, FO371/11433, E4677/20/91.
56. Minute by V. A. L. Mallet, August 10, 1926, FO371/11433, E4677/20/91.
57. Sékaly, *Congrès du Khalifat*, 210.
58. Rida (Mecca) to Arslan, July 8, 1926, in Arslan, *Sayyid Rashid Rida*, 446–49.
59. Rida (Cairo) to Arslan, September 16, 1926, in Arslan, *Sayyid Rashid Rida*, 454.
60. Rida to Arslan, December 10, 1926, in Arslan, *Sayyid Rashid Rida*, 461.
61. Shah, "The Meccan Conference," 310.
62. Memorandum to Wakely on request of Ikbal Ali Shah, dated April 5, 1927, L/P&S/10/806. This file contains various offers of services from Iqbal ᶜAli Shah, all of which were rejected.
63. Henry Fitzmaurice (Batavia), dispatch of October 8, 1926, FO371/11476, E6347/1511/65. Rashid Rida expressed his satisfaction; see *al-Manar* (November 5, 1926), 27(8): 638–40.
64. Rida to Arslan, September 16, 1926, in Arslan, *Sayyid Rashid Rida*, 455.
65. *Al-Muqattam*, March 4, 1927.
66. Wahba to Amin Bey [Tawfiq], October 22, 1926, *MRJ*, file 1480, part 1.

67. The Soviet Muslim delegates described collection of the money necessary for the journey. See the interview in *al-Siyasa,* June 16, 1926.

68. Rida (Mecca) to Arslan, June 19, 1926, in Arslan, *Sayyid Rashid Rida,* 445.

69. Jordan (Jidda), enclosure in dispatch of July 31, 1926, L/P&S/10/1115, E4937/367/91. The Tawfiq Report also gives the sums of various gifts, and the identical figure of £1,000 for Amin al-Husayni.

70. For details on the campaign, see *al-Manar* (October 17, 1926), 27(7): 548–55. See also the unsigned memorandum entitled "The Khilafatist Wahabi Case," Jerusalem, January 8, 1927, *ISA,* division 65, file 31. Rashid Rida's reply to Muhammad ᶜAli appeared in *al-Manar* (June 18, 1928), 29(3): 162–80.

71. Intelligence Report no. 31, Government of India, FO371/11433, E5595/20/91.

72. Text in Norman Mayers (Jidda), dispatch of January 9, 1927, L/P&S/10/1155, P. 1527.

73. Shafiq, *Aᶜmali baᶜda mudhakkirati,* 285–86.

74. Sirdar Ikbal Ali Shah to Shuckburgh, August 8, 1928, FO371/13043, E4125/2492/65.

75. Shakib Arslan, *al-Irtisamat al-lutaf fi khatir al-hajj fi aqdas mataf.*

76. Ahmad al-Sharabasi, *Amir al-bayan Shakib Arslan,* 2: 522.

77. There was some confusion in 1928, as many thought this was the overdue second congress. The choice of this site may have been intended to leave that impression. See Muhammad al-Saᶜid (Jidda), dispatch of June 5, 1928, in *DWQ,* ᶜAbdin: al-khilafa al-islamiyya, uncatalogued box; unsigned draft dispatch (Cairo), May 31, 1928, *AFC,* carton 131, file 26/3; *Umm al-qura,* June 8, 1928.

11. IN DEFENSE OF JERUSALEM

1. Muhammad ᶜAli al-Tahir, *Nazariyyat al-shura fiᵓl-ahwal al-sharqiyya al-hadira,* 96–100, 162–66, 189–93, 203–8, 226–31, 234–40. On the author, see Khayriyya Qasimiyya, "Muhammad ᶜAli al-Tahir, qalam filastini fi Misr."

2. *Al-Manar* (February 1932), 32(2): 113–32; (March 1932), 32(3): 193–208; (April 1932), 32(4): 284–92. See similar account in *al-Shihab* (February 1932), 8(2): 80–95.

3. Muhammad ᵓIzzat Darwaza, *Hawla al-haraka al-ᶜarabiyya al-haditha,* 75–82. Darwaza for a time was the trustee of the congress archives. See *al-Jamiᶜa al-ᶜarabiyya,* December 18, 1931.

4. ᶜAjaj Nuwayhid, "al-Hajj Muhammad Amin al-Husayni. Hadha al-muᵓtamar al-islami al-ᶜalami fiᵓl-Quds awakhir 1931 judhuruhu fi Makka 1926."

5. H. A. R. Gibb, "The Islamic Congress at Jerusalem in December 1931." See also Louis Jovelet, "L'évolution sociale et politique des Pays Arabes," 575–88; Eugène Jung, *Le réveil de l'Islam et des arabes,* 15–31, 99–107; and Michael Assaf, "Die musulmanische Konferenz in Jerusalem und der Panislamismus."

6. The major general accounts are those by Uri M. Kupferschmidt, "The General Muslim Congress of 1931 in Jerusalem"; ᶜAdil Hasan Ghunaym, "al-Muᵓtamar al-islami al-ᶜamm, 1931"; Yehoshua Porath, *The Palestinian National Movement,* 2: 8–13; and Yuval Arnon-Ohanna, *The Internal Struggle Within the Palestinian Movement 1929–1939,* 77–90 (in Hebrew).

7. Ahmad al-Sharabasi, *Amir al-bayan,* 2: 584–86. Amin al-Husayni said that he had left the autobiography, entrusted to him by Arslan for publication, among the congress papers, but Sharabasi did not find it. Years later another copy surfaced in Beirut, and was published as Arslan, *Sira dhatiyya.* My own search for the archive yielded no results. The permanent secretariat also had planned the publication of a detailed book on the congress and its antecedents, but no such volume ever appeared. For a description of the planned volume, see *al-Jamiᶜa al-ᶜarabiyya,* July 3, 1932.

8. On this plan, see Secret Political Report, dated Cairo, February 22, 1929, in FO371/ 13749. For a contemporary's reminiscences of Muhammad ʿAli and his involvement in the cause of Palestine, see ʿAjaj Nuwayhid, "Mawlana Muhammad ʿAli al-zaʿim al-hindi, 1878–1931."

9. Texts of telegrams from Amin al-Husayni (Jerusalem) to Shawkat ʿAli (London), January 7, 1931, and texts of replies, in *al-Rabita al-sharqiyya* (January 1931), 3(4): 5–18. Further details of the ceremony in Afzal Iqbal, *Life and Times of Mohammed Ali*, 387–93.

10. Resolutions in *al-Manar* (December 12, 1928), 29(8): 628–32. The Syrian publicists Shakib Arslan, Ihsan al-Jabiri, and Riyad al-Sulh, were signatories to a petition to the League of Nations Permanent Commission on Mandates, "in the names of, and as representatives of, the Muslim congress recently held in Jerusalem." Text of petition dated December 11, 1928, in FO371/13745, E1629/204/65.

11. For the text of the standard invitation, see *al-Manar* (February 1932), 32(2): 117–18; translated texts of invitations intercepted by postal authorities in India, in L/P&S/ 10/1314, file 350.

12. Mameli (Italian ambassador) memorandum to British Foreign Office, November 17, 1931, FO371/15282, E5725/1205/65.

13. Note by O. G. R. Williams (Colonial Office) on his meeting with Foreign Office and India Office representatives, November 17, 1931, CO732/51, file 89205, part 1. Minutes of the meeting on November 16, 1931, in FO371/15282, E5711/1205/65.

14. Government of India to Secretary of State for India, November 23, 1931, CO732/ 51, file 89205, part 2.

15. Minute by G. F. A. Warner, November 25, 1931, FO371/15283, 5831/1205/65.

16. Wauchope to Cunliffe-Lister, November 21, 1931, FO406/68, E5831/1205/65.

17. Wauchope to Cunliffe-Lister, FO406/68, E6040/1205/65.

18. Text in FO371/15283, E6087/1205/65.

19. Haim Arlosorov (Jerusalem) to Brodetsky (London), August 24, 1931, *CZA*, S25/ 5689.

20. Arlosorov to Brodetsky, November 13, 1931, *CZA*, Z4/10042.

21. The journalist was Taysir Duwaji, an Istiqlalist who volunteered his services to the Jewish Agency Arabist, Haim Kalvarisky. See Duwaji's letters to Kalvarisky in *CZA*, S25/ 5789; and Haim Arlosorov's political diary for September 30, October 27, and December 4, 1931, *CZA*, Z4/3663 (II-III). The published version of Arlosorov's diary conceals Duwaji's identity, as it does the identities of many Arab interlocutors. See Haim Arlosorov, *Yoman Yerushalayim*.

22. On the opposition and the congress, see the general remarks of Rashid Rida in *al-Manar* (February 1932), 32(2): 124–26.

23. Typescript of the manifesto, with a full list of signatories, in uncatalogued file entitled "Hisab jari maʿa al-bank al-ʿarabi fiʾl-quds," *ISA*.

24. Refutation in *al-Jamiʿa al-ʿarabiyya*, November 25, 1931; Arabic text of Amin al-Husayni's rebuttal in *al-Fath* (Rajab 23, 1350), 6(279): 10–11.

25. *Al-Jamiʿa al-ʿarabiyya*, December 4, 1931.

26. On Saʿid, see G. Kampffmeyer, "Egypt and Western Asia." For the course of the negotiations, see *al-Muqattam*, December 5–8, 1931; and review of the entire process, December 18, 1931. For a copy of the December 4, 1931 proclamation of Shawkat ʿAli and Saʿid on the progress of negotiations, see *ISA*, division 65, file 43. Rashid Rida gave his own version of the dispute, in which he, too, attempted to mediate, in *al-Manar* (February 1932), 32(2): 128–32.

27. For accounts of the counter-congress, see Wauchope (Jerusalem) to Cunliffe-Lister, January 30, 1932, L/P&S/10/1314, file 206; and the hostile account in *al-Jamiʿa al-ʿarabiyya*, December 23, 1931.

28. Quoted in Alfred Nielsen, "The International Islamic Conference at Jerusalem," 343.

29. Interview in al-Muqattam, December 12, 1931.

30. Hüseyin Nakib (Nice), secretary to Abdülmecid, proclamation/letter of November 14, 1931, translated in al-Muqattam, December 31, 1931.

31. The subject of Egypt and the congress has been studied by Thomas Mayer, "Egypt and the General Islamic Conference of Jerusalem in 1931"; and Kedourie, "Egypt and the Caliphate," 195–97.

32. Nur al-islam (Cairo) (October–November 1931), 2(6): 464.

33. Amin al-Husayni to King Fuʾad, October 29, 1931, DWQ, Prime Ministry, al-khilafa al-islamiyya, uncatalogued box.

34. Copy of proclamation of October 27, 1931, MRJ, file 1935. Text also published in al-Jamiʿa al-ʿarabiyya, October 29, 1931.

35. See his remarks as reported in al-Jamiʿa al-ʿarabiyya, November 9, 1931.

36. Zawahiri, al-Siyasa waʾl-Azhar, 318. For another version of their meeting, see Tahir, Nazariyyat al-shura, 99–100.

37. Al-Manar (February 1932), 32(2): 121–24.

38. Al-Jamiʿa al-ʿarabiyya, November 12, 1931. See FO141/728, file 1132, for the discrete Egyptian protest against the article, made to British authorities.

39. Al-Ahram, November 6, 1931; al-Jamiʿa al-ʿarabiyya, November 9, 1931.

40. Text of letter in al-Jamiʿa al-ʿarabiyya, November 11, 1931; CO732/51, file 89205, part 2. For Fuʾad's disparaging views of these assurances, see report on audience, in Sir Percy Loraine (Cairo), dispatch of November 17, 1931, CO732/51, file 89205, part 2.

41. Sir Percy Loraine (Cairo), cable to Jerusalem, November 30, 1931, CO732/51, file 89205, part 2.

42. Egyptian consul (Jerusalem), undated dispatch (c. late October 1931), MRJ, file 1935; another copy in ISA, division 65 (captured archive of the Egyptian consulate in Jerusalem), file (old number) 1068; Egyptian consul (Jerusalem), dispatch of November 2 or 3, 1931, in same file.

43. Chargé d'affaires (Jidda), telegram of November 14, 1931, FO371/15282, E5667/1205/65.

44. For the text of the belated Saudi letter to Amin al-Husayni, see al-Muqattam, January 10, 1932.

45. The Hijazi minister of war, Jamal al-Ghazzi, was the medium for this rumor. See interview in al-Muqattam, December 4, 1931.

46. Münir Bey appeared at the ministry on October 23, 1931, and the exchange of views was described in a report on plans for the Jerusalem congress, condensed from "diverse sources," and circulated internally in the ministry on December 3, 1931; see AFC, carton 71, file 13/4.

47. Sir George Clerk (Ankara), dispatch of November 12, 1931, FO406/68, E5784/1205/65.

48. Cunliffe-Lister (London) to Wauchope (Jerusalem), November 18, 1931, FO406/68, E5742/1205/65.

49. Rendel's notes on meeting, November 20, 1931, FO371/15283, E5770/1205/65. The India Office was reportedly in agreement with this conclusion, but an undated draft letter from the Undersecretary of State for India to the Undersecretary of State for Foreign Affairs offered that "the refusal of a passport to Abdul Majid might have unfortunate effects on [Shawkat ʿAli's] behaviour during his visit to Palestine for the Conference." L/P&S/10/1314.

50. Wauchope (Jerusalem) to Cunliffe-Lister (London), November 20, 1931, FO371/15283, E5785/1205/65.

51. Cunliffe-Lister (London) to Wauchope (Jerusalem), November 30, 1931, FO406/68, E5920/1205/65.

52. G. Clerk (Ankara), dispatch of November 12, 1931, FO406/68, E5784/1205/65.

53. Clerk, dispatch of December 1, 1931, FO406/68, E6050/1205/65.

54. Chambrun (Ankara), dispatch of December 14, 1931, *AFC,* carton 66, file 12/2.

55. Egyptian consul (Jerusalem), dispatch of December 3, 1931, *ISA,* division 65 (captured' archive of the Egyptian consulate in Jerusalem), file 1068.

56. James Morgan (Ankara), dispatch of December 8, 1931, FO406/68, E6172/1205/65. For the Turkish text, see Tevfik Rüştü Aras, *Lozanın İzlerinde 10 yıl,* 138–39.

57. *Al-Fath* (January 15, 1932), 6(285): 545–48, 557–59; *La Nation arabe* (November–December 1931) (no. 10–11): 9–13.

58. See lists in Kupferschmidt, "The General Muslim Congress," 158–62; FO371/16009, E753/87/65; and *La Nation arabe* (November–December 1931) (no. 10–11): 14–19.

59. For his role in Jerusalem and his activities on behalf of the Hijaz railway, see Muhammad Saᶜid al-Jazaʾiri, *Mudhakkirati ᶜan al-qadaya al-ᶜarabiyya waʾl-ᶜalam al-islami,* 240–60, 270–71.

60. For a translation into Arabic of his Urdu address, see *al-Jamiᶜa al-ᶜarabiyya,* December 16, 1931. On that occasion, he said: "You have seen that I have not participated much in your deliberations, because of my lack of familiarity with Arabic."

61. On İshaki, see the volume by Tahir Çağatay, et al., *Muhammad Ayaz İshaki.* See also his pamphlet submitted to the congress, entitled *Risala khatira ila al-muʾtamar al-islami al-ᶜamm . . . ᶜan halat al-muslimin fiʾl-Rusiya,* a copy of which is preserved in *MRJ,* file 1951.

62. See his proclamation to the congress entitled *Bayan ila al-muʾtamar al-islami al-ᶜamm . . . ᶜan halat al-muslimin fiʾl-Qafqas,* a copy of which is preserved in *MRJ,* file 1951. Also preserved here is a letter from İshaki and Şamil to King Fuʾad of Egypt, appealing for material and political aid for Russian Muslims. Their agitated remarks to the congress on Soviet policy appear in *al-Jamiᶜa al-ᶜarabiyya,* December 20, 1931. The presence of two leading Russian expatriates evoked a Soviet polemic against the congress by L. I. Klimovich, *Musul'manam daiut khalifa,* summarized by N. A. Smirnov, *Ocherki istorii izucheniia islama v SSSR,* 232–33.

63. Agha Buzurg al-Tihrani, *Tabaqat aᶜlam al-shiᶜa, nuqabaʾ al-bashar fiʾl-qarn al-rabiᶜ ᶜashar,* 1(4): 1437–41.

64. *Muhawarat al-imam al-muslih Kashif al-Ghitaʾ,* 52–53.

65. Muhammad al-Husayn Al Kashif al-Ghitaʾ, *al-Murajaᶜat al-Rayhaniyya.*

66. Tihrani, *Tabaqat,* 1(2): 613–15.

67. *Muhawarat al-imam al-muslih Kashif al-Ghitaʾ,* 55.

68. For a defense of his role as prayer leader to a Sunni congregation, see Hashim al-Daftardar al-Madani and Muhammad ᶜAli al-Zuᶜbi, *al-Islam bayna al-sunna waʾl-shiᶜa,* 1: 56–57. For criticism by Rashid Rida on the way in which Shaykh Muhammad al-Husayn conducted himself on this occasion, see *al-Manar* (September 1933), 33(5): 394–95.

69. For the text of his address, see the pamphlet *al-Khutba al-taʾrikhiyya.* This was published under the auspices of the congress itself.

70. H. A. R. Gibb wrote that the invitation to Shiᶜis was a "striking innovation, inasmuch as it was the first outward manifestation of a new spirit of co-operation (born in part of common adversity) which held out the hope of healing the age-long breach between the Sunni and Shiᶜah branches of Islam." Of this "fanciful and premature" observation, Elie Kedourie wrote that, "needless to say, this spirit of cooperation between Shiᶜites and Sunnis was visible neither then nor since." Gibb, "The Islamic Congress at Jerusalem," 101–2; Kedourie, *Chatham House Version,* 384–85.

71. The altercation occurred between ᶜAbd al-Rahman ᶜAzzam, of Wafdist affiliation, and Sulayman Fawzi, a journalist of royalist sympathies who was in the pay of the Egyptian consulate in Jerusalem. The incident attracted much attention. See the account

of the Egyptian consul (Jerusalem), dispatch of December 8, 1931, *ISA*, division 65 (captured archive of the Egyptian consulate in Jerusalem), file 1068. The file also includes Fawzi's own handwritten account of the incident, dated December 7, 1931, and a dispatch from the Egyptian consul of December 13, 1931, reporting the disbursement of £30 to Fawzi. For the published account, see *al-Jamiʿa al-ʿarabiyya*, December 7, 1931.

72. Statement by Shawkat ʿAli at Palace Hotel, December 5, 1931, in presence of ʿAbd al-Hamid Saʿid and others, *ISA*, uncatalogued file entitled "Hisab jari maʿa al-bank al-ʿarabi fiʾl-quds."

73. Tahir, *Nazariyyat al-shura*, 190.

74. For the disruptive activities of this group, which even included smoking in the congress hall where this was prohibited, see Tahir, *Nazariyyat al-shura*, 106–7. It was apparently Kalvarisky who wrote to the Jewish Agency that "I arranged that a group of four people in the congress hall would conduct affairs such that there would always be disaffection among the participants." Those named overlap the list given by Tahir. Letter of December 10, 1931, *CZA*, S25/5689.

75. Account of ʿAzzam's explusion in Wauchope (Jerusalem), telegram of December 17, 1931 and attached communiqué, FO371/15283, E6296/1205/65.

76. Notes of mufti's interview with Wauchope, December 17, 1931, FO371/16009, E87/87/65.

77. Gibb, *Whither Islam?*, 362–63.

78. George Antonius, Annual Report to the Institute of Current World Affairs for year ending September 30, 1932, in Antonius-Oxford; also copy in *ISA*, division 65 (Antonius Papers), file 707.

79. Haim Arlosorov (Jerusalem) to S. Brodetsky (London), November 13, 1931, *CZA*, Z4/10042.

80. Wauchope (Jerusalem), dispatch of March 26, 1932, L/P&S/10/1314.

81. Report on proceedings of the congress, enclosed in dispatch from Foreign Ministry to Gaillard (Cairo), January 29, 1932, *AFC*, carton 66, file 12/2.

82. The discussion on this issue is drawn from *al-Jamiʿa al-ʿarabiyya*, December 16, 1931.

83. Ibid.

84. Ibid., December 17, 1931, for the results of the voting. For the full list of those elected, see *Muqarrarat al-muʾtamar al-islami al-ʿamm fi dawratihi al-ʾula*, 24–25.

85. Quoted by Nielsen, "The International Islamic Conference at Jerusalem," 344.

86. *Al-Jamiʿa al-ʿarabiyya*, December 15, 18, 1931.

87. Described by Donald N. Wilber, *Riza Shah Pahlavi*, 39–55.

88. For his involvement, see Hidayat Allah Hakim Ilahi Fariduni, *Asrar-i siyasi-yi kudata: zindigani-yi aqa-yi Sayyid Ziyaʾ al-Din-i Tabatabaʾi*, 109–14, 118.

89. Charles Hart (Teheran), dispatch of December 30, 1931, *NA*, RG59, 867n.00/138.

90. Hart, dispatch of January 15, 1932, *NA*, RG59, 867n.00/143.

91. Arslan, *Sayyid Rashid Rida*, 641–42.

92. French text of charter in *AHP*, 36:165ff.; Arabic text in *al-Manar* (March 1932), 32(3): 209–12.

93. *Al-Manar* (March 1932), 32(3): 194–95.

94. A. J. Kingsley, Assistant Deputy Commandant C. I. D., to Chief Secretary for Palestine, July 30, 1932, L/P&S/10/1314, file 5326.

95. Ziyaʾ al-Din himself gave an account of the beginning of his activities in a lengthy circular letter to members of the executive committee, dated August 14, 1932, *ISA*, uncatalogued file apparently from seized papers of ʿAwni ʿAbd al-Hadi (hereafter: Tabatabaʾi Report).

96. Typescript copy in *ISA*, division 65, file 707; another copy appended to Tabatabaʾi Report.

97. For texts, see *Filastin*, June 11, 1932.

98. Typescript copy in *ISA*, division 65, file 707; another copy appended to Tabatabaᵓi Report.

99. For a list of branches, see Tabatabaᵓi Report, appendix 1. For Ziyaᵓ al-Din's remarks, see *Filastin*, August 13, 1932.

100. For Ziyaᵓ al-Din's detailed account of the various options for proceeding with the university, see his undated letter to the members of a committee for the university, in *ISA*, division 65, file 864; another copy is appended to the Tabatabaᵓi Report.

101. *Al-Jamiᶜa al-ᶜarabiyya*, November 23, 1932.

102. Record of conversation of March 16, 1933, between Amin al-Husayni and Charles Crane, as recorded by George Antonius, *ISA*, division 65 (Antonius Papers), file 854. Numerous schemes to raise money—most based on some sort of tax for services provided by the Supreme Muslim Council of Palestine—were aired during the congress itself. See *al-Jamiᶜa al-ᶜarabiyya*, December 12, 1931.

103. *Filastin*, December 4, 1932. For examples of appeals, see Tabatabaᵓi (Jerusalem) to King Fuᵓad (Cairo), May 16, 1932, *MRJ*, file 1935; Tabatabaᵓi (Jerusalem) to ᶜAbbas Hilmi, June 26, 1932, *AHP*, 125:16–17.

104. Departure detailed in *Filastin*, May 5, 6, 1933.

105. Antonius, Annual Report to the Institute of Current World Affairs for the year ending September 30, 1934, in Antonius-Oxford. For accounts of the mission, see *Oriente Moderno* (1933), 13: 293–95, 336–39, 558–60, 402–4. ᶜAlluba has left an account of his journey to India, in *al-Fath* (June 21, 1935), 9(450): 1220–21; (June 28, 1935), 10(451): 14–17.

106. D'Aumale (Jerusalem), dispatch of May 9, 1935, *AFC*, carton 66, file 12/1. For earlier evidence of ᶜAlluba's interest in making Egypt the center of the congress functions, see *Filastin*, January 14, 1933. For an account of the mediation mission to Arabia, see *al-Manar* (July 1934), 34(3): 232–35.

107. Secret police report, Palestine, no. 13/33, April 22, 1933, L/P&S/12/2118; Ely Palmer (Jerusalem), dispatch of March 6, 1935, *NA*, RG59, 867n.00/238; *Palestine Post* (Jerusalem), January 16, 1935.

108. For a view of the secretariat as essentially closed, see Antonius, Annual Report to the Institute of Current World Affairs for year ending September 30, 1935, Antonius-Oxford.

109. Paulo Boneschi, "Une fatwà du Grande Mufti de Jérusalem."

110. *Al-Muqattam*, February 7, 1937.

111. George Wadsworth (Jerusalem), dispatch of February 19, 1937, *NA*, RG59, 867n.00/440.

112. Enclosure no. 1 in R. Bullard (Jidda), dispatch of March 9, 1937, FO371/20839, E1868/201/25.

113. Fritz Grobba, *Männer und Mächte im Orient*, 273.

12. Swiss Exile

1. Sharabasi, *Amir al-bayan*, 2: 815–17.

2. Ihsan El-Djabri, "Le Congrés Islamique d'Europe"; *La Tribune d'Orient*, October 31, 1935, for what the sponsors regarded as a "compte-rendu exact."

3. "Der Muslimische Kongress von Europa, Genf September 1935" (republishes account of *La Tribune d'Orient*, October 31, 1935, with introduction); Virginia Vacca, "Il Congresso dei Musulmani d'Europa a Ginevra" (based on the Damascus *al-Ayyam*).

4. [Iqbal ᶜAli Shah], "European Muslim Conference at Geneva." The authorship of this anonymous piece has been deduced from its contents.

5. The Swiss materials cited here originated in the Ministère public fédéral, and were obtained through the Swiss Federal Archives in Bern. Unfortunately, it was impossible to locate any federal police file on the actual proceedings, although it seems unlikely that the event would have escaped surveillance.

6. Mahmoud Salem, *Le Congrès Islamo-européen de Genève (Août 1933)*, 3–7.

7. Ibid., 9.

8. Ibid., 15–18; *La Nation arabe* (April–May–June 1933) (no. 4–5–6): 5–7.

9. On Arslan's political career, see E. Lévi-Provençal, "L'Emir Shakib Arslan (1869–1946)"; Juliette Bessis, "Chekib Arslan et les mouvements nationalistes au Maghreb"; Antoine Fleury, "Le mouvement national arabe à Genève durant l'entre-deux-guerres," 345–53; and a forthcoming biography of Arslan by William Cleveland.

10. *Filastin,* July 1, 1933.

11. Arslan to Rida, July 29, 1933, in Sharabasi, *Amir al-bayan,* 2: 815; announcement of postponement in *La Tribune d'Orient,* July 15, 1933.

12. Chekib Arslan, *Aucune Propagande au monde ne peut défigurer le portrait d'un Homme,* 9.

13. On Ghayati and his journal, see Fleury, "Le mouvement national arabe à Genève," 339–45; Trefzger, *Die nationale Bewegung Ägyptens,* 109-20.

14. Zaki Ali, *Islam in the World,* dedication page.

15. Salem, *Le Congrès Islamo-européen,* 5.

16. Arslan to Rida, July 29, 1933, in Sharabasi, *Amir al-bayan,* 2: 816.

17. Ibid., 817.

18. Rida (Cairo) to Arslan (Geneva), August 10, 1933, in Arslan, *Sayyid Rashid Rida,* 717–18.

19. Minutes by A. K. Helm, September 19–20, 1934, FO371/17831, E5873/5873/65; British legation (Bern), dispatch of September 29, 1934, FO371/17831, E6124/5873/65.

20. Procureur général de la Confédération (Bern) to Conseiller d'Etat, Dépt. de Justice et Police (Geneva), March 8, 1935, *SFA,* C.10.3.

21. Declaration by Hakky Bey at the Commissariat de Police, Geneva, March 19, 1935, *SFA,* C.10.3.

22. Procureur général de la Confédération (Bern) to Police fédérale des Etrangers (Bern), June 17, 1935, *SFA,* C.13.108; Chef de la Division des Affaires Etrangères (Bern) to Procureur général (Bern), July 11, 1935, *SFA,* C.10.3.

23. Arslan letter of August 14, 1935, quoted by Conseiller d'Etat, Dépt. de Justice et Police (Geneva) to Procureur général (Bern), August 21, 1935, *SFA,* C.10.3.

24. Chef de la Division des Affaires Etrangères (Bern) to Procureur général de la Confédération (Bern), August 23, 1935, *SFA,* C.10.3.

25. Procureur général de la Confédération (Bern) to Conseiller d'Etat, Dépt. de Justice et Police (Geneva), August 26, 1935, *SFA,* C.10.3.

26. Arslan, *Aucune Propagande au monde,* 25.

27. For a translation of the letter—Arslan (Geneva) to Amin al-Husayni, February 20, 1935—see Esco Foundation for Palestine, *Palestine: A Study of Jewish, Arab and British Policies,* 2: 774–75. On the letter incident, see Sharabasi, *Amir al-bayan,* 1: 103–6; 2: 828–34.

28. Arslan (Geneva) to Rida, Safar 12, 1354, in Sharabasi, *Amir al-bayan,* 2: 829.

29. On Arslan's Italian affinities, see Bessis, "Chekib Arslan," 477–79; Mario Tedeschini Lalli, "La propaganda araba del fascismo e l'Egitto," 724–26.

30. On Durics and Mehmed Reszulovics, who accompanied him, see Alexandre Popovic, "Les musulmans de Hongrie dans la période post-ottomane," 181–82.

31. On Szynkiewicz, see "Der Muslimische Kongress von Europa," 103–4. On his community, see Maciej Konopacki, "Les Musulmans en Pologne." A few years later, Szynkiewicz gained some notoriety when German occupation authorities installed him as mufti of all *Ostland,* the German-occupied areas of the Soviet Union.

32. On these communities, see the sources provided by Alexandre Popovic, "Les Musulmans du Sud-Est européen dans la période post-ottomane."

33. On Misali's relationship with Arslan, see Bessis, "Chekib Arslan," passim; for his recollection of the congress, see Messali Hadj, *Les mémoires de Messali Hadj,* 195–99.

34. [Shah], "European Muslim Congress," 396–97.

35. Prentiss B. Gilbert (Geneva), dispatch of October 2, 1935, *NA,* RG59, 540.4 V1/4.

36. *Oriente Moderno* (1935), 15: 564.

37. [Shah], "European Muslim Conference," 396.

38. "Le Congrès Musulman d'Europe," *La Nation arabe* (October-November 1935), 7(7): 419. On Barbiellini, see *Oriente Moderno* (1932), 12: 72–73.

39. [Shah], "European Muslim Conference," 396–97; similar report in *Oriente Moderno* (1935), 15: 503.

40. Arslan, *Aucune Propagande au monde,* 8.

41. "Discours de Ihsan Bey El-Djabri, prononcé au Congrès Musulman d'Europe," *La Nation arabe* (July-August-September 1935), 5(6): 379–85.

42. Ibid., 376.

43. *La Nation arabe* (October-November 1935), 5(7): 422.

44. *Al-Muqattam,* October 9, 1935; *Oriente Moderno* (1935), 15: 566–67.

45. Prentiss B. Gilbert (Geneva), dispatch of October 2, 1935, *NA,* RG59, 540.4 V1/4.

46. An exception also was made for the Viennese Turcologist Herbert Jansky, who also attended the congress.

47. British consulate (Geneva) to Chancery (Bern), October 2, 1935, FO371/18925, E6005/5696/65.

48. *La Nation arabe* (October-November 1935), 5(7): 423-24; "Il Congresso dei Musulmani d'Europa a Ginevra."

49. *Filastin,* September 19, 1935; *al-Fath,* September 26, 1935; *Oriente Moderno* (1935), 15: 503–4.

50. *Al-Muqattam,* October 9, 1935; *Oriente Moderno* (1935), 15: 565–66.

51. Transcript of Arslan's interrogation by the Police de Sûreté, Geneva, October 6, 1938, *SFA,* C.10.7.

52. Mussolini's speech of March 12, 1937, and Ciano's speech of May 13, 1937, in Royal Institute of International Affairs, *Documents on International Affairs 1937,* 267, 283.

13. Congresses of Collaboration

1. Sir Muhammad Iqbal, *The Reconstruction of Religious Thought in Islam,* 151.

2. Ibid., 151–52.

3. Activities of the Indian Muslim delegation reported by W. A. Smart (Cairo) to P. C. Bamford (Simla), October 28, 1938, FO371/21884, E6732/10/31. See also the reports from the delegates to Jinnah in Atique Zafar Sheikh, ed. *Quaid-e-Azam and the Muslim World,* 27–41, 65-76.

4. On the congress, see Ettore Rossi, "Il Congresso interparlamentare arabo e musulmano pro Palestina al Cairo (7–11 ottobre)"; and the organizer's own account in Muhammad ᶜAli ᶜAlluba, *Filastin wa-jaratuhu,* 7–9, 115–16.

5. For an informative if overwrought account of this policy, see O. S. S. Research and Analysis Report 890, "Japanese Infiltration among Muslims throughout the World," May 15, 1943, *NA,* RG59.

6. On Ibrahim's career in general, see the sources cited in ch. 1, *n.* 34. On Ibrahim's early activities in Japan, see Abdürreşid İbrahim, *Âlemi İslâm ve Japonya'da istişarı İslâmiyet;* Nakaba Wakabayashi, *Kaikyo sekai to Nihon,* 8–10, passim; and Ettore Rossi, "Le relazioni tra il Giappone e il monde musulmano e l'opera di ᶜAbd er-Rashīd Ibrāhīm." On the impression made upon Muslims by the Japanese victory over Russia, see Klaus Kreiser,

"Der japanische Steg über Russland (1905) und sein Echo unter der Muslimen."

7. On the structure of the Tatar Muslim expatriate community in Japan, see O. S. S. Research and Analysis Report 890.2, "Japanese Attempts at Infiltration among Muslims in Russia and her Borderlands," August 1944, pp. 31–37, NA, RG59; M. Abdul Aziz, *The Crescent in the Land of the Rising Sun*, 11–25; and Berthold Spuler, "Die Lage der russland-türkischen Emigation im Fernen Osten."

8. For an account of the opening, see R. Craigie (Tokyo), dispatch of May 9, 1938, FO371/22193, F6413/5214/23.

9. Internal Report on Financial Aid to the Greater Japan Muslim League (for 1939), April 19, 1940, *JMFA*, reel S328, frame 1039. I am indebted to Tetsuo Masuda for his translation of official Japanese documents.

10. On the Manchukuo League, see O. S. S. Research and Analysis Report 890.1, "Japanese Infiltration among Muslims in China," May 15, 1944, pp. 43–44, 96, NA, RG59.

11. Ibid., 31–43, on the All China Muslim League; see also Yang Ching-chih, "Japan—Protector of Islam!" 476–77.

12. On Muzakkir, see Mitsuo Nakamura, "M. Professor Haji Kahar Muzakkir and the Development of the Muslim Reformist Movement in Indonesia." On Kasmat and Ma'ruf, see Benedict R. O'G. Anderson, *Java in a Time of Revolution*, 419, 424–25.

13. For a day-by-day account of the activities as viewed by an Indonesian participant, see H. M. Farid Ma'roef, *Melawat ke Japan*, 1–17. The author provides the names of other guests at the exhibition, and a brief account of the congress convened on November 18, 1939. I am indebted to Benedict Anderson for translating passages from this pamphlet. For evidence of the request, see Greater Japan Muslim League to Islamic Office of Army, Navy, and Foreign Ministries, April 26, 1940, *JMFA*, reel S328, frame 1051.

14. Greater Japan Muslim League to Islamic Office of Army, Navy, and Foreign Ministries, April 26, 1940; Islamic Affairs Committee of Foreign Office to Greater Japan Muslim League, May 9, 1940; both in *JMFA*, reel S328, frames 1050–51; Foreign Ministry to Consul General in Batavia, *JMFA*, reel S328, frame 1048.

15. Abdürreşid İbrahim (Tokyo) to Amin al-Husayni (Berlin), Mufti Files, p. 00094.

16. Netherlands Information Bureau, *Ten Years of Japanese Burrowing in the Netherlands East Indies*, 26.

17. See Harry J. Benda, *The Crescent and the Rising Sun*, 103–31.

18. Adolf Hitler, *Mein Kampf*, 747.

19. Grobba memorandum on the Arab question, March 7, 1941, in *Documents on German Foreign Policy, 1918–1945*, ser. D, 12: 235.

20. On the Berlin period of his career, see Lukasz Hirszowicz, *The Third Reich and the Arab East*, 211–313; Anthony R. De Luca, " 'Der Grossmufti' in Berlin: The Politics of Collaboration"; and Daniel Carpi, "The Mufti of Jerusalem, Amin el-Husseini, and His Diplomatic Activities during World War II (October 1941-July 1943)."

21. Arslan (Geneva) to Amin al-Husayni, Dhu al-Hijja 29, 1361, Mufti Files, p. 00295.

22. Ibid., June 1, 1944, Mufti Files, p. 00317.

23. Ibid., Jumada II, 13, 1362, Mufti Files, p. 00356.

24. Undated memorandum to Amin al-Husayni ("our demand must rest upon the following foundations"), Mufti Files, pp. 00423–24.

25. Amin al-Husayni (Berlin) memorandum [to Ribbentrop], October 20, 1943, Mufti Files, pp. 00201–5. The memorandum reiterates a program presented still earlier to the German Foreign Office.

26. On the history of Berlin's Muslim organizations, see M. S. Abdullah, *Geschichte des Islams in Deutschland*, 23–34.

27. On the Zentralinstitut, see Erwin Ettel (Berlin) to Ernst Woermann, December 11, 1942, *GFO*, reel 392, frames 930/297972–73. I am indebted to Daniel Dishon for his assistance in reading German diplomatic documents.

28. Erwin Ettel (Berlin) to Ernst Woermann, December 11, 1942, *GFO,* reel 392, frame 930/297977.

29. Mustafa al-Wakil to Ernst Woermann, [December 14, 1941], *GFO,* reel 392, frames 930/297960-61.

30. Abd al-Halim Naggar and Mansooruddin (Berlin) to Amin al-Husayni, December 14, 1942, *GFO,* reel 392, frame 930/297955.

31. Woermann (Berlin) to Kurt Prüfer, December 14, 1942, *GFO,* reel 392, frame 930/297958.

32. Minute of Bose-Ribbentrop meeting, October 14, 1942, *Akten zur deutschen auswärtigen Politik, 1918-1945,* ser. E, 4: 84-87; Reimund Schnabel, *Tiger und Schakal: Deutsche Indienpolitik, 1941-1943,* 277-78.

33. *Hamburger Fremdenblatt,* September 24, 1942.

34. Woermann memorandum, December 12, 1942, *GFO,* reel 392, frames 930/297968-69.

35. Wilhelm Melchers (Berlin) to Woermann, December 16, 1942, *GFO,* reel 392, frames 930/297948-50. On the incident, see also Grobba, *Männer und Mächte im Orient,* 308.

36. Islamische Zentralinstitut, *Die Rede Seiner Eminenz des Grossmufti Anlässlich der Eröffnung des Islamischen Zentral-Institutes zu Berlin,* in *GFO,* reel 392, frames 930/297941-45; *Völkischer Beobachter* (Berlin), December 19, 1942.

37. Amin al-Husayni to Hitler, [December 1942], *GFO,* reel 396, frame 930/304371.

38. For an account of this activity, see S. Wiesenthal, *Grossmufti—Grossagent der Achse,* 29-30.

39. Amin al-Husayni (Oybin) to Ribbentrop, November 12, 1944, Mufti Files, pp. 00187-88. The official was Wilhelm Melchers.

40. On these activities, see Ladislaus Hory and Martin Broszat, *Der kroatische Ustascha-Staat 1941-1945,* 154-61. It was this more consequential collaboration that led the Yugoslav government in July 1945 to place Amin al-Husayni on the United Nations' list of war criminals.

41. On the SS and Turkic Muslims, see Patrick von zur Mühlen, *Zwischen Hakenkreuz und Sowjetstern,* especially 139-69. On the Wehrmacht's efforts in this field, which preceded those of the SS, see Joachim Hoffmann, *Die Ostlegionen, 1941-1943,* especially 136-46 on religious guidance.

42. Amin al-Husayni (Berlin) to Japanese Foreign Minister, n.d. [1943], Mufti Files, pp. 00919, 00947-48.

43. Ibid., June 22, 1944, Mufti Files, pp. 00917-18, 00949.

44. *The Testament of Adolf Hitler. The Hitler-Bormann Documents, February-April 1945,* 71.

45. Viceroy to Secretary of State, India Office, July 14, 1940, L/P&S/12/2118.

46. Minute by R. Peel, July 17, 1940, L/P&S/12/2118.

47. L. Baggallay (Foreign Office) to R. Peel (India Office), August 1, 1940, L/P&S/12/2118.

48. R. Peel (India Office) to Viceroy, August 4, 1940; Viceroy to Peel, August 5, 1940, L/P&S/12/2118.

49. For Maraghi's view of Amin al-Husayni, see M. P. Waters, *Mufti over the Middle East,* 9.

50. Muhammad Husayn Haykal, *Mudhakkirat fiʾl-siyasa al-misriyya,* 2: 197.

51. Allan A. Michie, *Retreat to Victory,* 145.

52. On the mosque and the war, see A. L. Tibawi, "History of the London Central Mosque and the Islamic Cultural Centre 1910-1980," 197-204.

CONCLUSIONS

1. El-Djabri, "Le Congrès Islamique d'Europe," 373.

BIBLIOGRAPHY

PRIVATE AND PUBLIC ARCHIVES

Colonial Office Archives, Foreign Office Archives, Public Record Office, London.
Political and Secret Archives, Public and Judicial Archives, India Office Records, London.
State Department Archives, National Archives, Washington.
Political Archives of the German Foreign Office, Microcopy T-120, National Archives, Washington.
Archives of the French Embassy, Cairo.
Mahfuzat Ri³asat al-Jumhuriyya (Archives of the Presidency of the Republic), Cairo.
Dar al-Watha³iq al-Qawmiyya (Egyptian National Archives), Cairo.
Japanese Ministry of Foreign Affairs Archives, Microforms Division, Library of Congress, Washington.
Records of the Ministère Public Fédéral, Swiss Federal Archives, Bern.
Israel State Archives, Jerusalem.
Political Department Archives, Central Zionist Archives, Jerusalem.
Records of the General Islamic Congress for the Caliphate in Egypt, Azhar Mosque Library, Cairo.
Wilfrid Scawen Blunt Papers, West Sussex County and Diocesan Record Office, Chichester.
Wilfrid Scawen Blunt Papers, Fitzwilliam Museum, Cambridge.
Hardinge Papers, Cambridge University Library, Cambridge.
Abbas Hilmi II Papers, Durham University Library, Durham.
Hajj Amin al-Husayni Wartime Papers, Israeli Foreign Ministry, Jerusalem.
George Antonius Papers, St. Antony's College, Oxford.

PUBLISHED OFFICIAL DOCUMENTS

Akten zur deutschen auswärtigen Politik, 1918–1945.
Documents diplomatiques français, 1891–1914.
Documents on British Foreign Policy, 1919–1939.
Documents on German Foreign Policy, 1918–1945.

MAJOR PERIODICALS AND NEWSPAPERS

Al-Ahram, Cairo.
Al-Fath, Cairo.
Filastin, Jaffa.
Al-Jami³a al-ᶜarabiyya, Jerusalem.

Al-Liwaᵓ al-misri, Cairo.
Majallat al-muᵓtamar al-islami al-ᶜamm lᵓl-khilafa bi Misr, Cairo.
Al-Manar, Cairo.
Al-Muqattam, Cairo.
Muzaffari, Bushhir and Mecca.
Al-Nahda, Cairo.
La Nation arabe, Geneva.
Oriente Moderno, Rome.
Qanun, London.
Al-Qibla, Mecca.
Al-Rabita al-sharqiyya, Cairo.
Revue du monde musulman, Paris.
Al-Shihab, Constantine.
Sırat-ı müstakim/Sebilürreşad, Istanbul.
Al-Siyasa, Cairo.
Tercüman, Baghchesaray.
Umm al-qura, Mecca.
Al-ᶜUrwa al-wuthqa, Paris..
Al-Zahra, Cairo.

BOOKS AND ARTICLES

Abdullah, M.S. *Geschichte des Islams in Deutschland.* Graz, 1981.
Abu-Manneh, B. "Sultan Abdulhamid II and Shaikh Abulhuda Al-Sayyadi."
    Middle Eastern Studies (May 1979) 15(2):131–53.
——"Sultan Abdülhamid II and the Sharifs of Mecca (1880–1900)." *Asian and
    African Studies* (1973) 9(1):1–21.
Adamec, Ludwig W. *Afghanistan, 1900–1923: A Diplomatic History.* Berkeley, 1967.
Adamiyat, Faridun. *Andishehha-yi Mirza Aqa Khan Kirmani.* Teheran, 1346 solar/
    1967.
Affan, Seljuk. "Relations between the Ottoman Empire and the Muslim King-
    doms in the Malay-Indonesian Archipelago." *Der Islam* (1980) 57(2):301–10.
Afshar, Iraj, and Asghar Mahdavi. *Majmūᶜa-yi asnad va-madarik-i chap nashuda dar
    bara-yi Sayyid Jamal al-Din mashhur bih-Afghani/Documents inédits concernant Seyyed
    Jamāl-al-Din Afghānī.* Teheran, 1342 solar/1963.
Agerọn, Charles-Robert. *Les Algériens musulmans et la France (1871–1919).* 2 vols.;
    Paris, 1968.
Ahmad, Aziz. "Afghānī's Indian Contacts." *Journal of the American Oriental Society*
    (July-September 1969) 89(3):476–504.
——*Studies in Islamic Culture in the Indian Environment.* Oxford, 1964.
Akün, Ömer Faruk. "Nâmık Kemal'in Kitap Halindeki Eserlerinin İlk Neşirleri."
    Türkiyat Mecmuası, (1973–1975) 18:55–66.
Alexander, J. *The Truth about Egypt.* London, 1911.
Algar, Hamid. *Mīrzā Malkum Khān. A Study in the History of Iranian Nationalism.*
    Berkeley, 1973.
——"Shiᶜism and Iran in the Eighteenth Century." In Thomas Naff and Roger

Owen, eds. *Studies in Eighteenth Century Islamic History* (Carbondale, Ill., 1977), 288–302.

Ali, Zaki. *Islam in the World.* Lahore, 1938.

ᶜAlluba, Muhammad ᶜAli. *Filastin·wa-jaratuha.* Cairo, 1954.

Almez, *H.O.S. Tjokroaminoto.* Jakarta, 1952.

Altunsu, Abdülkadir. *Osmanlı Şeyhülislâmları* Ankara, 1972.

ᶜAmara, Muhammad. *al-Aᶜmal al-kamila liᵓl-imam Muhammad ᶜAbduh.* 1: *al-Kitabat al-siyasiyya.* Beirut, 1972.

Anderson, Benedict R. O'G. *Java in a Time of Revolution: Occupation and Resistance, 1944–1946.* Ithaca, 1972.

ᶜAqqad, Mahmud ᶜAbbas al-. *al-Rahhala "Kaf":* ᶜAbd al-Rahman al-Kawakibi. Cairo, 1959.

——*Rijal ᶜaraftuhum.* Cairo, 1963.

Aras, Tevfik Rüştü. *Lozanın İzlerinde 10 yıl.* Istanbul, 1935.

Arlosorov, Haim. *Yoman Yerushalayim.* 2d ed.: Tel Aviv, 1949.

Arnon-Ohanna, Yuval. *The Internal Struggle within the Palestinian Movement 1929–1939.* Tel Aviv, 1981. (in Hebrew)

Arslan, Chekib. *Aucune Propagande au monde ne peut défigurer le portrait d'un Homme.* Annemasse, 1936.

Arslan, Shakib. *al-Irtisamat al-lutaf fi khatir al-hajj fi aqdas mataf.* Cairo, 1350/1931.

——*Sayyid Rashid Rida aw ikhaᵓ arbaᶜin sanna.* Damascus, 1356/1937.

——*Sira dhatiyya.* Beirut, 1969.

Asadabadi, Mirza Lutf Allah Khan. *Sharh-i hal ve asar-i Sayyid Jamal al-Din Asadabadi maᶜruf bih Afghani.* Tabriz, 1326 solar/1947–48.

Assaf, Michael. "Die musulmanische Konferenz in Jerusalem und der Panis-lamismus." *Palästina* (1932), 15(1–2):34–43.

Atatürk'ün Söylev ve Demeçleri, vol. 1, Istanbul, 1945.

Atatürk'ün Tamim, Telegraf ve Beyannameleri, vol. 4, Ankara, 1964.

Axenfeld, K. "Geistige Kämpfe in der Eingeborenenbevölkerung an der Küste Ostafrikas." *Koloniale Rundschau* (November 1913), 647–73.

Aybek, Zafer Hasan. "Ubayd-Allah Sindhi in Afghanistan." *Journal of the Regional Cultural Institute* (Teheran) (Summer-Autumn 1973) 6(3–4):129–36.

Aydemir, Şevket Süreyya. *Makedonya'dan ortaasya'ya: Enver Paşa, 1914–1922.* Istanbul, 1972.

Aziz, M. Abdul. *The Crescent in the Land of the Rising Sun.* London, 1941.

Azoury, Negib. *Le Réveil de la nation arabe.* Paris, 1905.

Badger, George Percy. "The Precedents and Usages Regulating the Muslim Khalifate." *Nineteenth Century* (September 1877) 2(7):274–82.

Baha, Lal. "The Activities of the Mujāhidīn, 1900–1936." *Islamic Studies* (Islamabad) (Summer 1979) 18(2):97–168.

——"Activities of Turkish Agents in Khyber during World War I." *Journal of the Asiatic Society of Pakistan* (Dacca) (August 1969) 14(2):185–92.

Bakri, Muhammad Tawfiq al-. *al-Mustqabal li ᵓl-islam.* 2d ed.; Cairo, n.d.

Baldry, John. "Al-Yaman and the Turkish Occupation, 1849–1914." *Arabica* (1976) 23(2):156–96.

Balyuzi, H.M. *Edward Granville Browne and the Bahāᵓí Faith.* London, 1970.

Bardin, Pierre. *Algériens et Tunisiens dans l'Empire Ottoman de 1848 à 1914.* Paris, 1979.

"The Basmachis: The Central Asian Resistance Movement, 1918–24." *Central Asian Review* (1959) 7(3):236–50.

Battal-Taymas, A. "Ben Onu gördüm (İsmail Gaspıralı hakkında notlar)." *Türk Kültürü* (Ankara) (July 1968) 6(69):649–52.

——*Musa Carullah Bigi.* Istanbul, 1958.

Bayan ila al-mu^(?)tamar al-islami al-^(c)amm . . . ^(c)an halat al-muslimin fi^(?)l-qafqas. Jerusalem, n.d.

Baysun, M. Cavid. "Şirvanî-zade Ahmed Hulûsi Efendi'nin Efganistan elçiliğine âid vesikalar." *Tarih Dergisi* (Istanbul) (September 1952) 4(7):146–58.

Bayur, Hikmet. *Türk inkılâbı tarihi.* 3 vols.; Istanbul-Ankara, 1946–53.

Benda, Harry J. *The Crescent and the Rising Sun. Indonesian Islam under the Japanese Occupation 1942–1945.* The Hague, 1958.

Bennigsen, Alexandre, and Chantal Lemercier-Quelquejay. *La presse et le mouvement national chez les musulmans de Russie avant 1920.* Paris, 1964.

Bessis, Juliette. "Chekib Arslan et les mouvements nationalistes au Maghreb." *Revue historique* (April-June 1978) no. 526, 467–89.

Blunt, Wilfrid Scawen. *The Future of Islam.* London, 1882.

——*Gordon at Khartoum.* London, 1912.

——*India under Ripon.* London, 1909.

——*My Diaries.* 2 vols.; London, 1920.

——*Secret History of the English Occupation of Egypt.* London, 1922.

——"The Sultan's Heirs in Asia." *Fortnightly Review,* n.s. (July 1880) 163:16–30.

Boneschi, Paulo. "Une fatwà du Grande Mufti de Jérusalem Muhammad ^(?)Amin al-Husaynī sur les ^(c)Alawites." *Revue de l'histoire des religions* (Paris), (July-August 1940) 122(1):42–54; (September-December 1940) 122(2–3):134–52.

Boratav, Pertev. "La Russie dans les Archives ottomanes. Un dossier ottoman sur l'*imam* Chamil." *Cahiers du monde russe et soviétique* (July-December 1969) 10(3–4):524–35.

Bourgeot, André. "Les échanges transsahariens, la Senusiya et les révoltes twareg de 1916–17." *Cahiers d'études Africaines* (1978) 18(1–2):159–85.

Bouvet, L. "Un Projet de Parlement musulman international." *Revue du monde musulman* (March 1909) 8(3):321–22.

Boyer, Pierre. "L'Administration française et la règlementation du pèlerinage à la Mecque (1830–1894)." *Revue d'histoire maghrebine* (July 1977) 9:275–93.

Browne, E. G. "Pan-Islamism." In F. A. Kirkpatrick, ed. *Lectures on the History of the Nineteenth Century* (Cambridge, 1904), 306–30.

——*The Persian Revolution of 1905–1909.* Cambridge, 1910.

——*The Press and Poetry in Modern Persia.* Cambridge, 1914.

Burke, Edmund. "Moroccan Resistance, Pan-Islam and German War Strategy, 1914–1918." *Francia* (Munich) (1975) 3:434–64.

——"Pan-Islam and Moroccan Resistance to French Colonial Penetration, 1900–1912." *Journal of African History* (1972) 30(1):97–118.

Çağatay, Tahir, et al. *Muhammad Ayaz İshaki hayatı ve faaliyeti, 100. doğum yılı dolayısıyla.* Ankara, 1979.

Canard, M. "L'Impérialisme des Fātimides et leur propagande." *Annales de l'Institut d'Etudes Orientales* (Algiers) (1942–47) 6:156–93.

Carpi, Daniel. "The Mufti of Jerusalem, Amin el-Husseini, and His Diplomatic Activity during World War II (October 1941-July 1943)." *Studies in Zionism* (Tel Aviv) (Spring 1983), no. 7, 101–31.

Carr, E. H. "Radek's 'Political Salon' in Berlin 1919." *Soviet Studies* (Oxford) (April 1952) 3(4):411–30.

Cebesoy, Ali Fuat. *Moskova Hatıraları.* Istanbul, 1955.

Chenoufi, Ali. *Un savant tunisien du XIXème siècle: Muhammad as-Sanusi, sa vie et son oeuvre.* Tunis, 1977.

Chenoufi, M. "Les deux séjours de Muhammad ʿAbduh en Tunisie." *Cahiers de Tunisie* (Tunis) (1968) 16:57–96.

Ching-chih, Yang. "Japan—Protector of Islam!" *Pacific Affairs* 15(4):471–81.

"Il Congresso dei Musulmani d'Europa a Ginevra." *Annali del R. Istituto Superiore Orientale de Napoli* (October 1935) 8(1):132–33.

Crecelius, Daniel. "The Emergence of the Shaykh al-Azhar as the pre-eminent Religious Leader in Egypt." *Colloque international sur l'histoire du Caire* (Cairo, 1972), 109–23.

Cromer [E. Baring]. *Modern Egypt.* 2 vols.; New York, 1908.

Cruickshank, A. A. "The Young Turk Challenge in Postwar Turkey." *Middle East Journal* (Winter 1968) 22(1):17–28.

Daftar, Muhammad Hadi al-. *Safha min rihlat al-imam al-Zanjani wa-khutabuhu fi ʾl-aqtar al-ʿarabiyya waʾl-ʿawasim al-islamiyya.* Najaf, 1366–77/1947–57.

Dahhan, Sami al-. *ʿAbd al-Rahman al-Kawakibi.* Cairo, 1964.

Dale, Stephen F. *Islamic Society on the South Asian Frontier: The Mappilas of Malabar, 1498–1922.* Oxford, 1980.

——"The Mappilla Outbreaks: Ideology and Social Conflict in Nineteenth-Century Kerala." *Journal of Asian Studies* (November 1975) 35(1):85–97.

Darwaza, Muhammad ʿIzzat. *Hawla al-haraka al-ʿarabiyya al-haditha,* vol. 3, Sidon, 1951.

Davison, Roderic H. *Reform in the Ottoman Empire, 1856–1876.* Princeton, 1963.

Dawn, C. Ernest. "Ideological Influences in the Arab Revolt." In his *From Ottomanism to Arabism* (Urbana, 1973), 1–53.

De Luca, Anthony B. " 'Der Grossmufti' in Berlin: The Politics of Collaboration." *International Journal of Middle East Studies* (February 1979) 10(1):125–38.

Deny, Jean. "Instructeurs militaires turcs au Maroc sous Moulay Hafidh." *Mémorial Henri Basset* (Paris, 1928), 219–27.

Desparmet, J. "La turcophilie en Algérie." *Bulletin de la société de géographie d'Alger et l'Afrique* (Algiers) (1916) 21:1–25; (1917) 22:1–83.

Dictionary of National Biography, 1912–1921. London, 1966.

Dijwi, Yusuf al-. *al-Islam wa-usul al-hukm waʾl-radd ʿalayhi.* Cairo, n.d.

Djabri, Ihsan El-. "Le Congrés Islamique d'Europe." *La Nation arabe* (July-August-September 1935) 5(6):369–74.

Dumont, Paul. "L'axe Moscou-Ankara. Les relations turco-soviétiques de 1919 à 1922." *Cahiers du Monde russe et soviétique* (July-September 1977) 18(3):165–93.

——"La fascination du bolchevisme: Enver pacha et le parti des soviets populaires." *Cahiers du Monde russe et soviétique* (April-June 1975) 6(2):141–66.

Edib, Eşref. "Meşhur İslam seyyahı Abdürreşid İbrahim Efendi." *İslâm-Türk Ansiklopedisi Mecmuası* (1945) 2(53–54):3–4.

Ende, Werner. "Iraq in World War I: The Turks, the Germans and the Shīʿite Mujtahids' Call for Jihād." *Proceedings of the Ninth Congress of the Union Européenne des Arabisants et Islamisants, Amsterdam, 1–7 September 1978* (ed. Rudolf Peters; Leiden, 1981), 57–71.

——"Sayyid Abū al-Hudā, ein Vertrauter Abdülhamid's II. Notwendigkeit und Probleme einer kritischen Biographie." *XIX. Deutscher Orientalistentag 1975, Vorträge* (ed. Wolfgang Voigt; Weisbaden, 1977), 1143–55.

Ertürk, Hüsameddin. *İki devrin perde arkası.* Istanbul, 1957.

Esco Foundation for Palestine. *Palestine: A Study of Jewish, Arab and British Policies.* 2 vols.; New Haven, 1947.

Fahim, Mohammad. "Afghanistan and World War I." *Journal of the Pakistan Historical Society* (Karachi) (April 1978) 26(2):107–15.

Fahmi, Mahir Hasan. *Muhammad Tawfiq al-Bakri.* Cairo, 1967.

Farid, Muhammad. *Awraq Muhammad Farid. 1: Mudhakkirati baʿda al-hijra.* Cairo, 1978.

Fariduni, Hidayat Allah Hakim Ilahi. *Asrar-i siyasi-yi kudata: zindigani-yi aqa-yi Sayyid Ziyaʾ al-Din-i Tabatabaʾi.* Teheran, 1322 solar/1943–44.

Faruqi, Ziya-ul-Hasan. *The Deoband School and the Demand for Pakistan.* London, 1963.

Fleury, Antoine. "Le mouvement national arabe à Genève durant l'entre-deux-guerres." *Relations internationales* (Geneva) (Autumn 1979) no. 19, 329–54.

Fuglestad, Finn. "Les révoltes des Touareg du Niger (1916–17)." *Cahiers d'études Africaines* (1973) 13(1):86–89.

Fursat, Muhammad Nasir Mirza. *Kitab-i asar-i ʿajam.* Bombay, 1353/1933.

Ghazzi, Kamil al-. " ʿAbd al-Rahman al-Kawakibi." *al-Hadith* (Aleppo) (June-July 1929) 3(6–7):405–20, 445–50.

Ghunaym, ʿAdil Hasan. "al-Muʾtamar al-islami al-ʿamm, 1931." *Shuʾun filastiniyya* (Beirut) (September 1973) No. 25, 119–35.

Gibb, H.A.R. "The Islamic Congress at Jerusalem in December 1931." In Arnold J. Toynbee, ed. *Survey of International Affairs 1934* (London, 1935), 99–109.

——"Lutfi Paşa on the Ottoman Caliphate." *Oriens* (1962) 15:287–95.

——*Studies on the Civilization of Islam,* eds. Stanford Shaw and William Polk. Boston, 1962.

——*Whither Islam?* London, 1932.

Goldschmidt, Arthur J. "The Egyptian Nationalist Party: 1892–1919." In P. M. Holt, ed. *Political and Social Change in Modern Egypt* (Oxford, 1968), 308–33.

Green, Arnold. *The Tunisian Ulama, 1873–1915.* Leiden, 1978.

Grobba, Fritz. *Männer und Mächte im Orient. 25 Jahre diplomatischer Tatigkeit im Orient.* Göttingen, 1967.

Hadj, Messali. *Les mémoires de Messali Hadj, 1898–1938.* Paris, 1982.

Haim, Sylvia G. "The Abolition of the Caliphate and its Aftermath." In Thomas W. Arnold, *The Caliphate* (2d ed.: London, 1965), 205–44.

——"Alfieri and al-Kawākibī." *Oriente Moderno* (July 1954) 34(7):321–34.

——*Arab Nationalism: An Anthology.* Berkeley, 1962.

——"Blunt and al-Kawākibī." *Oriente Moderno* (March 1955) 35(3):132–43.

——"The Ideas of a Precursor, ᶜAbd al-Rahmān al-Kawākibī (1849–1902), in Relation to the Trend of Muslim-Arab Political Thought." Doctoral dissertation, Edinburgh, 1953.

Hairi, Abdul-Hadi. *ShīᶜIsm and Constitutionalism in Iran.* Leiden, 1977.

Halim, A. "Russo-Turkish War of 1876–77 and the Muslims of Bengal." *VI. Türk Tarih Kongresi* (Ankara, 1967), 526–32.

Hamka (Hadji Abdul Malik Karim Amrullah). *Ajahku. Riwayat hidup Dr. Abd. Karim Amrullah dan perdjuangan kaum agama.* Jakarta, 1950.

Hardinge, Arthur H. *A Diplomatist in the East.* London, 1928.

Hartmann, Martin. "Der Islam 1907–1908." *Mitteilungen des Seminars für Orientalische Sprachen zu Berlin* (1908) 11(2):207–33; (1909) 12(2):33–108.

Hartmann, Richard. "Zum Gedanken des 'Kongresses' in den Reformbestrebungen des islamischen Orients." *Welt des Islams,* o.s. (1941) 23:122–32.

Haykal, Muhammad Husayn. *Mudhakkirat fiᵓl-siyasa al-misriyya.* 2 vols.; Cairo, 1953.

Heine, Peter. "Salih ash-Sharif at-Tunisi, a North African Nationalist in Berlin during the First World War." *Revue de l'Occident musulman et de la Méditerranée* (Aix-en-Provence) (1982), no. 33, 89–95.

Hirszowicz, L. "The Sultan and the Khedive, 1892–1908." *Middle Eastern Studies* (October 1972) (3):287–311.

——*The Third Reich and the Arab East.* London, 1966.

Hostler, Charles. *Turkism and the Soviets.* London, 1957.

Hourani, Albert. "The Syrians in Egypt in the Eighteenth and Nineteenth Centuries." *Colloque international sur l'histoire du Caire* (Cairo, 1972), 221–33.

——"Wilfrid Scawen Blunt and the Revival of the East." In his *Europe and the Middle East* (Berkeley, 1980), 87–103.

Hitler, Adolf. *Mein Kampf.* Munich, 1942.

——*The Testament of Adolf Hitler. The Hitler-Bormann Documents, February-April 1945.* London, 1961.

Hoffmann, Joachim. *Die Ostlegionen, 1941–1943. Turkotataren, Kaukasien und Wolgafinnen im deutschen Heer.* Freiburg, 1976.

Hory, Ladislaus, and Martin Broszat. *Der kroatische Ustascha-Staat 1941–1945.* Stuttgart, 1964.

Hurgronje, C. Snouck. "Les confréries religieuses, la Mecque, et le Panislamisme." In his *Verspreide geschriften* (Bonn-Leipzig, 1923) 3:189–206.

——"Eenige Arabische strijdschriften besproken." In his *Verspreide geschriften* (Bonn-Leipzig, 1923) 3:149–88.

İbrahim, Abdürreşid. *Âlemi İslâm ve Japonya'da intişarı İslâmiyet.* Istanbul, 1329/1910–11.

İnalcık, Halil. "The Socio-Political Effects of the Diffusion of Fire-arms in the Middle East." In V. J. Parry and M. E. Yapp, eds. *War, Technology and Society in the Middle East* (Oxford, 1975), 195–217.

India, Government of. *Sedition Committee Report, 1918.* Calcutta, 1919.

Iqbal, Afzal. *Life and Times of Mohamed Ali.* Delhi, 1978.

Iqbal, Sir Muhammad. *The Reconstruction of Religious Thought in Islam.* Oxford, 1934.

Ivanow, W. "The Organisation of the Fatimid Propaganda." *Journal of the Bombay Branch of the Royal Asiatic Society*, n.s. (1939) 15:1–35.

Jäschke, Gotthard. "Nationalismus und Religion im türkischen Befreiungskriege." *Welt des Islam*, o.s. (1936) 18:54–69.

——"Le rôle du communisme dans les relations russo-turques de 1919 à 1922." *Orient* (Paris) (1963), no. 26, 31–44.

——"Ein scherifisches Bündnisangebot an Mustafa Kemal. Ein Beitrag zur Geschichte der arabisch-türkischen Beziehungen." *Der Orient in der forschung: Festschrift für Otto Spies* (Wiesbaden, 1967), 371–94.

Jaza᾿iri, Muhammad Saᶜid. *Mudhakkirati ᶜan al-qadaya al-ᶜarabiyya wa᾿l-ᶜalam al-islami.* 2d ed.; Algiers, 1387/1968.

Jindi, Anwar al-. *ᶜAbd al-ᶜAziz Jawish.* Cairo, 1965.

——*al-Imam al-Maraghi.* Cairo, 1952.

Jisr, Husayn al-. *al-Risala al-hamidiyya.* Damascus, 1352/1933–34.

Jong, F. de. "Abu᾿l-ᶜAzā᾿im, Muhammad Mādī." *EI²* Supplement (1980), 18.

——"al-Bakrī, Muhammad Tawfik b. ᶜAlī b. Muhammad." *EI²* Supplement (1980), 122–23.

——"Turuq and turuq-opposition in 20th century Egypt." *Proceedings of the VIth Congress of Arabic and Islamic Studies, Visby 13–16 August, Stockholm 17–19 August 1972* (Stockholm, 1975), 84–96.

Jovelet, Louis. "L'évolution sociale et politique des Pays Arabes (1930–1933)." *Revue des études islamiques* (1933) 4:425–644.

Jung, Eugene. *Le réveil de l'Islam et des arabes.* Paris, 1933.

Kalam, Javahir. "Hujjat al-Islam vala Shahzada Abu al-Hasan Mirza Shaykh al-Ra᾿is Qajar." *Iran-i Abad* (1959) 1(11):27–29.

Kampffmeyer, G. "Egypt and Western Asia." In H.A.R. Gibb, ed. *Whither Islam?* (London, 1932), 103–54.

——"Urkunden und Berichte zur Gegenwartsgeschichte des arabischen Orients." *Mitteilungen des Seminars für Orientalische Sprachen zu Berlin* (1927) 30(2):140–60.

Karabekir, Kâzım. *İstiklâl Harbimiz.* Istanbul, 1960.

——*İstiklâl Harbimizde: Enver Paşa ve İttihat Terakki Erkânı.* Istanbul, 1967.

Karpat, Kemal H. "The Status of the Muslim under European Rule: The Eviction and Settlement of the Cerkes." *Journal Institute of Muslim Minority Affairs* (Jidda) (Winter 1979-Summer 1980), 7–27.

Kashif al-Ghita᾿, Muhammad al-Husayn. *al-Murajaᶜat al-Rayhaniyya.* Beirut/Sidon, 1331/1913.

Kawakibi, ᶜAbd al-Rahman al-. *Umm al-qura.* Port Said, n.d.

Keddie, Nikki R. "Pan-Islam as Proto-Nationalism." *Journal of Modern History* (March 1969) 41(1):17–28.

——"Religion and Irreligion in Early Iranian Nationalism." *Comparative Studies in Society and History* (April 1962) 4(3):265–95.

——*Sayyid Jamāl ad-Dīn "al-Afghānī": A Political Biography.* Berkeley, 1972.

Kedourie, Elie. "Afghani in Paris: A Note." *Middle Eastern Studies* (January 1972) 8(1):103–5.

——"Egypt and the Caliphate, 1915–52." In his *Chatham House Version and other Middle Eastern Studies* (London, 1970), 177–207.

——*In the Anglo-Arab Labyrinth.* Cambrídge, 1976.

——"The Politics of Political Literature: Kawakibi, Azoury and Jung." In his *Arabic Political Memoirs* (London, 1974), 107–23.

Kelidar, Abbas. "Shaykh ᶜAli Yusuf: Egyptian Journalist and Islamic Nationalist." In Marwan R. Buheiry, ed. *Intellectual Life in the Arab East* (Beirut, 1981), 10–20.

Kelly, J.B. *Britain and the Persian Gulf.* Oxford, 1968.

Kerr, Malcolm H. *Islamic Reform: The Political and Legal Theories of Muhammad ᶜAbduh and Rashīd Riḍā.* Berkeley, 1966.

Khalid, Detlev. " ᶜUbayd-Allāh Sindhī." *Islamic Studies* (Islamabad) (June 1969) 8(2):97–114.

——" ᶜUbayd-Allah Sindhi and Muslim Nationalism." In *Main Currents of Contemporary Thought in Pakistan* (ed. Hakim Mohammed Said; Karachi, 1973) 2:300–28.

——" ᶜUbayd-Allāh Sindhi in Turkey." *Journal of the Regional Cultural Institute* (Teheran) (Winter-Spring 1973) 6(1–2):29–42.

Al-Khuṭba al-taʾrikhiyya allati alqaha fīʾl-jalsa al-thaniyya ᶜashara min jalsat al-muʾtamar al-islami al-ᶜamm samahat al-ᶜallama al-jalil al-imam al-hujja al-mujtahid al-shaykh Muhammad al-Husayn Al Kashif al-Ghiṭāʾ. Jerusalem, 1932.

Klimovich, L.I. *Musul'manam daiut khalifa.* Moscow, 1932.

Konopacki, Maciej. "Les Musulmans en Pologne." *Revue des études islamiques* (1968) 36:115–30.

Kraiem, Mustapha. "Au sujet des incidences des deux séjours de Muhammad ᶜAbduh en Tunisie." *Revue d'histoire maghrebine* (Tunis) (January 1975) no. 3, 91–94.

Kramer, Martin. "Egypt's Royal Archives, 1922–52." *American Research Center in Egypt Newsletter* (Winter 1980), no. 113, 19–21.

——"Shaykh Marāghī's Mission to the Hijāz, 1925." *Asian and African Studies* (March 1982) 16(1):121–36.

Kreiser, Klaus. "Der japanische Steg über Russland (1905) und sein Echo unter der Muslimen." *Welt des Islams,* n.s. (1981) 21(1–4):209–39.

Kupferschmidt, Uri M. "The General Muslim Congress of 1931 in Jerusalem." *Asian and African Studies* (March 1978) 12(1):123–62.

Kutay, Cemal. *Kurtuluşun ve cumhuriyetin manevi mimarları.* Ankara, 1973.

Kuttner, Thomas. "Russian *Jadīdism* and the Islamic World: Ismail Gasprinskii in Cairo—1908." *Cahiers du monde russe et soviétique* (July-December 1975) 16(3–4):383–424.

Lalli, Mario Tedeschini. "La propaganda araba del fascismo e l'Egitto." *Storia Contemporanea* (December 1976) 7(4):717–49.

Landau, Jacob M. "Al-Afghānī's Pan-Islamic Project." *Islamic Culture* (July 1952) 26(3):50–54.

——*The Hejaz Railway and the Muslim Pilgrimage: A Case of Ottoman Political Propaganda.* Detroit, 1971.

Laoust, Henri. *Le califat dans la doctrine de Rashīd Riḍā.* Beirut, 1938.

——"Le réformisme orthodoxe des 'Salafiya' et les caractères généraux de son orientation actuelle." *Revue des études islamiques* (1932) 6:175–224.

Lazzerini, Edward J. "Ibragimov (Ibrahimov), Abdurreşid." *The Modern Encyclopedia of Russian and Soviet History* (Gulf Breeze, Fla., 1979) 14:111–13.

——"Ismail Bey Gasprinskii and Muslim Modernism in Russia, 1878–1914." Doctoral dissertation, University of Washington, 1973.

Le Chatelier, A. *Les Confréries musulmanes du Hedjaz.* Paris, 1887.

Lee, Dwight E. "The Origins of Pan-Islamism." *American Historical Review* (January 1942) 47(2):278–87.

——"A Turkish Mission to Afghanistan, 1877." *Journal of Modern History* (September 1941) 13(3):335–56.

Lemercier-Quelquejay, Ch. "Un réformateur tatar au XIXᵉ siècle: ᶜAbdul Qajjum al-Nasyri." *Cahiers du monde russe et soviétique* (January-June 1963) 4(1–2):117–42.

Lévi-Provençal, E. "L'Emir Shakib Arslan (1869–1946)." *Cahiers de l'Orient contemporain* (1947–48) no. 9–10, 1–15.

Lewis, Bernard. "The Ottoman Empire in the Mid-Nineteenth Century: A Review." *Middle Eastern Studies* (April 1965) 1(3):283–95.

Lewis, Geoffrey. "The Ottoman Proclamation of Jihād in 1914." In *Arabic and Islamic Garland* [Tibawi Festschrift] (London, 1977), 159–65.

Lockhart, L. *Nadir Shah.* London, 1938.

Longford, Elizabeth. *A Pilgrimage of Passion: The Life of Wilfrid Scawen Blunt.* London, 1979.

Lorimer, J.G. *Gazetteer of the Persian Gulf.* Vol. 1; Calcutta, 1915.

Macfie, A.L. "The British Decision regarding the Future of Constantinople (November 1918-January 1920)." *Historical Journal* (June 1975) 18(2):391–400.

Madani, Hashim al-Daftardar, and Muhammad ᶜAli al-Zuᶜbi. *al-Islam bayna al-sunna waᵓl-shiᶜa.* Beirut, 1369/1950.

Madani, Husayn Ahmad. *Safarnama-yi Shaykh al-Hind.* Lahore, 1974.

Mardin, Şerif. *Jön Türklerin siyasî fikirleri 1895–1908.* Ankara, 1964.

Margoliouth, D.S. "Mohammedan Explanations of the Failure of Mohammedanism: A Conference at Meccah." *The East and the West* (London) (October 1907) 5:393–402.

Ma'roef, H. M. Farid. *Melawat ke Japan.* Jogjakarta, 1940.

Martin, B.G. "Maî Idrîs of Bornu and the Ottoman Turks, 1576–78." *International Journal of Middle East Studies* (October 1972) 3(4):470–95.

——"Notes on Some Members of the Learned Classes of Zanzibar and East Africa in the Nineteenth Century." *African Historical Studies* (1971) 2(3):524–45.

Mashriqi, ᶜInayat Allah Khan. *Khitab-i muᵓtamar-i khilafat.* Rawalpindi, 1974.

Massignon, Louis. "L'entente islamique internationale et les deux congrès musulmans de 1926." *Revue de science politique* (October-December 1926), 481–85.

Mathur, Y. B. *Muslims and Changing India.* New Delhi, 1972.

Mayer, Ann Elizabeth. " ᶜAbbās Hilmī II: The Khedive and Egypt's Struggle for Independence." Doctoral dissertation, University of Michigan, 1978.

Mayer, Thomas. "Egypt and the General Islamic Conference of Jerusalem in 1931." *Middle Eastern Studies* (July 1982) 18(3):311–22.

Mende, Gerhard von. *Der nationale Kampf der Russlandtürken.* Berlin, 1936.

Merad, Ali. *Ibn Bādis, commentateur du Coran.* Paris, 1971.

——*Le Réformisme musulman en Algérie de 1925 à 1940.* Paris, 1967.

Metcalf, Barbara Daly. *Islamic Renewal in British India: Deoband, 1860–1900.* Princeton, 1981.

Miège, Jean-Louis. *Le Maroc et l'Europe.* Vol. 4; Paris, 1963.

Minault, Gail. *The Khilafat Movement: Religious Symbolism and Political Mobilization in India.* New York, 1982.

Mousa, Suleiman. "A Matter of Principle: King Hussein of the Hijaz and the Arabs of Palestine." *International Journal of Middle East Studies* (May 1978) 9(2):183–94.

Mühlen, Patrick von zur. *Zwischen Hakenkreuz und Sowjetstern. Der Nationalismus der sowjetischen Orientvölker im Zweiten Weltkrieg.* Düsseldorf, 1971.

Muhammad, Shan. *The Khaksar Movement in India.* Meerut, 1973.

Muhawarat al-imam al-muslih Kashif al-Ghitaʾ al-shaykh Muhammad al-Husayn maʿa al-safirayn al-baritani waʾl-amriki bi munasabat ziyaratihima li-samahatihi fi madrasatihi fiʾl-Najaf. Najaf, 1373/1954.

Muqarrarat al-muʾtamar al-islami al-ʿamm fi dawratihi al-ʾula. Jerusalem, n.d.

Muqarrarat muʾtamar al-ʿulamaʾ al-awwal. Damascus, 1357/1938.

Murad, Mehmed. *Tatlı Emeller Acı Hakikatler.* Istanbul, 1330/1911.

"Der Muslimische Kongress von Europa, Genf September 1935." *Welt des Islams* (Berlin), (1935) o.s. 17(3–4):99–111.

Nakamura, Mitsuo. "M. Professor Haji Kahar Muzakkir and the Development of the Muslim Reformist Movement in Indonesia." In *Religion and Social Ethos in Indonesia* (Clayton, Victoria, 1977), 1–20.

Nallino, C.A. "La Fine del così detto califfato ottomano." *Oriente Moderno* (1924) 4:137–53.

Netherlands Information Bureau. *Ten Years of Japanese Burrowing in the Netherlands East Indies.* New York, 1942.

Nielsen, Alfred. "The International Islamic Conference at Jerusalem." *Muslim World* (October 1932) 22(4):340–54.

Niemeijer, A.C. *The Khilafat Movement in India, 1919–1924.* The Hague, 1972.

Noer, Deliar. *The Modernist Muslim Movement in Indonesia, 1900–1942.* Kuala Lumpur and Oxford, 1973.

Nuwayhid, ʿAjaj. "al-Hajj Amin al-Husayni fiʾl-muʾtamar al-islami al-ʿamm fi Makka." *al-Adib* (Beirut) (August 1975) 34(8):32–37.

——"al-Hajj Muhammad Amin al-Husayni. Hadha al-muʾtamar al-islami al-ʿalami fiʾl-Quds awakhir 1931 judhuruhu fi Makka 1926." *al-Adib* (Beirut), (September 1975) 34(9):32–36.

——"Mawlana Muhammad ʿAli al-zaʿim al-hindi, 1878–1931." *al-Adib* (Beirut) (April 1978) 37(4):2–18; (May 1978) 37(5):44–49.

O'Mahoney, H. "Le Congrès Panislamique." *Revue de l'Islam* (Paris) (1896) 1:17–18.

Ochsenwald, William. *The Hijaz Railroad.* Charlottesville, Virginia, 1980.

——"A Modern *Waqf*: The Hijaz Railway, 1900–48." *Arabian Studies* (1976) 3:1–12.

——"Ottoman Subsidies to the Hijaz, 1877–1886." *International Journal of Middle East Studies* (July 1975) 6(3):300–307.

Orhonlu, Cengiz. "Osmanlı-Bornu münasebetine âid belgeler." *Tarih Dergisi* (Istanbul) (March 1969) 23:111–30.

Osuntokun, Jide. "Nigeria's Colonial Government and the Islamic Insurgency in French West Africa, 1914–1918." *Cahiers d'études Africaines* (1975) 15(57):85–93.

Özön, Mustafa. *Namık Kemal ve İbret Gazetesi.* Istanbul, 1938.

Peters, Rudolf. *Islam and Colonialism: The Doctrine of Jihād in Modern History.* The Hague, 1979.

Pinson, Marc. "Russian Policy and the Emigration of the Crimean Tatars to the Ottoman Empire, 1854–1862." *Güney-Doğu Avrupa Araştımaları Dergisi* (1972) 1:37–56.

——"Ottoman Colonization of the Circassians in Rumili After the Crimean War." *Etudes Balkaniques* (Sofia) (1972) 8(3):71–85.

Popovic, Alexandre. "Les musulmans de Hongrie dans la période post-ottomane." *Studia Islamica* (1982) no. 55, 171–86.

——"Les Musulmans du Sud-Est européen dans la période post-ottomane." *Journal asiatique* (1975) 262(3–4):317–60.

Porath, Yehoshua. "The Palestinians and the Negotiations for the British-Hijazi Treaty, 1920–1925." *Asian and African Studies* (1972) 8(1):20–48.

——*The Palestinian National Movement,* 2: *From Riots to Rebellion.* London, 1977.

Pouwels, Randall Lee. "Islam and Islamic Leadership in the Coastal Communities of Eastern Africa, 1700 to 1914." Doctoral dissertation, UCLA, 1979.

Powell, A.A. "Maulānā Raḥmat Allāh Kairānawī and Muslim-Christian Controversy in India in the Mid-19th Century." *Journal of the Royal Asiatic Society* (1976) no. 1, 42–63.

Protokoll des III. Kongresses der Kommunistischen Internationale. Moskau, 22. Juni bis 12. Juli 1921. Hamburg, 1921.

Qasimiyya, Khayriyya. "Muhammad ᶜAli al-Tahir, qalam filastini fi Misr." *Shuᵓun filastiniyya* (Beirut), (November 1974), no. 39, 150–63.

Qunaybir, ᶜAbd al-Nabi. ᶜ*Abd al-ᶜAziz Jawish, 1872–1929.* Benghazi, 1968.

Ramsaur, E.E. *The Young Turks. Prelude to the Revolution of 1908.* Princeton, 1957.

Rathmann, Lothar. "Ägypten im Exil (1914–1918)—Patrioten oder Kollaborateure des deutschen Imperialismus?" In *Asien in Vergangenheit und Gegenwart. Beiträge der Asienwissenschaftler der DDR zum XXIX. Internationalen Orientalistenkongress 1973 in Paris* (Berlin, 1974), 1–23.

Raymond, André. "Tunisiens et Maghrebins au Caire au dix-huitième siècle." *Cahiers de Tunisie* (1959) 7(26–27):335–71.

Reid, Anthony. *The Contest for North Sumatra: Atjeh, the Netherlands, and Britain, 1858–1898.* Kuala Lumpur and Oxford, 1969.

——"Indonesian Diplomacy. A Documentary Study of Atjehnese Foreign Policy in the Reign of Sultan Mahmud, 1870–4." *Journal of the Malaysian Branch of the Royal Asiatic Society* (Kuala Lumpur) (December 1969) 42(2):74–114.

——"Habib Abdur-Rahman az-Zahir (1833–1896)." *Indonesia* (Ithaca) (April 1972) no. 13, 37–59.

——"Nineteenth Century Pan-Islam in Indonesia and Malaysia." *Journal of Asian Studies* (February 1967) 26(2):267–83.

——"Sixteenth Century Turkish Influence in Western Indonesia." *Journal of Southeast Asian History* (December 1969) 10(3):395–414.

Rida, Rashid. "Mudhakkirat muᵓtamar al-khilafa al-islamiyya." *al-Manar* (June

11, 1926) 27(3):208–32; (July 10, 1926) 27(4):280–94; (August 18, 1926) 27(5):370–7; (September 7, 1926) 27(6):449–58.

——"al-Muʾtamar al-islami al-ʿamm fi bayt al-maqdas." *al-Manar* (February 1932) 32(2):113–32; (March 1932) 32(3):193–208; (April 1932) 32(4):284–92.

——*Taʾrikh al-ustadh al-imam al-shaykh Muhammad ʿAbduh.* 2 vols.; Cairo, 1350/1931.

Risala khatira ila al-muʾtamar al-islami al-ʿamm . . . ʿan halat al-muslimin fi ʾl-rusiya. Jerusalem, n.d.

Robinson, Francis. *Separatism among Indian Muslims: The Politics of the United Provinces' Muslims 1860–1923.* Cambridge, 1974.

Roff, William R. "Indonesian and Malay Students in Cairo in the 1920's." *Indonesia* (Ithaca) (April 1970) no. 9, 73–87.

Rorlich, Azade-Ayse. "Fellow Travellers: Enver Pasha and the Bolshevik Government 1918–1920." *Asian Affairs,* n.s. (October 1982) 13(3):288–96.

——"Transition into the Twentieth Century: Reform and Secularization among the Volga Tatars." Doctoral dissertation, University of Wisconsin—Madison, 1976.

Rossi, Ettore. "Il Congresso interparlamentare arabo e musulmano pro Palestina al Cairo (7–11 ottobre)." *Oriente Moderno* (November 1938) 18(11):587–601.

——"Le relazioni tra il Giappone e il mondo musulmano e l'opera di ʿAbd er-Rashīd Ibrāhīm." *Oriente Moderno* (May 1942) 22(5):181–5.

Royal Institute of International Affairs. *Documents on International Affairs 1937.* Oxford, 1939.

Rustow, D.A. "Enwer Pasha." *EI*²(1965) 3:698–702.

——"Politics and Islam in Turkey, 1920–1955." In Richard N. Frye, ed. *Islam and the West* (the Hague, 1957), 69–107.

Sadr Hashimi, Muhammad. *Tarikh-i jaraʾid va majallat-i Iran.* 4 vols.; Isfahan, 1327–32 solar/1948–53.

Safaʾi, Ibrahim. *Rahbaran-i mashruteh.* Teheran, 1344 solar/1966.

Şah, Razaulhak. "Açi Padişahı Sultan Alâeddin'in Kanunî Sultan Süleyman'a Mektubu." *Tarih Araştırmaları Dergisi* (Ankara) (1967) 5(8–9):373–409.

Salem, Mahmoud. *Le Congrès Islamo-européen de Genève (Août 1933).* Paris, 1933.

Sands, C.E.W. *Report on the Silk Letter Conspiracy.* Naini Tal, 1917.

Schnabel, Reimund. *Tiger und Schakal: Deutsche Indienpolitik, 1941–1943.* Vienna, 1968.

Sékaly, Achille. *Le Congrès du Khalifat et le Congrès du Monde Musulman.* Paris, 1926.

Seydahmet, Cafer. *Gaspıralı İsmail Bey.* Istanbul, 1934.

Shafiq, Ahmad. *Aʿmali baʿda mudhakkirati.* Cairo, 1941.

——*Hawliyyat misr al-siyasiyya.* Vol. 4. Cairo, 1348/1929.

[Shah, Iqbal ʿAli]. "European Muslim Conference at Geneva." *Great Britain and the East* (September 26, 1935), 396–97.

Shah, Sirdar Ikbal Ali. "First Moslem Congress." *The Times* (London), July 21–23, 1926.

——"The Meccan Conference." *Contemporary Review* (London) (September 1926) 130(9):304–11.

Shamir, Shimon. "Midhat Pasha and the Anti-Turkish Agitation in Syria." *Middle Eastern Studies* (1974) 10(2):115–41.

Shanufi, ʿAli al-. "Fasl min al-rihla al-hijaziyya li-Muhammad al-Sanusi: al-khabar ʿan al-tunisiyyin biʾl-Astana." *Hawliyyat al-jamʿa al-tunisiyya* (Tunis) (1970) no. 7, 79–111.

Shanufi, al-Munsif al-. " ʿAlaʾiq Rashid Rida, sahib al-Manar, maʿa al-tunisiyyin." *Hawliyyat al-jamʿa al-tunisiyya* (Tunis) (1967) no. 4, 121–51.

Sharabasi, Ahmad al-. *Amir al-bayan Shakib Arslan.* 2 vols.; Cairo, 1963.

——*Rashid Rida, sahib al-Manar.* Cairo, 1389/1970.

Sharqawi, Mahmud. "Dirasat wathaʾiq ʿan muʾtamar al-khilafa al-islamiyya 1926." *al-Katib* (Cairo) (August 1970) 10(113):115–22; (September 1970) 10(114):132–37; (October 1970) 10(115):156–61; (February 1971) 11(119):151–58.

Shawish, ʿAbd al-ʿAziz. *al-ʿAlam al-islami.* Vol. 1. Istanbul, 1330/1913.

Shaykh al-Raʾis, Abu al-Hasan. *Ittihad-i Islam.* Bombay, 1312/1894–95.

——*Muntakhab-i nafis az asar-i hazrat-i Shaykh al-Raʾis.* Bombay, 1312/1894–95.

Sheikh, Atique Zafar, ed. *Quaid-e-Azam and the Muslim World: Selected Documents 1937–1948.* Karachi, 1978.

Shukla, R.M. *Britain, India and the Turkish Empire 1853–1882.* New Delhi, 1973.

Shuqruf, ʿAbd al-Munʿim Muhammad. *al-Imam Muhammad Madi Abu al-ʿAzaʾim.* Cairo, 1972.

Siddiqi, M. Mazheruddin. " ʿObaid-Ullah Sindhi." *The Islamic Literature* (Lahore) (July 1956) 8(7):15–25.

Sindi, ʿUbayd-Allah. *Ilham al-rahman fi tafsir al-Qurʾan.* ed. Musa Carullah Bigi, Karachi, 195–.

Singhal, D.P. "A Turkish Mission to Kabul—A Forgotten Chapter of History." *Journal of Indian History* (Trivandrum) (December 1961) 39(3):489–502.

Smirnov, N.A. *Ocherki istorii izucheniia islama v SSSR.* Moscow, 1954.

Smith, Grace Martin. "The Özbek Tekkes of Istanbul." *Der Islam* (1980) 57(1):130–39.

Spuler, Bertold. "Die Lage der russlandtürkischen Emigration im Fernen Osten." *Osteuropa* (Berlin) (1936–37) 12:541–45.

Steppat, Fritz. "Khalifat, *Dār al-Islām* und die Loyalität der Araber zum osmanischen Reich bei Hanafitischen Juristen des 19. Jahrhunderts." *Actes, Vᵉ congrès international d'Arabisants et d'Islamisants* (Brussels, c. 1970), 443–62.

—— "Nationalismus und Islam bei Mustafā Kāmil." *Welt des Islams,* n.s. (1956) 4(4):241–341.

Stoddard, Philip H. "The Ottoman Government and the Arabs, 1911 to 1918: A Preliminary Study of the *Teşkilât-ı Mahsusa.*" Doctoral dissertation, Princeton University, 1963.

Suwaydi, ʿAbdallah Efendi ibn Husayn al-. *al-Hujjaj al-qatʿiyya li-ittifaq al-firaq al-islamiyya.* Cairo, 1323/1905–6.

Tahir, Muhammad ʿAli al-. *Nazariyyat al-shura fiʾl-ahwal al-sharqiyya al-hadira.* Cairo, 1351/1932.

Taillardat, F. "Les congrès interislamiques de 1926." *L'Asie française* (Paris) (January 1927) 27(246):9–13; (February 1927) 27(247):54–60.

Tansel, Fevziye Abdullah. *Mehmed Akif: Hayatı ve Eserleri.* Istanbul, 1945.
—— "Mizancı Murad Bey." *Tarih Dergisi* (Istanbul) (1950–1) 2(3–4):67–88.
—— *Namık Kemal'in mektupları,* 2: *Midilli mektupları.* Ankara, 1969.
Tapiero, Norbert. *Les idées réformistes d'al-Kawākibī, 1265–1320-1849–1902.* Paris, 1956.
Tarrazi, Philippe de. *Taʾrikh al-sahafa al-ʿarabiyya.* 4 vols.; Beirut, 1913–33.
Thabit, Muhammad Saʿid Al. *al-Wahda al-islamiyya aw al-taqrib bayna madhahib al-muslimin.* Baghdad, 1384/1965.
Tibawi, A.L. "History of the London Central Mosque and the Islamic Cultural Centre 1910–1980." *Welt des Islams* n.s. (1981) 21(1–4):193–208.
Tidrick, Kathryn. *Heart-beguiling Araby.* Cambridge, 1981.
Tihrani, Agha Buzurg al-. *Tabaqat aʿlam al-shiʿa, nuqabaʾ al-bashar fīʾl-qarn al-rabiʿ ʿashar.* Najaf, 1375/1956.
Tlili, Béchir. "La Grande Guerre et les questions tunisiennes: le groupement de la *Revue du Maghreb* (1916–1918)." *Cahiers de Tunisie* (Tunis) (1978) 26(101–2):91–108.
—— "Au seuil du nationalisme tunisien. Documents inédits sur le panislamisme au Maghreb (1919–1923)." *Africa* (Rome) (June 1973) 28(2):211–36.
Togan, Z.V. "Gasprali (Gasprinskii), Ismāʿīl." *EI²* (1965) 2:979–81.
Toynbee, Arnold J. *Survey of International Affairs 1925,* 1: *The Islamic World since the Peace Settlement.* Oxford, 1927.
Trefzger, Marc. *Die nationale Bewegung Ägyptens vor 1928 im Spiegel der Schweizerischen Öffentlichkeit.* Basel and Stuttgart, 1970.
Tschelebi, Hadsch Moh. Nāfiʿ. "Die Bruderschaft Arabiens und der islamische Weltkongress zu Mekka 1926." *Welt des Islams,* o.s. (1927–29) 10:33–42.
Tunaya, Tarık Z. *Türkiyede siyasi partiler, 1859–1952.* Istanbul, 1952.
Vacca, Virginia. "Il Congresso dei Musulmani d'Europa a Ginevra." *Oriente Moderno* (1935) 15:501–4, 563–67.
Vasiqi, Sadr. *Sayyid Jamal al-Din Husayni.* Teheran, 1348 solar/1970.
Vernier, Bernard. *La politique islamique de l'Allemagne.* Paris, 1939.
Vogel, Renate. *Die Persien- und Afghanistanexpedition Oskar Ritter v. Niedermayers 1915/16.* Osnabrück, 1976.
Wahba, Hafiz. *Arabian Days.* London, 1964.
—— *Jazirat al-ʿarab fīʾl-qarn al-ʿishrin.* Cairo, 1375/1956.
Wakabayashi, Nakaba. *Kaikyo sekai to Nihon.* Tokyo, 1938.
Waters, M.P. *Mufti over the Middle East.* London, 1942.
Weit, Gaston. "Son altesse le Prince Omar Toussoun." *Bulletin de l'Institut égyptien* (1944) 26:1–19.
White, Stephen. "Communism and the East: The Baku Congress, 1920." *Slavic Review* (September 1974) 33(3):492–514.
Wiesenthal, S. *Grossmufti—Grossagent der Achse.* Salzburg-Vienna, 1947.
Wilber, Donald N. *Riza Shah Pahlavi: The Resurrection and Reconstruction of Iran.* Hicksville, N.Y., 1975.
X. "Doctrines et programmes des partis politiques ottomans." *Revue du monde musulman* (1913) 22:151–64.
Yakan, Wali al-Din. *al-Maʿlum waʾl-majhul.* Cairo, 1327/1909.

Yusuf, ᶜAli. *Bayan fi khitat al-Mu ᵓayyad tujaha al-dawla al-ᶜaliyya al-ᶜuthmaniyya.* Cairo, 1909.

Zawahiri, Fakhr al-Din al-Ahmadi al-. *al-Siyasa wa ᵓl-Azhar, min mudhakkirat Shaykh al-Islam al-Zawahiri.* Cairo, 1364/1954.

Ziadeh, Nicola. *Origins of Nationalism in Tunisia.* Beirut, 1962.

Zolondek, L. "Sabunji in England 1876–91: His Role in Arabic Journalism." *Middle Eastern Studies* (January 1978) 14(1):102–15.

Index